SOCIETY TIES

SOCIETY TIES

A HISTORY OF THE

JEFFERSON SOCIETY

AND *Student Life* AT THE

UNIVERSITY OF VIRGINIA

---

*Thomas L. Howard III and
Owen W. Gallogly*

FOREWORD BY JOHN T. CASTEEN III
President Emeritus of the University of Virginia

PUBLISHED BY THE
WILLIAM R. KENAN JR. ENDOWMENT FUND FOR THE ACADEMICAL VILLAGE
DISTRIBUTED BY THE UNIVERSITY OF VIRGINIA PRESS

Distributed by the University of Virginia Press.

© 2017 by Thomas L. Howard III and Owen W. Gallogly
All rights reserved. Published 2017
Printed in the United States of America
21 20 19 18 17   1 2 3 4 5

ISBN-13: 978-0-8139-3981-0

This paper meets the requirements of ANSI/NISO Z39-48
1992 (Permanence of Paper).

TO

Society members,
past, present, and future

FOR

Thomas L. Howard Jr.
In loving memory

AND

Carol, Michael, and Karen
With thanks

Contents

APPENDICES

Color gallery of images follows page 212

I thus pay a last long tribute to the Jefferson Society, gentlemen, because I honor, venerate and love her; because some of my happiest moments and most instructive hours have been spent within these walls; because I have learned here what one cannot acquire from the lips of professors, nor gather from the pages of books; and lastly because, viewed as an instrument, a means of intellectual education and advancement, I regard this society as . . . a bright literary store of potent influence.

WILLIAM ROANE AYLETT, 1854

Foreword

JOHN T. CASTEEN III

President Emeritus, University of Virginia

Few discussions of the University of Virginia's history omit mention of the Jefferson Society. There are many reasons for this. The Society is old—essentially as old as the University itself, a student invention during the University's first year. The two institutions share nearly two hundred years of generally peaceful coexistence. The Society's members have included a good number of students who subsequently became persons of some fame, many among our most noted and best alumni—people who, after their years in Jefferson Hall, lived on to become leaders and shapers of the culture born during the period of national identity-building that coincided with the University's first few years.

From the start, the Jefferson Society's meetings have been for the purpose of debate and for the exploration of differences in opinion, knowledge, and judgment. More so than, for example, the Faculty Senate and its predecessors, the Student Council, and other similar organizations, the Jefferson Society has been the University's open forum. That it serves the students who own it accounts in large part for its durability and its impact. Its speakers have included persons of all kinds—mainstream figures in public and cultural life, and occasionally obscure persons, seeking to promote their projects, their hopes, or their fears to an audience of students. From time to time, the forum has also accommodated persons perched out on the extreme poles of public opinion and at any point between the extremes. Over time, many, many students have come to be heard for all kinds of reasons, and persons high and low, serious and sometimes silly, have found in Jefferson Hall on Friday nights a likely forum for the expression of their ideas.

Through all of this—and especially in recent times as more and more students have wanted to join—this common forum's fit with the community it serves has been uneasy. It may seem contradictory that an organization that retains the right to choose its own members should serve as an open forum. Jefferson Hall in 1825 within a university of about a hundred students may be one thing, but the same Hall in 2017 in a university of 21,985 students may in fact be something quite different. The University is in some sense diminished because few other open forums have come into being since 1825 aside from the Jefferson Society. Exclusivity in the forum itself seems to me to threaten, perhaps to undercut, the democratic inclusiveness that Jefferson intended within his university. And yet the Jefferson Society endures, a beating heart at the center of the University.

How did the Jefferson Society come to be selective, or exclusive, and still fulfill this role? This volume provides several commonsensical explanations: the limited number of spaces available for new members, in the University generally and in the Hall, combined over these two centuries with the Jefferson Society's dominance in sponsoring the most notable venues—the Hall itself, occasionally Old Cabell Hall, and other places for heavily subscribed events—and its accepted function in student literary life. The Jefferson Society sponsored contests of various kinds, the student newspapers, the old *University of Virginia Magazine*, and other periodicals. Its original competitor, the Washington Society, and other similar student societies struggled and usually failed. Students at one time created more forums, more points of entry into the larger dialogue or debate, safe spaces in which they could argue the composition and shape of the brave new world to which the University itself was a gateway. No doubt some enjoyed prestige or prominence at one time.

Perhaps there are more reasons. But the common forum is in first assumption open: it invites and welcomes discourse of all kinds, including more than a few topics that flourish only because the First Amendment protects them. Where else but in a university, in an open forum, ought the culture's extremists be heard and seen in their various, often least favorite postures? Their very existence makes the point that unconstrained public discourse, our civic means of pursuing truth, ultimately strengthens the university community.

The University's distinctive culture had its origins in Jefferson's declaration, in a letter written in 1820 to the English historian and abolitionist William Roscoe, that his new, as yet unopened university would be dedicated to the "illimitable freedom of the human mind." From one era to another, the University may or may not achieve its founder's lofty purpose. Jefferson himself came to have doubts about students' actual conduct during the University's first year. In our own time, unsorted, sometimes unanalyzed notions about behavioral or political correctness seem to be at odds with the First Amendment. And yet universities in this country reside in the province of free discourse, of contrary opinions arranged, however briefly and imperfectly, with whatever passion or dispassion might motivate a debater's positions, in dialectical opposition, and here, in the common forum that students own. This forum flourishes in its capacity to "tolerate any error" (Jefferson's term) in the marketplace of ideas "so long as reason is left free to combat it."

Ultimately, none of this happens without the open forum at the University's core. The records of the University's early years are full of evidence that chaos reigned, at least from time to time. Every undergraduate learns some version of the murder of Professor John Davis, then chair of the faculty, the university's presiding officer, during a pointless student riot on the Lawn on the night of November 12, 1840—an event commonly said to have led eventually to the creation of the honor system. One should, perhaps, read the history and myth of this period agnostically. Students of the 1840s may not be fairly represented in the record. They turn up in actions taken by the professors to curb their misconduct, in faculty resolutions and actions taken by the rector and the Board of Visitors, for example, but generally not in their own words. Whatever the case may be, surely some public debate occurred, after the murder if not before, and then continuing through the 1840s as professors argued that a culture of lawlessness had the University in its grip. Evidence suggests that academic cheating was rampant, and during a decade of remarkable self-examination and often bitter dialogue, it largely supplanted student violence on the faculty's list of concerns.

Throughout the nineteenth century, and despite remarkable threats and adversities—the murder of Professor Davis, strained University finances, the Civil War and Reconstruction, the generation-long contest over the University's identity following Reconstruction—the University emerged from the sectionalism and frequent isolation of the old South to become a national institution, and the Jefferson Society somehow sustained its function as the open forum. In turbulent times, it attracted members who wanted a culture defined in some part by academic pursuits, by the *Literary* of the Society's name, and by the dialectical reasoning implicit in unconstrained debate. This history essentially tells what is known of the Society's existence in these years and in the century that came after. In some regards, the factual history is rich. Members' names, some evidence of life or activity within the Hall, occasional resolutions, and other materials exist, the ravages of fire in 1895 and periodic neglect of the material record notwithstanding. In other respects, the record is frustratingly sparse. Jefferson Hall's actual engagement in the large process of institutional evolution is difficult to document because few or no records survive of the relevant debates. Students would have had opinions. These would have been debated in the Hall, but without leaving documentary records. Relations between the Jefferson Society and its rivals—the Washington Literary Society and Debating Union, housed at least during its prosperous periods in Hotel B, and the Patrick Henry Society from which the sixteen original student members of the Jefferson Society departed on July 14, 1825, to create a new and different society— are not especially well documented. We infer or speculate when thinking about why the Jefferson Society endured in turbulent times while its competitors did not. Perhaps what matters is that it endured with its self-declared mission intact.

The names of nineteenth-century student organizations imply at least two different mainstreams in student life, one likely classical or neoclassical in its intentions (the Philomathean Society, the Parthenon), and the other determinedly American (Jefferson, Washington, Patrick Henry). That both mainstreams supported literary activity seems clear enough. The Latinate names, literary contests, and later student literary magazines establish this. They suggest that students assumed ownership of these forums and wanted the University to be culturally or intellectually expansive and serious. At least some wanted to be something other or in addition to rowdy. Evidence as to how the open forum, intellectual life, and argumentative fervor implied by the naming after Jefferson and Henry, perhaps even Washington, despite obvious differences between these three eponymous figures, is sparse, except that this more civic stream *endured*—essentially always in Jefferson Hall, and less consistently but tenaciously in Washington Hall with its history of coming back to life at least twice after long periods of inactivity. Students wanted the experience of these halls. Students created them and made them survive.

I joined, *was admitted to*, the Jefferson Society in 1962. It was in those days a place of discourse and revelry, a society if you will, a place of debate and speaking on Friday nights. The scene differed from all of the other student organizations, and yet it did not. The president, generally a grave person and sometimes also witty or sly, always with a gavel at hand and ready for use, presided on the dais behind the railings, with the secretary nearby, his papers spread out on a desk in front of him, and the speaker's podium below the rail and in front of the first row of chairs. Generally, the room was full on Friday nights, or nearly so. When the program lagged or one speaker stood down and another took the podium, and often during probationary speeches, disorder threatened, and the president's gavel rang out to pull the meeting back to order. When the weather allowed the door to be open, it was. Members and others drifted outside to stand on the steps or the walkway under the porch, to attend to personal matters, sometimes to go find a missing friend who might enjoy or be provoked by the evening's program. The keg generally sat on a chair in the center of the room. Probationary members giving their first speech, some visibly alarmed by their always skeptical, always volatile audience, usually seemed to want to please, although probably as many provoked as charmed, and not all enjoyed their first time in front of the room. Most probationaries faced hecklers. Guest speakers were better treated. As a guest was introduced, conversation would stop, and members almost always listened intently, if only to prepare for the debate that generally followed.

More or less fixed as the Society's internal rhythm or decorum was, unanticipated events occurred: a probationary might receive vigorous applause and perhaps an ovation; sometimes the sequence of events changed at the whim of the president or of the group as a whole. Regardless, guest speakers of every kind found energetic, if not always compliant and sometimes combative, listeners. The great topics of the period were debated there—attacks on coeducation and, later, defenses of it; any number of arguments about the war in Vietnam; the merits of Faulkner's *The Reivers*, which was current while I was an active member; attacks, most of them silly but all of them passionate, on the University's perceived future; seemingly endless, often boring diatribes about "*the old U*" or "*the Old Hall*," both imagined as somehow different from and *better than* current times. Several spoke off and on throughout the first half of the 1960s against what they styled "creeping state U-ism." I remember the scene as dimly lit, sometimes smoke-filled as pipes or cigars flavored, and no doubt contaminated, the air that came through the door and front windows, the chairs comfortable but not too much so, the beer not the best but adequate.

The keg resting on the chair in the back of the Hall raises another issue. I have wondered throughout my life whether our determination to control or stamp out student consumption of alcohol ever succeeds. The keg on its chair seems to me to have done little harm. Very few of us had cars, so few drove after drinking. Police officers and deans dealt with genuine misbehavior, but their attitudes toward us and the attitudes of the adult culture generally were more parietal than one sees now. Laws and corrective or enforcement practices have changed. It is hard to imagine ABC enforcement officers in those days resorting to violence to enforce the legal drinking age, but easy to remember being told to get back to our rooms and stay there until we were presentable. In Jefferson Hall on Friday nights, certainly some people became drunk, but in truth not many. The biannual cocktail parties were memorable, but for their cordiality and occasional silliness, not for rowdiness. The setting itself, the Hall, and the Society's traditions imposed and enforced a version of order, even of decorum, on those Friday nights.

The coming and periodic dominance within the forum, the Society, and the University, of minority persons and women, coincidental with desegregation and coeducation, surely improved the Hall regardless of any laws or regulations. As the 1960s advanced, the Jefferson Society and the University emerged from a period of torpor—between the time when ex-GIs making up for lost time made the community serious in new ways and the era of coeducation and desegregation that followed, and the emergence of today's vigorous, ambitious, remarkably wise student culture. My own observation over time has been that minority students, women students, and international students rarely come to the University of Virginia to waste time or squander opportunities.

This history deals well with those developments. Like any telling of the often unrecorded history of student life in prior times, it involves a certain amount of folklore, a good bit of it credible. This version entails little false nostalgia and quite a lot of restraint with regard to tales that cannot be proved. Yet it records some myths, known stories, in order to understand the Jefferson Society's temperament and durability over time. Warts and all, this is a tale of the best visions accomplished by students during these two hundred years.

Introduction

This volume offers the first in-depth look at the rich history of Jefferson Literary and Debating Society written for a public audience. It grew out of a conversation in Room 7, West Lawn, where the Society was founded in 1825. My coauthor and I were wearing tuxedos, having just returned from the annual Founder's Day Banquet in the Dome Room of the Rotunda, and in that moment we were both captivated by the spirit of the Society and a burning desire to learn as much about its history as we could. The next five years took us on an incomparable journey through dusty archives in the basement of Alderman Library at the University of Virginia (and beyond). We read documents that, in many cases, had not been read since they were placed there almost one hundred years ago, and we discovered a story far richer than either of us could have imagined.

Every project of history is aided by certain happy accidents—pieces of information handed down through the most unlikely circumstances or discovered in the most fortuitous coincidences. For us it was a set of notes hastily scribbled on the back of a financial document. At first disregarded, upon closer scrutiny they proved to be debate notes on the Jefferson Society's decision to integrate, offering reasons for and against the election of Wesley Harris, a young engineer from Richmond, Virginia, as the Society's first African American member in 1962. The notes had been saved from the wastebasket simply because they were written on the back of a budget. This fascinating glimpse into the inner workings of an organization that counts the likes of Woodrow Wilson and Edgar Allan Poe among its members is just one of the many moving and sometimes deeply personal stories that make up the Society's larger history.

Why study the history of the Jefferson Society? Why focus with a fine lens on this one particular organization when there have been countless others of importance at the University of Virginia and elsewhere? What makes this one special? One of the Jefferson Society's past chroniclers, Karl Saur, opened his article on the Society's history with the words, "the history of the Jefferson Society is, in large measure, the history of the University of Virginia." One cannot understand the history of the Jefferson Society without also understanding a much broader history of student life at the University of Virginia, and vice versa. The Society was founded just four months after the University opened its doors to students in March 1825. In a very short time, the Society was at the center of intellectual and social life for students. In 1837, it moved into the home it has occupied ever since—Hotel C on the West Range, which is now named in its honor: Jefferson Hall. The Society's place in the heart of Thomas Jefferson's Academical Village plays no small part in its identity and its centrality to life at the University—as well as its continued success.

For almost a century, the Jefferson Society was doubtless the most important and most prominent student organization at the University. Along with the Washington Society, the two generated almost all of the student activities for years, but by the turn of the twentieth century, collegiate literary societies had begun to slip from the position of prominence on college campuses that they had occupied for more than a century. Fraternities and athletic contests competed for students' attention, and membership dropped low enough to force some societies to fold. The Jefferson Society survived this wholesale decline by adapting to the times—staying interesting and compelling to students at the University of Virginia while preserving many of its distinctive traditions and cherishing its rich history. Over time, the Society evolved from an organization that demanded loyalty and exclusivity of its members to one that serves as a forum for students who come from all corners of the University. It is in large part this evolution that has saved the Jefferson Society from obscurity and allowed it to continue to prosper.

As the University grew, the Jefferson Society grew with it, organizing elaborate Final Celebrations beginning in the 1830s. These celebrations, which essentially amounted to graduation exercises, were the biggest date on the University's social calendar. After the Civil War, the Society and its members played a foundational role in a number of literary efforts that would eventually become institutions at the University. Among these were the *Virginia University Magazine* (later the *University of Virginia Magazine* and the *Virginia Spectator*) and the student newspaper *College Topics* (later the *Cavalier Daily*). The formation of a student council also traces its roots to the Society. The University was not the only party to benefit from such industry; in 1913 the Society formed the Virginia High School

League with the help of the Washington Society, intended to cultivate debating in high schools across the state.

Much like the University of Virginia itself, progress for the Jefferson Society has not always come without its obstacles and challenges. In the early years, the faculty placed limitations on student speeches in response to inflammatory remarks advocating abolition from a Jefferson Society orator. First the texts of speeches had to be approved by the faculty, then public speeches were forbidden altogether for a time. Membership in the Society reached critically low numbers during the Civil War and both World Wars, threatening the very existence of the organization. In 1926, the Society was reprimanded by University president Edwin Alderman for the release of an issue of the *University of Virginia Magazine* containing a story entitled "Mulatto Flair." The Society again tripped over the stumbling block of racial prejudice roughly fifty years later when the *Spectator* put out a Jim Crow issue. The Society did not integrate until 1963, nor did it become coeducational until 1972, the last major group on the Grounds to accept women. More recently, in the late 1980s and the early 1990s, the Society was rocked by allegations of sexual discrimination and improper alcohol consumption, and it was barred from Jefferson Hall for one semester as a result.

Despite the challenges the Jefferson Society has faced over the course of its almost two hundred years in existence, its impact on the University community and higher education is palpable and lasting, and its history offers insight into the social transformations that have taken place as the University of Virginia has modernized and asserted its status as an elite public institution. The Society, like the University of Virginia, has changed from generation to generation and has demonstrated commitment to harmonizing storied traditions with a spirit of progress.

———

Writing in the two-volume 1974 study *The University in Society*, historian James McLachlan gave the seminal appraisal of the importance and impact of literary societies as they thrived in the nineteenth century at universities across the country:

The student literary societies engrossed more of the interests and activities of the students than any other aspect of college life. Elaborately organized, self-governing youth groups, student literary societies were, in effect, colleges within colleges. They enrolled most of the students, constructed—and taught—their own curricula, granted their own diplomas, selected and bought their own books, operated their own libraries, developed and enforced elaborate codes of conduct among their members, and set the personal goals and ideological tone for a majority of the student body.[1]

In the late eighteenth and early nineteenth centuries, literary and intellectual societies flourished. Finding their roots in Benjamin Franklin's philosophical group for mutual improvement, which he called the Junto, they are a prime expression of the American ideals of democracy, popular participation in government, and personal intellectual improvement. When he founded the American Philosophical Society in 1743, Franklin sought to expand the ideals of the Junto into an organization that would become the premier learned society in the colonies, connecting the American intellectual community across the growing continent. The American Philosophical Society provided a valuable forum for communication and collaboration between early American intellectuals in an age when such opportunities were few and far between. Its members came to include the first four presidents and many who signed the Declaration of Independence and helped draft the Constitution.

It was not long before young, promising students sought to emulate the political leaders they looked up to. At Princeton University, students founded the American Whig and Cliosophic Societies in 1769 and 1770, respectively. James Madison was one of the founders of the Whig, and Aaron Burr was among the founders of the Clio. Modeled after representative legislative bodies, their aims included a desire to provide political training to their members, giving them the tools to enter public life. Other college literary societies quickly followed, notably the Dialectic and Philanthropic Societies at the University of North Carolina in 1795. These two societies were particularly enthusiastic in their promotion of debate, a key tool used by college societies to learn about and discuss the salient issues of the day. Like Princeton before it, North Carolina fostered two societies, not as rivals but as complements to each other, pairings that would prove mutually beneficial in practicing debate and maintaining a presence in their respective university communities. For historian Timothy Williams, literary societies were one way for students to pursue "intellectual manhood," growing into thinking, working men who could contribute to the world around them. It was also a way for students to shape part of their education to suit their own ends. While "intellectual histories seldom treat these subjects from a student perspective," he writes, "students were *always* agents in the development of educational culture."[2]

In addition to the political training students sought to gain by participating in literary societies, they also provided valuable oratorical training to the public figures of the nineteenth and early twentieth centuries. Scheduled debates and orations on important, pressing issues provided the dual benefit to students of political instruction and training in public speech. Countless notable orators, legislators, and politicians honed their oratorical talents in literary societies, and many of them identified their time and activities in societies as formative to their desire to enter public life.

Following the example of those detailed above, it is no surprise that the students at the University of Virginia soon formed literary societies of their own. The first was the Patrick Henry Society, a short-lived, politically radical exemplar of student organization. Taking on the name of the University's venerated founder, the Jefferson Society soon grew from the foundation of the Patrick Henry, and it quickly rose to prominence. True to form, students formed a counterpart, the Washington Society, in 1831. Since its founding in 1825, the Jefferson Society has never folded, making it the oldest student organization at the University of Virginia. To this day it remains the most prominent literary society at the University, as well as one of the most notable in the United States. The Washington Society has been less fortunate, fading in and out of existence at various points in its own storied history, but it remains relevant as a counterpart and occasional rival to the Jefferson Society.

Robert M. T. Hunter was an early member of the Jefferson Society who would later go on to a remarkable political career, serving as Speaker of the United States House of Representatives and secretary of state of the Confederacy. During a speech he delivered to the Patrick Henry Society in 1829, he referred to the predecessors in whose path the Jefferson Society followed, as well as the goals they pursued, as he implored students to invest themselves in the work of literary societies:

And are there any then who deign the efficiency of our means for the promotion of these great ends? Will any say that such societies are devoid of utility, and there is no improvement to be derived from them? Let us refer him to the illustrious examples which sanction our undertaking. Let us beg of him to analyze the principles of action which are thus brought into play and to consider the great necessity there is for practice in order to mark any degree of proficiency in either the arts or the sciences. Was it not in societies of this sort that the youthful minds of a Robertson a Franklin and a Madison were disciplined? And has not their importance been so generally acknowledged that they have been incorporated with the very existence of almost all other American colleges, and their exercises become among the chief of the institution?[3]

The Jefferson Society has played a significant role in the formation of political and literary leaders, like Hunter, the world over. Its sons and daughters include a president of the United States, a handful of cabinet officials, five of the sixteen men who served in Jefferson Davis's Confederate Cabinet, many governors, senators, congressmen, jurists, and Pulitzer Prize winners, among other notable individuals (see the appendices for listings). Honorary members add even more names to the roll of honor.

The Jefferson Society is certainly a classic example of the "colleges within colleges" character of literary societies so aptly described by James McLachlan. In its earliest days, the Society counted more than a quarter of the students enrolled at the University of Virginia among its members, another quarter of whom were members of the Washington Society. The Society kept and maintained a library and hosted debates, oratorical contests, and an annual moot court. Much like the formal departments of the University of Virginia, the Jefferson Society played an official role in the University's Final Exercises and in the celebration of Thomas Jefferson's birthday. The membership certificate or "shingle" the Society awards to its members is even modeled after the diploma issued by the University of Virginia as early as 1833. The Society also worked hard to ingratiate itself with the University administration, offering honorary membership to many of the original Board of Visitors, most notably Thomas Jefferson. He declined in order to avoid the impression of bias. The Society had better luck initiating James Madison and James Monroe, both of whom accepted.

The chroniclers of the University of Virginia—Paul Brandon Barringer, Philip Alexander Bruce, Virginius Dabney, and Garry Wills, among others—all recognize the importance of Mr. Jefferson's University and its past. The two most important works detailing the history of the University are those authored by Philip Alexander Bruce and Virginius Dabney, both of which aided in the preparation of this volume. Bruce, a noted

Virginia historian, wrote his *History of the University of Virginia, 1819–1919: The Lengthened Shadow of One Man* in the last decade of his life as a commemoration of the University's centennial. His five-volume work published in 1921 is often credited with expanding the understanding of Jefferson's educational philosophy and remains the seminal work on the subject. Bruce was followed in 1981 by Virginius Dabney, who carried the narrative forward through the Vietnam era. One final notable work is a history of the University by Paul Brandon Barringer, a former chairman of the faculty, which provides a detailed appraisal of the structure of the University's departments, as well as short biographical sketches of notable alumni. Barringer's work was published in 1904. We also owe a consummate debt to Charles Wall, without whose doctoral dissertation, "Student Life at the University of Virginia, 1825–1861," we would have been lost.

While the history of the University of Virginia is quite well documented, comparatively little has been written about the Jefferson Society itself. Each of the historians mentioned above devote some attention to the Society in their accounts of the University of Virginia, which hints at the importance of the Jefferson Society in the University's identity but more importantly invites inquiry into the history of the Society.

Among the ranks of the Society's members have been many amateur historians who preserve the rich oral tradition of legend, tales, and anecdotes about the Society's past—some of which have proven to be true, the rest of which live in the hearts of Society members the world over and capture the spirit of the Society in a legendary form. Those who have attempted to record its history have produced a handful of articles, the most important of which are John Moore's "History of the Jefferson Society, 1825–1957" and Karl Saur's "Historical Sketch of the Jefferson Society of the University of Virginia." These shorter glimpses into the Society's history are valuable in their own right and have been helpful in the preparation of this manuscript, but they too leave greater depth and analysis to be desired.

The following pages represent an attempt to build upon what these men started, to capture the effect the Jefferson Society has had on the young men and women who it has counted as members, and to examine the vitally important role the Society has played in the University of Virginia's history. This volume could very well be considered a group biography of sorts. It will focus not only on describing the Jefferson Society, but also, and perhaps more importantly, the role the Society has played in the University of Virginia community and the greater world of American higher education—borrowing ideas from similar organizations at other universities and providing a powerful example for others to follow. It will highlight the contributions the Society has made to the University, and the place the Society holds within the community of higher learning, including key similarities and differences in development when compared to other collegiate literary societies. This work covers a lot of ground in a very short space and thus will not often pause to dwell on specifics of daily life in the Society or the actions of individual members. It would not be possible to even begin to capture the full breadth of the lively characters who have called themselves members of the Society. Rather, this book will examine the Society from the inside looking out upon the rest of the world. The exception to this rule is chapter 4, which primarily considers Woodrow Wilson and will give us the opportunity to examine the internal function of the Society in greater detail. Wilson drafted a constitution for the Society that, once adopted, has essentially remained in force to this day, with a handful of notable differences. We are fortunate, because of Wilson's stature, to have a great deal of source material pertaining to his college years. The period of less than two years he spent in the Society was an exciting time, and his quick rise through the ranks of leadership is a testament to the force of his personality.

The drafting of this volume has presented significant challenges. First, as with all institutional history related to the University of Virginia, the tragic Rotunda Fire of October 27, 1895, destroyed much of the records of the Society and of the University—valuable information that is lost forever and is nearly impossible to derive from other sources. Second, the records of the Jefferson Society that do survive are fragmented, incomplete, and often extremely difficult to comprehend. Important papers are often missing, damaged, or removed from context. The minutes of the Society are nearly complete dating back to 1875. The vast bulk of them are detailed and informative, but at times they are unfinished, irrelevant, or composed to be humorous rather than substantive. Despite its deficiencies, the Society's archives provide a fairly complete picture of the second half of the Jefferson Society's history. This volume, which relies heavily on these records, reflects our best understanding of the nature, trends, and meaning emerging from careful examination of the entirety of the Society's archives, the first such examination to be published. We were also aided by rich archival collections and memoirs from the University's early alumni, complete collections of the *University of Virginia Magazine* and its precursors, as well as *College Topics* and the *Cavalier Daily*.

As this volume goes to press, student members of the Jefferson Society have undertaken efforts to catalogue and digitize much of the Society's archival holdings, which had previously been disorganized and closed to the public. This project, supported by a grant from the Jefferson Trust and led by Jack Chellman, will dramatically improve the accessibility of these materials for future research and ensure that they are well preserved for the benefit of future generations by transferring them to the Albert and Shirley Small Special Collections Library at the University of Virginia. We hope that these efforts will, together with this volume, encourage more research on the history of student life at the University of Virginia and in American higher education more broadly.

Acknowledgments

The advice of several historians, scholars, and friends has been invaluable throughout the entire process of producing *Society Ties*. Peter S. Onuf has provided us with guidance, wisdom, and helpful criticism from the outset. He has put up with our constant bombardment and has kept us from too much navel-gazing. The mark that he has left on this work and our development as scholars is indelible. We are forever indebted to his direction, input, skepticism, and encouragement, and we hope that we have produced a work of which he can be proud.

The input of Elizabeth Varon, Alexander "Sandy" Gilliam, Al Brophy, Jon Kukla, A. E. Dick Howard, David O'Brien, and David Fontana has had a lasting impact on the quality of this volume. The contributions of several individuals have made the demanding research effort easier: Lara Morris has read every word of this book at least twice (along with many more she cut out), constantly pushing us both to be better writers. Without her continual aid and encouragement, this book would still be just a pile of incomprehensible notes shoved in a box somewhere. David Ensey and Catherine Creighton both made valuable contributions with key research assistance. We are incredibly grateful to President John T. Casteen III for providing the foreword to this volume, and to Wesley Harris and Judge Barbara Lynn for their willingness to share their experiences.

This book would never have become a reality without the generous support of the William R. Kenan Endowment Fund of the Academical Village. A Kenan Fellowship supported the early stages of our research, and the endowment rose to the occasion to support its publication with an outpouring of generosity greater than we could have ever expected. Lucy Russell, Brian Cullaty, and others at the Center for Undergraduate Excellence and the Mary and David Harrison Institute for American History, Literature, and Culture were tireless supporters in their administration of the Kenan Fellowship. We are eternally grateful to the Kenan

Endowment, and we hope that generations at the University will benefit as much as we did from the opportunities it makes possible.

We would also like to thank the Jefferson Literary and Debating Society for access to its archives; David Mattern of the Papers of James Madison, for his help uncovering the Society's letter to James Madison; as well as Alderman Library and the Albert and Shirley Small Special Collections Library at the University of Virginia, the Virginia Historical Society, the Library of Virginia, and the Albemarle Charlottesville Historical Society, all of which hold significant resources used in drafting this volume. The staffs of these institutions are the unsung heroes of the historical craft.

Last, I would like to thank Sean O'Brien and Jennifer Patja of the Robert H. Smith Center for the Constitution at James Madison's Montpelier. I did a large part of my writing in the Center's Gupton Library during a few stays in the picturesque Constitutional Village before I joined the Center staff, and when the last chapter seemed like it would never be finished, Jen encouraged me to keep writing. Her support kept me going until the last words found their way onto the page, and she inspires me to be the best writer I can be. I am fortunate to call them both colleagues, and more importantly friends.

Charlottesville, Virginia
Thomas Howard
May 11, 2016

CHAPTER ONE

The Founding

1825–1829

A chorus of young voices rings out through the crisp night air on the University of Virginia's West Range. They proudly proclaim, in the sort of imperfect unison only achieved by the cadence of a familiar call and response:

holding it to be true, that opinions, springing out of solitary observation and reflection, are seldom, in the first instance, correct; that the faculties of the mind are excited by collision; that friendships are cemented, errors corrected and sound principles established by society and intercourse; and, especially in a country where all are free to profess and by argument maintain their opinions, that the powers of debate should be sedulously cultivated.[1]

The students conclude their happy oath with a pledge to associate "themselves under the name of the Jefferson Society of the University of Virginia." Then the pounding of a gavel rings out, and in a moment dozens of eager shouts begin to call for the attention of the chair to be recognized for a chance to speak at the lectern. This scene has repeated itself, verbatim, at the beginning of each term since 1825, as students have gathered to devote themselves to literary pursuits and the art of debate as part of the University of Virginia's oldest student organization, the Jefferson Society.

The Sage of Monticello settled back in his chair and gazed out over the Lawn. It was the last of June 1826. In the waning days of his life, Thomas Jefferson often journeyed the three miles from his mountaintop home at Monticello to the University he fathered to check in on the newly opened institution. On this particular occasion, he sat for over an hour in the doorway of the Rotunda, in a chair a student had provided for him. He observed a feverish pitch of activity. Workmen were lifting the first of twelve marble Corinthian capitals that had just arrived from Italy. Students crisscrossed the Lawn from their dormitories to their classes in the ten pavilions that dotted the colonnade. Jefferson's long-held dream had finally become a reality.[2]

That dream, to build a University of Virginia, dated back almost half a century. In 1778, a much younger Jefferson introduced to the Virginia General Assembly his "Bill for the More General Diffusion of Knowledge," a plan to create several free public schools across the Commonwealth.[3] Although the bill failed to pass, it offers us an early glimpse into Jefferson's belief in the importance of public education. After his retirement from politics in 1809, Jefferson turned to this project in greater earnestness. Over the next decade, Jefferson, aided by his close friend and legislative ally Joseph C. Cabell, sought to convince the Virginia Legislature to fund a new public university in Virginia.[4]

Jefferson had grand goals for this new university. First and foremost, he believed it would become "the most eminent" institution of higher learning in the United States and "draw to it the youth of every state."[5] He was convinced that such an institution would be invaluable in promoting and developing the "natural aristocracy" of future political leaders.[6] Beyond the simple desire to educate young Americans, however, Jefferson hoped that the University of Virginia would serve as a southern counterweight to northern schools such as Harvard and Yale. He feared that "if our legislature does not heartily push our University, we must send our children for education to Kentucky or Cambridge. The latter will return them to us fanatics and tories, the former will keep them to add to their population. If however we are to go a begging any where for our education, I would rather it should be to Kentucky than any other state, because she has more of the flavor of the old cask than any other."[7]

Jefferson's design for the University of Virginia was just as grandiose as his goals for its success. Instead of constructing one large building to house students, dining facilities, and classrooms, as did most schools of the time (like his own alma mater William and Mary), Jefferson imagined a different configuration. His vision was of an Academical Village, two long rows of student dormitory rooms interspaced with ten pavilions, which would serve as faculty residences and lecture halls. These buildings would face a central, grassy Lawn, at the head of which would be the

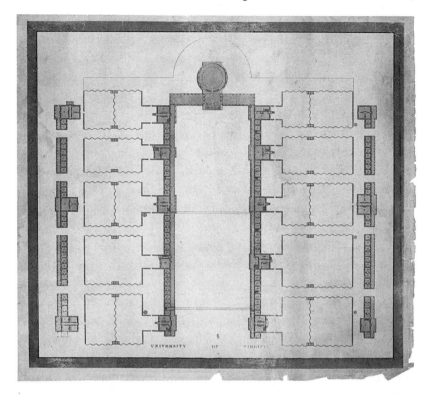

FIGURE 1. The Peter Maverick engraving of the Academical Village shows Jefferson's plans for the Lawn enclosed by student rooms and pavilions with the Rotunda at the head, which would serve as a library. Image courtesy of the Albert and Shirley Small Special Collections Library at the University of Virginia, *Peter Maverick Plan of the University, 1825*, Accession #6552 and 6552-a.

Rotunda, a large, classically designed building which would serve as the library. Unlike almost all colleges and universities of the age, Jefferson insisted that a library, not a church or chapel, should be the focal point of the University of Virginia. Two additional rows of student rooms and six "hotels," or boarding facilities, faced outward to form the Ranges, which enclosed working gardens and completed the Academical Village.[8]

Jefferson and Cabell made their first great stride toward establishing the University in 1816 when the Virginia General Assembly granted legal status to Jefferson's Central College in Charlottesville, Virginia. The state legislature then passed a bill in February 1818 providing funds for a University of Virginia and establishing what came to be known as the Rockfish Gap Commission to select a location for the school.[9] Jefferson, one of the twenty-one commissioners on the panel, was able to convince the commission both to locate the University at his Central College and to adopt his educational philosophy for the new school. Unlike most contemporary institutions of higher education, "the new University would award as much emphasis to the modern sciences and modern languages as it did to the ancient languages, and as much to useful information derived from their study as to reasoning faculties developed from such studies."[10] Students could elect to take coursework from any of the eight original faculty chairs in ancient languages, mathematics, medicine, natural philosophy, modern languages, moral philosophy, law, and chemistry.[11] Each subject area had its own requirements for the completion of a degree. With this innovative philosophy and design, and with Thomas Jefferson as rector, the University officially opened its doors to students in March 1825.

The students who fell under Jefferson's watchful gaze in June 1826 were a small, rowdy bunch. There were only about one hundred of them, all but a handful of whom lived in the rooms on the Lawn and on the Ranges. In the early days of the University of Virginia, violence and misbehavior among the students were common. On one notable occasion, for example, a student threw a brick at Professor John P. Emmet, an Irishman, during a small riot over the presence of foreign professors.[12] Almost immediately after the University opened its doors in 1825, a major student revolt, complete with armed students and terrorism of the faculty, erupted in quiet Charlottesville.[13] The faculty responded by instituting strict rules for conduct, requiring students to keep to a nine p.m. curfew. They forbade drinking, gambling, and smoking and required students to wear a drab grey uniform on school days.[14] One reason for this early disorder was the distinct lack of student activities in the years immediately after the University opened its doors, leaving young, brash Southern gentlemen with little to do outside of the classroom but cause trouble.

Students at universities everywhere in the United States in the early years of the country sought to capture some authority to regulate their own affairs outside of the classes they were required to take by the faculty and trustees, as well as to relieve the tedium of lectures, examination, and recitation. They began to organize their own activities and groups, which according to historian of higher education John Thelin, "meant that if students found the formal curriculum to be stultifying, they at least had reasonable odds of finding or initiating pursuits outside of the classroom and the formal course of study."[15] One of the early activities that emerged were student-initiated literary societies. At most universities in the seventeenth and eighteenth centuries, the curriculum was rigidly prescribed by the faculty, often centering on classical texts. Students did not enjoy a great amount of autonomy, and they found their education to bear little relation to the world around them. They created literary societies "as a means to training themselves to think, write, and speak."[16] Described by historian Thomas Harding as "virtually little republics, with their own laws and a democratically elected student administration," literary societies "furnished a climate of opinion and a forum for developing talents and personalities unequalled by any other facet of college life or instruction—then or now."[17] They also provided an escape from the monotony of attending class and a way to form lasting bonds with classmates.

Students at the University of Virginia followed the example of their counterparts at other major universities across the country in forming student groups. Among these were the American Whig and Cliosophic Societies, founded at the College of New Jersey (Princeton) in 1769 and 1770, respectively, and the Dialectic and Philanthropic Societies at the University of North Carolina, both founded in 1795.[18] Whig and Clio were both modeled after representative legislative bodies, and members partook in debate to pass "legislation" reflective of the aggregate view of the body. This process was meant to provide political training to their members, giving them the tools to enter public life after graduating. The Dialectic and Philanthropic Societies at North Carolina promoted debate enthusiastically, recognizing its utility in engaging students with the salient issues of the day. In England, the Oxford Union, perhaps the most famous collegiate literary society, was founded in 1823.[19] Given this trend, it is not surprising that the students at the University of Virginia, the sons of the leading families in the Commonwealth and across the antebellum South, would want to follow any example they felt would provide them advantages later in life.

The first literary society at the University of Virginia was the Patrick Henry Society, which was founded only days after students arrived. Very little is known about this short-lived organization other than its reputation for boisterous, disorganized meetings, which reflected student conduct of the period. A very large portion of the student body took part in the proceedings of the Patrick Henry Society, whose meetings were open to the public and frequently visited by curious residents of Charlottesville.

Some members of the Patrick Henry Society soon became dissatisfied with the chaotic conduct of the organization. These young southern
gentlemen sought a model similar to the formal, prescribed meetings
of the Whig and Clio Societies at the College of New Jersey. They also
hoped to keep out the local Charlottesville rabble by restricting attendance at meetings to the members only. On July 14, 1825, sixteen members
of the Patrick Henry Society met in Room 7, West Lawn, to form a new
literary society for the University of Virginia, one they would name after
the University's founder—the Jefferson Society. The Society would prosper over the next two centuries, becoming one of the most notable and
important student organizations at the University of Virginia, a position
it still occupies today.[20]

The identities of several of the sixteen founders are lost to history, but
the names of nine of the faction that split from the Patrick Henry Society are recorded for posterity: Edgar Mason, John W. Brockenbrough,
Mann A. Page, John H. Lee, J. N. Tazewell, William G. Minor, Robert A.
Thompson, Robert Saunders Jr., and Thomas Barclay were among those
who met in Room 7 on July 14.[21]

In the following months, the original sixteen would do much to define
the Jefferson Society as a young but promising organization, setting it on
the course that would carry it through the next two hundred years. Much
of what they decided and many of their actions still lie at the heart of the
Jefferson Society in its meetings, identity, and lore. They chose mottos,
designed emblems, selected colors, adopted Greek letters, and elected
honorary members, all of which helped to capture and mold the spirit
of the organization they were striving to create. They drew upon what
they knew, following the example of other literary societies, colleges, and
political leaders across the country and the world.

Four days after the first meeting, on July 19, a committee consisting of
Mason, Lee, and Minor met next door in Room 5, West Lawn, and drafted
the Society's first constitution, a document that unfortunately does not
survive.[22] Presumably, the initial constitution laid out basic structure for
the Society's meetings, qualifications for membership, and a statement
of purpose. Meetings followed accepted rules of order (*Robert's Rules of
Order* would not be published until 1876) and likely kept to a strict agenda.
The president would call the meeting to order and invite the secretary to
call the roll and read the minutes of the last meeting. Applicants for membership would learn of their fate early in the meeting, as voting on new

members seems to have been one of the first orders of business. Members chosen as debaters would then discuss a predetermined question, debates that quickly gained a reputation for being hotly contested, divisive, and theatrical. They would often go on for hours as members fought to voice their opinion over the roar of the crowd. Before the meeting adjourned, the Society would take care of any administrative business and select a question for debate at the next meeting. All of the decisions made by the Society were governed by painstakingly delineated processes allowing for a particular number of speakers on any question and differing voting ratios depending on the nature of the question being considered.[23]

The aspiring young statesmen of the new Jefferson Society showed such an obsession with the mechanics of the constitution in the formative days that meetings often became bogged down in discussion of proposed amendments. Eventually, members who proposed an amendment that ultimately failed to pass were fined one dollar for wasting the Society's time.[24]

Because of the desire to rectify the disorder the founders perceived in the Patrick Henry Society and the student body, rules for meeting procedure and behavior were instituted in the Jefferson Society. In February 1827, a strict policy of secrecy was imposed upon the membership, with expulsion as the penalty for violation. When they were inducted, members were placed under "the most solemn injunction not to divulge any of its proceedings, or, anything which may occur within its walls."[25] This would remain the policy of the Society for many years. The rowdy spirit of the students could not be quelled however, and the Society took still more efforts to regulate meetings. It convened a regular court after each meeting, presided over by two judges, which heard all appeals and issued fines, a custom that continued until 1838.[26]

At the meeting on July 19, 1825, the members chose their first officers. Edgar Mason was elected moderator; John H. Lee, vice-moderator; Mann A. Page, secretarius; and J. N. Tazewell, bibliothecarius.[27] These titles for officers fell out of use at some point in the following ten to fifteen years, and they became known by their present, more conventional names, such as president and secretary, as they appear in the constitution drafted in 1837, the oldest surviving version.[28] These positions, along with their presumptive functions, are consistent with those adopted by almost every other literary society at the time.[29]

It is worth noting that the bibliothecarius, or librarian, a position that no longer exists, would have been charged with maintaining the Society's

library. Building a library for the use of its members was a major function of any early college literary society because of the prohibitively high
price of books. Most college libraries had strict rules regulating the use
and accessibility of books, and separate libraries maintained by literary
societies provided a more convenient alternative for students. They contained volumes of greater interest to students, such as literature and history—a departure from the regimented holdings of university libraries,
which kept strictly to the established curriculum. Libraries maintained
by literary societies could also be updated more quickly, and they held
subscriptions to periodicals of interest to students.[30] At the University
of North Carolina, the Dialectic and Philanthropic Societies maintained
a large library of approximately ten thousand volumes, which became
the foundation for building the University of North Carolina library collections after the Civil War. While it was in all likelihood not as large
as its North Carolina counterpart, by the middle of the nineteenth century the Jefferson Society's library was in its own right one of the largest
academic libraries not directly associated with a university on the East
Coast. The Society donated its library to the University of Virginia in
the 1850s, after which it was housed in the Rotunda. Unfortunately, the
entire library burned in the Rotunda Fire of 1895, along with most of the
Society's records.[31]

Edgar Mason called the first meetings to order every Monday evening "at candlelight." This soon changed to every fortnight, as the Society
adjusted to how much business it needed to conduct. The place and time
of early meetings varied widely, adapting to the availability of university
buildings. The first meetings were held in Pavilion I on the west side of
the Lawn. Later they moved to Pavilion IV, which was not in use as a
residence, and Pavilion VII, the modern-day Colonnade Club. The Jefferson Society continued to compete with other societies, such as the
Washington Society, as well as with classes for a more permanent place
to meet, frequently petitioning both the faculty and the Board of Visitors
for a meeting room. Such a space was finally granted in 1837, when the
Society was allowed to meet in Hotel C on the West Range, the building
it has occupied ever since.[32]

As did most literary societies of the day, these early members designed
a badge, or seal, that could be used on official documents and to brand
the Society. It would also have been worn on certain occasions to denote
membership. The Jefferson Society's original badge consisted of "a scroll,

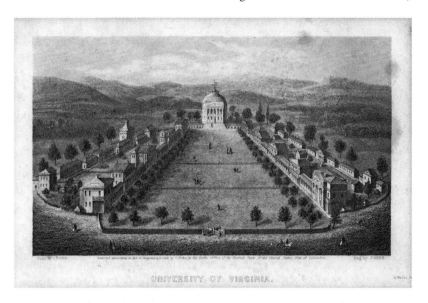

FIGURE 2. This engraving by John Sertz from 1856 shows a view of the Lawn from the south. Early generations of students lived, worked, and studied in Jefferson's Academical Village. The Lawn was a lively space which placed them in regular contact with faculty, who lived and taught in pavilions interspersed among the student rooms. Image courtesy of the Albert and Shirley Small Special Collections Library at the University of Virginia, University of Virginia Visual History Collection, U.Va. Prints and Photographs File, RG-30/1/10.011, Print 00018.

on which appeared the Declaration of Independence transversed by a spear, surmounted with the cap of Liberty; on the reverse shall be the name of the Society, its date of birth, encircled by a wreath of laurel."[33] On the front of the badge appeared the first motto of the Society: *"Pro Patria, Pro Libertate, atque Pro Litteris,"* or "For Country, for Liberty, and for Literature."[34]

Over the course of the nineteenth century at the University of Virginia, other organizations used a variety of methods to signal membership, including pins, ribbons, and colored clothing. Ribbons were by far the most popular devices, and a number of early student organizations became known as "ribbon societies," the most notable of which were Eli Banana and T.I.L.K.A. While the Jefferson Society was never known as a ribbon society proper, members often wore a "bunch of ribbons, the colors of which [were] to be Blue, White, and Pink, to be worn on the left Lapelie of the coat," probably simply because of the popularity of ribbons among the student body.[35]

Like many of the institutions at the new University, all of these particular symbols adopted by the Society would eventually change. The
color of the Society was designated as blue alone in 1834, by which time
the Washington Society had adopted white as its color and another society had taken pink.[36] The badge and motto were changed in 1848 to their
current forms.[37] The seal now features a silhouette of Jefferson with two
quills crossed behind it and the Greek letters of the Society, all enclosed
in a triangle.

The Society's new motto was "*Haec olim meminisse iuvabit.*" This
famous quote, taken from Virgil's *Aeneid*, is commonly translated as "In
the future it will be pleasing to remember these things." At the time, many
college students felt that they were "poised on the brink of adult responsibilities and tribulations," and "they sadly felt that the joys they experienced as students would be gone forever."[38] In these early days, University
students rarely stayed longer than two years, with many leaving after one
or two sessions. They saw their college days as brief but blissful respites
before entering the long, difficult battle that was adult life. This new motto
reflected the ephemeral nature of college life and future longing to return
to the "sunny hours of youth" after leaving the University.[39]

The Greek letters adopted by the Jefferson Society in the 1820s are the
only original identifiers still in use today. It is unclear exactly when they
were adopted, but they were doubtless embraced within the first three
years of the Society: *Phi*, for *philoi*, meaning brotherhood; *Pi*, for *patris*,
meaning fatherland; and *Theta*, for *theos*, meaning divinity. In the early
nineteenth century, it was quite rare for an organization to adopt Greek
letters; such a convention was not widely practiced until the middle of
the century.[40] When the Jefferson Society was founded, only one notable
organization had done so: Phi Beta Kappa, founded in 1776 at the College
of William and Mary. The first social fraternities followed soon after the
Jefferson Society, likewise adopting Greek letters. Most were founded in
the north, such as the Kappa Alpha Society (1825) and Sigma Phi (1827),
both at Union College in Schenectady, New York.[41]

Honorary Members

The expectation of political and oratorical training brought students to
the sessions of the Jefferson Society, but the only way the young orga-

nization could retain membership and operate effectively was to build credibility for itself in the eyes of both the students and the community. The first members employed a powerful tool to enhance the prestige of the Society and define it as an organization: the election of prominent public figures to honorary membership. This was a common practice for nineteenth-century literary societies, serving to stake out intellectual and political territory and lending credibility as they made a name for themselves.[42] Notable individuals who accepted honorary membership often came in person to one or more meetings of the organization, particularly if they had ties to the school. Honorary members also often shared their thoughts on the value of literary associations with the student members, either in person or by letter. Young students thus gained an invaluable opportunity to affiliate with the political elite of the day while simultaneously enhancing their society's prestige.

The Jefferson Society's earliest members appreciated the political training they received in the Society and at the University, and sought to enrich it through association with elite Virginia figures. "From the beginning the founders of the University of Virginia focused on the specific task of educating Virginia's youth to take charge of Virginia's political destiny," efforts that were reinforced by a close relationship between the University's Board of Visitors and the Jefferson Society.[43] Three of the first individuals elected to honorary membership in the Jefferson Society— Jefferson himself, James Madison, and James Monroe—were members of the Board of Visitors and the most important members of Virginia's national political dynasty after George Washington died in 1799.

The first Jefferson Society members were the sons of wealthy planters, so naturally they hoped to model themselves after the prominent Virginians on the Board of Visitors. To promote these relationships, "they wrote letters to them, commemorated their achievements as a body, and practiced their statesmanship on the friendly confines of the university campus."[44] Electing these prominent men to honorary membership was a strong expression of a desire to build ties with them and emulate their example in public life. Jefferson was the first elected, on the motion of Robert A. Thompson, one of the original sixteen members.[45] On August 11, 1825, a committee of three drafted a letter to express the good news to Jefferson:[46]

University of Va, Aug. 11 1825

We, a committee of the Jefferson Society of the University of Virginia, appointed for that purpose, have the honour to inform you of your election as an honorary member of that Society; And in doing so, permit us to express, in the name of that Society, of which we are the organ, and for ourselves individually, the sincere respect which we entertain for your character as a man, and the profound gratitude with which we are impressed for your imminent services as a patron of science, a politician and a philanthropist. We are, with sentiments of the highest esteem and veneration, Your obedient servants,

Committee—

Edgar Mason
John W. Brockenbrough
Robt. Saunders Jr.

The Society received Mr. Jefferson's reply the next day. He declined honorary membership, appealing to the responsibilities he held to all the students at his University, not wanting to show favor, preference, or undue support to any one group or segment of students. He wrote in handwriting cramped by his old age:[47]

Monticello, Aug. 12, 1825

I am very thankful, gentlemen, for the honor done me by the society of which you are a committee, in electing me one of its honorary members. I could decline no distinction conferred by them, nor service I could render them, but on reasons of still higher importance to themselves, on maturely weighing the general relation in which the law of the University and the appointment by its visitors have placed me as to every member of the institution, I believe it my duty to make no change in those relations by entering into additional and different ties with different associations of its members. The duties with which I am charged require that in all cases which may arise, I shall stand in an equal position as to every person concerned, not only that I may preserve the inestimable consciousness of impartiality to all, but the equally inestimable exemption from all suspicion of partialities. Your kind expressions towards myself ensure to me, I hope, an equally kind acceptance of the reasons on which I act, and I can add with truth on behalf of my colleagues of the visitation, that the highest reward they can receive from their joint cares and exertions on behalf of this institution, is the anticipated hope and relief that they are rearing up in science and in virtue those on whom the hopes of their country rest for future government and prosperity. For myself, I pray you to accept assurances of my sincere affections and best wishes,

Th. Jefferson

Despite feeling constrained by his position as rector of the Board of Visitors, Jefferson was likely very pleased to see the development of a budding literary society at the University, believing strongly as he did in the ideals of self-improvement and democracy such organizations promoted. This sentiment is confirmed by Jefferson's service as the president of the American Philosophical Society, a position he occupied for no less than eighteen years.[48]

Neither James Madison nor James Monroe felt such constraint, and both accepted their offers of honorary membership. Madison was notified (perhaps for a second time) of his election on May 5, 1827, in a letter similar to the one Jefferson received:[49]

University of Virginia, May 5th 182[7]

Dear Sir,

The documents of our society having been misplaced and we not being able to ascertain whether you have been informed that you were elected an honorary member of the Jefferson society as a committee have the honour to announce to you your appointment, and that we shall feel ourselves much gratified whenever you visit the University to be honoured with your attendance—We are Sir with respect and esteem Your Obt. Sevts.

John Willis
Thos. S. Gholson
R. Howerton

Both Madison and Monroe would serve longer on the Board of Visitors than Jefferson, who died in 1826, and along with the rest of the board, both would support the Society in that capacity. On July 17, 1827, for example, the Board of Visitors responded to the Society's request for a meeting place by allowing that "while the board cannot permanently appropriate to their use, the room which they now occupy, they will not be unnecessarily disturbed in the use of it, but will be permitted to occupy it as heretofore, till it shall be required for some other purposes of the University."[50] Both Madison and Monroe were in attendance at that session of the Board of Visitors, with Madison serving as rector.

A more charming offer of honorary membership was extended to the Marquis de Lafayette, a celebrity in the United States because of his assistance in the American Revolution. While he was in the United States, Lafayette was invited to the University of Virginia; his visit culminated with a public dinner in the Rotunda on August 20, 1825. Before the dinner, John H. Lee, one of the original sixteen who was then serving as president, approached Lafayette on the Lawn and informed him of his election to honorary membership. In good humor, Lafayette replied,

> While under the auspices of a name equally cherished and venerated by all of us, gentlemen, I am initiated to the honour of a fellowship in your institution, I find myself under an additional obligation to your juvenile kindness. I am happy, my dear sir, in those testimonies of affection, to recognize your feelings towards us, the soldiers of independence and freedom—and your attachment to the republican principles for which we have had the honor to fight and bleed. With the most lively gratitude, I accept, and shall ever keep the favour you have been pleased to confer upon me, and while I most cordially reciprocate your friendly wishes on my behalf, I beg you to accept my affectionate acknowledgements.[51]

After dinner, Lafayette toasted the University, saying, "The University of Virginia: May it more and more diffuse through every part of mankind, the principles, the feelings, and the benefits of true knowledge, general philanthropy and unalloyed republicanism."[52]

The Jefferson Society further defined itself politically by who it did not select as an honorary member. We know of at least one more early American statesman who was considered, but ultimately rejected for honorary membership in the Jefferson Society: John Randolph of Roanoke. Randolph had earlier split with Jefferson and formed his own faction of the Democratic-Republican Party and opposed Monroe's candidacy for president. Randolph went so far as to refer to Jefferson as "St. Thomas of *Canting*bury," a reference to St. Thomas of Canterbury, bemoaning the indiscriminate manner with which he felt Americans followed Jefferson's overly idealistic view of democracy.[53] When his name was brought up, the Society denied him membership out of deference to both Jefferson and Monroe. By rejecting Randolph, the Society clearly displayed its political loyalties.

By 1825, Madison, Monroe, and Jefferson occupied a well-defined political niche. At first pass, the Jefferson Society cast its lot in favor of the Democratic-Republican philosophy of these three men and their emphasis on the role states were meant to play in their conception of Union. While the political makeup and leanings of the Jefferson Society would be quite fluid by nature because of high student turnover from year to year, Jeffersonian ideals of republicanism remained central to the political socialization that occurred in the Jefferson Society.[54]

Edgar Allan Poe

One of the young men who joined the Jefferson Society in the early days was Edgar Allan Poe. He came to the University of Virginia in its second session, which began on February 1, 1826. When Poe arrived at the University, the student body had grown slightly from the previous term, to 177 students. Poe matriculated on February 14, one of five students to do so on that day.[55] According to Miles George, a student at the time, Poe first lived briefly on West Lawn, but no records survive to indicate in which room.[56] We do know, however, that he later moved to 13 West Range, the room that has now become famous as the poet's residence for the majority of the one year he spent at the University.

Poe was likely encouraged to attend the University of Virginia by General John H. Cocke, a member of the first Board of Visitors as well as a friend and associate of John Allan, Poe's foster father. Allan provided for Poe while he was at the University, sending him clothes and other necessities.

As a young man, Poe displayed a penchant for languages, both ancient and modern. The early curriculum of the University of Virginia allowed students to choose their course of study, selecting "tickets," or classes in the subjects they wanted to take, the exams for which would be administered at the end of the session by the Board of Visitors.[57] Poe took "tick-

FIGURE 3. A young Edgar Allan Poe, from an oil portrait by H. Inman. Image courtesy of the Albert and Shirley Small Special Collections Library at the University of Virginia, University of Virginia Visual History Collection, U.Va. Prints and Photographs File, RG-30/1/10.011, Print 15791.

ets" in Latin, Greek, French, Spanish, and Italian from George Long, the Chair of Ancient Languages, and George Blaetermann, the Chair of Modern Languages. Together, the two would teach Poe his full slate of classes. Long came to Virginia from Trinity College at Cambridge where he was a fellow. At the University, he established a strong standard of linguistic scholarship during his brief tenure, which lasted until 1828. If Long was one of the stars of the original faculty, Blaetermann achieved considerably less success, as he was ultimately dismissed from his chair in 1838 by request of the student body, after gaining a reputation as a violent and easily angered man. He appears, however, to have been a competent instructor.[58]

By all accounts, Poe was an excellent student and attended class regularly. A report authored in January 1827 by the Board of Visitors and delivered to the Virginia General Assembly tracked the progress of the students enrolled in the new University. Poe appears twice in the report, once ranked fourth in the Senior Latin class, and again ranked sixth in the Senior French class. Poe's translation of Tasso in the Modern Languages Pavilion even earned him the praise of the cantankerous Professor Blaetermann.[59]

Records of Poe's reading in the University library allow us to get a sense of the young author's literary interests. In the early days of the University, independent reading was an important part of the curriculum, as students spent relatively little time in the classroom. The library itself, however, was strictly regulated: to borrow books students were required to request them in advance and pick them up on the one day per week the library was open. The library records show six volumes that Poe drew from the shelves: Charles Rollin's *Ancient History*, William Robertson's *America*, John Marshall's biography of George Washington, Voltaire's *Histoire Particulière*, and Nicholas Dufief's *Nature Displayed*.[60] By no means do these five titles constitute the extent of Poe's reading. William Wertenbaker, the first University librarian, reported seeing him frequently at work in the library. He probably also purchased several volumes from local booksellers, such as the copy of Byron that Thomas Bolling, one of Poe's fellow students, reported buying with him.[61] It is also likely that Poe partook of the fledgling Jefferson Society library, which members had begun to compile by the time Poe was a student.

Much speculation surrounds Poe's personal life while he attended the University as well as the reasons for his early exit from school. For example, his friend William Wertenbaker claimed that Poe never drank in Charlottesville, or if he did, he did so sparingly.[62] On the other hand, Edwin Alderman, the first president of the University of Virginia, who served from 1904 to 1931, had a different opinion. In a memorial speech given in Poe's honor, he speculated, "it is certain that Poe gambled and drank at the University," but went on to explain, "it should be understood that he was not expelled, dismissed, or disciplined in any fashion whatever."[63] T. G. Tucker, one of Poe's neighbors on West Range, described Poe's alcoholism: "His passion for strong drink was even then of a most marked and peculiar character. He would always seize the tempting glass, generally unmixed with sugar or water—in fact, perfectly straight—and without the least apparent pleasure, swallow the contents, never pausing until the last drop had passed his lips."[64] It is clear that Poe's lifelong battle with addiction had already begun during his time at the University of Virginia. We also know that Poe gambled—John Allan was forced to take a trip to Charlottesville to settle many of Poe's debts, which reportedly amounted to roughly $2,500.[65]

By all descriptions, Poe moved through his student days as a loner, but he seems to have found a home and companionship in the Jefferson Society. The intellectual discourse of the Society was probably a haven for the young artist, both to display his budding literary abilities and to find some reprieve from the chaos of 1820s student life. He was elected to membership on June 17, 1826, at the tail end of the Society's first year of existence.[66] By that time, the Jefferson Society had come into its own, counting thirty-two young men as members.[67] Unfortunately, we know little of Poe's activities in the Society compared to those of other famous alumni.

Shortly after he joined the Society, Poe delivered an essay entitled "Heat and Cold," the text of which does not survive. He was active in the meetings of the Society and presumably as regular in his attendance as he was to his classes. At one meeting, Poe served as secretary pro tempore and recorded the minutes for that evening.[68] Poe's signature attesting to the accuracy and completeness of his minutes was clipped from the minute book and stolen by Lancelot Minor Blackford, a member in the late 1850s. The signature was purchased at auction by a group of alumni and returned to the Society in 1988.[69]

Of those who knew Poe from the Jefferson Society, John Willis wrote most extensively. "Poe had many noble qualities," Willis recalled, "and nature had endowed him with more of genius, and a far greater diversity of talent, than any other whom it had been my lot to have known ... His disposition was rather *retiring* and he had few intimate associates."[70] Willis concluded, "in the days of his youth, when first entering upon manhood," Poe's "bosom was warmed by sentiments of the most generous and noble character."[71]

Poe thrived in the intellectual environment of the Jefferson Society. He would often host readings of poetry or short stories in his room on the West Range, where his friends, many of whom were Society members, would sit for hours and listen to Poe dramatically deliver his work. Poe's listeners generally admired his presentations, but

on one occasion Poe read a story of great length to some of his friends [likely Jefferson Society members] who, in a spirit of jest spoke lightly of its merits, and jokingly told him that his hero's name, "Gaffy" occurred too often. His proud spirit would not stand such rebuke; so in a fit of anger ... he flung every sheet into a blazing fire.[72]

It is not surprising that Poe cultivated such a following in the Society, which since its founding has enjoyed a lively and close-knit intellectual community both inside, and perhaps more importantly, outside of Jefferson Hall. Its members hold a diverse variety of interests, and the time spent in the Society forges strong bonds of friendship that extend into all corners of the lives of its members. It is likely that Poe laid the seeds of some of his closest friendships as he read to Society members late at night in his room on the West Range.

Poe was also fond of drawing, which he almost never did on paper, but rather on the walls of his room. Miles George recalled,

Poe, as has been said, was fond of quoting poetic authors and reading poetic productions of his own, with which his friends were delighted & entertained, then suddenly a change would come over him & he would with a piece of charcoal evince his versatile genius by sketching upon the walls of his dormitory, whimsical, fanciful, & grotesque figures.[73]

Poe's sudden mood swings would mark the end of the night for his friends, who would leave the troubled youth to draw in solitude until the next reading occurred.

Poe leaves vivid reminiscences of the University and the surrounding countryside in his work. His short story "A Tale of the Ragged Mountains," though not written while Poe was a student, is based heavily on his time in Charlottesville and begins with the line, "During the fall of the year 1827, while residing near Charlottesville, Virginia, I casually made the acquaintance of Mr. Augustus Bedloe." Bedloe's wanderings in the Blue Ridge Mountains paralleled Poe's own experience.[74] Images of Charlottesville appear through his work, sometimes directly, other times only as part of a larger picture, but it is very apparent that Charlottesville made a powerful and enduring impression on the young poet.

Poe left the University of Virginia on December 15, 1826, when the term expired. He had accumulated such a monumental debt that John Allan refused to send him back to the University for a second session. His debts included, among many other things, expenses for a servant who attended to his room (as every student was expected to have in those days) and bills from local Charlottesville merchants.[75] Allan paid Poe's "legitimate debts" but refused to pay off his gambling obligations. Despite the fact that Poe considered his gambling losses to be "debts of honor" and often voiced his intention to repay them, it is unlikely that he was ever able to do so.

Poe is remembered fondly by the Jefferson Society. In 1861, the Society undertook to raise money to support Maria Clemm, Poe's ailing and poverty-stricken mother-in-law.[76] Later, on January 16, 1909, the Society hosted an event to commemorate the centenary of Poe's birth. The event drew considerable attendance and featured a slate of speakers, each of whom detailed a different aspect of Poe's life. "Poe Night," as it became known, was celebrated annually until the 1940s, when a change in the academic schedule put the date during the winter recess.[77] The Society still actively commemorates Poe's time as a member by hosting Poe reading contests and referring to the secretary's chair in Jefferson Hall as the Poe Chair.

In a 1907 speech on Poe delivered by Edwin Alderman, himself an honorary member of the Jefferson Society, the University president said of the poet, "Poe has endowed his alma mater with immortal distinction, and left it a legacy which will increase with the years. It is not the endowment of money, for there was no scrip left in his purse, but simply the endowment of a few songs and a fund of unconquerable idealism."[78] Alderman went on to say,

True he is no exemplar to whom we can point our youth, but the fact that there is a little room on West Range in which dwelt a world poet, who never wrote an unclean word and who sought after beauty in form as passionately as a coarse man might seek after gain, has contributed an irreducible total of good to the spirit which men breathe as well as a wide fame to his alma mater that will outlive all disaster, or change, or ill-fortune.[79]

Poe's memory lives on in the Society, helping to define its spirit of literary creativity from its earliest days.

———

Poe's contemporaries in the Jefferson Society distinguished themselves academically as well. In the same report on the progress of students that places Poe near the top of his French and Latin classes, a handful of other students known to be members of the Jefferson Society are recorded excelling in a variety of different classes. Robert M. T. Hunter, who would later become Speaker of the House of Representatives, finished third in the Junior Mathematics class and first in the Moral Philosophy class. John Willis placed fifth in Junior French, Chapman Johnson sixth in Natural Philosophy, and Mann A. Page, one of the original sixteen, fifth in Law.[80]

Outside of the classroom and in the sessions of the Society, these men cultivated close, personal relationships. Rebecca Lomax, a close friend of Robert M. T. Hunter, recommended her "Cousin Mann Page, to you, as an acquaintance. He will deliver this letter to you. And from what I have told him in respect to you, he is anxious to cultivate your acquaintance."[81] It is entirely probable that the introduction to Page was the reason Hunter joined the Jefferson Society. Friendships begun in the Jefferson Society in these early days proved lasting, just as they would for future generations of Society members. Hunter served alongside William Ballard Preston, another early Jefferson Society member, as senators from Virginia in the Confederate Senate. In 1860, a delegation of three men who had been members of the Jefferson Society—Preston, Alexander H. H. Stuart, and George W. Randolph—met with President Lincoln in an effort to head off conflict before the Civil War.[82] Close, working relationships born in the Jefferson Society continue to characterize the organization to the present day.

With the Jefferson Society firmly established, over the following years it moved into the position of prominence it would come to occupy at the heart of the University of Virginia community. It rapidly grew in membership, eventually comprising almost half of the student body, and played an ever-increasing role in the events and happenings of the University. The Jefferson Society's celebrations at Final Exercises became the highlight of the University social calendar just a few years after the Society was founded. The Society also began publishing a magazine, filling the void of literary pursuits and journalism that existed at the young University. Soon, the Jefferson Society had moved into the mainstream of University life, a position it would occupy for years to come.

CHAPTER TWO

The Antebellum Era

1830–1860

The First Students

The University of Virginia opened its doors in 1825 to great fanfare and promise. Though the initial enrollment of students, 175, was slightly less than the aged Thomas Jefferson had anticipated, the young men who took up residence on the Lawn and Ranges in those early years were exactly the type of students that he had hoped the new University would attract.[1] His wish that the University be attended by men "especially of the South and West" was fulfilled by each successive class of students. Their presence allayed Jefferson's fear about the lack of quality education available in Virginia he had expressed in a letter to James Breckenridge a few years earlier: "We are now trusting to those who are against us in position and principle, to fashion to their own form the minds & affections of our youth . . . we must have there at all times 500 of our sons imbibing opinions and principles in discord with those of their own country. This canker is eating on the vitals of our existence, and if not arrested at once will be beyond remedy."[2] The University of Virginia would quickly become a place where elite southerners invested deliberately in their own future.

The matriculates in the first year and throughout the antebellum period were by and large the scions of wealthy planting families—the sons of the southern aristocracy, sent off to school to learn how best to occupy their position of high social standing and to complete their proper training as antebellum gentlemen. Historian Lorri Glover describes the process by which "southern sons" grew into elite southern gentlemen at the University of Virginia and institutions like it across the South: "Universities served a vital social function for southern elites: they were the setting for young men to begin the arduous, practiced process of acquir-

FIGURE 4. This iconic engraving by Edward Sachse in 1856 shows the University of Virginia from the west, looking down from Lewis Mountain; it includes a view of the Rotunda, the Annex, the Lawn and Ranges, and the Anatomical Theatre. Image courtesy of the Albert and Shirley Small Special Collections Library at the University of Virginia, University of Virginia Visual History Collection, U.Va. Prints and Photographs File, RG-30/1/10.011, Print 00017.

ing the reputation of gentlemen. Early republican southerners evinced a passion (verging on obsession) for social status and believed that a young man's future hung on public perceptions."[3] According to John Thelin, who also emphasizes the importance of the "stamp" a particular college placed on its graduates, "the University of Virginia had become successful at transmitting the distinctive code and culture of the nineteenth-century Virginia gentleman to its students and the South's future leadership."[4]

It was these privileged young men who would come to define both the Jefferson Society and the University itself over the next four decades, and almost every step they took on the Grounds of the University of Virginia was a deliberate posture to achieve this mark of gentlemanly stature. Their parents, who had lived through the American Revolution, perceived

that the persistence of the Republic depended on the talents and diligence of this generation of American sons. Elites also needed their boys to preserve family wealth and prominence. Without dutiful, accomplished sons, families foundered. For these sons, then, good was never good enough. Boys hoping to earn affirmation as men had to be great—precociously talented.[5]

Unlike many northern colleges, where a larger portion of the students were poor, the University of Virginia student body was almost entirely made up of the sons of rich, prominent families. The cost of attending the University of Virginia is evidence of their wealth. Including spending money and books, a University of Virginia student in the 1840s could easily expect to spend over $400 in a year. Compared to the annual expenses of attending Yale, Princeton, and Harvard—$195, $226, and $245, respectively—the high cost gives us a fair picture of the wealth of University students and their families.[6]

Another measuring stick with which we may grasp the affluence and power of these young men, this one quite graphic, is an appraisal of their most prized property: slaves. The families of the vast majority of students owned slaves in large numbers. Of thirty families from Virginia counties who sent their sons to the University of Virginia in 1830, thirteen owned twenty or more taxable slaves, and twelve more owned between ten and nineteen.[7] Slaves were the most valuable asset to an antebellum southern family. The high percentage of slave ownership among University students' families placed these young men solidly in the upper echelon of southern society. Glover remarks that slaveholding, almost as a matter of course, was closely related to the rituals of manhood undertaken in college. Southern status was "built of elites' domination of slaves," and they were concerned with preserving their upper-class slaveholding tradition, for "their experiences with educating their sons pushed state loyalties and then regional distinctions to the forefront of elite consciousness."[8]

It was not only a gentlemanly stamp of education that encouraged southern families to choose the University of Virginia as a destination for their sons; sectionalism also figured prominently in their thinking. Sectional tensions between North and South had been brewing in the United States since the nation's founding, and as time wore on they only intensified, exacerbated by events like the Missouri Crisis. Rich southern families were concerned that sending their sons to northern colleges would return them as abolitionists or proponents of a powerful central government, both of which were anathema to the southern planter class. They saw the University as an ideal alternative, a school that would train their future leaders in the southern mindset. Richard McIlwaine, a law student at the University in the 1850s and a Jefferson Society member, recalled a conversation with his father regarding where he should study law:

I expressed a preference for Harvard University . . . when he spoke up with great positiveness and said, "My son, those people in Boston do not agree with us either in politics or religion. You expect to live in the South and I advise you to continue your education among your own people. Any place that you choose south of Mason & Dixon's line will be acceptable to me." [I]t did not take me a minute to change my mind and to say "the University of Virginia," to which he responded, "That is all right. You will be there among your own people, who think as we do."[9]

The choice of an institution like the University of Virginia becomes particularly important when one considers, as noted historian of higher education Frederick Rudolph does, that a college education is not only a personal and social investment, but also a vehicle by which the dedicated graduates of a particular institution could serve civil society.[10] The penchant of southern parents for sending their sons to like-minded institutions would harden even further after the sectional crisis of 1850, causing the University's enrollment to expand rapidly until the onset of the Civil War.

The young men who attended the University of Virginia were concerned to the point of obsession with their conception of honor, as it related to themselves personally, to their families, and to their southern identity. As a result, they carried themselves in a manner which could only be described as haughty and arrogant to a contemporary observer, or worse, a northerner, but which would have seemed quite natural to them. They did not think twice about talking down or acting disrespectfully to those they saw as their inferiors, especially slaves, free blacks, poor whites, and foreign professors. Much to the chagrin of their parents, they were "typically rash and brash," according to Glover, and "largely rejected parental appeals to moderate public expression of their feeling. Instead they reveled in peer culture that lauded bravado and often resulted in indecorous, headstrong displays."[11]

An example of such behavior at the University occurred in 1839, when two students, Franklin English and Madison McAfee, got involved in an altercation with several free blacks. When a slave of Professor Charles Bonnycastle named Fielding tried to intervene, English became enraged that a slave would have the audacity to attempt to interfere with the affairs of a white man and promptly beat Fielding. When Bonnycastle himself tried to intervene and resolve the situation, the students became even more upset that the professor had tried to stop what they saw as "merited chastisement" of the slave. Instead of stopping the beating, one student held Bonnycastle back while the other beat Fielding until the slave "humbled . . . himself and English expressed himself satisfied."[12]

The antebellum students at the University engaged in a host of "pranks" which could perhaps better be described as assaults or riots. Almost nightly, groups of students would run the length of the Lawn yelling, singing, setting off fireworks, and even firing pistols. These displays were sometimes more pointed, directed against specific professors, as in 1833 when a student filled an ink bottle with gunpowder and tried to detonate it outside the window of the faculty chairman's house.[13] Such incidents greatly disturbed the faculty, who lived in close proximity to the students on the Lawn. Professors routinely attempted to have the students moved farther away from the dormitories on the Lawn, but to no avail. One such request argued that having faculty so close to the student living areas "provokes a spirit of defiance, and renders many disorderly for no other reason than to show they are not afraid to be so."[14]

It was often the professors' attempts to control and discipline students that provoked such outbursts. The wealthy planters' sons who attended the University at that time saw themselves as young gentlemen equal or superior in class and social standing to their professors, and they expected to be treated as such. The harsh rules imposed by the faculty on dress code, alcohol consumption, and daily schedules grated on the students' sense of propriety. They often felt that the faculty was treating them disrespectfully, something they would not stand for, especially from the many foreign professors teaching at Virginia. As antebellum historian Charles Wall notes, "coming from prominent, slave owning families, they were accustomed to command and to expect deference, not to being watched, summoned, and ordered about."[15]

Violence and misbehavior were not limited to student-faculty or student-servant interactions; student-on-student violence was also prevalent. Always prepared to respond to any perceived slight to their sense of honor and propriety, small matters between students often exploded into violence. The final recourse in disputes between southern men was the duel, which Glover calls "the ultimate defense of reputation and display of status among adult southern gentlemen."[16] In his comprehensive study, *The Shaping of Southern Culture,* preeminent southern historian Bertram Wyatt-Brown observes that duels publicly divided "respectable gentlemen from the rest of society."[17]

Whether with pistols, knives, or simply their fists, antebellum students saw a duel as the final arbiter of disputes and determinant of a man's honor. Wharton J. Green, a student in the 1850s argued that the duel was a "fair stand-up fight where neither has the advantage."[18] The urge to fight was so prevalent at the University that in only two months in 1836 the minutes of the faculty record four fights, all of which involved either dirks, pistols, or both.[19] University students believed that their personal and family honor was at stake in almost every daily interaction and that dueling, even to the death, would bring them great respect. For example, Charles Ellis, a Jefferson Society member in the mid-1830s, recorded that fellow Society member Louis Wigfall challenged another man to a duel while shouting "that his father and brother had been each shot in a duel and it was his wish to die thus also."[20]

Students and the Jefferson Society

Early students at the University clearly abhorred any form of regulation or action that they felt was disdainful to their honor or autonomy. Why, then, did these young men form and join literary societies and subject themselves to rules of membership and behavior, coupled with political organizational structures? The early meetings of the Jefferson Society were highly regulated, with fines imposed for everything from interrupting the speaker to leaving the meeting before it ended.[21] It would seem that these haughty southern gentlemen should find such rules and regulations repulsive to their natures. But in fact, the early literary societies— and the Jefferson Society in particular—offered a plethora of reasons for these men to desire membership.

The Jefferson Society existed in the highly nuanced world of what Rudolph has termed the "Collegiate Way," or "the notion that a curriculum, a library, a faculty, and students are not enough to make a college."[22] These intangible and unofficial elements of what defined the unique experience at any institution "became so much the language of colleges that in time it was difficult to separate the real thing from the myth which collegians and colleges created out of the college way."[23] Rudolph goes on to say, "adherents of the collegiate way became ecstatic over the beneficial influence which classmates exerted on one another, over the superiority of the college community as an agency of education over mere studies. They pointed with satisfaction to the extracurriculum, to the whole range of social life and development" that existed as part of the collegiate way.[24] Thelin builds on this concept by observing "the central feature of undergraduate life was that is was intricately organized by and for students, with a system of rewards and punishments that persisted regardless of the college administration's attitudes. The vitality of the extracurriculum served as a buffer to the demands of coursework and examinations."[25] In some respects, for students in the "elaborate world . . . within and alongside the official world of the college . . . compliance with the formal curriculum was merely the price of admission into 'college life.'"[26] Students fervently pursued the rewards of success in the insular collegiate way, and at the University of Virginia, the Jefferson Society was their first stop. More recently, historian Timothy Williams has understood the antebellum college experience as a pursuit of "intellectual manhood," or the careful, reasoned mastery of self in preparation for entering the public life. Literary societies were one way that students could shape their own educational experience outside of the classroom.[27]

The most obvious reason for students first to form and later to join the Jefferson Society was a distinct lack of any other activities to speak of at the University. Unlike modern colleges and universities where opportunities for student activities and engagement abound, catering to every niche and fine degree of student interest, the University of Virginia in the antebellum years had virtually no such institutions. Student activities were essentially limited to class attendance and whatever they could find to pass the time in town. As a result, literary societies sprang up to help students entertain themselves when not focused on schoolwork or attending classes.

The Jefferson Society also afforded students the opportunity to participate in and govern an organization with little or no interference from the faculty, something that Rudolph and Thelin both agree was an important factor that led students to create literary societies at colleges and universities across the country.[28] Students suffered under the close control of staff and professors in almost every aspect of their collegiate lives, and literary society involvement offered them a respite from such rules. As Wall notes, the literary societies were important "for ante-bellum University students precisely because they were theirs—student created and operated."[29] He goes on to argue that at "a time when the Faculty tried to maintain strict supervision of student routine yet did not provide any positive alternatives to forbidden behavior . . . the literary societies in particular satisfied some of their need for organized debate and sociability."[30] Students flocked to these havens of self-governance, keen on regulating their own affairs as young citizens.

The Jefferson Society served as a training ground in oratorical skill, something that was not taught at the University but was considered critically important to a southern gentlemen, especially one entering the popular fields of law or statesmanship. Glover tells us of displays of oratory, students everywhere "understood that such rituals publicly tested not only their oratorical skills, but their manhood as well. By displaying their speaking skills, grace, and self-assurance—all traits required of southern gentlemen—students demonstrated their preparedness to join the exclusive ranks of confident, commanding southern men."[31] According to Williams, "literary societies were sources of validation of speech. By learning how to captivate, convince, and perhaps even silence their peers, young men enacted a society in which power emanated from men and for men."[32]

James McLachlan notes, in his comprehensive study of collegiate literary organizations, that they often served as "colleges within colleges," teaching students skills that could not be gained from class attendance. Both Richard McIlwaine and Albert Howell, students during the antebellum period, cited the necessity of joining a literary society if one wished to go into law. Training in rhetoric was essential to a legal career, to Howell a "lawyer without a tongue is no lawyer at all," and at the time this training could only be obtained under the auspices of literary societies.[33] One can imagine the members of the Society preparing and rehearsing in Jefferson Hall for the debates that they would later engage in on the floor of statehouses across the South or in the United States Congress. William Roane Aylett, a graduating member of the Jefferson Society, described the importance of Society membership to a student's education in his valedictory address in 1854:

I thus pay a last long tribute to the Jefferson Society, gentlemen, because I honor, venerate and love her; because some of my happiest moments and most instructive hours have been spent within these walls; because I have learned here

what one cannot acquire from the lips of professors, nor gather from the pages
of books; and lastly because, viewed as an instrument, a means of intellectual
education and advancement, I regard this society as . . . a bright literary store of
potent influence.[34]

Membership in the Jefferson Society was not simply a way for students
to while away the time in between classes; rather, it was an educational
forum where they prepared and tested each other for future endeavors.
According to historian Kenneth Greenberg, oratory "was the public display of a superior personality" and allowed gentlemen to display their
"superior intelligence and virtue."[35]

Validation of gentlemanly worth was perhaps the most crucial factor
driving young men to join the Jefferson Society. Literary society membership was a conspicuous indicator of gentlemanly status, as young southern men were expected to be well versed in rhetoric, oratory, debate,
and literature and able to display that excellence whenever possible. If
southern students were given "an exhaustive list of activities required to
act the part of gentlemen," then the Jefferson Society was a place where
they could engage in many of them, and perhaps most importantly, they
could do so in public. As Glover notes, while the rituals of the southern
elite "varied from the superficial, including dress, to the intimate, such
as emotional expressions, they shared one thing in common: all these
coached behaviors were for public show."[36]

Attendance at Jefferson Society meetings was all part of a gentlemanly
act for Thomas H. Malone. A student between 1852 and 1855, Malone had
a very specific routine designed to practice the activities of a gentleman.
He would first attend the Jefferson Society meeting, retire to play whist,
and then enjoy a late-night supper—served by slaves.[37] Membership in a
literary society was a mark of distinction that men cherished throughout
their time at the University and beyond.

Not only was literary society membership important to one's own
sense of gentlemanly status, it also served as a forum for sons of important southern families to socialize and form lasting connections. Almost
all students at the antebellum University were rich, but this was especially true of members of the Jefferson Society. The high initiation fee to
join the Society, set at ten dollars throughout the 1850s, precluded less
well-to-do students from considering membership.[38] This was the same
amount required to use the University's bathhouses for an entire term in

that same year.[39] Henry C. Allen, a student in 1855, wrote his father that many prospective members were deterred from applying as a result of the expense. The high cost of becoming a member did help limit the Society to the upper echelon of southern society. In the thirty-five years of the University's existence before the Civil War, numerous United States senators and representatives, governors, and members of the Confederate government passed through the doors of Jefferson Hall. Hundreds more served in their respective state legislatures. Though obviously not all in attendance at precisely the same time, many of these young men would almost certainly have met and formed associations that would become important for their future political ambitions during their time at the University. In this way, the Society served not only as a training ground for young southern leaders, but also, as the oath taken by every member envisioned, a place where "friendships are cemented."[40]

Antebellum students saw the Jefferson Society as a forum to compete and prove their superiority beyond the classroom. The debates, orations, and officer elections in the Society were intellectual duels where young gentlemen could display and build their self-worth. As a result, members often took their commitments to the Society very seriously. For example, Green recounted his week after being assigned to debate on the appropriate limits of the federal government's power:

Goodbye to text books for the week to follow. I was too full on the fate of Rome, and more especially of another great kindred Republic, to give time or thought to trivialities or puerilities. Page after page, if not quire after quire, of foolscap was spoiled to connect the line of thought. The Madison papers were analyzed and dissected by paragraph in order to give the true intent of the "Framers," and so the "Resolution" of '97 and '98, the Missouri Compromise and its legitimate offspring in the base born bastardy, fitly dubbed the "Omnibus Bill," were torn into tatters and scattered to the four winds. Then long walks were taken morning, noon, and at nightfall, memorizing the sublimity of thought on paper.[41]

His performance, though shaky at first, ended to resounding applause and even earned him a nomination for the presidency of the Society.[42] Such a successful presentation would have brought great honor to the debater and thus was a compelling reason for men to join the Society.

Such competitiveness extended to the elections for officers and valedictory orators of the Society as well. Charles Venable, a student and member in 1845, recalled that the "Jeff . . . had great capacity for getting up excitements at election time."[43] The races were fierce, and with haughty young men competing for the honors, they often resulted in outrage and wounded dignity. Venable recalled such an instance when "the defeated aspirants for the office of final orator in the Wash. and Jeff. withdrew in disgust and formed a third society called the Philomathean."[44] He went on to note that this new society of malcontents "died in its infancy."[45] These electoral challenges represented opportunities to hone political skills that would be useful in later life.

The seriousness with which many members took Jefferson Society affairs, combined with their excitable juvenile personas, often made the hall of the Society a place for pompous and dramatic displays. Charles Ellis, another member, recalled attending a meeting at which he "heard an Essay, of a very flaming character, from the right honorable Mr. Pierce Lewis of Georgia."[46] He also lamented the overtly arrogant exhibitions of several members, saying that there was

too much etiquette, and a disposition to browbeat every person who may not be of superior talents or impudence enough to overlook their sneers; perhaps 'tis better that such a spirit should exist in college; it gives one a foretaste of what he may expect in the world, but it represses the inclination for improvement which might otherwise break out.[47]

The Jefferson Society provided a venue for young students to display their pompous manner, which was otherwise restricted in forced deference to the faculty. While some such as Ellis clearly found this overwhelming, it would have been a significant draw to other southern gentlemen ready to display their own sense of self-importance. This was perhaps the clearest manifestation of the Jefferson Society's place in the "collegiate way."

Regardless of which of these reasons for joining the Society attracted them, hundreds of students became members throughout the antebellum period. Similarly, the Washington Society, the longest-lived counterpart to the Jefferson Society, also achieved a significant degree of prominence in the years after its founding in 1831. But while the Washington Society participated in many of the same activities in the University community, it was certainly the Jefferson Society that enjoyed the most success, perhaps because of its claim to the name of the University's founder. Many members became deeply affectionate toward and committed to the Society. Aylett stated that "it is natural that I should feel for [the Society] an attachment, it is natural that I should cherish its interests and prosperity; it is right that I should regard her lofty pre-eminence in this University with pride, and feel proud also, of the humble membership which I have enjoyed."[48] Jefferson Society membership was a fundamental part of many students' identity during their time at the University and was at the heart of their collegiate experience. It was this attraction and commitment that made the Jefferson Society one of the largest and most influential institutions in the earliest years of the University of Virginia.

Institutional Foundations

While the Jefferson Society certainly had no shortage of prospective and interested members, it was lacking one necessity early in its existence—a permanent meeting place. With space at a premium in the rapidly expanding University, the Board of Visitors found it difficult to find room for students to meet.

After the Society was founded in 1825, it was shuffled between several meeting spots as the Board of Visitors tried in vain to cope with the constant demand for space in the new University. The Society first met in the basement of Pavilion I on the Lawn; however, they were soon shifted around to several other pavilions.[49] The Society petitioned the Board of Visitors several times for more secure meeting space, most notably in 1831 when the Board forwarded their request to the Executive Committee to "extend to the Society such accommodations as may be found practicable."[50] As late as 1837, however, it was meeting biweekly in various pavilions, including Pavilion IV, but none of these served as permanent residences.[51]

Finally, in September 1837, the University granted the Society the use of Hotel C, West Range, as a meeting place "until it shall be wanted for the purposes of the University under such restrictions as the Chairman may deem necessary to preserve it from injury."[52] Jefferson had originally designed the hotels as dining halls; however, by this time a few of them were no longer used for that purpose and had become general meeting space. The acquisition of Hotel C was a great advantage for the young Society, as it provided a reliable location for weekly meetings and a home for the hitherto transient organization. This continuity guaranteed the Society much needed stability that was often lacking in the antebellum

University and that had been nonexistent in their previous meeting places. In 1841, the Board of Visitors granted the Society additional control over the building, allowing the members to take down the interior walls that had previously divided the hall into several rooms.[53] This created a large, open meeting area quite similar to what is currently in use by the Society and also marks when the building became known as Jefferson Hall.

For twelve years the Jefferson Society was the only student society with a permanent meeting place. It took the Washington Society until 1849 to secure their meeting room in Hotel B on the East Range. In 1852, they received permission of the Board of Visitors to enlarge the room, which Philip Alexander Bruce tells us is the same year Hotel B became known as Washington Hall. It was not until 1869, when the Washington Society had reorganized after the Civil War, that they took over the entire building.[54]

Permanent control of Hotel C also allowed the Society to begin and sustain its own library, as many other literary societies of the time did. A notable example is the University of North Carolina, where the Dialectic and Philanthropic Societies took an active role in expanding and managing their university's library after donating their sizeable collection in 1886, which by then totaled over 15,000 volumes. Williams, in *Intellectual Manhood*, makes a strong case for the impact that the student collections at UNC had on the intellectual development of the members of the societies in Chapel Hill, and it is likely students at the University of Virginia experienced similar benefits.[55]

While the Jefferson Society's library did not approach the size of that of the Dialectic and Philanthropic Societies, likely because the University of Virginia did more than its counterpart in North Carolina to support its own library, the Society's library nonetheless played a significant role in its development. The 1837 constitution of the Jefferson Society lists "Librarian" as one of the elected officers of the Society, and it enumerates several fines and disciplinary measures to be taken against members who failed to return borrowed books.[56] This library would have been convenient for members of the Society, as the operating hours of the University library at the time were woefully insufficient. Charles Ellis recalled one evening when "after Dinner [I] went into the Jefferson Hall and took a Book out of the Library."[57] The University library would have been closed at this time, so Society members, with access to their own private collection of books, would have had a considerable advantage over other students. Furthermore, we can gather that the Jefferson Society library likely contained books that complemented rather than paralleled the University library.[58] This would have allowed Society members an even wider range of literary options than were available to the average student, which they would have used to study for classes, to prepare for debates, and to support their own literary compositions. The Jefferson Society gave their entire library to the University in the 1850s, and unfortunately the collection burned in its entirety in the Rotunda Fire of 1895.[59]

At about the same time it acquired Hotel C, the Jefferson Society obtained another prized possession—the portrait of Thomas Jefferson by Thomas Sully. The legendary early American portrait artist painted five portraits of Jefferson in his later years. Of these five, the whereabouts of four are known: one is currently in the possession of the American Philosophical Society, one is held by the United States Senate, one is displayed at West Point Military Academy, and one is owned by the Jefferson Society. It is somewhat unclear how the Society came into possession of this rare item, though it is understood that James Monroe once owned the Jefferson Society's portrait.[60] It is possible the painting was willed to the Society by Monroe or his descendants, or that it was purchased by the Society, as some sources suggest, for an amount between fifty and five hundred dollars.[61] Regardless of how it was acquired, the painting quickly increased in value. In the 1920s it was transferred from Jefferson Hall to the safekeeping of the University after it suddenly disappeared from Jefferson Hall (President Alderman had taken the portrait after finding it unattended while the doors to Jefferson Hall stood wide open).[62] Shortly thereafter, the painting, which is now valued at $600,000, was placed on loan to the Rotunda and is hung in the Upper West Oval Room.[63]

Society Activities

During the antebellum period, as now, the bulk of the Jefferson Society's activities took place during their weekly meetings, which usually occurred on Saturday nights. While the minutes of meetings prior to the 1870s were lost in the Rotunda Fire, we are able to reconstruct meeting activities from other contemporaneous sources. For example, the 1837 constitution indicates that meetings followed a specific order of business.[64] Each session began with the calling of the roll by the secretary, the election and initiation of any new members present, and the reading of the previous meeting's minutes. The Society then moved on to the literary portion of the meeting, consisting of an oration or essay and a debate, which usually occupied the bulk of the time. Finally, the meeting concluded with committee reports, any other necessary administrative duties, and a final roll call.

Usually the longest and most interesting part of each meeting was the literary portion, during which members engaged the Society on a variety of topics. The constitution specified that each week, "a member shall be elected . . . who shall, as he may choose, read an essay, or deliver an oration, two weeks from the day of his election." These speeches were often substantial and covered a wide variety of topics from metaphysics to the powers of the federal government and the origins of language.[65] Essays were often submitted to one of the University publications after first being presented to the Society.

Following the oration or essay, the Society proceeded to its weekly debate. In order to ensure that every member participated in debate from time to time, the constitution specified "members of the society shall be divided, alphabetically, into four classes, one of which shall debate at each regular meeting of the society." Each week one of these classes would be selected to debate a resolution decided upon by the Society. There was only one formal rule for debate: clearly anticipating the long-windedness of certain members, the constitution prohibited individuals from speaking more than twice on a topic without consent of the president and never more than three times.

Like the speeches and essays, there was a wide selection of resolutions for debate. Williams notes that students at UNC debated "every great public question" and most commonly examined resolutions regarding "current affairs; philosophy and morality; government and political economy; history and biography; and education, arts, and sciences."[66] Frequent specific topics would have dealt with internal improvements, public education, and slavery. Whatever the subject, "students believed that weekly literary society debating was an important part of the broader cultural process of mental and moral improvement occurring during college. Moreover, they felt it was an effective way to find meaning for their emerging mental maturity, or intellectual manhood: to use their education for the betterment of their families, society, state, and nation."[67]

The discussion often became heated and disorganized. Charles Ellis recalled a night on which the meeting was "disorderly" as a result of "much speaking on the question under Debate, 'whether West Point ought to be abolished or not.'"[68] Other debates considered such questions as: "Ought capital punishment to be abolished?" "Are short terms of political office desirable?" and "Was the English Government justified in banishing Napoleon to St. Helena?"[69] After the debate was concluded, a vote would be taken by roll call to determine which side was victorious. The only other occasion that required a time-consuming roll call vote was the election of new members, which indicates the value placed on these debates.

The dark cloud of sectionalism that hung over the University throughout the antebellum years also found its way into these collegial contests. Unrestricted by University rules regarding political speech, southern fire-eaters such as Louis Wigfall saw these debates as opportunities to voice their radical secessionist views. The evening he joined the Society, Wigfall "joined in the debate with a good deal of ardor; and plunged headlong into nullification and secession at the bare mention of S. Carolina's course in 1832."[70] Robert G. H. Kean, a student and Jefferson Society member in 1853, wrote in his journal that the Society had engaged in a heated debate over slavery.[71] It should also be noted that the Jefferson Society did give at least some credence to both sides of the question of union. This is evidenced by the invitation it extended to Daniel W. Voorhees, a pro-union speaker, in July 1860, even though most of the members were decidedly pro-southern by then. According to historian Thomas Harding, literary societies across the country, particularly those located at colleges and universities in the South, debated questions of slavery and secession with greater frequency as the likelihood of war increased.[72] As did all Americans, members of the Jefferson Society found the question of a possible civil war a troubling one, and tensions rose as armed conflict became more and more likely.

While the Jefferson Society meetings were remarkably well disciplined in comparison to the University as a whole, a fair amount of chaos interrupted the orderly flow of business. The noise and uproar caused by several Society meetings brought the faculty to the brink of permanently suspending its activities in the late 1830s.[73] In December 1858 a member fired a bullet through the door of the Hall during a meeting without warning.[74] While the Society specified rules for decorum during meetings in its constitution and by-laws, it is clear that these were not always obeyed, and meetings could descend into the youthful rowdiness that consumed the University at the time.

Society meetings and activities offered young men the chance to compete with each other in both oratorical and political skill beyond regular
debates during meetings. University president Edwin Alderman commented that in the first half century of its existence, the "supreme honor
of the University" was "to be the president of the Jefferson Literary Society."[75] The elections for the presidency of the Society were hard-fought
battles that lived up to Alderman's estimation of the office's worth. The
editors of the *Collegian*, one of the college magazines at the time, published this description of a Jefferson Society campaign:

For several days before-hand, friends of the various candidates might have been
seen bustling around, hunting up recruits, soliciting votes, praising their candidate's genius, and peculiar fitness for the post . . . urging his claim on green
academics and unsophisticated meds, with the warmth and fluency worthy of a
political campaign against the Know-Nothings. Each separate clique had a man,
who was, by all odds, the smartest fellow and best speaker in college. The only
topic in all circles for a week beforehand was the election. Every other man you
met wanted to bet you a box of Havanas, a bottle of Johannesburg, or anything
else from a basket of champagne to a double breasted brandy smash, that his
candidate would be the successful one.[76]

While the students clearly found these campaigns exciting projects, the
faculty was less pleased. They complained that the elections "were accompanied by such turbulence as to degrade the reputation of the University,
cause dangerous personal feuds and divert the members' attention from
their normal studies."[77] Regardless of the outcome, it was clear that Jefferson Society elections were the highlight of each academic term and
were fiercely contested by men who each felt his personal honor was at
stake in the race.

Another area of competition focused on the oratorical abilities of
members. The Jefferson Society elected orators for various University-
wide ceremonies throughout the academic year, and the competition for
the post of Final Orator, and thus the privilege to speak at the University
Final Celebration in June, was especially heated. The Final Celebrations
were large affairs hosted over the span of a few days. Major student organizations such as the Jefferson Society, the Washington Society, and the
newer Society of Alumni, would each host their own celebrations before a
larger, University-wide event, when those students who had finished their

degrees would graduate.[78] The Jefferson Society's Final Celebration was always the largest. The *Virginia University Magazine* always took notice and would publish a description of the proceedings much like this one:

At 8 ½ o'clock the band began to play in the orchestra. There was a momentary lull, and the tramp of the marshals and committeemen was heard at the door, and soon along the long aisle they came, escorting the Professors and Board of Visitors and other distinguished persons to the rostrum. They reach the rostrum and take their seats and look out upon the audience.[79]

The agenda would then proceed with a litany of energetic speeches:

After the last strains of "Dixie" had died away, and long before there was any indication of the cessation of the hum of voices in the audience, the President introduced as the "best debater" of the Jefferson society, for the session of 1872-3, Mr. J. Sharp Williams, of Memphis, Tennessee, and in a very appropriate speech of a few minutes length, presented him with the medal of the society.[80]

Prominent speakers often graced the Society with their presence. For example, in 1850, former president John Tyler spoke at the Final Celebration.[81] As one can imagine, the honor of speaking alongside a former president of the United States or some similar dignitary as the Final Orator pushed Society men to extreme action. In 1858, for example, a competitor for Final Orator received four challenges to duels before he went to bed and two more upon waking the next morning.[82] Naturally, the political campaigning for the honor was just as intense as it was for the office of Society president: the editors of the *Virginia University Magazine* wrote that "in some respects, a Jefferson election for final Orator, etc., is a rare piece of fun; but, in others, it presents the observer with a display of the baser portions of man's nature, and the darker shades of character rather melancholy to behold."[83] After the election, those who supported the winner carried him to a local tavern, where he was expected to buy "lager beer, whiskey, or brandy, until the whole number should become almost too fuddled to reshoulder him."[84] So, while election as Final Orator was a great honor, it was also a great burden for the victor.

In 1857, another yearly competition was added alongside the election for Final Orator: the Debater's Medal.[85] The Debater's Medal was a fifty dollar gold medallion engraved with striking scenes of the Lawn and

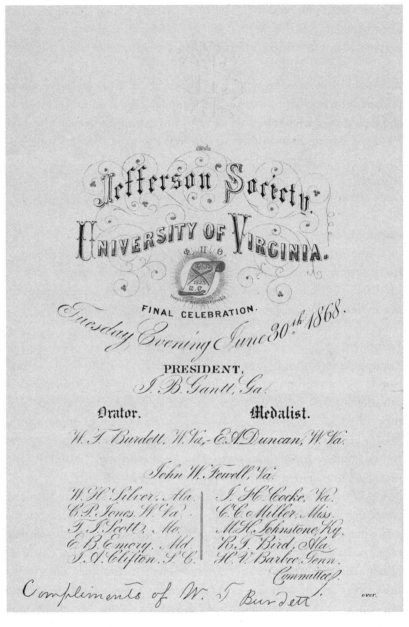

FIGURE 5. This elaborate invitation to the Jefferson Society Final Celebration in 1868 is characteristic of those distributed by the Society each year to what was the most important event on the University social calendar. Image courtesy of the Albert and Shirley Small Special Collections Library at the University of Virginia, Broadside 1868 .U752.

Rotunda and inscribed with the winner's name and year. It was originally awarded each spring to one member of the Jefferson or Washington Societies who distinguished himself in an intersociety debate, though later it would be awarded through a variety of different systems, and other medals would be introduced. The first winner of the Debater's Medal from the Jefferson Society was Thomas C. Nelson.[86] The Debater's Medal was the only medal awarded by the Society before the Civil War; afterward an Orator's Medal was instituted as a complement.

The University community and the Jefferson Society also began hosting elaborate yearly celebrations of Thomas Jefferson's birthday during the antebellum years. Known as the "Anniversary Celebration" or the "Intermediate Celebration," these events occurred around April 13 each spring beginning in 1832 and continued until 1870, when they were eliminated to save money.[87] Though not quite as elaborate as the Final Celebration, the Jefferson Society selected an "Anniversary Orator" or "Intermediate Orator," as well as someone to read the Declaration of Independence for the occasion. Not limited to members of the Society, the Intermediate Celebration was a rite of spring for denizens of the Charlottesville community. The *Jefferson Monument Magazine* took note on the occasion of the 1851 Intermediate Celebration:

The chapel was crowded to overflowing. Almost all the pretty girls in the vicinity were present, looking most enchanting and making conquests by the score. The liberality of the Society had procured a fine brass band from Richmond, to perform on the occasion, and so fine music was an additional pleasure.[88]

These events were a highlight of the year for many Society members, and they offered a chance both to reflect on the life of the University's founder and to simply unwind and celebrate the return of spring. The Intermediate Celebration, after being discontinued in 1870, eventually morphed into an annual Jefferson Society banquet, which continues today as the Founder's Day Banquet. The practice of reading the Declaration of Independence was revived in 1960.[89]

These exciting competitions and entertaining celebrations, as with any opportunity to capture the public eye, were almost immediately injected with political overtones. At the first Intermediate Celebration in 1832, the Society selected Merritt Robinson, a student and member, to present the public oration. Robinson gave a speech on the immorality of

FIGURE 6. The literary societies frequently hosted formal balls in the Rotunda, such as the one depicted here in the 1894 edition of *Corks and Curls,* for students and the ladies of Charlottesville and the surrounding area. Image courtesy of the Albert and Shirley Small Special Collections Library at the University of Virginia, University of Virginia Visual History Collection, U.Va. Prints and Photographs File, RG-30/1/10.011, Print 00080.

slavery and the need for emancipation, enraging many students and faculty alike.[90] As a result the faculty proclaimed that "no distracting question of state or national policy, or theological dispute should be touched in any address."[91] The Board of Visitors went even further in 1837 by banning all public speeches by students.[92] The *Collegian* protested this ban, saying with "our debating societies indirectly prostrated . . . cold science and scholastic plodding will then gloom this proud fabric of the American Sage."[93] While the board reversed itself in 1840, the message was clear: public speakers and ceremonies should be celebratory, not political.

The Final Celebrations did not escape their share of political controversy either. In 1858, in the heat of the sectional crisis, the Jefferson and Washington Societies jointly invited Henry Winter Davis, an alumnus of the University and member of Congress from Maryland, to address their joint finals event.[94] Davis, while a respected congressman, was also an abolitionist. Lancelot Minor Blackford, a member of the Society at the time, recalled that this "excited at once a storm of disapproval," as the "sectional feeling . . . was already intense, and it was, if possible, stronger among the professors than the students."[95] After several days of intense deliberations, the faculty informed the Societies that they could not use University property to host Davis and that they should withdraw their invitation immediately. Davis was apparently quite taken aback by this sudden rejection, and he wrote a "caustic rebuke" to both Societies in response to the action.[96] Therefore, while these celebrations and orations were often times for merriment, they also highlighted the rising tide of strife between the North and South, which would culminate soon in the devastating Civil War.

Magazines

The Jefferson Society played a leading role in the establishment of a literary publication for the students of the University of Virginia. In the antebellum years, student publications were rare and were viable only at a select few colleges, mostly in the North, and more often than not sponsored by the literary societies.[97] Generally issued monthly, a magazine was an outlet for student publication of essays, literature, and university news, both humorous and serious. Beginning in 1838, the Jefferson Society was actively involved in the effort to create a student magazine. After a few abortive attempts, by 1856 the Jefferson Society had finally put their weight behind a publication that would serve the University community more permanently: the *Virginia University Magazine*.[98] The Jefferson Society was instrumental in founding, funding, and providing many of the editors and contributors to all major iterations of an antebellum student publication.

The first two notable efforts to fulfill the literary needs of the University were the *Collegian* and the *Jefferson Monument Magazine*. Both struggled from lack of interest and enthusiasm on the part of the student body, and each only survived for a few years. The *Collegian* was published from 1838 to 1842, and the *Jefferson Monument Magazine* ran from 1849 to 1851.[99] Of the *Collegian* very little information survives, and it is unclear how its editorial board was selected. However, all five members of its first editorial board were members of the Jefferson Society, strongly suggesting that the Society was closely tied to the publication.[100]

The next major effort toward establishing a magazine, the *Jefferson Monument Magazine* had a novel purpose and clear editorial structure. It was founded with the intent that "the proceeds of the publication are to be appropriated to the creation of a fund, which . . . shall at some future day

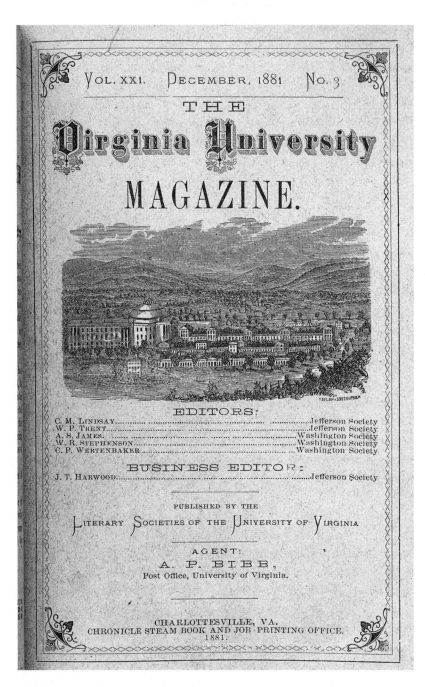

VOL. XXI. DECEMBER, 1881 NO. 3

THE

Virginia University

MAGAZINE.

TAYLOR & SMITH PHILA

EDITORS:

C. M. LINDSAY..Jefferson Society
W. P. TRENT..Jefferson Society
A. S. JAMES..Washington Society
W. R. STEPHENSON..Washington Society
C. P. WERTENBAKER...Washington Society

BUSINESS EDITOR:

J. T. HARWOOD...Jefferson Society

PUBLISHED BY THE

LITERARY SOCIETIES OF THE UNIVERSITY OF VIRGINIA

AGENT:

A. P. BIBB,
Post Office, University of Virginia.

CHARLOTTESVILLE, VA.
CHRONICLE STEAM BOOK AND JOB PRINTING OFFICE.
1881.

FIGURE 7. An early cover of the *Virginia University Magazine*. Image courtesy of the Albert and Shirley Small Special Collections Library at the University of Virginia, *Virginia University Magazine* 21, no. 3 (December 1881).

serve to erect at the University of Va. a Monument to JEFFERSON."[101] Each of the four literary societies of the time elected one person to the editorial board, with a fifth being elected by the University at large. While it was focused toward a noble purpose, the *Jefferson Monument Magazine* suffered from a disease that afflicted almost all student publications at the time, a lack of subscribers. In October 1850, the publication had only 300 subscribers among students, faculty, alumni, and community members.[102] It was forced to shut down less than a year later before accumulating any funds for the statue of Jefferson.

The most successful antebellum student publication was the *Virginia University Magazine*, which began publication in 1856. The *Magazine*, as we will refer to it going forward, was cosponsored by the Jefferson and Washington Societies, though its editorial board was separate from the Societies' regular officers. Contests for editorial positions were as fierce as other Society elections, especially prior to the Civil War when only two or three editors were needed to run the *Magazine*. By 1872, the *Magazine* had become such a venerated tradition at the University the editors were pleased to find a "Memento of Long Ago":

In looking over the archives of the Jefferson Society, we came upon a cloth bag, and upon further examination found it to be the waste bag of the Jefferson Monument Magazine ... made of fine red woolen stuff, lined with cambric, and notwithstanding the lapse of twenty-three years—for the date worked upon it is 1849—is in a good state of preservation. We carried it to our office, and are now using it to receive our exchanges.[103]

Though sporadically suspending publication and occasionally assuming different names, the *Magazine* survived well into the second half of the twentieth century. After the failure of the Washington Society, its operations were taken over by the Jefferson Society alone, which supported it as long as possible, until it folded in the 1960s. Having provided a literary outlet for students for more than a century, it will forever be one of the Jefferson Society's most important and enduring contributions to the University community.[104]

The reasons for starting a magazine were as varied as those for joining the Jefferson Society in the first place. The principal motivation was to make up for a lack of formal training in literary composition offered by the University. The *Collegian* argued that, in reference to speech and composition, "both of these branches of education, so indispensably necessary to every accomplished American, are entirely disregarded in the exercises of this Institution."[105] A magazine would provide a forum for student publication that was previously missing at the University and encourage students to hone their composition and literary skills.

In the absence of a daily student newspaper, a magazine was the only source of college news. Each issue of the *Virginia University Magazine* featured a section called "Collegiana" and an "Editor's Table," in which the editors described and commented on current events around the University. The February 1870 issue of the *Virginia University Magazine* described exactly why "Collegiana" was so cherished, with a bit of self-deprecating humor:

Our college is a miniature world. Among its five hundred students, of all sizes, shapes, and ages, may be found almost every variety of character and condition. But, unfortunately for some of us, it is such a miniature that whatever of interest that transpires within her limits is known throughout the University long before it can appear in print in our columns. This is unfortunate, as it makes the "Collegiana" not a medium of "news," but simply a few pages of whatever readable or unreadable the poor editors can get up.[106]

In both of these sections, students could find information such as the dates and times of school-sponsored dances, upcoming speakers to the University, and news of elections in the literary societies. They also included humorous tales of University antics that would not have been permitted in a faculty-sanctioned or censored newspaper. For example, one story detailed the revels of one of the editor's drinking parties, which were strictly prohibited under University regulations.[107] The *Magazine* could also publish articles that would have been frowned upon by the faculty but were popular among students, like the article "Drinks and How They are Made."[108] The independence of the *Magazine* allowed the editors a much wider degree of freedom to publish items of interest to students that would normally have been removed by the faculty sponsors often associated with student publications at other schools.

Finally, as with most Jefferson Society activities then and now, the presence of a magazine enticed both contributors and readers with the thrill of competition. The *Virginia University Magazine* offered a $100 prize medal, similar to the Debater's Medal, for the best original essay submitted each term. The editors selected a panel of three professors to read, review, and judge the submitted articles, which added to the prestige of being selected as the winner. The *Magazine* announced the medal in "Mensaila," a precursor to the more aptly named "Collegiana":

It has been determined, by a consultation of the committees from the three Literaries [*sic*] Societies of the University, to offer a medal of the value of one hundred dollars, to be awarded to the writer of the best essay, to be published in the Magazine during the next session. The design is, after the nine numbers have been issued, to place them in the hands of three learned Professors of the University—Profs. J. B. Minor, W. H. McGuffey, and G. F. Holmes—and get them to decide as to the respective merits of the articles, and award the medal to the most worthy.

This is, it has been thought, to be a means at least by which the Magazine may be made a real index of the talent of the University, as the honor of such an award will awake the ambitious energies of all.[109]

The first winner of this medal was a member of the Society, John Johnson of South Carolina, for his article "Drudgery and Leisure." He was awarded his medal at the Jefferson Society Final Celebration in 1857 to great fanfare.[110] The value of the medal dropped to $50 when the Columbian Society withdrew from the editorial board, but even so, the medal quickly gained prominence, and a great degree of excitement surrounded the committee's decision every year.[111] The editors of the *Magazine* smugly boasted:

Let us then, fellow students, urge upon you the importance of giving special attention to original composition, and neglect no longer this important branch of education. Be no longer deceived by the false impression, that all your time should be devoted to class studies . . . The medal awarded to the author of the best article in the Magazine is now regarded as the highest literary honor of the University.[112]

The opportunity to compete clearly enticed students to participate, as the medal, colloquially referred to as the "Mag Medal," continued to be highly coveted for many decades.

Sectional and racial animosity found its way into the pages of these collegiate publications, much as it did into the Society's debates. An 1850 editorial in the *Jefferson Monument Magazine* encouraging further subscription and contribution from the students called on southern students to unite around a southern publication.[113] After complaining of various other distractions that prevented students from submitting to the magazine, such as visiting young women, the editor vehemently attacked the readers' supposed lack of southern pride:

Have you no [southern] *pride*, fellow students? . . . Will you let it be said that *by three hundred and fifty-five* SOUTHERN STUDENTS at the University of Virginia a monthly Magazine of 32 pages octavo *could not be supported?* Have you no more sectional pride than this? Are YOU *the southern sons, of southern sires*, and permit this, when you see your Northern brethren sending out, from almost every college north of Mason's and Dixon's line, a worthy periodical? *Will you,* CAN YOU as SOUTHERNERS yield the palm of literary attainment without a struggle? We know that there is not one true son of the South from whom the *indignant* NO does not all at once come.[114]

While the effectiveness of this appeal is impossible to judge, it made it clear that a magazine was not simply a publication for the enjoyment of the students; it was also a tool in the constant southern fight against perceived northern aggression and oppression.

Sectional tempers flared again in 1859 when several Yale students invited the Jefferson and Washington Societies to join with them in the publication of a national undergraduate magazine known as the *Undergraduate Quarterly*. The Jefferson Society was interested in joining the endeavor; however, the two parties reached an impasse when the issue of race arose. Fearing that their name would be associated with institutions that supported abolition, both the Jefferson and Washington Societies responded that they could only participate "on condition that all institutions of learning which practically ignore the distinction between the white and black races, shall be excluded from the association."[115] Yale could not agree to those terms, so the Jefferson Society abandoned its interest in assisting the publication. Once again, racism and sectionalism subverted an exceptional opportunity for meaningful intellectual engagement by the Society.

The Jefferson Society and the University

It should not come as a surprise that the Jefferson Society was the University's premier institution throughout the antebellum period. It served as the main college activity for hundreds of students, and it only grew in membership as the Civil War approached. One hundred and thirty-two students were Society members during the 1857–1858 school year out of a school population of roughly 600, and by 1859–1860 that number had swelled to 241 out of 600.[116] With so many members, the Society was able to reach into every corner of the University community, visible in the eyes of students, faculty, and the community. Not until social fraternities started appearing in the late 1850s would the Jefferson Society and other literary societies face any kind of real competition for the attention of students.

When other social organizations, such as fraternities and the Young Men's Christian Association, did begin to emerge in the 1850s, they served as complements to rather than competition for the Society. While fraternities were mainly social organizations, one of their primary functions was as political parties to win Jefferson Society elections for officers, magazine editors, and orators, while the Society itself retained the dominant place in University life it had always enjoyed.[117] John M. Strother, a student and member of Delta Kappa Epsilon fraternity recalled a particularly contentious set of Society elections in 1857, which pitted his fraternity against Beta Theta Pi, Phi Kappa Psi, and the West Range party.[118] Unfortunately for Strother, his fraternity was soundly defeated this election cycle and thus excluded from "Society honors." It was not until after the Civil War that such organizations would emerge as competition for the Jefferson Society in terms of membership and social standing at the University.

The Jefferson Society's influence at the University of Virginia extended beyond the social scene. The Society also helped shape the University curriculum at the time. Literally serving as the "college within a college" that James McLachlan described, the Society was an intellectual training ground to complement the schoolwork of each member. University President Alderman later remarked that the Society "has been a splendid department of political science and government."[119] In reaffirming the Society's right to use of Jefferson Hall, the Board of Visitors remarked that they "entertain[ed] a high opinion of the importance of the literary societies as agents of education."[120] Members of the Jefferson Society were exposed to intellectual engagement and challenges that other students never had the opportunity to experience.

Outside of the walls of Jefferson Hall, the Society had a great impact on the curriculum and learning environment of the University as a whole. They brought notable speakers to the University to enrich the existing curriculum and instituted University magazines, which served as rare examples of literary outlets for students. After noticing that the University did not have a chair of literature, the Society, through the mouthpiece of the *Magazine*, lobbied the Board of Visitors and faculty to institute such a position. Though their original plan to raise enough money to endow the chair themselves failed, they were finally successful in convincing the Board of Visitors to create one. The *Magazine* announced the good news in October 1857:

We may congratulate our readers that the anti-progressive Board of Visitors have at last established a Professorship of Literature, and in the selection of Geo. Fred. Holmes, a name already quite eminent in the periodical literature of the country, they have given very general satisfaction. The absence of literary culture, strictly speaking, has long been an objection to the University course of instruction.[121]

This helped fill a large hole in the curriculum during the antebellum period and advanced the study of literature at the University. Above all, the Society was both the social and intellectual hub of the University of Virginia during the antebellum period. "Students' experiences with their literary societies reveal," writes Williams, "that southern peer groups did not always work at cross-purposes with university faculty, but in tandem with the shared values of restraint and intellectual manhood."[122]

Hotheaded Southerners

As the 1850s wore on, sectional tensions, which had formed the backdrop of the national and University political scene for decades, moved to the forefront of discussion. As the nation began to debate issues such as slavery and secession vigorously, so did the University literary societies. Although the records of the Jefferson Society from this period are lost, we can get an idea of what was likely discussed from the minutes of the

Washington Society. For example, in 1859 that society voted twelve to four that a state has the right to secede.[123] Secessionist fire-eaters now filled the halls of both societies, calling on southern men to recognize their duty to their homes and support the slowly forming rebellion. While the Jefferson Society discussed secession at the University, Society alumni such as Robert M. T. Hunter, Robert Toombs, and Alexander H. H. Stuart, who would all emerge as prominent national figures by the Civil War, helped guide the national negotiations and debates. The sectional crisis had truly consumed Society members past and present.[124]

As the storm of secession gathered, the Society found itself a direct participant in national affairs. In May 1856, spurred on by sectional anger, United States Representative Preston Brooks of South Carolina savagely beat Senator Charles Sumner of Massachusetts almost to death with his cane on the floor of the United States Senate. Brooks shattered his cane in the process, and the Jefferson Society, "fully approv[ing] the course of Mr. Brooks" resolved to purchase him a "splendid" new cane.[125] The Society convened a mass student meeting on May 29, just one week after the caning. Taking up a collection from many students, the Society purchased a cane which was "to have a heavy gold head . . . and also bear upon it a device of the human head, badly cracked and broken."[126] At the meeting, several members of the Society spoke at length about Brooks, the conditions in Kansas and Nebraska, and the political landscape of slavery. They ultimately expressed appreciation for Brooks's actions.

Brooks stood resolute in the face of criticism from the North, relishing the praise that was pouring in from across the South. In a letter to his brother Ham the day after the incident, he wrote:

Abolitionists are like a hive of disturbed bees . . . I have been arrested of course and there is now a resolution before the House, the object of which is to result in my expulsion. This they can't do. It requires two thirds to do it and they can't get a half. Every Southern man sustains me. The debate is now very animated on the subject.[127]

The Jefferson Society's gift was a sign that the members conceived of themselves and the University as preeminent southern institutions, bound to defend the honor of their brethren when called or provoked. They stood by Brooks and inscribed their cane with his own words: "Every southern man sustains me."

As the Civil War approached rapidly, many University students felt the need to leave school and enlist in support of the southern cause. Charles Wall notes that "the eagerness of the students in rallying to the cause and to military service was in considerable measure an expression of their southern gentleman's code of personal behavior, their romantic quality, and their youthful enthusiasm and recklessness."[128] After the election of Abraham Lincoln, University students quickly formed two military companies, the Southern Guard and the Sons of Liberty.[129] These companies drilled with muskets on the Lawn until April 1861, when, on Founder's Day, the faculty received news that Fort Sumter had surrendered to South Carolina troops. Almost immediately, the student soldiers were called upon to seize the federal arsenal at Harper's Ferry.

The Civil War drastically altered life at the University for the worse. The student population shrank, professors abandoned the institution, both the Jefferson Society and the University were ruined financially, and five hundred former University students died on the fields of battle.[130] While the antebellum period had been a golden age of activity, influence, and prominence for the Jefferson Society, such stability was threatened with the entrance of Virginia into the Civil War. The young southern aristocrats who characterized the Society's first thirty-five years risked their entire way of life in a bloody conflict with their fellow citizens. This, their ultimate duel for gentlemanly honor, ended with the utter destruction of the land they loved so well. It would take years for the South and the Society to recover what it lost on the battlefields of the Civil War.

CHAPTER THREE

Civil War and Reconstruction

1860–1878

Preparing for War

The University of Virginia community entered the Civil War like many Virginians: with apprehension of what was to come. At the beginning of 1861, even the political leadership of the state that would eventually be home to the capital of the Confederacy was unsure if secession was the best course of action. Above all, they knew that if war broke out, Virginia would be the main theater and would likely suffer the greatest ravages. It should not come as a surprise that in the years leading up to the war, a fever pitch of activity engulfed the University of Virginia, as students and faculty weighed questions of union, secession, and the fate of slavery and prepared themselves for the conflict.

By 1859, the University of Virginia claimed more students than Harvard or Yale. As sectional conflict heightened and the Civil War seemed imminent, "Southerners called for greater self-sufficiency and expressed confidence in their own institution."[1] The *Richmond Enquirer* proclaimed both the South and the University to be incomparable models for the nation to emulate. It smugly boasted:

The University of Virginia is probably superior to any in the Union. Under these circumstances, it surprises us, that moral, conservative, and religious men at the North, who can afford it, do not send their sons to Southern schools. Their training would [be] moral, religious, and conservative, and they would . . . learn . . . pure morality, the right of property, the sacredness of marriage, the obligations of law, the duty of obedience to government.[2]

Half a century after Thomas Jefferson wrote in support of the need for an institution to educate the sons of the South and cultivate enlightened southern political leaders, Virginia faced the very real prospect of being cut off from the North, its institutions of higher learning, and the security it provided. As the University of Virginia positioned itself at the forefront of educated southern culture, the Jefferson Society moved to help solidify the uniquely southern identity of Mr. Jefferson's University.

In the years leading up to the war, the Society shifted its political temper considerably. While always decidedly sympathetic to southern interests and reflective of the southern planter aristocracy throughout most of the prewar period, the Jefferson Society nevertheless sponsored orators of opposing political backgrounds. To be sure, at the University of Virginia in 1860, "one word was mentioned repeatedly and ominously—secession."[3] The town and the University favored the preservation of the Union, as did most Virginians until well into 1861, "and viewed dissolution as a harbinger of civil war."[4] But as the tensions escalated and the cannons of Fort Sumter loomed in the distance, the likelihood that Virginia would remain in the Union rapidly diminished, and with it went the willingness of the Jefferson Society to hear those who would advocate otherwise.

On July 4, 1860, less than one year before Virginia's secession, Daniel W. Voorhees, the Indiana federal district attorney, addressed the literary societies in a joint session on "The American Citizen." Voorhees, who had recently defended one of John Brown's coconspirators against charges of murder and treason, took a pro-union stance in his speech, which he certainly understood would be unpopular in Charlottesville. Nonetheless, after praising Virginia for her leadership in the creation of the Union in spite of fierce antifederalist opposition to ratification of the Constitution, he warned of the dangers of secession:

Remembering her early struggles and sacrifices, calling to mind the precious memories which bind her to the American Union . . . Virginia turned her back on the Tempter of Disunion . . . May each State profit by her example! May her wise precepts govern the public mind as in the days of Madison and Henry! May the Union never be destroyed, but in any event and under all circumstances may the American citizen be true to his race, and true to liberty as it is recognized in the American Constitution![5]

Virginia, for the time being, seemed determined to stay in the Union. Its convention to consider secession met on February 13, 1861, nine days after the first seven states to secede had formed a provisional Confederate government. On April 4, a motion to secede was defeated by an overwhelming majority, 88 to 45. But the attack on Fort Sumter and, more importantly, Abraham Lincoln's April 15 request that the state raise troops to aid in suppressing the rebellion pushed Virginians to reconsider, and on April 17, they voted by similarly large margin, 88 to 55, to secede from the Union. In the span of just two weeks, the situation had changed enough to drive Virginia from the nation it had played such an important role in creating.

Along with those of Virginia, the sentiments of the Society shifted decidedly in favor of secession, and the membership became unwilling to hear either northern or antislavery orators. The guest who had been invited to speak at the joint celebration with the Washington Society on July 4, 1861, was David Paul Brown, an avowedly abolitionist lawyer from Philadelphia. On April 15, on the motion of R. C. M. Page, a member of the Washington Society, the literary societies revoked their invitation, disapproving of recent public comments Brown had made and entering their decision in the minute book of the Jefferson Society. John Shelton Patton, an early historian of the University, remarks that

evidently David Paul Brown was ugly about it, for this minute appears as a description of the action taken by the joint assembly of the societies upon the correspondence: "Mr. Brown was deemed to have offered a great indignity to the body, and the committee [was] instructed to forward to him a letter which, upon being read before the body, was deemed expressive of their views on the matter."[6]

In the span of just a few months, both the Jefferson Society and its members experienced a remarkable political transformation. The traditional willingness to hear speakers of any persuasion that had been a mark of pride for the Society vanished in the face of sectional conflict and civil war, giving way to unabashed southern pride and verbal sparring with anyone who found themselves on the opposite side of the issue.

The Society's southern fervor also engulfed their literary endeavors in the *Virginia University Magazine*. Since 1859 the Society had awarded the Everett Medal to the student who submitted the best published biographical piece to the *Magazine*. That year, Edward Everett, a Massachusetts Whig who had served as secretary of state under Millard Fillmore, had visited the University and spoken before the Society. He delivered what was by all accounts "a striking lecture, the proceeds of which he turned over to the literary societies of the University with the expressed hope that the interest would be used in providing a medal to be bestowed upon the writer of the best article on American biography published in the *University Magazine*."[7] Despite running for vice president on John Bell's Constitutional Union Party ticket in 1860 (Bell won Virginia), in early 1863 Everett began campaigning vigorously for President Lincoln's reelection. The Jefferson Society reacted by unequivocally showing their opposition to Everett's course of action.

Of course the societies disdained Mr. Everett's medal after learning his pronounced sentiments; Mr. Pendleton moved to abolish it forever, and the motion was carried unanimously. Then Mr. Falligant moved to return the fund to Mr. Everett. Mr. Underwood moved to appropriate it to the defense of the state and this substitute was adopted.[8]

The question was reconsidered again, and finally the funds were deposited with the proctor to be returned as soon as hostilities cooled. It is unclear what ultimately became of the money.

The debate over the fate of the Everett Medal, which never reemerged after the Civil War, reaches into the wartime sentiments of the Society. As an organization of proud southern men defending their homeland and way of life, the Jefferson Society had taken steps to remove all doubt about where its loyalties lay well before discontinuing the Everett Medal.

The Jefferson Society Enters the Civil War

The prospect of fighting a war was naturally very exciting for the young men at the University of Virginia, many of whom had grown up hearing stories of glory and conquest in the Mexican-American War from their fathers. As the political leaders of the South voted one by one to secede from the Union, the students eagerly anticipated the opportunity to prove their own worth on the battlefield, and as the war effort gathered momentum, students became more and more enthusiastic about the Confederate cause. Randolph H. McKim, a student at the University in 1861, who does not appear to have been a member of the Jefferson Society, recalled: "On a bright morning in the month of April, 1861, there is a sudden explosion of excitement at the University of Virginia. Shouts and cheers are heard from various precincts . . . all eyes turned to the dome of the rotunda from whose summit the Secession flag is seen waving."[9] The convention convened in Richmond to consider secession had voted to remain in the Union only a few days before. But to the students in Charlottesville that was unimportant; to them the South was on an irreversible path to war, and they wanted to be there to seize the glory that only battle could offer. McKim, who claimed to be one of the students who broke into the Rotunda, offered as his explanation: "It was the *threat of invasion* that revolutionized the position of the State of Virginia."[10]

The students rallied under the banner of secession, and the excitement mounted as the day went on. Students left their classes, unable to resist the temptation of rallying in favor of the Confederate cause. Despite the best efforts of professors to keep their pupils' attention, by midday McKim reported that "a great throng of students is presently assembled on the lawn in front of the lofty flight of steps leading up to the rotunda, and one after another of the leaders of the young men mounts the steps and harangues the crowd in favor of the Southern Confederacy, and the Southern flag waving proudly up there."[11] William Randolph Berkeley, the recently elected Final Orator of the Jefferson Society, was foremost among those proselytizing to his fellows from the steps of the Rotunda, pressing them to support the Confederacy. The ardor of secession had caught fire at the University.

The chairman of the faculty, Socrates Maupin, a former Jefferson Society member, recorded the incident in the minutes: "The Rotunda was broken into last night and the Confederate flag erected on the dome by persons unknown."[12] Even though Maupin himself was sympathetic to the Confederate cause, he ordered that the flag be removed, as Virginia had not yet seceded. Six days after the surrender of Fort Sumter, and three days after Virginia seceded, the faculty itself ordered that the Confederate flag be raised over the Rotunda, reflecting official University support of Virginia's departure from the Union.[13]

With Virginia finally in the Confederate camp, the Jefferson Society and the University of Virginia began supporting the war effort in earnest. Just eight days after Virginia voted to secede, "on motion of R. M. C. Page, the Final Celebration of the [Washington] society was dispensed with 'in view of the probable suspension of lectures at the University growing out of the disturbed condition of political affairs.'"[14] The Jefferson Society did the same soon after, believing that the Society's resources could be put to better use than a celebration, given the impending armed conflict. A few days later, the literary societies took their support one step further, and both the Jefferson Society and the Washington Society independently voted to donate the entirety of their treasuries to the governor of Virginia for the defense of the Commonwealth. Together, the societies wrote:

University of Va., May 10, 1861

Sir,

The Literary Societies of the University of Va. in separate session, having resolved to appropriate their surplus funds to the cause of the South, we the undersigned were appointed committees of the Jefferson & Washington Societies respectively, to forward to you at Richmond the enclosed checks for $516.61, viz: $316.61 from the Jefferson and $200 from the Washington Societies, the whole amount of the funds of the Societies after meeting all Existing liabilities—and to request you to employ the same in such manner as in your judgment shall most advance the interests of our common cause—the defense of the South.

We would also state that the Annual Celebrations of the Societies have been suspended for the present Session by a unanimous vote, that we might contribute our all towards that cause.

Our only regret is that the condition of our finances at present will not allow us to render more efficient service in this respect. Very Respectfully,

Yours,

Committee of Wash. Soc.	Committee of Jeff. Soc.
D. R. Barton	W. W. Minor, Jr.
S. W. Bozeman	S. M. Garnett
E. H. DeJarretts	A. B. Wooldrige[15]

Both literary societies knew full well the disastrous effects that handing over these funds might have on their future prosperity, but the defense of Virginia and the South was far more important. Many of the activities that had brought them prestige in the past, such as the publication of the *Virginia University Magazine* and the grandiose Final Celebrations, depended on the financial largesse of the literary societies, and their continuation was threatened by the uncertain outcome of the war.

Student Life at the University of Virginia during the War

When a nation goes to war, its universities and schools are often severely affected. The younger generation takes up the burden of war, leaving school to risk their lives for their country. For the University of Virginia, the Civil War hit especially hard, as its students organized into companies and then marched onto the battlefield. The University had a military presence as early as 1827, when it had been authorized by state and local governments to house a small armory on the Grounds and train students in military strategy and drills. In 1831, a captain named Partridge took over the command of the military school at the University, and the students formed their own military company, the University Volunteers.[16] However, the presence of an armed battalion of students in the early, boisterous days of the University proved troublesome, and its existence was short lived.

At the outbreak of the Civil War, University students petitioned to organize militarily once again. They formed three companies: the Sons of Liberty, with seventy-four students, formed in late 1860; the Southern Guard, one hundred strong, was founded in January 1861; and finally sixty-four students rallied under the old name of the University Volunteers in April 1861.[17] University students did not receive unqualified support for their military exercises; some professors preferred them to remain in school and focus on their studies and leave the fighting to others. At the urging of Professor Maupin, Governor John Letcher refused a petition on the part of the Southern Guard and the Sons of Liberty to be accepted into state service, arguing that there was far "too much talent to be risked in one body."[18] The student companies continued to drill on the Grounds, sometimes foraying out to participate in local skirmishes, and many students eventually left to join regular companies.

Enrollment at the University of Virginia dipped to frighteningly low numbers during the war. Just sixty-six students attended the sessions of 1861–1862, and forty-six attended the next year in 1862–1863, only eight of whom graduated. In 1863–1864, the enrollment remained dangerously low at fifty students. The faculty struggled along with their students, as professors' salaries were pegged to the enrollment totals in their classes. The combination of an extremely small student population and the plummeting value of paper money, which made their salaries worth even less in real terms, deeply reduced faculty standards of living.[19] Although the possibility of closing the University was discussed at length, the Board of Visitors fought to keep the school open as long as there were still some students in classes. In addition to ensuring these remaining students could continue their studies, the board was concerned that the Grounds would be inundated with wounded soldiers and hospital beds if the school were to shut down entirely.[20]

The faculty maintained strong leadership throughout the war. Maupin continued to serve as chairman, a position he had held since 1854, striving to hold together the faculty and the University through the austerity brought on by the war. Through his efforts the University stayed open despite threateningly low enrollment and slashed funding. He earned the heartfelt respect of the faculty members who remained at their posts through the war.[21] It was Maupin who led the effort to save the University from being razed by Union forces when they captured Charlottesville. On March 3, 1865, as federal troops approached the University, Maupin, accompanied by a contingent of professors and local government officials, met General George Custer's scouts near where the University Chapel stands today, waving a flag of truce. After a few tense moments, Maupin, appealing to the memory of Thomas Jefferson, was able to convince Custer to spare the University, "for it would always be a national asset." Custer agreed and posted guards to protect the University's buildings from damage during the occupation.[22]

Charlottesville was home to one of the largest war hospitals in Virginia. The Charlottesville General Hospital began operations on July 15, 1861, with a capacity of five hundred beds. Dr. James Lawrence Cabell, professor of medicine at the University, was the chief surgeon for most of the war. Housed in various buildings throughout Charlottesville and the University, the hospital remained an active facility for four years, discharging its last patient in March 1865. Charlottesville was an ideal location—the city was served extensively by rail lines, was in close proximity to Richmond for supplies and aid, and was secluded in the foothills of the Blue Ridge Mountains, making it relatively safe from attack.[23] At the University, patients were housed in the Rotunda and Annex, in rooms on the Lawn and the Range, and in the hotels. For the most part, the pavilions on the Lawn remained the private residences of professors and were used for the few classes that continued to meet. Jefferson Hall was among the buildings used to house patients, seeing thousands of wounded soldiers

FIGURE 8. Socrates Maupin was president of the Jefferson Society as a student in 1831, before joining the faculty later in his life. He served as chairman of the faculty from 1854 to 1870, during which time he played a major part in saving the University from being burned during the Civil War. Image courtesy of the Albert and Shirley Small Special Collections Library at the University of Virginia, University of Virginia Visual History Collection, U.Va. Prints and Photographs File, RG-30/1/10.011, Print 10195.

over the four years of conflict, thus temporarily displacing the Jefferson Society from its traditional home.

Meanwhile, the Jefferson Society continued to meet throughout the war, albeit irregularly. After sending their entire treasuries to Governor Letcher, the Jefferson and Washington Societies struggled financially to support their activities. (It is likely that none of the members expected the University to continue to sustain enrollment after the war began.) The next year, a few members of the Washington and Jefferson Societies met together as the University Literary Society, holding their meetings in Washington Hall. The combined organization met only for one session, after which the Jefferson Society was reorganized and continued to meet with only a few interruptions during the war.[24]

It is quite remarkable that the Jefferson Society survived the war. The low number of students attending the University would have made it extremely difficult to sustain the debates and meetings of the Society, which thrived on high participation from students. The financial troubles and material threats of wartime rendered many of the other traditional functions of the Society—including hosting balls, celebrations, lectures, and producing student publications—completely impossible.

We know very little about what the actual meetings of the Jefferson Society were like during the war. Jefferson Hall being unavailable, the Society likely met informally in one of the classrooms in the Rotunda Annex or a pavilion. Records survive of a single Jefferson Society president from the war years: Gratz Cohen. He reported home to his family in a letter dated November 26, 1863, "I was elected unanimously President of the Jefferson Society at their last meeting."[25] Cohen, who had earlier served in the Confederate Army as a member of the Savannah Artillery, was the first documented Jewish student to attend the University of Virginia. His Confederate war record and sympathies undoubtedly made him a favorite among the ranks of the Society.[26] He reported often to his parents and sisters at home, keeping them apprised of his studies and the small but hardy group of students at the University of Virginia. Cohen had great respect for the students who continued their studies throughout the war and often spoke highly of them, though he never mentioned the Society again after his earlier letter.[27]

The Jefferson Society and the Confederacy

Much like their forebears in antebellum years, the members of the Jefferson Society continued to look up to the political figures of their day and sought to model themselves after Virginia and Confederate statesmen. But now the young Society members had a much more personal link to their role models—many of the Confederate leaders they eagerly watched had themselves been Jefferson Society members in their student days. A popular student custom in the antebellum and war periods was to keep autograph books, booklets containing names and remembrances of the other students they met during the term. One can imagine the signatures that would have graced the pages of these books when the Grounds of the University teemed with future politicians.

Society members during the war could look to myriad examples of statesmen who had paced Jefferson Hall and spoken from behind the same lectern in their student days. On April 12, 1861, just before the outbreak of war, the Virginia government sent three former Society members as a delegation to Washington, DC, in an attempt to quell hostilities. Alexander Hugh Holmes Stuart, William Ballard Preston, and George Wythe Randolph found President Lincoln unwilling to back down from his resolve to hold federal forts in the South. The three men returned to Richmond by April 15, where they led the call for secession at the Virginia Convention.

Of the eighteen men who served in Jefferson Davis's cabinet, five were Jefferson Society members. At least twelve more filled the ranks of the Confederate Congress. For example, Robert Toombs, a former president of the Jefferson Society, served as the first Confederate secretary of state. Earlier, as a United States senator from Georgia, Toombs was instrumental in creating the short-lived Constitutional Union Party. By the time Lincoln was elected, however, he had lost all faith in the ability of North and South to coexist. In a farewell speech to the Senate on January 7, 1861, he railed against the Republican political agenda, proclaiming, "We want no negro equality, no negro citizenship; we want no negro race to degrade our own; and as one man [we] would meet you upon the border with the sword in one hand and the torch in the other."[28] Retuning to Georgia, he led the call for secession, bringing with him his old-line Whig supporters. Toombs also aspired to the presidency of the new Confederacy. When he lost to Jefferson Davis, he became a critic of the Confederate government, opposing the attack on Fort Sumter and ultimately resigning from his position as secretary of state after just five months in office.

Another alumnus of the Jefferson Society called to service in the new Confederate government was Robert Mercer Taliaferro Hunter. Hunter, a student in 1826, was one of the earliest members of both the Jefferson Society and the Patrick Henry Society. He then took Toombs's place and served as the second Confederate secretary of state from July 1861 to February 1862, before serving as a Confederate senator from Virginia for the remainder of the war. Hunter was a Democrat, initially drawn to the politics of John C. Calhoun. As a talented young politician, Hunter was elected the Speaker of the House of Representatives in 1839, the position from which he would launch his long political career. Then, as a Confederate, he proved to be a vocal critic of Jefferson Davis. He attended the Hampton Roads Conference in February 1865, a failed attempt by

FIGURE 9. Confederate currency featuring Jefferson Society members: Clement Clay on the $1, Robert M. T. Hunter on the $10, and George Wythe Randolph on the $100. Image courtesy of the Albert and Shirley Small Special Collections Library at the University of Virginia, Currency Collection, ACHS 856.

a moderate southern delegation to negotiate an end to hostilities with President Lincoln.

Toombs and Hunter were joined in Jefferson Davis's cabinet by Society members Thomas H. Watts, who served as the third attorney general, and George W. Randolph, the third secretary of war. James Alexander Seddon later replaced Randolph to become the fourth secretary of war. Clement Clay, another notable member of the Society from the late 1830s, served as head of the Confederate secret agents while in office as a senator from Alabama. Members of the Jefferson Society active in government during the Civil War followed what might be described as a typical Virginian course of action, whether or not they were Virginia natives. Vigorously supportive of the Confederate cause, though sometimes critical of the government itself, they often attempted to quell hostilities and were frequently critical of their more radical compatriots.[29]

Of the hundreds of University of Virginia students who were killed or wounded in the Civil War, a great portion of them were Society members—a devastating loss that would be felt for years, and from which the Society would be hard-pressed to recover. In late 1865, a group of Society members began to advocate for a monument to honor the fallen Confederate soldiers who had been University students. "The Jefferson Society, with whom the Washington united, by a series of resolutions which did much credit to the students of 1865–1866, inaugurated a movement to erect a monument in the soldier's cemetery, as yet an unenclosed space. The movement failed [for the time being] on account of the impoverished state of the South."[30] On February 19, 1890, *College Topics,* the new student newspaper, joined a renewed clamor for a monument honoring the Confederate war dead, and a bronze statue was finally unveiled on June 7, 1893.[31] The Jefferson Society has since been particularly vigilant in its efforts to remember fallen members from all wars, installing plaques in Jefferson Hall to honor those killed in the two World Wars and later commemorating the centenary of the Civil War with a ceremony.

Reconstruction

The Civil War crippled the South for generations. Families that had enjoyed enormous wealth were suddenly impoverished. Entire cities were razed by Union armies, leaving little more than ashes. The single

most valuable capital investment in the United States, the wealth represented by slaves, had been wrested from the hands of southerners by the
great "Army of Emancipation." The men who died fighting for the Confederacy numbered 258,000, and another 200,000 were wounded. The 39
percent casualty rate these numbers represent all but wiped out a generation of southern men.[32] It would take years for the South to recover from
the physical, financial, and human cost of the Civil War. But as historian
Frederick Rudolph observed, "the Civil War in many ways clarified the
dimensions and prospects of the American experiment. It swept away the
pretensions of the southern plantation aristocracy and all the dreams that
had sustained it."[33] The southern colleges, in the face of this new national
paradigm and "laid waste by war, impoverished, robbed by death and
poverty of the college-going generation . . . like the South itself, could but
hold on, hold on to romantic dreams of an Old South that never was or
hold on until the day when the Union might become one again."[34]

Like most universities in the South, the University of Virginia was
slow getting back onto its feet. Strapped for funding of any kind, it struggled to ensure that facilities were adequate, professors were well qualified,
and students had much needed resources available to them.[35] Abused
by the heavy use associated with the Charlottesville General Hospital
and wartime wear and tear, many University buildings had leaking roofs
and damaged floors and needed repainting. It would be several months
before some of the buildings needed for classrooms were serviceable
again. Those professors who remained at their posts after the war took
out loans on their personal credit to pay for many of the expenses the
University incurred in resuming operations. The Board of Visitors had
difficulty finding new professors who were qualified to teach and was
often unable to pay those few who were hired. The students did not fare
much better—many veterans attended class in tattered old uniforms.[36]
On October 18, 1864, Maupin wrote to Secretary of War James Alexander Seddon, a fellow Jefferson Society member, pleading for rations and
pensions for disabled former Confederate soldiers at the University to
ensure they could continue their studies. Seddon granted his request.[37]
The University and the Jefferson Society lost an important leader and
supporter when, on October 19, 1871, Maupin died following an accident.
He was buried in the University cemetery.[38] He had been instrumental
in restoring the school's financial condition and reputation after the war,
but although enrollment at the University had climbed steadily under his

watch, it was a continuing struggle to support the new students. The loss of Maupin was keenly felt.

Like the University itself, the Jefferson Society faced an uphill battle to regain the vitality and interest among students it had enjoyed before the war, but it recovered remarkably well given the challenges it was up against. In just three years, the literary societies were stable enough to resume publication of their antebellum literary endeavor, the *Virginia University Magazine*. The first postwar number of the *Magazine* appeared in October 1868. In just a few years, the Final Celebrations were also back in full force. As was the case before the war, major organizations on the Grounds hosted celebrations to honor their graduating members and recap their activities of the year. The largest celebrations were hosted by the literary societies and, eventually, the YMCA. The celebrations continued to be massive undertakings, including grandiose decorations, distinguished guests, and many speakers.

The following account of the 1873 Jefferson Society Final Celebration was typical of what appeared in the *Magazine*'s first issue every fall about the events of the previous spring:

The bright, cheerful day argued conspicuously for the success of the celebration of the Jefferson Society that night. Long before the appointed time, the Public Hall, brilliantly illuminated with a thousand gas-jets encircling the galleries and gorgeous chandeliers suspended from the ceiling, was thronged almost to its full capacity. There was assembled the beauty and fashion of Virginia and her sister states who had come to grace the occasion with their presence, and encourage by their smiles the efforts of the orators of the evening, the *lions* of a night, and to inspire the ambitious Jeffersonians with a manly emulation to win the honors due to labor and talent.[39]

This cheery scene was repeated time and again for the more than one hundred years that the Jefferson Society hosted their end-of-year celebration. It is hard to believe that this iteration of the Final Celebration could be at all subdued compared to those that occurred before the Civil War. The description of the proceedings offered a glimmer of hope that the South was on the road to recovery and that the Jefferson Society could still capture the attention of the students at the University of Virginia.

After the last strains of "Dixie" had died away, and long before there was any

FIGURE 10. The Public Hall in the Rotunda Annex, shown here decorated for Founder's Day on April 13, 1867, was the site of many of the public lectures and celebrations hosted by the Jefferson Society in the second half of the nineteenth century. Visible is a reproduction of Raphael's *School of Athens*. Image courtesy of the Albert and Shirley Small Special Collections Library at the University of Virginia, University of Virginia Visual History Collection, Accession #6436.

indication of the cessation of the hum of voices in the audience, the President introduced as the "best debater" of the Jefferson society, for the session of 1872–3, Mr. [John] Sharp Williams, [a future US senator] of Memphis, Tennessee, and in a very appropriate speech of a few minutes length, presented him with the medal of the society.[40]

Even though they were able to revive their Final Celebrations, the societies were forced to adapt to make ends meet, and the less important Intermediate Celebration fell by the wayside. As described in chapter 2, both societies had traditionally hosted this celebration in April to commemorate Jefferson's birthday, and it had been one of the biggest dates on the University social calendar. These daylong festivities were expensive propositions, often including decorations, musical accompaniment, and a prominent speaker. In 1870, however, the literary societies together "decided to abolish the system of separate intermediate celebrations, and to institute, in their stead, a joint celebration of the two societies, at which, in lieu of orations, a public debate should constitute the exercises of the occasion."[41] In the face of tight budgets, the Intermediate Celebrations were cast aside in favor of maintaining the more important Final Celebrations at the end of each academic year.

Despite the success of restarting the Final Celebrations, the Society apparently continued to languish in its meetings and debates for some time longer: "The Jeffersonians seem to have lost all sight of the original object of the organization. Debating has come to be utterly ignored, and declamation is the order of the day," read "Collegiana" in March 1873.[42] One reason that meetings may have been slow to pick back up after the war was that the postwar student body was very different from the one that had attended classes in 1860. The sons of the antebellum planter elite had been replaced by older, war-hardened veterans and a new crop of men too young to have served in the war but old enough to feel the devastating loss it caused.

In some ways literary society membership was less attractive to post-war students, who felt less compelled to earn the gentlemanly stamp of the old University or perform the same rituals of southern manhood that had sent students flocking to Jefferson Hall before the war, and those who signed their names to the membership rolls seemed to participate with less enthusiasm and excitement than in the Society's antebellum prime. The *Magazine* bemoaned the lack of student interest in literary societies in the February 1871 issue:

Out of the five hundred students who annually attend the University, about one hundred and sixty join each of the two debating societies. Now, it does appear strange that there should be found nearly two hundred men who deliberately deny themselves advantages scarcely second to the benefits which they derive from their academic studies.[43]

The Reconstruction years were a far cry from the days when the Society enjoyed the presence of almost half the student body in Jefferson Hall and engaged in friendly competition with the other half who joined the various other literary societies at the University.

In order to be an attractive destination for postbellum students, the Jefferson Society needed to examine its purpose deeply and adapt its activities and identity to fit their needs and desires. Over the three decades following the war the Society changed from a bastion of southern privilege to focus much greater attention on the cultivation of oratory and debate, as well as literary composition. The social rituals that characterized the Society before the war gave way to more intense training in these arts for all students at the University, with the aim of creating new leaders for the Commonwealth.

The process of change after the war was not easy, however, and balancing the traditional character of the Jefferson Society with a renewed energy for debate proved quite difficult. As they struggled to attract new members during Reconstruction, the role and position of literary societies in the University community was debated at length. The issue was on students' minds, particularly as they began to form fraternities and participate in athletics, and appeared as a topic quite frequently in the pages of the *Virginia University Magazine*. In October 1869, "Collegiana" observed that at the commencement of a "new year of literary societies . . . most of the new students seem to appreciate the benefits to be derived from them, and have determined to join one or the other. The same good will and fraternal feeling, generous rivalry and emulation, without envy or jealousies, exist between the societies that have ever *peculiarly* characterized these associations of our University when compared with those of other colleges."[44] Then, in April 1870, the *Magazine* editors confronted this question:

How are literary societies to be conducted so as to fulfill their design, and not be converted into jangling political bodies? This is a question which we have seen discussed in many of our exchanges, and especially in those from larger institutions. With us too it has been for some time under discussion . . . It must be confessed that our societies have been sadly perverted from their original design, and in their present design do little or nothing towards the promotion of literary culture among their members.[45]

Questions about the purpose of literary societies did not remain confined to the editor's column of the *Magazine*. Both the Washington and Jefferson Societies made frequent changes to the way they operated during Reconstruction in an attempt to remain popular with students. The Jefferson Society in particular experimented widely, trying everything from inviting public figures as speakers, opening their meetings to Charlottesville residents, changing the order of business conducted at meetings, and offering awards to members for various pursuits.

Near the end of the 1869–1870 session, the societies again made their proceedings secret, hoping that doing so would restore the element of mystery that surrounded them in their earliest days, when members were laid "under the most solemn injunctions not to divulge any of its proceedings, or, anything which may occur within its walls."[46] The change must not have been very successful, however, because by November 1870, the editors of the *Magazine* reported that "an attempt has been made in both societies to reverse the action taken by them towards the end of last session, closing the doors of their halls against all but members."[47] It was not long before the doors were thrown open again, and those who participated in debates hosted by both the Jefferson and Washington Societies became more skilled at engaging with their opponents. Debate and oratory played a major role in reinvigorating the Jefferson Society, and in just a few short years would draw a young Woodrow Wilson to walk through the doors of Jefferson Hall.

After the Civil War, the Jefferson Society also made a concerted effort to support, promote, and enrich literary education in the postbellum South. The editors of the *Magazine* and the Jefferson Society recognized the pressing need to return as quickly as possible to the promotion of literature and writing. The new crop of student-veterans attending the University had not enjoyed the same opportunities to practice composition as their antebellum counterparts, to say nothing of the business of running a magazine. Furthermore, the ravages of war had destroyed many private libraries and other collections of books, upon which the development of young writers relied. The Society worked diligently to bolster the quality of the literary environment at the University, as is evidenced by the content of the *Magazine* in the years following the Civil War. Chief among these efforts, of course, was the *Virginia University Magazine* itself. The "Editors Drawer" of the February-March 1869 issue spent a considerable amount of space commenting on the state of the publication. The very fact that two months were combined in one issue suggests that the Society was having trouble reinvigorating the *Magazine*:

The Virginia University Magazine, before the war held a high rank among Southern periodicals, and was unquestionably the best college magazine in America; it was complimented from all quarters, and brought credit as well upon the University as upon the students by whose efforts it was sustained. This position was not gained in the first, nor in the second session of its existence, and if we wish to re-establish its former precedence, we must work patiently and persistently toward that end. With its revival last session, the "Magazine" began life anew. All the experience which had been gained by those who had formerly conducted it was lost.[48]

In 1868, the literary societies took a key step to promote the *Magazine* and its popularity among the students. They reintroduced the Magazine Medal for the first time after the war, to be awarded to the best contributor over the course of the year. Given the success of the medal in raising student interest and excitement in contributing to the *Magazine* during the antebellum period, the Society hoped this iteration would do the same. Decisions regarding the winner were administered by a committee of the faculty that included Professors Gildersleeve, Holmes, and Schele de Verre. The editors forwarded the eligible articles to the committee, and the professors (all three of whom served in this capacity for several years) chose the best submission and wrote a short letter detailing their impressions and including a citation for the winner. The medal itself was presented at the Final Celebration of the society of which the winner was a member, or at the Jefferson Society celebration if the winner was not a member of a literary society.

The first medal awarded after the war, in 1868, went to A. W. Miller, a member of the Jefferson Society.[49] Unfortunately, the next year did not go as smoothly. The committee did not find an article worthy of recognition and wrote in their report, "The committee have diligently read and estimated the articles submitted to their judgment, and reluctantly, but unanimously and decidedly, recommend the societies to reserve their medal for another year, to be the reward of more manifest accomplishment."[50] The subsequent letters from the Magazine Medal committee, however, show that the quality of articles ultimately did improve, and their choice became more and more difficult from year to year, a testament to the success of the medal in promoting the *Magazine* among the students.

In pursuit of literary excellence, the Society was quite active at times in its management and oversight of the *Magazine*. On December 23, 1875, members of the Society debated an article which was to appear in the January issue of the *Magazine* entitled "Pseudo-Chivalry." Some members believed its critique of college manners deviated too far from the accepted aims of the *Magazine*, which might have been described as: "to cultivate literary composition." They proposed removing the article from every copy of the *Magazine* before it was distributed, and, after lengthy discussion, the motion to do so was carried 17 to 1.[51]

The Jefferson Society did not limit its efforts to the *Magazine* in promoting literary education. A few years after the Civil War, the Society began a campaign to increase access to printed material for students. The *Magazine* editorialized:

It seems to us that it would be a good idea for the Literary Societies to establish a Reading Room on the Lawn, where the members might have access to the leading reviews and other periodicals of England and America. If the societies will not establish such a resort, it ought to be done by the University.[52]

A Reading Room Association was formed soon after, and this group met regularly in Jefferson Hall.[53] The establishment of a reading room would have had several benefits for University students. Beyond simply increasing access to current periodicals and news, in the years of Reconstruction the hours of the University library were still quite limited, and a student-run reading room would have often been much more convenient. As such, it was an idea discussed at considerable length, even though it would have been a fairly expensive proposition. First proposed in the *Magazine* in 1869, it was still under consideration in 1878, when on November 23, the Jefferson Society appointed a representative to a conference committee with the YMCA to discuss funding the project.[54] That the Societies were involved in accomplishing this goal shows the place they continued to hold in the ethos of the University community.

The literary societies also functioned as custodians of the history and records of the University. The December 1871 issue of the *Magazine* indicates that the Jefferson Society, at the suggestion of one of its members, Moses Wicks, collected all of the back issues of the *Magazine* to be bound and placed in the University library. Furthermore, they strongly urged future editors to forward copies of forthcoming issues directly to the library so that they might be added to the collection.[55]

The Jefferson Society Strives to Move Forward

The earliest surviving minutes of the Jefferson Society are recorded in a minute book that dates to the end of 1875. They pick up the narrative of the Society at the meeting on December 18, 1875.[56] On the first page of the leather-bound tome is a quickly scrawled note that bears bad news for curious minds: "Minutes previous to these contained in this book (1875–1894) were placed in the University Library for safe-keeping and were destroyed in the Great Fire, Sunday Oct. 27, 1895."[57] These minutes and other accounts of meetings soon after the war show some signs of life in the recovering Society. It had returned to debating regularly, inviting speakers, and enjoying the company of fellow members.

The Jefferson Society endured many of the same growing pains as the South during Reconstruction, grappling with the difficult questions of how the South might best get back on its feet after the Civil War. For example, on February 12, 1876, they debated the question: "Should the South remain an agricultural people or should she turn her attention to manufactures?"[58] On October 20, 1877, the question presented before the Hall was "Ought Va to repudiate her State-Debt?" The same pressing question occupied the attention of the state legislature at the time.[59]

Some of the accounts of meetings are amusing. In 1871, a member entered a plea of insanity at the tribunal held at the end of meetings to adjudicate fines; the *Magazine* was happy to report that it was accepted.[60] In 1873 the editors were "glad to notice that, this session, there is a tendency to discard manuscript altogether and to speak extemporaneously."[61] Extemporaneous speaking had long been seen as one of the virtues and useful skills taught by the Jefferson Society.

The *Magazine*'s editors also bemoaned the lack of energy and electioneering in Jefferson Society politics during the winter of 1874 to 1875, yet another sign to the observer that students might be losing interest in the Society's activities. The next year showed some signs of hope for the old rabble-rousing elections of the Hall.

The old spirit of electioneering, which they had thought so entirely annihilated under the new regime, has again manifested its existence. The election of the Final President caused the repetition of the old scenes . . . for two whole weeks books were neglected and the all absorbing talk was with reference to the chances of the various candidates. There was actually a caucus![62]

Some felt that to regain their former prominence at the University, the literary societies needed bolstered support from the University:

But before the most conscientious course on the part of the societies can be productive of the best results, they need some assistance and encouragement from the University authorities. Granting that every student in the societies is there for the purpose of self-improvement, he does not know how to accomplish the desired end without instruction in the art of speaking . . . There is an obligation and a right existing between the University and the societies in this matter. The University owes the members of the societies the means of learning how to speak, and has the right to demand of them to put forward good speakers on all public occasions.[63]

At the end of the Reconstruction era the literary societies at the University of Virginia began to see competition from other organizations on Grounds for the first time. Students joined fraternities by the dozens, and the number of chapters represented multiplied quickly. Even the *Magazine* took notice and began to keep track of the new organizations, periodically publishing a register of the various fraternities and societies and their respective memberships.[64] The Young Men's Christian Association, better known as the YMCA, which was founded in 1856, greatly increased in membership after the war. It began to fulfill some of the roles in the University community that the Jefferson Society had traditionally performed, such as hosting large events and facilitating student publications. The YMCA even briefly sent an editor to the *Virginia University Magazine* in 1868.[65] While the Jefferson Society still enjoyed one of the largest memberships of any student organization at the University, its position at the center of student life was threatened by athletics, fraternities, and especially, the YMCA.

During Reconstruction the Jefferson Society sometimes struggled to find direction and purpose, but ultimately it made a strong recovery after the Civil War. Quick to reestablish its most important functions in Final Celebrations and the *Virginia University Magazine,* it was still faced with a lack of resources and faltering student interest. In the years following the war the Society shifted from a place where young southern men could come to practice at becoming gentlemen, to an organization that focused more of its time and energy on debate and literary improvement. In the face of increasing competition, the Jefferson Society would need strong, decisive leadership to help it maintain its position of prominence in the University of Virginia community. That leadership would come from a scrawny Virginian from Staunton named Woodrow Wilson.

CHAPTER FOUR

Woodrow Wilson and the Society

1879–1882

Wilson Arrives at the University of Virginia

When a young Thomas Woodrow Wilson decided to pursue the study of law after graduating from Princeton University in 1879, he returned to his native Virginia and enrolled at the University of Virginia School of Law. Already a successful student at both Princeton University and Davidson College, Wilson hoped that an education in law would allow him to pursue a career in politics.[1] He would later write to Ellen Axson, his fiancée, "The profession I chose was politics, the profession I entered was law. I entered one because I thought it would lead to the other."[2] In the year and a half he spent at the University, Wilson found an environment where his budding political and oratorical skills were tested, honed, and enriched.

During his first year at the School of Law, Wilson took up residence on Dawson's Row.[3] These six brick cottages at the west end of the University's Lawn and Ranges were built as student dormitories in 1859, as the student body outgrew the existing facilities.[4] Wilson lived in Room 158 of House F throughout his first year of study.[5] His room was on the ground floor, looking out onto a scenic view of Reservoir Road.[6] Though the rooms were small, Wilson enjoyed their close proximity to the center of the University while avoiding the bustle of the central Grounds.

Almost as soon as he arrived in Charlottesville, Wilson immersed himself in the University community and began taking part in a variety of activities. Archibald W. Patterson, a fellow student who was to become one of Wilson's best friends at the University, recalled that Wilson "had an excellent tenor voice and one of his first activities was to join the Chapel choir and assist in organizing a Glee Club."[7] Part of a long and storied tradition at the University, a capella groups and glee clubs have been important to University social life since shortly after the Civil War, and countless clubs continue to serenade students in Charlottesville to this day. In Wilson's time, these groups sang at regular Sunday church services, were featured in commencement ceremonies, and even performed at large public concerts in Charlottesville.[8] Patterson recalled long evenings that he, Wilson, and the other six members of their glee club would spend singing ballads to Charlottesville girls under the direction of their leader, Duncan Emmett.[9]

Beyond his musical inclinations, Wilson sought an outlet for his other passions—debate and oratory. He displayed his oratorical skill soon after he enrolled at the University when he was given the opportunity to present a medal to a successful acrobat at the Gymnasium on the East Range in front of a rather large crowd.[10] When Wilson rose to speak and present the medal to Tom Phister of Maysville, Kentucky, most of the crowd had no idea who the aspiring young statesman from Staunton was.[11] Wilson delivered a short but serious address, which he topped off with an amusing poem he had composed, displaying his immense capacity for both powerful oratory and cunning wit.[12] The audience was "captivated," and "he had spoken only a few minutes when his reputation as an orator was established."[13] With one short speech, Wilson had begun to make a name for himself in a student body that was still relatively small and within which reputation meant everything.

Wilson delivered several more such speeches at athletic and other University events, but he found his true oratorical home on the West Range at the meetings of the Jefferson Society. Wilson was no stranger to college literary societies when he arrived at the University. To truly understand the impact they had on his life and his political career, it is illuminating to trace Wilson's formative years before he came to Charlottesville, and the experiences which he brought with him when he arrived. During the year he spent at Davidson College, Wilson became enamored with the Eumenean Society, a literary society founded there in 1837. He was elected to membership almost immediately upon his arrival in October 1873, attending meetings with regularity, a custom that would mark his penchant for literary societies throughout his college years. He participated in several debates, read many original compositions, and was elected corresponding secretary of the organization.[14]

Wilson also took an active role in revising the society's constitution, displaying his long-held, intense interest in constitutions, rules of order, and other governing documents.[15] Wilson historian Ray Stannard Baker noted that Wilson had been captivated by constitutions "from the time when he was a lad of twelve or thirteen in Augusta, organizing the Lightfoots and writing out the rules of order."[16] While it is unclear exactly how much influence Wilson had on any particular revisions to the Eumenean Society constitution, the society did vote to commend him for "valuable assistance in the work" of revising the new document.[17] Wilson would later bring his fervent interest in constitutional revision and improvement to the Jefferson Society, helping to complete the Society's recovery from the Civil War.

Wilson remained an active member of the Eumenean until illness forced him to withdraw from school a year later; his stay at Davidson was cut short by digestion issues that would plague him for the rest of his life.[18] By the time he arrived in Charlottesville in the fall of 1879, Wilson was already a frail young man—Patterson described him as "rather thin" with a "reddish complexion [that] gave evidence of the dyspeptic trouble which followed him through life."[19] These health difficulties eventually curtailed Wilson's stay at Virginia, as they had at Davidson, but he was apparently comparatively free of ailment early in his stay in Charlottesville.[20]

One year after leaving Davidson, in 1875, Wilson entered Princeton University at the age of nineteen. There he found a similar forum to practice his rhetorical skills in the American Whig Society. Founded in 1769, the Whig Society (along with its counterpart, the Cliosophic Society) rested at the epicenter of undergraduate activities at Princeton until the late nineteenth century.[21] Wilson was admitted to membership in September 1875 and remained active until his graduation four years later in 1879. As a member, Wilson took part in a wide variety of oratorical and debating activities. His first speech before the group was delivered in October 1875 and was entitled "Rome Was Not Built in a Day."[22] This and many similar stellar presentations helped to catapult the young Wilson into prominence in the Whig Society.

Never one to miss an opportunity to engage in politics, Wilson used the politically charged atmosphere in Whig Hall as a training ground for future political endeavors, both in other literary societies and later in his professional career. While at Princeton he trained himself for "the bar, the pulpit, the stump, the Senate Chamber, [and] the lecturer's platform."[23] He was elected to serve as speaker of the society, as its first comptroller, and as historian during his tenure at Princeton.[24] He was also involved in a commission to improve the physical appearance of the society's meeting place and sat on a committee that recommended raising $10,000 to fund an endowment for Whig Hall, notable for the central place it occupied on campus at Princeton as well as its grandeur.[25]

Not only did Wilson figure prominently in the American Whig Society, but he also founded his own literary society at Princeton, which he named the Liberal Debating Society. He authored its first constitution, yet another example of his propensity toward and interest in founding documents.[26] The constitution demonstrated Wilson's affinity toward the British cabinet system of government, as it divided executive power between a president and a secretary of state, effectively a prime minister.[27] Wilson later adopted a similar approach when revising the constitution of the Jefferson Society. Nor was he about to sacrifice political control: he served first as secretary of state and secured his close friend's election as president, then later served in that capacity himself.[28]

Wilson also sought an outlet for his literary talents at Princeton and found it in the *Princetonian*, the college newspaper. He was elected to the board of editors in March 1877, quite soon after the paper's formation in 1876.[29] In that capacity, he wrote a series of comprehensive editorials, often on political issues of national importance. Later he was elected managing editor, an experience that would influence his views on the organization of the *Virginia University Magazine*, Virginia's equivalent of the *Princetonian*.[30] The *Princetonian* had an elaborate system for electing its large editorial board, it separated the duties of literary editors and fiscal managers, and it required editors to have successfully contributed articles to the publication in the past.[31] The *Virginia University Magazine* had no such organizational structure, something that both appalled and motivated the young Wilson to advocate change upon his arrival at the University. He went on to alter the composition and duties of the *Magazine*'s editorial board substantially while at Virginia.

The political training Wilson's contemporaries were receiving in the Whig Society was not lost on them. In pursuing their goals, Wilson and his friends in Whig often made light of their political aspirations. While trading letters, on more than one occasion he signed "Thomas Woodrow Wilson, Senator from Virginia," and his friends did likewise.[32] It may seem odd that Wilson chose to describe himself as a Virginian when his family moved from Staunton to Augusta, Georgia, while "little Tommy" was just a toddler, but Wilson's southern heritage was always important to him. Thus it came naturally that Wilson should look to the University of Virginia to continue his studies. He officially enrolled at the University on October 2, 1879, signing his name as T. W. Wilson.[33]

Shortly after he arrived in Charlottesville, Wilson joined the Jefferson Society. The roll books of the Society first bear Wilson's name on the night of October 18, 1879, when he was formally elected into membership.[34] To become a member in 1879, Wilson would have had to receive the approval of three-fourths of all members present and voting.[35] The by-laws of the Society at that time also specified the form of voting on membership to be *viva voce*, probably in order to ensure an even higher degree of selectivity and exclusivity.[36] It is not clear whether Wilson had friends in the Society or if it was on merit alone that he gained membership, but given his extensive experience and interest in collegiate literary societies, it was a natural fit for Wilson.

Wilson as a Politician

Wilson was considered by many to be a rather reserved young gentleman, but in the Jefferson Society he found a group of men who became his close friends during his tenure at the University and throughout his life. Archibald Patterson recalled that while Wilson had many acquaintances, "his circle of familiar friends was small."[37] Chief among these were Patterson, who later became the commissioner in chancery in Richmond; Charles W. Kent, later professor of English literature at the University; Richard Heath Dabney, later professor of history and dean of graduate studies at the University; Walter Lefevre, later professor of philosophy at the University; and Walter D. Toy, who became professor of Germanic languages at the University of North Carolina—all Society members.[38]

Dabney in particular was one of Wilson's closest friends and confidants. They were also fraternity brothers in Phi Kappa Psi, and the letters between them are among the most interesting glimpses into Wilson's private life, especially in his early adulthood. Patterson portrayed Wilson as an almost giddy schoolboy when recalling the long late-night strolls Wilson so enjoyed taking with his group of friends:

On these strolls Wilson was at his best. Putting aside the reserve which characterized his general bearing, he would yield himself utterly to fun and frolic, like a boy out of school. He had an inexhaustible store of anecdotes and was a very prince of story-tellers, always suiting the action to the word. When in one of these moods, he was as good as a circus.[39]

Meetings of the Jefferson Society and the close relationships he enjoyed with friends he met there were probably a welcome respite for Wilson from his studies. While he was a strong student, he admitted to being "most terribly bored by the noble study of law sometimes."[40] He was so much more interested in his extracurricular activities that "Wilson's class-work was a matter of secondary importance . . . lesson study and recitation seemed to be a sort of treadmill process, lacking the enthusiasm always exhibited in his forensic and literary endeavors."[41]

Beyond their tight-knit friendship, this group of gentlemen served as Wilson's closest allies and confidants in the Jefferson Society, his newest drawing board for political development. The Jefferson Society would prove to be Wilson's most engaging training ground so far; while he had certainly participated in political dealings in collegiate literary societies in the past, he honed his art and achieved his greatest level of success in that arena as a member of the Jefferson Society. In just over a year, Wilson adroitly climbed the ranks of Society leadership, aided by Dabney and the rest, and effected important and long-lasting change on the Society's structure and governance.

Wilson fully immersed himself immediately in the Society's affairs. Patterson remembered that Wilson "took a lively interest from the outset, attending its sessions with noticeable regularity and often participating in the debates."[42] It appears that his level of activity did not go unnoticed, as he was quickly appointed chairman of one of the Society's committees.[43] Shortly thereafter, Wilson secured an appointment to serve as the Society's secretary. Each incoming president had the power to appoint one member as secretary and one as assistant secretary, who together were charged with the duty to "record and read the proceedings, conduct the correspondence, and carefully preserve all records and documents of the Society."[44] That office was clearly an integral position in the day-to-day functioning of the Society, despite being unelected.

Benjamin Abney of South Carolina was inaugurated as the president of the Society for his second term on November 22, 1879, and "after a few appropriate and impressive remarks," he appointed Wilson as secretary, an important stepping-stone in Wilson's rise through the ranks of the Jefferson Society.[45] Although he had served in office before and had impressed the Society with his skill in oratory and debate, this was his first time in a constitutionally prescribed position.[46] As Wilson's last office before ascending to the presidency of the Society in the fall of 1880, serving as secretary certainly helped catapult him into prominence in Jefferson Hall.

No explanation from Wilson's pen survives detailing how he attained the presidency; however, it is likely that the steps he took to get there can be attributed to the respect he had earned in the eyes of the other Society members and partially to the power of his fledgling political machine. Patterson and Dabney served as secretary and assistant secretary respectively in the term prior to Wilson's appointment as secretary, and while the president, Benjamin Abney, is not mentioned as one of Wilson's close friends or confidantes, it is probably safe to assume that the advice of the immediate past secretary and assistant secretary would carry some weight in his appointment decisions.[47] Furthermore, Walter Lefevre, yet another of Wilson's intimate classmates, served on the influential Question Committee, which decided the weekly topic for debate, making his advice also unlikely to have been overlooked.[48] Aside from the strength of Wilson's friendships, his punctilious attendance at the meetings of the Jefferson Society as well as his reputation as a steadfast, hardworking young man doubtless influenced Abney's decision to trust him as his secretary.

From there—only one year after arriving at the University—Wilson was poised to rise higher in the Jefferson Society than he had ever had the opportunity to in the Whig Society at Princeton: to the office of president. At the beginning of his second year at the University, Wilson relocated from Dawson's Row to Room 31, West Range.[49] His new room was much closer to Jefferson Hall and only three doors down from Heath Dabney.[50] On October 9, 1880, the Society held its first regularly scheduled election of the fall term. The meeting proceeded as usual, starting with a call to order with "Mr. Wilson in the chair. Election of Officers being first in order of business, upon nomination by Mr. Lefevre of Mr. T. Woodrow Wilson for president, the latter gentleman was unanimously elected to that office."[51] Once in office, he got right to work: "Mr. Wilson gave notice that he would at some future time introduce a resolution to appoint a committee for revising our constitution."[52]

Wilson's control over the Society was nearly complete. He had been elected unanimously to the office of president, which was no easy accom-

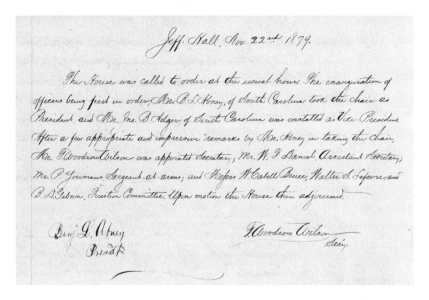

FIGURE 11. Woodrow Wilson was appointed secretary of the Jefferson Society on November 22, 1879. This excerpt shows the meticulous handwriting Wilson used to take minutes during the session and his elegant signature. Image courtesy of the Jefferson Society.

plishment and a fairly significant honor in and of itself. Just a few years after Wilson left the University, in 1883, a presidential contest became so heated that it devolved into blows between one of the candidates and his opponent's most ardent supporter.[53] In 1925, as University president Edwin Alderman remarked, at one time "the supreme honor of the University" was "to be the president of the Jefferson Literary Society."[54] But on the nomination of his longtime friend and ally, Walter Lefevre, Wilson was elevated to that cherished office without a single dissenting voice.[55] This indicates both the closeness and the influence Wilson's political coalition had gained by the time he was elected president.

As president of the Society, Wilson focused on two key objectives—securing political power in his circle of allies and reforming the Society's constitution and by-laws, two goals which often intersected and overlapped. To aid in his revision of the constitution, he harnessed the talents of Dabney as a "floor leader" of sorts for the project, trusting him to make the requisite motions and ultimately to shepherd the final product to passage.[56] Dabney spearheaded the constitutional reform effort admirably, and on October 23, 1880, the Society passed his motion to appoint a committee to draft a new constitution and by-laws.[57] This committee was composed of Dabney, Lefevre, a nondescript Mr. Andrews, and Wilson himself as chairman *ex officio*.[58] In one fell swoop, he had placed two of his closest allies in visible and important positions with critical roles in a major constitutional overhaul.

Together, Wilson, Dabney, and Lefevre smoothly piloted the effort to pass a new constitution and by-laws for the Society even though Wilson's term as president expired before the final passage of the document. Rather than rush the proceedings, Wilson ensured that Lefevre would succeed him as president, and, in what must have been an astonishing bit of political maneuvering, Lefevre was also unanimously chosen as president on November 20, 1880.[59] With a friend safely in the president's chair, Wilson and Dabney were able to present and pass the vast majority of their desired constitutional changes—all but one of Wilson's constitutional revisions had been brought to the floor by Dabney and passed by January 15, 1881.[60]

Wilson built one of the first and best-recorded political machines in the history of the Jefferson Society. It appears that for several sessions, anything that happened in the Society Wilson either had a hand in or a connection to. Dabney also served as editor-in-chief of the *Virginia University Magazine* during Wilson's term, further consolidating their control.[61] For Wilson, the Jefferson Society, and literary societies in general, were meant to be training grounds for future leaders, and always the consummate politician, he took full advantage of these training opportunities for his future career while at the University.[62] His efforts and the efforts of his companions went a very long way toward ensuring that the Society found solid footing after the Civil War. With changes like a new emphasis on debate and new types of students after the war, Wilson sought to bring its constitution up to date with the postbellum character of the Society.

Wilson's Constitution

"So infectious was Wilson's interest in the new constitution," wrote Baker, "that we find most of the meetings for many weeks devoted to the discussion of its principles."[63] While certainly a long and arduous project, taking almost four months to complete from proposal to passage, Wilson's constitution proved a successful endeavor, the results of which left an indelible mark on the organization and governance of the Society.

The impetus for Wilson's reform of the Jefferson Society's constitution and by-laws likely stemmed from the woefully inadequate and disorganized nature of the documents that had governed the Society since 1859. The previous constitution was composed of only seven short and rather disjointed articles followed by no less than forty-one by-laws.[64] Substantive provisions that should have been placed in the constitutional text seem to have been tacked on to the by-laws as afterthoughts.[65] Furthermore, the 1859 constitution contained very little on the governance of the *Virginia University Magazine,* one of the Society's most important contributions to the University community. It included only three short sections in reference to the *Magazine,* and it gave no guidance whatsoever as to the composition, structure, or powers of the editorial board.[66] On top of their structural deficiencies, the 1859 governing documents reflected the Society as it had existed before the war, when it (and the University itself) was made up almost exclusively of representatives of the southern aristocracy, an exceedingly homogeneous group among whom there was little disagreement over what the primary aims of the Society were. Wilson and his committee systematically reworked both the constitution and by-laws in order to address these issues as well as to modernize, clarify, and organize the documents.

While it is impossible to know for certain exactly what role Wilson played in the Constitutional Committee because no records of the committee's proceedings are extant, there are six major areas of revision that reflect significant Wilsonian influence.[67] The first of these relates to the structure and organization of the document itself. Wilson had an abiding belief in the importance of clarity and order, two words which certainly did not describe the 1859 Jefferson Society constitution and by-laws. The newly produced constitution provided a model of a clear structure. For example, it gave a detailed outline of the Society's governance and officers in article II, something the previous constitution sorely lacked.[68] The final product of Wilson's committee was an orderly, navigable document, far superior in structure to the hodgepodge of rules and regulations that constituted the 1859 document.

Second, not only did Wilson and his committee reorganize the documents for the sake of clarity, but also they undertook the challenging task of moving many provisions from the by-laws into the constitution.[69] The 1859 by-laws included many regulations that were better reserved for the constitution itself, due to either their permanence or centrality to defining the Society, and Wilson's committee transferred many of these sections into the new draft of the constitution. For example, the 1859 constitution did not require that applicants for membership be students at the University of Virginia; instead, that stipulation was stated in the by-laws.[70] In Wilson's new constitution, this important provision was featured prominently as article I, section 1.[71] Whereas the 1859 constitution was extremely short and incomplete, the new constitution was significantly longer and more substantive, comprising eleven articles and fifty-five sections.[72] Wilson and his committee successfully limited the content of their new by-laws to procedural regulations, a much clearer and more commonsensical approach than had previously been the case.[73]

Third, Wilson's belief in the importance of debate as a tool for developing young leaders and statesmen shone through in several significant additions to the new constitution, by which he hoped to make the Society more attractive for students at the University. In article V, the committee expanded the weekly debates of the Society to include all members, where previously only certain selected members debated a topic chosen by the Society at each meeting.[74] In the new constitution, after the selected debaters had spoken, "the question shall be open to the house for debate" before a vote could be taken on which side had won.[75] In the same article, the committee ensured that these debates would not be shortened or ignored by an early adjournment of the meeting. Article V specified that no vote could be called on the debate question prior to "half-past ten o'clock."[76] This meant that these debates would carry on for two to three hours at minimum. Furthermore, the new constitution specified that no member could be elected as Final president or vice president of the Society, both highly coveted positions, without having either debated or presented a speech before the Society at least twice.[77] While the 1859 constitution had exalted oratory over debate, Wilson's influence and opinions effected a complete reversal of their positions in the 1880 document.[78]

Beyond simply encouraging debate, Wilson sought to promote a specific sort of debate. Archibald Patterson remembered that Wilson had always been "especially happy in suggesting subjects for discussion" in the Society, but that he "would insist upon having some fresh and practical theme about which people were thinking."[79] Wilson believed it was important that young men not debate highly theoretical and impractical topics such as "Who was the greatest general, Napoleon or Caesar?" which was apparently a favorite at the time.[80] Instead, he hoped they would discuss relevant, timely questions of public policy, a consideration he felt was so important to the survival and relevance of collegiate literary societies that he enshrined it in the new preamble to the Society's constitution:

We, the members of the Jefferson Society of the University of Virginia, in order to form a more perfect organization, provide for our common improvement in the art of debate, promote general culture amongst ourselves and those around us, and drill ourselves in all those exercises which strengthens for the free duties of citizenship, do ordain and establish this Constitution for our government.[81]

The gravity that Wilson and the other framers sought to place on debate in relation to one's obligations as a citizen is obvious. Wilson's preamble remains the opening passage of the Jefferson Society constitution today, reflecting the continued importance of debate in molding successful young citizens.

Wilson also had an important role in creating the greatly expanded governing structure in the new constitution.[82] The 1859 constitution included virtually no details about establishing standing committees, and it had placed much discretion and authority in the hands of the officers.[83] Wilson helped create four new committees under the 1880 constitution that would handle various aspects of the Society's activities: the Ways and Means Committee, the Conference Committee, the Judicial Council, and the Finals Committee.[84] These bodies created a much more functional governing structure, as duties were both dispersed and clearly delineated to specific officers and committees. Many of the functions charged to these committees, for example, the Final Celebration, had become too large and complicated to be administered by the Society as a whole, and it made sense to delegate them to specific groups of Society members.

For many years as a young man, Wilson harbored the belief that the British model of cabinet government was superior to the congressional government of the United States, a point of view he expressed in one of his earliest published works, "On Cabinet Government." Students at the University of Virginia would have seen this essay before Wilson arrived on the Grounds.[85] The diffused executive power in the new constitution and the increased powers held by the Society as a whole were probably a manifestation of this conviction.[86] In article II, "Outline of Government," the executive power of the Society is vested in all the officers and all the

standing committees instead of one president or executive officer.[87]
Wilson probably sought a more collective exercise of executive power,
especially befitting a smaller, close-knit organization such as the Jefferson
Society. In a similar vein, the new constitution weakened the power of the
Society officers; for example, it allowed for an appeal of the decisions of
the president to the whole Society and permitted the treasurer to make
disbursements only with the entire Society's authorization.[88]

Finally, Wilson's biggest changes were perhaps those that dealt with
the governance of the Society's publication, the *Virginia University Magazine*.[89] The 1859 constitution had only three short sections pertaining to
the *Magazine*, and all it mentioned in regard to the editorial board was
"that an editor be elected on the part of this Society to serve for a term of
three months."[90] Wilson, as a former managing editor of the *Princetonian*,
must have found this dreadfully insufficient. He drew on his experience
to greatly expand and improve the structure of the editorial board of the
Magazine. Notable changes included creating a bona fide editorial board,
lengthening the term and expanding the powers of the editor-in-chief,
and placing an editor specifically in charge of the finances of the *Magazine*.[91] The new constitution also bolstered the qualifications required of
the editorial staff by ensuring that "no member shall be eligible for the
position of literary editor of the Magazine who has not had at least one
prose article of his own composition accepted for publication in the Magazine."[92] The knowledge and experience Wilson brought to these reforms
were reflected in the final product, and it helped ensure the publication
would be under competent governance for the foreseeable future.

Wilson did not get everything he wanted out of the new constitution. One of Wilson's proposals, relating to the Society's medal for their
best debater, was defeated and a compromise was passed.[93] Under the
1859 constitution, only one medal was to be given each semester to the
Society's best debater.[94] However, by the time Wilson became a student,
custom dictated that two medals be awarded each year—the Debater's
Medal to the best debater and an Orator's Medal to the second-best
debater.[95] Wilson made it clear that he hoped the Society would give only
one medal each year to its best debater; however, the regular membership voted down this suggestion.[96] While the Society did indeed officially
institute a system of awarding two medals, Wilson won a small conces-
sion in that "whenever there [were] but two contestants no second medal
shall be given."[97] Later, at the turn of the century, the competition was

divided into separate debate and oratorical contests to determine the winner of the respective medals, logically differentiating them in character instead of merely by prestige.

Although Wilson's proposal for a single debater's medal failed, this was comparatively insignificant compared to the number and importance of his revisions that passed successfully. Wilson saw these changes as the culmination of his political legacy in the Society, writing to Dabney after leaving the University to inquire "what was the ultimate fate of the new Constitution in the Jeff?"[98] Wilson's political savvy and legal brilliance led to a document that has stood the test of time, as his 1880 constitution placed the Society back on firm footing after the Civil War and remains the basis of the current constitution of the Jefferson Society. Wilson not only reshaped the Society during his time as a student but also steered it onto a new, more resolute course that it would follow for years to come. Wilson helped to imbue the degree of interest in the affairs of the Society that had motivated students to contest its elections with uncommon vigor before the war, and soon (very soon) students were once again fighting over the presidency.

Wilson as a Debater and Orator

Woodrow Wilson's activity in the Jefferson Society went well beyond politics and constitutional reform; it also included debate, oratory, and literary performances. Archibald Patterson recalled that Wilson became quite interested in the oratorical activities of the Society almost immediately after becoming a member, participating in several debates that were both "spirited and impressive."[99] Only one week after being elected to membership in the Society, Wilson was called upon to debate the negative of the resolution "Is the Government of Great Britain better adapted to promote the welfare of society than that of the U.S.?"[100] Patterson noted that these were the types of questions that Wilson enjoyed debating, as opposed to the "hackneyed" and impractical questions that were often discussed at the time.[101]

Although Wilson's reputation as a speaker was growing at the University, he did not feel that it was merited. He believed that his speaking abilities were lacking, even saying that he was "surprised" at the reputation he had gained as an orator.[102] After he was chosen to deliver the Society's monthly oration, he wrote to his old friend Robert Bridges that

I am to deliver the March oration. Since my return from Washington I have found, much to my surprise and dismay, that at that meeting which took place during my absence, it was moved and unanimously carried that, inasmuch as several young ladies had expressed a desire to be present when my oration is to be delivered, the society be upon that evening thrown open to visitors! . . . I'm thoroughly scared. I took no very special pains with my oration and I'm beginning to tremble for its reception.[103]

At that time, Society meetings remained closed except to members, but apparently Wilson's reputation as a speaker had grown to the point that a significant number of guests were interested in attending. Wilson's fears were evidently misplaced, as the minutes of the Society concerning his speech state that "Mr. Wilson inspired by the bright eyes and approving smiles of many fair visitants delivered his oration with an earnestness and vigor that drew down much well deserved applause."[104]

The content of Wilson's March oration to the Society deserves some consideration, given that it is one of his first well-recorded statements on the Confederate cause and the Civil War. Though he was the son of a former Confederate army chaplain, Wilson displayed a remarkably progressive view for the time on the outcome of the Civil War and the fate of the Confederacy. The bulk of the speech itself was on John Bright, the British liberal politician, but toward the end Wilson raised the topic of the Confederacy.[105] Wilson began his discussion with the seemingly contradictory statement: "Because I love the South, I rejoice in the failure of the Confederacy."[106] He went on to detail several compelling reasons that the success of the Confederacy would have actually been ruinous to the South, including the resulting states' comparative weakness with the North, concluding that "even the damnable cruelty and folly of reconstruction was to be preferred to helpless independence."[107] Wilson touched on slavery only briefly, never condemning it as an immoral institution. Rather, he cited it as a hindrance to the southern economy and something that would have forever incited strife until it was eliminated.[108]

Although most of the speeches and debates of the Society were friendly, some became quite personal. Wilson developed an intense rivalry with William Cabell Bruce, later a United States senator from Maryland, which culminated in a climactic competition for the coveted Debater's Medal. Bruce and Wilson were both successful debaters and orators, and their competition led Bruce to later reflect that their rivalry "involved Wilson and me in an estrangement which I deeply regret."[109] Bruce was evidently a pompous young gentleman, whom Patterson recalled would rehearse his speeches in his room on the Range "without regard to the peace and dignity of the neighborhood."[110] Arrogant as he might have been, Bruce proved a formidable debate opponent for the young Wilson.

The two men were scheduled to meet for a debate on April 2, 1880, in Jefferson Hall, but the anticipated crowd was so great that the event had to be relocated to Washington Hall, the larger meeting place of the Washington Society.[111] Indeed, Patterson remembers that the hall "was packed almost to suffocation with an audience from far and near" who had come to watch Wilson and his teammate Junius M. Horner debate Bruce and Benjamin L. Abney.[112] The resolution of the debate was "Is the Roman Catholic Element in the United States a Menace to American Institutions?"[113] Wilson and Horner took up the negative of the resolution while Bruce and Abney argued the affirmative. The arguments on each side were fierce, but when the debate concluded, a faculty committee chaired by Dr. John W. Mallet declared Bruce the winner of the Debater's Medal and Wilson the winner of the Orator's Medal, which were, according to custom, the first place and second place medals, respectively.[114]

His defeat by Bruce was crushing to the future president of the United States. Apparently Wilson felt that he was a "debater or nothing" and that to accept the Orator's Medal would be below him.[115] He originally stated that his intention was not to accept the medal at all, as he wanted "first or none."[116] After some convincing by his friends, however, Wilson was persuaded to accept the medal, by virtue of which he was expected to deliver a speech at the Society's Final Exercises alongside his rival Bruce.[117]

It appears that the disgruntled Wilson may have challenged Bruce to a rematch of sorts later that same month. Wilson's papers from that time show extensive debate notes concerning the resolution "Was the Monroe doctrine founded upon a wise policy?"[118] Bruce later recalled that indeed this debate had taken place, but he did not remember the results of it.[119] Neither Wilson nor the extant records of the Society make any mention of the result, but Bruce later described what he felt were the reasons for his superiority to Wilson in debate, recalling, "I had a more commonplace, conventional mind than his . . . he was too abstract, too oracular for a debater. . . . Wilson, in my judgment, was much better fitted for the public platform than for a debating assembly."[120] If Bruce's explanation is to be believed, then we can assume that he also won this debate.

Before the end of the final term, Wilson was bested yet again by Bruce, who had become a bitter rival. Both men had submitted essays to the *Virginia University Magazine*'s writing competition; Wilson had submitted the text of his speech on John Bright and another on William Gladstone, while Bruce had submitted an essay on John Randolph of Roanoke.[121] A faculty committee chaired by Professor Francis H. Smith awarded the medal to Bruce but had several kind words to say about Wilson's "excellent articles."[122]

Wilson took these defeats and what must have been quite negative interactions with Bruce extremely personally. While Bruce would later write that he was glad their college rivalry did not result in "lasting bitterness" between them, Wilson did not share such feelings. In 1922, he wrote to Cordell Hull, then chairman of the Democratic National Committee, upon Bruce's nomination as a Democratic candidate for the United States Senate from Maryland, that "I have known [Bruce] since he was a young man and feel it my duty to say that . . . he is incapable of loyalty in any manner . . . is by nature envious and intensely jealous, and cannot take part in disinterested service of any kind."[123] It is by no means certain just how much of this can be attributed to their University interactions, but their former rivalry certainly did not endear Bruce to Wilson.

Bruce had thoroughly embarrassed Wilson in their previous contests, but Wilson had one last chance to upstage him at the Final Exercises of the Jefferson Society, held on June 29, 1880.[124] As the winners of the Society's medals, Wilson and Bruce were both expected to present speeches at the Final Celebration. Wilson, after humbly stating that he was "just learning to speak," dazzled the audience with what the *Richmond Daily Dispatch* declared "the best [speech] which has been delivered by a student here for many a year."[125] Richard B. Hubbard, a former Texas governor and the guest speaker at the 1880 commencement, pronounced after hearing Wilson speak: "That young man will be an honor to his State."[126] Wilson's delivery and content were so extraordinary that the *Dispatch* was driven to mention that Wilson's presentation "was a far better speech than the first medalist made, who evidently could not have fulfilled the promise his speech gave before the committee when he contested for and received the first honor over Mr. Wilson."[127] Wilson finally bested his rival in a contest of oratory on the biggest stage either of them would enjoy during their college years, the University of Virginia's Final Exercises.

FIGURE 12. Woodrow Wilson working at his desk. Image courtesy of the Albert and Shirley Small Special Collections Library at the University of Virginia, G. E. Thompson Collection of Woodrow Wilson Photographs, Accession #38-192-a, Photo #24.

Wilson's Legacy

Like many of his past and future endeavors, Wilson's term at the University of Virginia was cut short by illness. In the late fall and early winter months of 1880, Wilson's physical condition deteriorated substantially.[128] He had been examined by his doctor over Christmas vacation and, as he later wrote to Dabney, his digestive organs were found to be "seriously out of gear."[129] At the urging of his parents, he returned home to North Carolina to rest and regain his health. The *Virginia University Magazine* recorded his departure with a note of sadness in the January 1881 issue saying: "We regret to announce that Mr. T. W. Wilson, Orator of Jeff. Society 1880, has left the University on account of his health. Last session he distinguished himself as a writer and as a debater."[130]

His interest in the affairs of the Jefferson Society continued despite his premature departure from the University. Despite his health problems, he wrote to Dabney:

FIGURE 13. Woodrow Wilson and his wife, Edith Bolling Wilson, at a baseball game. Image courtesy of the Albert and Shirley Small Special Collections Library at the University of Virginia, G. E. Thompson Collection of Woodrow Wilson Photographs, Accession #38-192-a, Photo #31.

I miss you and the other boys of [Phi Psi] more than you would believe, Heath; and when Saturday night comes, I find myself wishing that I could drop in at the Jeff. again. Whom have you elected G. P. in my stead? And what was the ultimate fate of the new Constitution in the Jeff? To what fate did the medal question come? Are there any new candidates for any of the honors of the Society in the field? Tell me all you can about the frat. and about the Jeff. when you write—which do as soon as ever you can.[131]

Having only attended the University for one and a half years, Woodrow Wilson's tenure as a member of the Jefferson Society was remarkably short when considering what he achieved in that time. In less than half the time it takes to earn a modern college degree, he was able to form a powerful political machine, sweeping himself and his allies into power. Wilson's machine provided a model for future powerful political alliances, such as the coalition led by Robert Musselman in the 1930s. Machine politics dominated by a single charismatic leader have made repeated appearances in the Hall, which is at its very core a politically minded organization. Every subsequent political coalition, while disparate in goals and composition, could look back to Woodrow Wilson's close-knit team from the late 1880s for a model and inspiration.

Beyond playing at politics, Wilson left an even more permanent legacy in the new constitution for the Society that he was instrumental in passing. His efforts to modernize, expand, and clarify the Society's constitution and by-laws were overwhelmingly important. These reforms helped ensure the Society would have relatively stable governance and clear rules of procedure for years to come. As a result it did not falter after the Civil War or in the face of competition from other student organizations. Wilson's work in stressing the importance of competence on the editorial board of the *Virginia University Magazine* also had a great impact. The continued success of the *Magazine* under the Society's governance for almost a century after Wilson left the University can be attributed in no small part to the substantial improvements he pioneered in the 1880 constitution.

While Wilson's political and legal acumen constituted his greatest tangible contributions to the Jefferson Society, it was the message of his 1880 Final speech that left the most significant intellectual legacy to future members of the Jefferson Society and collegiate literary societies in general. In this address Wilson focused on the relevance of literary societies and their place in the rapidly changing America of the late nineteenth century.[132] At times pessimistic but also hopeful about the future of these organizations, Wilson argued that they needed to change and adapt to modern times. In brief, he stated:

The Jefferson Society was indeed once a literary society, but it is not now. Her journals contain entries bright as the records of immortality, but the case is altered now. . . . I do not taunt my Society, though its day of usefulness is nearly over. . . . The conditions which gave it and like organizations life have passed away. The scholastic standards have been raised. . . . College societies, if not vain and useless affairs, must prepare us for life. Life and its demands are different from what they once were, the societies must be different—they must be practical schools. In this death of old affairs I see signs of happy promise—it prefigures a new birth and a better existence.[133]

Wilson attempted to enshrine many of these necessary changes in his new constitution for the Jefferson Society. He believed that this document would help preserve the Society's relevance as a "practical school" for young Americans.

As Woodrow Wilson left the University of Virginia in December 1880, he hoped that many bright young men would follow him and be trained in the school that was the Jefferson Literary Society. In the "signs of happy promise" he spoke of in June 1880, he saw a new generation of leaders emerging from these societies who would be prepared to provide principled leadership for the rapidly expanding American republic. Over its long history and to this day, more than a century later, the Society fulfills Wilson's dream.

CHAPTER FIVE

The Jefferson Society
and a Changing University

1880–1925

Woodrow Wilson ushered in a new era at Jefferson Hall, one that saw political maneuvering and electioneering on the part of its members intensify. The new structure of his constitution, coupled with his popularity as a student, inspired renewed interest in the Society and a greater energy for debate. But politics was both a blessing and a curse for the Society, for while it stimulated activity among the membership and increased attendance at meetings, the other functions of the Society—like the important and visible orations at the Final Celebration—often fell by the wayside as Society members focused on who would win upcoming elections. A fine line separated the two possible effects of intense political campaigns. In December 1891, the *Magazine* lauded the energy that was being thrown into the present Jefferson Society election:

The "Jeff." has, during the past four weeks, begun to assume its old time aspect. That is to say, a political fight has been instituted, and every Saturday night the hall is filled with interested members . . . politics has been the stimulus, and really there is always something to learn in the "Jeff." during these political contests: the meetings abound in short debates on parliamentary practice, and constitutional points . . . looked upon in the light of a training school of parliamentary practice, the "political Jeff." is not a bad institution after all; and it would seem that debates on constitutional points is much to be preferred to the wearisome effusions of the ordinary literary society.[1]

But when things got too heated, the conflict could damage the Society. If the members were not careful, a bad campaign could leave the Society in a "state of coma" and "practically dead," with none of its members willing to put forth any effort after campaign season was over.[2] The above campaign, which the *Magazine* welcomed in December, posed a more frightening prospect by January. It had become disruptive to the Society's business, and the president who should have been selected by January 2 was not in place until January 23.[3] The editors remarked,

The Jeff. has never seen a similar contest; never before in all her history, stretching across nearly three quarters of a century, has there been such a political upheaval. That Society has been little better than a mere political machine for many years, but never before has she been controlled by an organization absolutely independently of any fraternity.[4]

This particular election began to unfold as usual, with several political factions aligning behind their chosen candidate. Fraternities, still relatively young organizations at the University, did not want to miss out on the opportunity to install one of their members in the coveted presidency of the Jefferson Society. Each put forth its own man, testing his strength against the field, then either dropping back to support some other agreeable candidate, or seeking to strike a bargain for the backing of enough other members to remain in the race. In this particular year, a collation nicknamed the "Farmer's Alliance" formed to take on the fraternities' control of the Society and gained significant ground. Both sides resorted to parliamentary trickery: delaying meetings and making efforts to change the makeup of eligible voters by placing restrictions on who could vote, the most effective of which dealt with tenure in membership. In the end, the Farmer's Alliance emerged victorious. But as Philip Alexander Bruce describes, when politics took over, as it sometimes also did in the Washington Society,

it was the general impression, at this time, that the two societies had failed to carry out the purpose for which they had been revived after the war . . . no one took any part in the current of so-called debate in these bodies . . . the members who possessed the leisure and energy to prepare such elaborate discourses were few in number, and it followed that the proceedings were meagre in thought and curtailed in extent.[5]

The next year, the political conflict reached its peak in the most contentious and violently disputed election the Jefferson Society has ever seen. Two candidates emerged as the chief competitors for the 1893 Final presidency: Mallory K. Cannon, who might be described as the more established candidate, was set to square off against the popular Murray M. McGuire, a star pitcher for the University Nine and leader of many other organizations on the Grounds. McGuire, who did not have enough support within the Society to win, recruited roughly thirty other students to join the Jefferson Society in time to vote for him in the election. Cannon's supporters realized McGuire's plan and countered with a cunning strategy of their own. They simply began adjourning each meeting of the Society before any business could be conducted, including the induction of new members. The conflict attracted attention from every corner of the University, including that of James P. C. Southall, an old Delta Kappa Epsilon fraternity brother of McGuire's who had recently begun to teach physics at the University. He recalled the chaotic events in his memoir, *In the Days of My Youth:*

As instructor in Physics it is doubtful whether I ought to have descended into the arena of college politics, but I was a violent partisan and could not keep out of it. As a matter of fact, I was the active manager of McGuire's campaign, and Breckenridge Robertson was my firm ally and efficient helper. "Mike" Cannon was a prominent student in college who had taken his M. A. Degree in June, 1892 . . . and who was now in the Law School. The political leader of the Cannonites was an Irishman from Clarke County, known as "Kit" Carson, and afterwards widely known in the Philippine Islands as Judge Adam C. Carson. He was a man of no mean ability, a born politician if ever there was one, clever, resourceful and adroit, affable, good-natured, and likable; but in my opinion he was absolutely untrustworthy and unscrupulous.[6]

Carson led the effort to keep McGuire's supporters out of the Society, the membership of which was still fairly small after the last politically tumultuous election, every week turning away the hundreds of students Southall and Robertson had assembled in front of Jefferson Hall. The tactics did not sit well with Southall:

We believed that the enemy had resorted to a mean subterfuge in order to escape certain defeat, and the feeling between the two parties was at fever-heat. Certain parliamentary questions were involved. The only copy of the new constitution of the Society which had been ratified and adopted but which had not yet been printed, disappeared mysteriously from the desk of the secretary where it had been kept, and was never afterwards found; the reason of its disappearance, as we alleged, was because this document explicitly forbade the employment of the tactics that had been adopted by our opponents.[7]

In the December 17, 1892, issue of *College Topics*, the nascent student newspaper, broadsides appeared arguing on behalf of both sides, Carson and his supporters claiming they had committed no wrong in adjourning meetings immediately, and Robertson making the plea for relief on the part of the challenger McGuire.[8] The publicity only increased the excitement around the contest, and according to Southall,

long before the appointed hour of the meeting of the Jefferson Society, the hall on West Range was already packed and jammed with members and applicants for membership so that not a bit of standing room was left, while outside a mob of students was assembled under the arcade. No pretence was made of calling the meeting to order.[9]

Robertson and Carson in turn fought their way through the crowd and attempted to rally support to their side. Both were powerful, commanding speakers, but the tension in the Hall had swelled to the point that no amount of smooth or stirring oratory would command the crowd. Southall was enraged as Carson concluded an impassioned defense of their actions over the preceding month:

It was all I could do to hear him in silence to the end, and when he finished, I looked him square in the face and told him that he was both a blackguard and a liar! Then pandemonium broke loose in the hall of the Jefferson Society. Tom Pinckney of South Carolina and Lee Marshall of Maryland, two of the gamest fighting cocks ever bred on earth, were close behind me on the platform, and had they not been held in leash at that moment, they would have leaped on Carson and saved me from my own fate. It was a tense moment which might easily have led to a free-for-all fight.

How the crowd dispersed that evening without riot and bloodshed, I cannot tell because I myself was so wrought up and so much in the thick of it that

I really never knew all that happened afterwards. Before the morning dawned, Carson and I had had a furious fist-fight upstairs in the old gymnasium at the end of East Range. That encounter lasted thirteen rounds, and was a bloody affair in dead earnest. Neither of the two combatants had the faintest notion of boxing, and each slugged the other with mortal hatred. Every blow landed full in the face, and then one of the so-called pugilists would pummel the other unmercifully pursuing him round and round the ring until the gong sounded. The mortification I experienced was far worse than the punishment I got, and I had plenty of both that night. The Irishman took a lot of punishment too, but in the end, I am sorry to say, he was the victor; for when in the last round I stumbled over a piece of furniture that was nailed to the floor and fell and was felled to the ground at the same time, that was the end of the battle.[10]

When the dust settled, Southall and Cannon's boxing match had in actuality settled nothing, and both parties agreed to submit their dispute to a committee of the faculty, chaired by the sage professor of moral philosophy Noah K. Davis. Over the course of the next two months, both sides traded extensive formal written briefs for the perusal of the faculty committee, which also included the chairman of the faculty, Dr. Paul Barringer. After initially attempting to lay the guilt on the shoulders of both sides, and being pressed by Robertson and Southall to issue a real judgment, Davis and Barringer came down on the side of McGuire. They issued their decision on February 18. It read:

"The friends of Mr. McGuire," having declined our request, that the moral rightness of their action in the premises be also submitted to our decision, we find ourselves limited to passing upon the single point submitted at the outset, namely, "the moral right of Mr. Cannon's friends in the Jefferson Society in having adjourned the Society at every recent meeting of the Society without the transaction of any business." Our judgment is, that this action of "Mr. Cannon's friends" was wrong.[11]

Thus with Murray Mason McGuire at the helm for the final term, the Society pressed forward. Yet a quickly changing college atmosphere and pressure from the University's administration to demonstrate increased academic merit posed unique challenges for the Society, weakened internally as it was. And in the next three decades, the Jefferson Society would see its previously uncontested position at the top of University social and academic life challenged by various elements competing for the interest of students, such as the YMCA, fraternities, and athletics.

Toward the Twentieth Century

The turn of the twentieth century was a time of great growth and change in the American university, a trend that the University of Virginia exemplified. At universities across the country, the new century "brought mushrooming enrollments, the advent of 'big time' college athletics with the building of giant stadiums and the fermentation of a youth culture dominated by college fraternities and sororities."[12] John Thelin tells us that the turn of the century marks the beginning of the rise of the comprehensive university based largely on the German model. The faculty of universities became more professionalized, known not only as teachers, but also as experts and pioneers in their fields. Administrative bureaucracy expanded dramatically, and educational leaders paid greater attention to the curriculum being taught at their schools.[13] The University of Virginia, in recognition that the old Jeffersonian model of governance with only a chairman of the faculty was no longer adequate to serve institutional interests, named its first president, Edwin Alderman, in 1904.

In this changing environment, it is not surprising that the activities of the Jefferson Society, particularly those most public in nature, should be subjected to scrutiny. The Board of Visitors was dissatisfied with the quality of the speakers that both societies put forth during the highly visible Final Celebrations; additionally, they doubted the capacity of the societies to award their customary Debater's and Orator's Medals to deserving recipients instead of political darlings. According to Bruce,

In 1893, Professor Venable suggested that the choice of final orators should be limited to candidates who had been recipients of degrees with honors. This indicated an extraordinary falling off in merit in comparison with the times when the most distinguished alumni were not the men who had won these degrees, but the men who had received the medals of the debating societies.[14]

His suggestion was never acted upon, but it demonstrates how tenuous the position of the Jefferson Society had become in a surprisingly short period of time. The faculty did insist that the content of the speeches delivered by the Final Orators be reviewed for intellectual rigor and appropriateness beforehand, in an effort to curtail the radical southern fervor that had featured prominently in the Society's speeches.

Two years after Professor Venable's suggestion with regards to the Final Orators, the Board of Visitors took action in their other area of concern: the awarding of the societies' medals. They appropriated $100 to award "Rector and Visitors' debating medals" to each society, following a public oratorical contest sponsored by the board itself.[15] It was no doubt of even greater concern to the board when

the energy displayed by the students towards the acquisition of these medals was so feeble that the Faculty requested the Board to abolish their award; and in June, 1899, this was done. But it was afterwards perceived by the Visitors that it was not entirely becoming for them to show indifference to what had once been such an important feature of the University's activities, and in November, 1901, they appropriated fifty dollars to be bestowed annually upon the best debater of the two societies.[16]

Even though the Society still awarded its own medals, they had been reduced, through politics, to little more than popularity contests. The *Magazine* half jokingly suggested, "Why not call things by their right name and to the man who makes most friends present a token of friendship instead of a debater's medal?"[17]

Other steps were taken in an effort to increase the quality of the Society's activities. In 1895, the constitution was amended to impose a fine on members who did not attend meetings.[18] The next year, another amendment, this one to combat growing influence of outside politics on the Society, restricted voting in elections: "No member who has not paid his dues or fines shall be qualified to vote for any Intermediate or Final Officer or magazine editor or be eligible for any of these offices."[19] The same amendment also adopted the use of *Robert's Rules of Order* to govern meetings in cases where it was not inconsistent with the Society's own by-laws and constitution. These changes were aimed at securing for the Society proper a greater degree of control in its own affairs.

The Rotunda

In the midst of these efforts, early Sunday morning on October 27, 1895, the history of the University of Virginia changed forever. Faulty wiring set fire to the Rotunda Annex, and by the end of the day, Jefferson's signature library was a smoldering shell of its former self. When the University outgrew the original Academical Village, the Board of Visitors commissioned architect Robert Mills to build an annex on to the north end of the Rotunda. Completed in 1853, it provided much needed classroom and office space. But the new building was connected to the Rotunda, which meant that when fire started in the attic early that Sunday morning, it spread quickly and easily to the Rotunda. Students and townspeople, summoned by the loud tolling of the bells in the University Chapel, rushed into the building in an attempt to save the books, papers, and paintings in the library, as well as the Alexander Galt statue of Thomas Jefferson. Beloved professor of engineering William H. Echols found some dynamite and heroically tried to sever the portico to the Rotunda and stop the spread of the fire. Echols's efforts were in vain, but the concussion succeeded in dislodging the Galt statue, which had gotten stuck in the curvature of the staircase as students tried to carry it outside.[20] The fire had too much fuel, and "soon the flames had gained possession of the Rotunda and nothing [was] now left standing but the bare and ruined walls."[21]

The University was devastated. It had lost the bulk of one of the largest libraries on the East Coast and along with it many of the records of the University. In response the Jefferson Society immediately called a special meeting to help the University respond. "The object of meeting to be the tender of our hall to the faculty for use as a lecture room owing to the destruction of our University by fire." The motion to do so was unanimously carried.[22] Classes were then held in Jefferson Hall until construction was completed on the new Rotunda.

The Rotunda was rebuilt with remarkable speed—alumni and philanthropists from across the country donated to fund the reconstruction and replenish the library collections. The University commissioned Stanford White of the renowned McKim, Mead, and White to lead the effort, and White's Beaux Arts–style reconstruction of the Rotunda was completed by 1897. The destruction of the original Rotunda was certainly a setback for the University, but the passion and dedication shown in the reconstruction effort reenergized the University as it moved toward the twentieth century.

A Changing University

Historian Daniel A. Clark, in his book *Creating the College Man*, examines changing conceptions of college education and the evolving conditions on college campuses at the turn of the century. Through the popular media, college came to be seen as a "stepping stone to success and manhood."[23] The "college man" became a recognizable image in American commercial culture. Evolving through the 1920s with the world around it, college-going became both more popular and more focused on business and skills rather than simply elite status.[24] Clark writes, "The late nineteenth century witnessed a profound transformation in American higher education, with the proliferation of institutions (both state and private), the emergence of electives, and the rise of technical, scientific, and professional courses. This metamorphosis coincided with the growth of a new middle class of urban professionals and managers."[25] Thelin writes:

college-going was rising in popularity, for several reasons. It was a means of socioeconomic mobility and hence an experience coveted by an increasing number of adolescents. In addition to increasing earning power, a bachelor's degree was perceived as a way for a nouveau riche family to gain social standing . . . the self-made man wanted his sons to have the shared campus experience that would position them to associate with young men from established, educated families.[26]

Universities were becoming less aristocratic and more meritocratic: no longer would attendance be the exclusive privilege of the very wealthy and the social elite. A college education could be used by more people to advance their standing and their career. While still seen as "a privileged place, college was also characterized in a decidedly middle-class fashion. In other words, campuses allowed for meritocratic opportunity."[27] The types of classes offered by universities began to change as more emphasis was placed on business acumen and modern sciences like economics. The meritocratic nature of education also permeated student life, as new student organizations quickly sprang up to accommodate the broadening range of student interests and values. Rudolph observes that

now what mattered for so many young men was not the course of study but the environment of friendships, social development, fraternity houses, good sportsmanship, athletics teams. The world of business was a world of dealing with people. What better preparation could there be than the collegiate life outside the classroom?[28]

Around the turn of the century, education-related issues and policy also saw increased attention from the public. Particularly in the south, public education at all levels became more widely available than ever before, and colleges and universities received greater funding and support from both the government and philanthropists. At the University of Virginia, enrollments were expanding, course offerings were greatly broadened, and new building projects changed the face of the Grounds. Running the affairs of the University became complicated enough that the old Jeffersonian system of academic governance by a chairman of the faculty was abandoned in favor of hiring a president as the chief academic officer. After offering the job to Woodrow Wilson, who by then was president of Princeton University, the Board of Visitors chose Edwin Alderman as the University's first president in 1904. Already a giant in southern education, Alderman had served as president of both the University of North Carolina at Chapel Hill and of Tulane University before coming to Charlottesville.[29] He played a foundational role in the southern education movement, which held "literacy and education [as] prospective cornerstones for the industrialization of the region. The attempt to create a 'New South' depended on the development of the new kind of Southerner, or at least a better educated Southerner."[30] He was renowned for his considerable political ability and oratorical skill; he was even encouraged to run for governor of Virginia at one point, but his opponent would have been the legendary Harry F. Byrd.[31]

In the south, education, particularly at the college level, was seen as a way to create a leading class and to further the industrial and political development of the region as it continued its recovery from Reconstruction. James Becker, whose doctoral dissertation covers Alderman and his place in southern education, writes:

Southerners who fought for public support of universal education desired to further their personal vision of the structure of Southern society. Unsuccessful in this social purpose, their institutional aims were largely achieved. They have generally been evaluated on their success establishing educational institutions, rather than their failure to re-make southern society according to their vision.

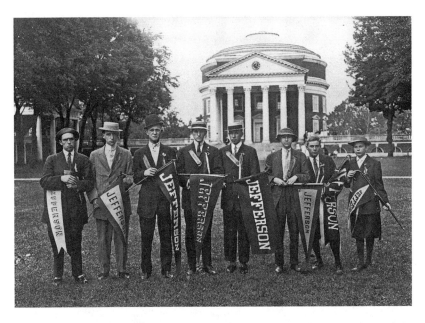

FIGURE 14. Jefferson Society members on the Lawn, circa 1910. Image courtesy of the Albert and Shirley Small Special Collections Library at the University of Virginia, Accession #9061-a.

FIGURE 15. Edwin Anderson Alderman served as the first president of the University of Virginia from 1904 to 1931. A world-renowned education leader of his generation, he was adored by students and elected an honorary member of the Jefferson Society several times over. He appreciated the sentiment, once saying, "the supreme honor of the University" was "to be the president of the Jefferson Literary Society." Image courtesy of the Albert and Shirley Small Special Collections Library at the University of Virginia, Holsinger Studio Collection, Accession #9862.

The story of the Southern education movement is a test of the relationship between educational development and the furtherance of social views, and the
ability of educators to use the schools to shape the future of society.[32]

Alderman, both by virtue of the fact that he was the first president of
the University and the leading role that he played in the southern education movement, changed the character of the University of Virginia
forever, greatly bolstering its public stature and mission. According to
Becker, "Alderman's projected role for the university, the training of
Southern Leadership for the future, was an extension and completion of
[the] concept of an aristocracy based on education."[33]

Alderman was revered by the students and became particularly supportive of the Jefferson Society, frequently attending meetings and events
and speaking with great reverence with respect to its history and traditions. He did not attend the University of Virginia and thus never had the
opportunity to be a member as a student, but on October 1, 1904, he was
elected an honorary member. The Society greeted him with great fanfare:
cards were printed up to advertise for the event, and

invitation[s] had been extended to every student of the University and the Hall
was filled with visitors and members. . . . The nominating speech was made by
Mr. J. Alfred Ritter. Mr. Ritter introduced Dr. Alderman in a way of which he
may well be proud, as his speech was eloquent, precise, and fitting. The nomination was seconded by Mr. J. S. Lawton in his usual graceful manner.[34]

Accordingly, "Dr. Alderman was unanimously elected to honorary membership in the Jefferson Literary Society. He was escorted to the front and
signed the roll. Dr. Alderman then delivered us an address in his own
graceful and charming manner. It was thoughtful, earnest, and full of
inspiration."[35] Alderman's legacy as an educational leader was cemented
over the course of the twenty-six years he spent as president, an office he
held until tuberculosis claimed his life in 1931. He was so respected by the
Jefferson Society that the membership elected him an honorary member
at least four more times, presumably unaware each time of the previous
election.[36]

Student Life

During this time, the Jefferson Society began to face greater competition for the attention of students. The first competitor to emerge was the Council of Friends of Temperance. Initially organized during the 1868–1869 school year by Professor John B. Minor and reorganized a few years later as the Temperance Union, it appealed to the Victorian sensibilities and growing opposition to drinking that were prevalent among students. The Temperance Union benefited greatly from having the use of their own private building, Temperance Hall, which was located near the present-day Corner.[37] Having their own space allowed them to compete for many of the social functions that traditionally fell to the Jefferson and Washington Societies, such as hosting public lectures and speaking contests.[38] By the last quarter of the nineteenth century, according to Bruce,

the membership [of the Temperance Union] was now large enough to allow room for the selection of young men of talent for all the leading parts on the public day. During the session of 1883–84, its enrollment was as long as that of the Washington Society, and in 1884–85 fell short by twenty names only of that of the Jefferson. At this time, the number of its members ran ahead of the number entered in the list of the Washington Society.[39]

The Temperance Union continued to grow and prosper through Prohibition—well into the 1920s—but with the passage of the Twenty-first Amendment repealing Prohibition, the Temperance Union, along with the movement it represented, faltered and fell into obscurity.

Another organization that attracted significant student involvement was the YMCA. Founded at the University in 1856, by no later than 1887 it had thirty more members than the Jefferson Society (103 and 73, respectively), and in March of the same year the *Magazine* began periodically to feature "YMCA Notes," a column dedicated exclusively to detailing the activities of the YMCA and recruiting new members.[40] Before 1887, only the literary societies had received regular dedicated coverage of their affairs.

Like the Temperance Union, the YMCA also enjoyed the use of their own building—constructing and occupying the building that is now Madison Hall in 1905.[41] What is currently Mad Bowl was the campus of the YMCA, where many of the University's sports teams played their games and students could run around the track and play field games. The

YMCA occupied Madison Hall and Mad Bowl until the 1950s when it was taken over by the University as an office building. It now houses the office of the University president.

Fraternities also grew steadily after the Civil War, and between 1865 and 1897 at least twelve new chapters were chartered at the University.[42] Before the turn of the century, fraternities were little more than clubs—loose associations between students who met regularly and supported each other in college politics. But in the new century they moved to engrain themselves more deeply in University life by building houses that would provide space for residence, dining, entertaining, and a library, exclusively for the use of brothers. Delta Kappa Epsilon was the first fraternity at the University to begin construction of a chapter house, in October 1899, and by 1902 most of the active fraternities had houses of their own.[43] In the 1910s, more than half of the students at the University of Virginia were Greek.

Closely related to the fraternities were the so-called ribbon societies, which in the words of Philip Alexander Bruce "aspired to lead the general society of the University, whether connected with themselves or not." Members would signify their membership by wearing a ribbon of a particular color or design. The first and most successful of these organizations was Eli Banana. Organized in 1878 at White Sulphur Springs, it drew members from leading fraternities and encouraged them to get involved in all aspects of the University. Eli quickly rose to great prominence, and with the help of the fraternities, its members successfully installed themselves in almost every major student leadership position within the decade.[44] Soon, another similar ribbon society, T.I.L.K.A., was organized to compete with Eli, also drawing its members from fraternities. Together with a third ribbon society, Zeta, which was founded in 1892 and was the progenitor of the Z Society, the ribbon societies sat at the pinnacle of student social life for several decades. The idea of a ribbon society became so powerful that members of the Jefferson Society began to wear dark blue ribbons to signify their membership, though by then the true ribbon societies had carved out their own space in the upper echelon of the University.

In 1883, students and local married ladies organized the German Club, intended to host German cotillions, dances featuring intricate social rituals and receptions. As it became more popular, the German Club began to challenge the Jefferson Society in its role as organizer of the University's most important social functions.[45] The German Club typically hosted their events, which by the turn of the century were essentially formal parties, in Washington Hall and Temperance Hall. In 1904, students and faculty organized the Raven Society to be the University's most prominent academic honorary society. While not strictly a ribbon society, the Raven Society also sought to identify and recognize the best students at the University.[46] Around the turn of the century, a number of other less significant organizations began to spring up as well, but they did not typically represent serious commitments on the part of students. These included a club for students from each state in the south and even a few in the north, as well as clubs for students from several of the high schools who sent appreciable numbers of students to the University, such as Virginia Episcopal School or Woodberry Forest. By the 1900s and 1910s, even more clubs had been organized according to students' interests, ranging from music, theater, and singing to horseback riding and fencing.[47] In 1916, the Virginia Union, a precursor to the present day student council, was organized for the general advancement of the University, and in time they would take over Madison Hall from the YMCA. Ultimately, every new club offered a new set of offices and elections to be contested by students, assembled another calendar of events to attend, and added another layer to the increasingly complex social life at the University, feeding the obsession with politics and social standing among the students. This proliferation of new student organizations created an entirely different student experience than the one enjoyed by the likes of Edgar Allan Poe or even Woodrow Wilson.

Finally, the biggest change in the University of Virginia around the turn of the century was the advent of big-time athletics. In the late 1800s, universities up and down the East Coast began organizing athletic teams comprised mostly of students and sending them to compete against teams from other universities. Soon students were flocking to see their classmates compete at football, baseball, track and field, and boxing. Accounts of out-of-town games were widely circulated among students, and scores for the latest games were often painted on the railroad bridge by the Corner as soon as the news came in.[48] Star players became heroes in the student body, and students started to look forward to big games more than any other event on the school calendar.[49] Clark writes:

The rise of manly sports on college campuses no doubt was the key factor in the transformation of the image of college. But the rise of new heroes like the athlete and college-educated leaders like [Theodore] Roosevelt—and their subsequent celebration in the media—also masculinized the gentleman of culture or the scholar, and posited the college as the location where such ideal, all-around men were formed.[50]

The advent of athletics had several important effects on the University of Virginia and on higher education in general. First, the changes happening on the Grounds went decidedly against the prominence of literary societies and the popularity of their leaders. Some of the time that students had previously devoted to literary societies or other organizations was now spent attending sporting events. Popular games conflicted with Society events, and students chose games over debates and speeches. Athletics also created a new breed of college celebrity—no longer was the president of the Jefferson Society the uncontested leader among his peers—a star pitcher, football player, runner, or boxer could command just as much, if not more, attention and respect. Students sometimes translated success on the field to political dominance in the Jefferson Society, as in the case of Murray McGuire, the baseball star who won the hotly contested 1893 presidential contest. The Jefferson Society itself got in on the action in 1904, fielding an intramural baseball team and defeating the Washington Society in their first game by a score of 14 to 13.[51]

On a broader level, sports, specifically football, became the primary reason many colleges had to interact with other schools. Universities in close proximity to one another created relationships to arrange games and other athletic contests on a yearly basis, informal at first, but later organized into conferences and rivalries. Football was so powerful that renowned historian of higher education Frederick Rudolph noted that it was because of football that in the 1890s Harvard worked with other schools for the first time since it was founded.[52] At the University of Virginia, students, faculty, and Charlottesville residents formed the General Athletic Association in 1887 to support the University's athletic teams. The organization contributed money for equipment and facilities and helped arrange games with teams from other schools.[53] Just like literary societies and fraternities before them, college athletics were another aspect of the extracurricular activities developed for students, by students.[54]

The proliferation of a wide variety of new student organizations was spurred in part by a growing proportion of middle-class men attending university—a marked departure from the nineteenth century. As evidence of their increasing importance relative to the literary societies, all of these organizations and activities received increasing coverage in the pages of the *Magazine* as their memberships grew and they assumed a greater role in University life.[55] The more additional organizations there were, the more contests and activities, and each one meant that the Jefferson Society defined the University experience to a slightly lesser degree.

Student Publications

One of the most important products of the expanding and changing University of Virginia was the creation of a student newspaper: *College Topics.* A college newspaper was a mark of prestige for any university, proving that it was large and important enough to take notice of and record its own events. Students at the University of Virginia felt theirs certainly merited such a periodical. Other universities had well-established papers by the time students at the University considered creating one in 1889: Harvard had started a paper in 1873, and Princeton created theirs in 1876.[56] Students believed that if the University of Virginia could support a paper, it would be further evidence that the school had recovered from the Civil War and again ranked among the elite universities in the country. They wanted a paper that would cover the events of their community faster than a monthly magazine, and they wanted to hear more about the sporting events their classmates were competing in under the banner of the University.

Even though the *Virginia University Magazine* endeavored to fill the function of "essentially a college-paper," which caused it to "pay special attention to Collegiana, as being the department to which the college community looks with the greatest interest," it simply was not well suited to cover the goings-on of the University community promptly, or even to be able to report on everything that happened, particularly the quickly multiplying athletic contests.[57] Faced with the prospect of a student newspaper, which might otherwise have seemed like a competitor, the editors of the *Magazine* welcomed its publication, viewing it as a fundamentally different undertaking: one that would focus on reporting interesting current events to the student body faster than a monthly magazine could. This would consequently take the pressure off the *Magazine* to report news, allowing it instead to focus on the literary elements of its publication. The editors of the *Magazine* saw significant differences in both the content of the two types of publications and the way they should be run, and they pointed these out to their readers:

There are several subjects of interest to the University which are not of such a nature as to admit of publication in a literary magazine, and so are excluded from our regular monthly, and, indeed, the greater part, perhaps, of the department devoted to Collegiana is out of place in that paper, for accounts of football and baseball games, descriptions of germans, college jokes, Y. M. C. A. notes, notices of students, etc., etc., do not properly fall within the province of a literary periodical.[58]

Accordingly, the call for a weekly student newspaper began in earnest in the pages of the *Magazine* itself in January 1889 after murmurs surrounding the idea had circulated among the students for a few months. In response to the question "Why should we not have a weekly?" the editors laid out the case for its creation:

Why should we not have a weekly paper published at the University? We cannot think of any satisfactory reason which can be assigned why we should not, while there are many which would justify the conclusion that we should. The University has been making such rapid strides, and its progress has been so great during the last three or four years, that we may confidently expect ere long, once more to stand in the days "'fore the war," in the very first rank among the educational institutions of this country, and such an undertaking as we suggest would be at once an effect of this progressive spirit, and an aid to still greater progress.[59]

The proposal seemed simple enough: for approximately $300, the University community could be furnished with a suitable paper in quarto format, eight pages long, and with a circulation of 300 copies.[60] But finding a stable base of subscribers was a difficult prospect. The *Magazine* had struggled since its inception to secure enough subscribers to consistently support publication. It was often able to, but when money got tight, the *Magazine* always fell back on the patronage of the literary societies. In 1883, the editors noted:

Our income this year will fall short of our outlay by about three hundred dollars. We have about two hundred subscribers whose subscriptions will amount to four hundred dollars, and about two hundred dollars in advertisements. It takes about nine hundred dollars a year to run the *Magazine*. The committee appointed by the Societies to solicit subscribers did their duty, but for some cause, not quite plain, the students, for the most part, were unwilling to subscribe.[61]

The Washington and Jefferson Societies never came close to allowing the *Magazine* to fail financially, consistently subsidizing its publication because its existence was central to their goals and aims. But healthy finances for a publication were difficult to sustain, and the effort to attract subscribers and advertisers was constant. The editors of the *Mag* once humorously remarked, "Our Mag. library contains three volumes, viz: one Webster's Unabridged, one Bible, one Cash Book. The W. U. is considerably worn, the B. moderately so and the C. B. scarcely at all. Delinquent subscribers and advertisers may find food for thought here."[62]

A weekly paper was farther afield from the accepted mission of the literary societies, and they were thus unlikely to support a college paper, even though their backing would certainly have ensured at least its initial success. The *Magazine* even pointed out how important the Jefferson Society's sponsorship would be to getting a paper started: "If the Jefferson Literary Society could be induced to make each of its members a subscriber—and its immense surplus fund of fifteen hundred dollars ought to prevent any trouble from that source, we could count on at least 300 subscribers."[63] But when the Society was approached in early 1889, it declined to offer its support on the belief that a paper was too financially dangerous.[64]

Three Jefferson Society members, however, were captivated enough by the idea to take it on themselves. Leigh R. Page, A. C. Carson (of boxing fame), and Stuart M. Beard stepped forward to head the operation, and with the help of two others, Hunt Chipley and John G. Tilton, they began publication of *College Topics* in January 1890 as a private undertaking. Chipley and Page left the publication early on, but two more students, Joseph McElroy and J. Breckenridge Robertson, another Jefferson Society member, joined the effort. At the end of the first year of publication, with Robertson as editor-in-chief, they had a $150 surplus.[65] By the close of the 1890–1891 term, the General Athletic Association (GAA) took control of *College Topics*. Their backing provided the stability and

FIGURE 16. The editorial board of the *University of Virginia Magazine* in the 1910 edition of *Corks and Curls*. Image courtesy of the Albert and Shirley Small Special Collections Library at the University of Virginia, *Corks and Curls* 23 (1910): 264–265.

fiscal support that *College Topics* needed to continue regular publication, which the Jefferson Society had declined to offer a year earlier. The GAA assumed responsibilities for the paper's financial security and for appointing its editors, in the process ensuring that the content would be largely athletic in nature.[66]

College Topics was enthusiastically received by the students, as evidenced by the surplus it ran during its first year. The editors of the *Magazine* also took notice, writing in their typically prolix fashion about other college publications:

The first number of *College Topics* lies before us. We cannot refrain from congratulating its editors of the dash and vim which they have displayed, not only in getting it up, but also in carrying it to a successful issue. The first number contains the essence of what with experience will prove a most valuable addition to college literature and fill a long felt want. The MAG. extends its most hearty congratulations and sincere hopes for a bright and brilliant future. May it ever live long and prosper.[67]

The next year brought similar approbation for *College Topics* on the part of the *Magazine*. On the same page though, the editors marked the passing of "Collegiana," an institution that had supplied University news for almost fifty years, and began the lengthy process of defining the space each respective publication would occupy moving forward:

The MAG. extends its heartiest greetings and congratulations to its bustling little contemporary, *College Topics*, which has apparently come to stay. Long may it flourish! We have room here at the University of Virginia for both publications; each one of them aids the other. *Topics* has gladly relieved the MAG. of the necessity of chronicling at length long past events, and thus we, the Editors, find ourselves more at liberty to make the MAG. a distinctively literary production and a fair exponent of the culture and refinement here. Hence the department of brief mention instead of the old "Collegiana," begun in this number. [68]

The *Magazine* thus began a marked transformation that lasted for the next five years—shedding much of the ancillary content it had typically provided about the University community and glimpses into the affairs of other colleges. One by one, the well-read headings of "Collegiana," "Intercollegiana," "YMCA Notes," "Athletic Notes," and even articles offering commentary about the conditions of the University or needed improvements to the curriculum disappeared from the pages of the *Magazine*. A "journal which [was] the mirror of University thought and feeling" transformed into a purely literary publication and offered little beyond poems, essays, and short stories, printed with an occasional biographical piece.[69] Now, instead of being a publication where every aspect of University life could find a place in its pages, its mission had narrowed: "The MAGAZINE is intended as a medium by which the best literary productions of the students at the University may be published, the exponent of her literary capabilities."[70] By 1892, the editors and the literary societies refocused attention on the idea that writing for the *Magazine* could improve the literary talents of students, if they would only give it a try:

There are plenty of men in college who have undoubted literary talent if there were only means to discover it . . . to be sure it brings a man into more prominence before college to have an article accepted by the MAG., which is supposed to contain all the literary talent that college affords.[71]

Charles W. Kent, a former president of the Jefferson Society who went on to serve as professor of English at the University, also made the case for the importance of cultivating literary talent:

So thoroughly am I persuaded of the value of and efficiency of college journals and literary societies, in so far as they are true to their natures that, if it were in my power, I would urge every man, who wishes to cultivate fluent speech or felicitous expression, to make use of the opportunities they afford. The MAGA-ZINE's "higher mission" is then to reach all such students, not solely as a read-ing public, but as actively enlisted coadjutors.[72]

Shifting toward literature did not signal a wholesale departure from the traditional content of the *Magazine*. It had always included works of literature from the pens of students and encouraged them to try their hand at writing; the elimination of a news function simply meant that it would now be entirely literary. There were reminders of that legacy offered to readers, like an article that appeared in 1898 entitled "Short Story in the University of Virginia Magazine," that reminded readers of stories that had appeared in the pages of the *Magazine* by authors who students might now recognize as famous. The focus on literary elements paid dividends for the *Magazine*, and it attained some recognition as a respectable literary vessel. In 1891, Thomas Nelson Page, a Jefferson Soci-ety member who achieved considerable fame as a southern author and literary critic, discovered a poem he attributed to Edgar Allan Poe and published it in the March issue of the *Magazine* that year.[73] The editors were thrilled to "to make [the] MAGAZINE the *medium* for conveying to the literary world so valuable a treasure-trove," and they were "confident that with so weighty an authority as Mr. Page that the theory exposed in these pages will stand successfully all critical literary fire!"[74]

After the creation of *College Topics*, the editors of the *Magazine* took a number of concrete steps to bolster and reinforce its literary nature beyond shifting its content. In 1890, they published a volume entitled *Arcade Echoes*, which compiled the best works of poetry that had appeared in the *Magazine* over the years. It would be updated and reissued at least once more a few years later.[75] In 1887, leaders of the Jefferson Society and the *Magazine*, one of whom was editor Thomas Longstreet Wood, created an organization called O.W.L., meant to increase the prestige of students engaged in literary activities—the editor-in-chief of the *Magazine* would automatically be a member, as would several other editors.[76] The O.W.L., which pursued these ends until it disappeared from existence in the 1930s, enjoyed prominence similar to the ribbon societies like Eli Banana and T.I.L.K.A. by virtue of the social standing of its members, who included the likes of Murray McGuire and beloved World War I aviator James Rogers McConnell.

In 1896, the year after he endowed a debate in his name, Professor James A. Harrison offered a monetary prize for the best original translation to appear in the *Magazine*.[77] Later the same year, Harrison offered a second prize, this one for the best poem, apparently based on success of his earlier offer.[78] Professor Harrison soon endowed both prizes to be awarded in successive years. The next year the Jefferson and Washington Societies split the traditional Magazine Medal into two medals, one awarded for the best story and the other for the best essay.[79] Finally, in 1889 William Jennings Bryan joined the philanthropic promotion of literary endeavors, providing the support for a Bryan Prize for the best article on the theory of government.[80] Two years earlier Bryan had spoken at the joint Final Celebration; the Conference Committee of the Jefferson and Washington Societies had invited him in January, and by February they had his favorable response. Not only did his scheduled address, "Thomas Jefferson Still Lives," reportedly draw 20,000, but also he surprised the members by dropping by a meeting of the Jefferson Society. The minutes from the June 15, 1897, meeting read:

After the speech made by the President and likewise Debater of the society, and the Orator, Hon. William Jennings Bryan was prevailed upon to speak. No one expecting to see Bryan, the house was not crowded, and when he had finished speaking, all thoroughly enjoyed shaking hands with the Hero of Democracy.[81]

In 1888, the enthusiasm students showed for publications spawned another institution, this time an annual, or yearbook, cleverly entitled *Corks and Curls*. In the students' slang, to cork was to perform poorly on a test or exam, to curl meant to do well, perhaps even with a flourish. According to Southall, the name was "invented by my honored friend Hampden Bagby, who was the first editor-in-chief. Well do I remember it was hailed with enthusiasm as a great and promising achievement."[82] *Corks and Curls* was organized by the fraternities, who each sent a representative to its editorial board. It quickly became an important chronicle of student life at the University, featuring essays about important events of the term and rosters of membership for student organizations. Yearbooks emerged at many universities at this time, most being "a lavishly bound collection of memorable events, inside jokes, light verse, fond recollections, and elaborate cartoons and caricatures."[83] Thelin holds student yearbooks up in contrast to the dry official catalogues of courses published by universities themselves to illustrate the continuing divide between the official college structure and the extracurricular activities.[84]

Members of the Jefferson Society were frequently involved in the publication of *Corks and Curls*. James Hay Jr. was the most notable, serving as president of the Jefferson Society the same year he was editor of *Corks and Curls*, in which capacity he would pen his famous poem "The Honor Men."[85] In 1912, the Jefferson Society began to send a representative to join the fraternities on the editorial board of *Corks and Curls*.[86]

A Changing Society

Just as the University of Virginia was growing and changing to become less aristocratic and more meritocratic, the turn of the century saw the Jefferson Society change likewise. In many ways, the Jefferson Society, even though it struggled against increased competition, exemplified the ideals of the southern education movement. Accordingly, the tone of the meetings changed, the Society redoubled its focus on debate, and it began several new events that would broaden its appeal and reach. The politics remained as intense as ever, fueling the energy that students poured into the almost century-old organization. According to the *Magazine*,

the societies meet every Saturday night. Their sessions rarely last more than two hours or two hours and a half, and often not so long. Each member is required to speak once in about six weeks in the Jefferson Society, with an average membership; in the Washington the frequency of debate is about the same.[87]

In response to greater competition from other student groups and the growing complexity of the University social life, the Jefferson Society began to regulate its membership more closely. Members were still elected frequently, almost every week. But it became harder to join the Society, and new members were expected to deliver "maiden speeches" on increasingly difficult topics.[88] For example, on October 30, 1897, a new member, Mr. Hofmayer, "volunteered and electrified the Society with his maiden speech," the very evening he was elected to membership.[89]

Recruiting qualified new members became a major priority, now that it could not be expected that the vast bulk of the student body would join a literary society as a matter of course—and that they might want to join something else instead. In 1901, it was "suggested that the President appoint a committee of five to look after the interest of our society and especially to get new members," and a month later the Society took out an advertisement in *College Topics* to recruit new members, something it never would have needed to do even a few years earlier.[90] Again in 1904 there was a "motion made and unanimously carried that each Jeff Society man who is to return to the University of VA next year be appointed as a committee of one to welcome, aid, and secure as many members for the Society from new men coming to the U. Va. next fall."[91]

In 1905, the Society began to host an event at the beginning of every term called "Pink Nimbus Night" to inform curious new students about what the Jefferson Society was and to recruit new members. Officers of the Society would give exciting speeches on the Society's history, how it contributed to the University community, and why it was a good idea for new students to join. The phrase "Pink Nimbus" alluded to the fact that the talks scheduled for these evenings would dispel the cloud of mystery that surrounded the Society for prospective members and give them a rosy view of the organization. Continuing into the 1950s, they resembled "a fraternity rush-talk, suffused with the roseate glow of the Society's consummate perfection and of the ineffable beatitude shared by those so fortunate as to be members."[92]

The membership of the Jefferson Society during this era was typically much smaller than it had been historically, relative to the size of the University. The roll featured somewhere between thirty-five and fifty names every term. For the most part, the activities remained lively, but sometimes there were not enough members present to conduct business, and meetings were adjourned early for lack of quorum on at least a handful of occasions at the turn of the century.[93]

The membership began to rebound by the 1910s. The Society weathered World War I particularly well: a report of the Membership Committee in 1917 read: "In spite of the disorganized condition of the University since the United States entered the War, the Society has maintained an average attendance of 30 during the term" and a roster of seventy-five members.[94] Meanwhile the enrollment of the University itself fell from approximately 1,000 down to 750. Even so, it weathered World War I far better than it had the Civil War, or than it would World War II, evidence of just how much of the war passed without the active involvement of the United States.[95] Only sixty-four students from the University of Virginia died in World War I. A plaque outside of Jefferson Hall lists the names of those members of the Jefferson Society "who lost their lives in the service of their country"; eleven names are cast in bronze.[96]

Meetings of the Society during this time typically followed the same basic structure. The first order of business was the calling of the roll and reading of the minutes from the previous meeting. The Society then began a "literary session," during which the membership would hear debates, orations, declamations, and original literary work. Following the literary session was a business session, during which the Society voted on new members, heard reports from the Society's officers, and discussed administrative matters. The business session was typically conducted in secret.

Meetings were held on Saturday nights, and the constitutionally defined time for the meeting changed several times—7:00, 7:15, 7:30, or 8:00 p.m. In reality, meetings were called to order at various times. Most meetings adjourned before midnight. Certain parts of the meeting were frequently disposed of, either because there was not enough business to make them worthwhile, or because members desired to attend a conflicting event, like a baseball game, a dance, or an engaging lecture. When interesting programs were held in either the Jefferson Society or the Washington Society, it was common for them to invite each other to their meeting. The two societies shared a conference committee to facilitate communication and any joint activities, like debates.

For most of this time, a monthly orator was elected to give a prepared speech at one of the meetings on a topic of his choosing. His speech would form the basis of the content for that evening. The minutes of December 4, 1897, give a good example of a typical oration, as well as a visit from the Washington Society: "Mr. Hofmayer, the orator for the night entertained and instructed in an able manner, a select audience of members of our own society, together with some members of our sister society, who came around to hear a good speech as a change from the discipline of listening to dry, noisy talks from the brilliant members of our Sister Society."[97] In addition to the monthly orators, members frequently spoke extemporaneously and tested their skills in oratorical contests.[98]

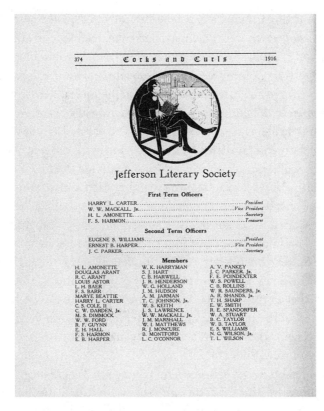

Jefferson Literary Society

First Term Officers

HARRY L. CARTER...President
W. W. MACKALL, Jr...Vice President
H. L. AMONETTE..Secretary
F. S. HARMON..Treasurer

Second Term Officers

EUGENE S. WILLIAMS...President
ERNEST B. HARPER..Vice President
J. C. PARKER..Secretary

Members

H. L. AMONETTE	W. K. HARRYMAN	A. V. PANKEY
DOUGLAS ARANT	S. J. HART	J. C. PARKER, Jr.
R. C. ARANT	C. B. HARWELL	F. E. POINDEXTER
LOUIS ASTOR	J. R. HENDERSON	W. S. POWELL
L. H. BAER	W. G. HOLLAND	C. B. ROLLINS
F. S. BARR	J. M. HUDSON	W. R. SAUNDERS, Jr.
MARYE BEATTIE	A. M. JARMAN	A. R. SHANDS, Jr.
HARRY L. CARTER	T. C. JOHNSON, Jr.	T. H. SHARP
C. S. COLE, II	W. S. KEITH	E. W. SMITH
C. W. DARDEN, Jr.	J. S. LAWRENCE	R. E. SPANDORFER
M. S. DIMMOCK	W. W. MACKALL, Jr.	W. A. STUART
W. W. FORD	J. M. MARSHALL	B. C. TAYLOR
R. F. GUYNN	W. I. MATTHEWS	W. B. TAYLOR
E. H. HALL	R. J. MONCURE	E. S. WILLIAMS
F. S. HARMON	B. MONTFORD	N. G. WILSON, Jr.
E. B. HARPER	L. C. O'CONNOR	T. L. WILSON

JEFFERSON LITERARY SOCIETY

FIGURE 17. The Jefferson Society in the 1916 edition of *Corks and Curls*. Image courtesy of the Albert and Shirley Small Special Collections Library at the University of Virginia, *Corks and Curls* 29 (1916): 374–375.

Each meeting featured a debate under constitutionally defined terms (the details of which were discussed and changed frequently during this time period). Topics for these structured debates would be presented by the Question Committee and chosen, along with the debaters, two to three weeks in advance. The question of the formal debate was often thrown open to the entire society for discussion afterward. In 1903, the content for the literary session was typically structured as follows: "From the roll of the members of the Society, arranged in the order in which they signed the Constitution, the Secretary shall divide the members of the Society into classes containing one member each, one of which classes shall read a selection, the other render a declamation, but that no member shall be required to debate, declaim, or read on the same night."[99] These weekly events kept the Society going despite its smaller membership. In 1904, the Society amended the constitution to allow for the appointment of a "critic" in an effort to raise the quality of presentations. The language dictated "that a critic be appointed by the Chair, who shall criticize the literary part of the program; who shall serve one month from the time of appointment whose report shall first be oral and shall be in writing on the Saturday night following."[100]

The Jefferson Society also began to invite speakers to meetings more frequently during this time, though visits were still relatively rare compared to later years. In December 1899, "Mr. Heard suggested that we follow the plan of some of the Northern colleges and invite speakers of note to address the Jefferson Society at stated intervals. Messrs. Monroe, Heard, and Stuart spoke strongly in favor of this. Mr. Bradshaw moved that Judge R. T. W. Duke be invited to speak before the Society on the 2nd Sat in Feb and Mr. Major Woods on the 2nd Sat in March. This motion was carried."[101]

Around the turn of the century the Society expanded upon the nascent bureaucracy that had been established under Woodrow Wilson. In 1895, the constitution was amended to allow for the election of the secretary.[102] He joined the president and vice president as officers elected every term (there were three terms in the academic year), with the treasurer serving for the full year. Standing committees attended to the bulk of the Society's business: namely the Ways and Means, Appropriations, Question, and Final Committees. The president frequently appointed special committees to take care of specific tasks. According to F. S. Harmon, president in 1916, "the day has passed when the Society has time to attend to the details of the organization. To be efficient the government must be one of committees."[103]

Notable Members

In 1905, amid an effort to renovate and redecorate Jefferson Hall, which had recently received heat and new electrical lights, the Society wrote letters to many of its famous alumni, requesting portraits that might hang in the Hall. John Randolph St. John, the chairman of the special committee charged with this task, wrote to a dozen individuals, all of whom had achieved some notoriety. These included John W. Daniel, a United States senator from Virginia; John Sharp Williams, minority leader of the US House of Representatives; Thomas Nelson Page, a noted southern author who would later go on to serve as ambassador to Italy under Wilson; Lyon G. Tyler, president of the College of William and Mary and son of President John Tyler; Charles W. Dabney, president of the University of Cincinnati; and James Keith, president of the Supreme Court of Appeals of Virginia. They also asked Alderman for a portrait. While most could not produce a portrait or afford to have one done, their responses were on the whole favorable, remembering fondly their time in the Jefferson Society and wishing success upon the present membership.[104] John W. Daniel, for example, wrote:

I am much honored by the request of the Jefferson Society to present them with my portrait. Neither the original nor the counterfeit could be placed in more agreeable associations than those to be found in the old "Jeff Hall." My purse is too short for me to send an oil portrait, but I will do the best I can in some other form to put myself in the good company to which I am invited. Please present my compliments to the Society, and receive them for yourself.[105]

In October 1911, the Jefferson Society again reached out to some of its most famous alumni, showing the same respect for the Society's favorite sons that previous generations had shown to the likes of Robert M. T. Hunter and Robert Toombs from the antebellum years. The Society drafted a series of "resolutions of respect to be sent by the Society to Woodrow Wilson, Claude A. Swanson, O. W. Underwood, John Sharp Williams, and Senator Culbertson of Texas."[106] Senator Oscar W. Underwood remembered his time in the Society fondly. He wrote in reply: "I had the honor at one time to be the President of the Jefferson Society. I often look back to it as the beginning of my public career. It was there that I first acquired an excellent knowledge of parliamentary law that has served me in good stead ever since . . . I hope that some time I may have the opportunity to again revisit the old hall."[107] Underwood would indeed get that chance, when he was invited to be the Society's featured speaker at the greatly anticipated Centennial Celebration in 1925.

Claude Swanson, the former congressman and governor and sitting senator from Virginia, who had taken John W. Daniel's seat when he retired, had similar sentiments: "The most pleasant and profitable associations of my university life were those connected with 'dear old Jeff Hall.' At that time college politics found expression through 'Jeff Hall.' Its sessions were lively, interesting, and exciting. No honor has come to me in my life that I prize higher than the orator's medal bestowed upon me by the Jefferson Society."[108]

Perhaps most effusive, however, was the resolution passed by the Society a few years later honoring Woodrow Wilson's presidency:

Whereas Woodrow Wilson is an alumnus of this University and a former member of this Society; and

Whereas he has achieved distinction as an educator of exceptional ability and a political thinker of keen perception and progressive principles; and

Whereas, finally, he has, in the last four years while President of the United States, secured the enactment of more constructive economic and humanitarian legislation than has ever before been passed within the same length of time in the history of the country, and has conducted our foreign relations in such a way as to keep an honorable peace with all the world to proclaim to the rest of the civilized world that this Republic respects the sovereignty and integrity of a benighted weaker state; therefore be it

Resolved, by the Jefferson Society of the University of Virginia, at its regular meeting, the fourth of November, nineteen hundred and sixteen:

1. That the Society heartily endorse the administration of the Federal Government under President Wilson; and
2. That the Society call upon all patriotic citizens who have the welfare of the country at heart to support President Wilson on Tuesday, the seventh of November; and

3. That a copy of this resolution be sent to President Wilson in the name of the Jefferson Society.[109]

Those members of the Jefferson Society who had gone on to successful careers in government and politics, Wilson first among them, continued to be an inspiration to the student membership, impressing the young men as to the worth of the activities they were participating in and the traditions they were preserving.

The Rise of Debate

As the University of Virginia expanded, the Jefferson Society expanded and adapted with it, fighting for the interest of students and searching for ways to further its goals of enriching oratory, debate, and literature at the University and elsewhere. The Jefferson Society focused particular attention on debate and established a number of events and institutions to cultivate debate among its members.

Following the trend begun in Wilson's time, the Jefferson Society pushed to debate more frequently and more vigorously. Professor of English Charles W. Kent was invited to deliver an address on the art of debate, sharing his thoughts on its virtues and offering insight about how members might improve their skills.[110] Amid concern about "the laxity shown by [the Society's] members in taking active part" in debates, the Society decided to publish the names of the scheduled debaters and their respective resolutions in *College Topics* in an effort to "improve attendance and preparation."[111] The minutes indicated that interest in debate was increasing: on November 24, 1897, they noted, "The debate was thrown open to the house and freely discussed. On the whole the debate was better than any other of this year, and it seems a new awakening has struck the society for every member with possibly one exception took part."[112]

The Society frequently wrestled with issues related to their immediate college environment, debating questions like "Resolved: That the Honor System in the University has deteriorated," "Resolved: that the University should have a President," "Resolved: that coeducation would be injurious to the University of Virginia," and "Resolved: That Greek Letter Fraternities of our Univs. and Colleges should be fostered by the esteem and patronage of all college men."[113]

Some years after Professor Kent's talk about the art of debate, the Society began to invite Charles Paul, a professor of speech and oratory to several meetings (recall that the Jefferson Society had some years earlier been instrumental in advocating the creation of this position). He gave advice to the young orators and debaters in Jefferson Hall and was soon elected an honorary member.[114] This allowed him greater ability to coach members, and he frequently served as critic after orations and debates.[115] In 1909, Paul recommended the most robust structure for formal debate and procedure the Society had ever adopted: "Resolved: That the Society devote whatever time may be necessary immediately after the regular debate on the second and fourth meeting in each month to parliamentary practice as outlined by Robert's Parliamentary Primer."[116]

The most important regular debate established during this time period was the Harrison Trophy. In 1895, James A. Harrison, professor of romance and Teutonic languages and an Edgar Allan Poe scholar, proposed to offer a trophy for a debate between the Washington and Jefferson Societies. At a meeting of the Jefferson Society on October 26, 1895, an amendment to the constitution was offered to create "a joint debater's contest between the Jefferson and Washington Literary Societies on the first Saturday night in March in which each society shall be represented by two selected debaters who will compete for the Harrison badge. The badge shall be held by the winning society as a trophy until recovered by the other society in a succeeding contest."[117] The value of Professor Harrison's prize was initially fifty dollars, but he increased it to one hundred because of the enthusiastic response from both societies.[118]

The first Harrison Trophy debate was held on May 1, 1896. George Nelms Wise and Pierce Bruns of the Jefferson Society and J. H. Barefield and Clyde Wise Pollock of the Washington Society disputed the question "Resolved, That the United States Legislators should vote according to the behests of their constituents," before a panel of judges that included Captain M. Woods, Hon. George W. Mooris, and Hon. J. W. Fishburne.[119] The Washington Society emerged victorious and claimed the handsome trophy that hung for the year in their hall. The second debate was held on June 12, 1897, and the Jefferson Society won, auguring the negative of the question: "Resolved that the Government should own and control the Railroad and Telegraph systems."[120] The Harrison Trophy debate continued until the Washington Society folded at the outset of the Great Depression, and it was revived as the Harrison

Cup shortly after the Washington Society was refounded in 1979.[121]

The Jefferson Society also began to join and participate actively in a number of intercollegiate oratorical and debating organizations, as well as engaging in individual debates with other universities and other debating societies, all in recognition that "the need for intercourse among the educational institutions of the South cannot be denied."[122] To regulate these activities, a debating and oratorical council representing the two literary societies at the University of Virginia was created. It comprised five members, two from each society, while the fifth was the professor of public speaking.[123] Together these five organized the medal debates and other contests between the two societies, as well as choosing the representatives for debates against other universities. Both societies, and thus by extension the University of Virginia, were members of three intercollegiate debating organizations. Two included universities from a number of states: the Southern Interstate Oratorical Association was made up of the universities of Texas, Alabama, South Carolina, Kentucky, Sewanee, and Vanderbilt, and the Central Oratorical Association included the universities of Chicago, Ohio, Wesleyan, Cornell, Columbia, Yale, and Princeton. The third organization, the State Intercollegiate Oratorical Association, included only schools in Virginia and was made up of Richmond, Randolph-Macon, Hampden-Sydney, Roanoke, and Emory and Henry colleges as well as Washington and Lee University.[124] Students who participated in the contests of these organizations or any that were independently arranged represented the University of Virginia, but in accordance with the University's Debating and Oratorical Council, representatives had to be chosen from the membership of either the Washington or Jefferson Societies, at least until January 17, 1914, when the Jefferson Society constitution was amended to allow any student to represent the University in debate.[125]

The Jefferson Society led the effort to establish the State Intercollegiate Oratorical Association, appointing a committee in December 1887 to look into the possibility and correspond with other colleges.[126] The first meeting of that organization was held in Asheville, North Carolina, on May 1, 1891, at which R. C. Crumpler of the Jefferson Society was elected the organization's first president.[127]

The structure of these organizations was quite complex and changed frequently as different universities and student organizations wanted to compete. There was frequent discussion, for example, in the Southern

Interstate Oratorical Association, about the method of choosing new colleges to be in the association.[128] Member organizations supplied officers for the associations on a rotating basis.[129] The Jefferson Society might expect to supply the president of the Southern Interstate Oratorical Association one year and the secretary the next, for example.[130]

From the piecemeal records of debates that the University of Virginia participated in during the first quarter of the twentieth century (which include the minutes of the societies, occasional newspaper accounts, and even more sparse personal accounts), it appears that the Jefferson Society sent its members as debaters more frequently than the Washington Society. Dozens of debates took place during that time period—in addition to the annual contests of the Southern Interstate Oratorical Association, the Central Oratorical Association, and the State Intercollegiate Oratorical Association, the University also debated against the University of North Carolina, Columbian University (today known as George Washington University), Tulane University, and many others.[131] In 1903, the Jefferson Society debated against students from the University of Pennsylvania, notable as the first time a southern school faced a university north of Washington, DC, in debate.[132] A picture of that debating team, taken for the Philadelphia newspaper and presented to the Society on May 9, 1904, hangs in Jefferson Hall to this day.[133]

These activities corresponded with an increasing interest in and awareness of what was going on at other universities, around the same time the *Magazine* began to publish a section entitled "Intercollegiana," which shared information and vital statistics about the goings-on and characteristics of other schools.[134] Ultimately, the energy put forth to cultivating debate in the Jefferson Society seems to have paid off: in 1916, the president, F. S. Harmon, wrote in a report at the end of his term: "A new impetus has been given to the literary society work. Never . . . have I seen so many members occupying chairs in this hall as during the past term; nor men more representative of all the elements of the student body fused into a working group."[135]

The Virginia High School Literary League

Out of a desire to share the experience of debating with a wider audience, in 1913 the Jefferson and Washington Societies began work on an ambitious project that would expand their goals of literary education into high schools in Virginia. They created a High School Debating Committee to consider the development of a program to cultivate debating skills among state high school students. The result was the formation of the Virginia High School Literary League, with a stated mission:

> to stimulate training in speaking and debating in secondary schools as well as to enlighten the public upon current problems which will be discussed in the course of the debates. The literary societies of the University, supported by the faculty and the Board of Visitors, thus hope to be of great service to the high schools as well as to the people at large throughout the state.[136]

The societies proposed their plan before a meeting of the Virginia State Teachers Association in Lynchburg, and it "was heartily endorsed by those present. It is heartily hoped that every high school in the state of Virginia, whether public or private, will become a member of this league."[137] The league also received the approbation of President Alderman, who found its aims very much in line with his own approach to public education. He offered words of encouragement to the societies as they continued their work: "Nothing more helpful has come out of this life of our students than this enterprise, for it has contained in it the true thought of the chief end of a university, public service and willingness and power to enrich the common life. I endorse the measure heartily."[138]

The chief responsibilities of the Washington and Jefferson Societies were first to "suggest a question to be discussed by the schools entering the league" and ultimately "furnish from the university library, free of cost, in pamphlet form, such material as will enable them to comprehend and discuss intelligibly the various points covered by the question presented." The second commitment represented a fairly large undertaking that would weigh heavily on both societies' members, but dissemination of resources located in the University library in a form digestible to high school students was a key hurdle in the success of the league. In 1914, the first resolution to be debated by the league was chosen: "Resolved, that a law be passed in Virginia compelling all children more than seven and less than fifteen years of age, who are not physically unable, to attend school at least sixteen weeks each year." The subject matter and the context, to the societies, seemed "well suited to the ability of the high school student, and furthermore, there is an abundance of material that may be secured on the subject."[139] The literary societies retained their responsibility for the league until 1926, when control was handed over to the constituent high schools. In March 1946, the league was reorganized after World War II as the Virginia High School Literary and Athletic League, and today is known as simply the Virginia High School League, which retains organizational responsibility for all competitive sports, debate, and forensics among Virginia high schools.[140]

The Society Expands Its Activities

While the University and its literary societies weathered World War I reasonably well, the conflict did claim the practice of hosting joint celebrations on July 4 with the struggling Washington Society, as well as hosting Final Orators, marking the passing of one of the last remnants of the former glory of the Jefferson Society. These grandiose celebrations were abandoned in 1918 in favor of conducting events focused more on the Society itself, rather than the whole University. The duties of the literary societies in organizing Final Exercises were at last handed over to the University administration in their entirety, and the Jefferson Society turned its attention inward.

The Jefferson Society's reverence for one of its most famous alumni, Edgar Allan Poe, continued unabated into the twentieth century. On September 30, 1899, "The Pres. informed the society of a formal invitation by the Pres. of the Poe Memorial Association to be present at the unveiling of the Poe bust. Mr. Heard moved that the society accept the initiation with thanks."[141] The University had commissioned a famous sculptor, George Julian Zolnay, to create a bust of Poe for the library, which was unveiled with much fanfare on October 17, 1899. The ceremony, led by Professor Kent, featured speeches on Poe's time as a student and his literary position, among many other topics.[142]

Beginning in 1908, the Jefferson Society formalized their own remembrance of Poe's life, attending to "the arrange[ment of] a memorial meeting in honor of E. A. Poe, former Secretary of the Society," to be known as "the Centenary of Edgar Allan Poe."[143] Held on January 16, 1909, the program, parts of which were suggested by Professor Paul, saw Jefferson Society members and guests give speeches on topics that ranged from a sketch of Poe's life to "Poe and the Jefferson Literary Society" to "The Pathos in the Lives of Our Southern Poets." The students clearly took inspiration from the unveiling of the Zolnay bust that had taken place just a few years earlier. The Washington Society was invited to participate, and students from across the University attended the evening which marked the centennial of Poe's birth.[144]

The Poe Centennial was well received; a news article described the evening as "most representative of the students of the events of the Poe Centenary. The Speakers were all students . . . Mr. Paul Micou, President of the Society, introduced each speaker in a few appropriate remarks." While the entire program "did not last much more than an hour . . . the seventy-five auditors, who had braved the swirling snowstorm, left with the hope that the Jeff. would see fit shortly to celebrate some more of the famous men who honor her rolls."[145]

News of the event traveled quickly, as well. William A. Poe, a descendent of the poet, read about the "elaborate series of exercises, . . . [to] be held at the University of Virginia, Edgar Allan Poe's Alma Mater in memory of the South's gifted son, and America's unequaled genius, to celebrate the Centenary of his birth." His sentiments were grateful, and he wrote: "Permit me gentlemen, as one of the nearest living relatives of Edgar Allan Poe, to express the highest appreciation of your intention to so greatly honor [him]."[146]

In 1904, the Society changed its emblem to the current design: "The badge of this Society shall be of gold and shall measure one-third by one half of an inch. It shall be two pens crossed upon which shall rest a profile (facing to the right) of Thomas Jefferson. At the top shall be the letters 'U. VA.;' on the left side (resting between the two pens) the figures '18;' and the right side (resting between the two pens) the figures '25' and at the bottom the Greek letters Phi Pi Theta."[147]

The year before the Poe Centennial, in 1908, the Society began the practice of hosting an annual banquet in commemoration of Founder's Day, a celebration of Thomas Jefferson's birthday, a practice that continues to this day.[148] The annual banquet became an excuse for Society members to dress up and enjoy an elegant evening, sometimes with a speaker, but always when the membership could put on its greatest airs. This event came in large part to replace the festivities of the abandoned joint and Intermediate celebrations with festivities intended for Society members only.

During this time the Law School had captured the fascination of students by hosting an annual moot court, a sketch comedy routine that took the form of a trial with humorous characters, situations, and encounters.

FIGURE 18. Jefferson Society members in costume for a moot court production, presented in Old Cabell Hall in 1927. Image courtesy of the Albert and Shirley Small Special Collections Library at the University of Virginia, University of Virginia Visual History Collection, U.Va. Prints and Photographs File, RG-30/1/10.011, Print 2700.

In 1898, the Jefferson Society, in an attempt to get in on the action, and to get a piece of the admission price that students were willing to pay to see such an event, began to host their own moot court.[149] Within a few years of its inception, the Society's version enjoyed popularity comparable to the Law School's production. The Society continued to put on a moot court well into the 1950s until student interest faded.

These events are evidence that despite the competition they faced, there was still a lively scene for the literary societies at the University of Virginia. As alluded to above, the Jefferson and Washington Societies frequently conducted activities together and supported each other's functions, until the latter folded at the outset of the Great Depression. One humorous example of the way that the Jefferson Society cooperated with the Washington Society (and also a good illustration of the tenor of some of the Society's more enjoyable meetings) involved an effort to borrow some chairs from Washington Hall.

Jefferson Hall being the smaller of the two buildings, sometimes there were not enough chairs for special events, which became a problem in 1915. Upon examination of the treasury, the Society did not have enough money to purchase additional chairs.

It was suggested that the conference committee proceed to Wash. Hall and invite that Society to the Smoker, at the same time asking a loan of thirty chairs. The committee was about to withdraw for that purpose, when Mr. B. C. Taylor stepped forward with a reminder to the Comm. that it was their duty not only to ask for the chairs but also to bring them over to our hall. Mr. Steger, chairman of the comm. was immediately on his feet in defense of the comm. No sooner had he taken his seat, than half the house was calling for the President's recognition. Mr. Banks was recognized, he called attention to the fact that . . . the little ant had been successfully modified in form for carrying heavy burdens, and that there was no reason why Mr. Steger could not be likewise modified. Mr. Steger was here given the floor and indignantly remonstrated against being compared to an insignificant ant. He offered to permit himself to be examined microscopically to prove his point, but no one took advantage of the opportunity.[150]

Steger, sensing his defeat, put forth an amendment to allow him to appoint an assistant who might help him carry the chairs. According to *Robert's Rules,* such an amendment should be put to a voice vote.

Owing to the volume of Mr. Taylor's voice, the vote had to be taken by standing. The amendment was carried. The original motion was again taken up. During this, the highest point was reached when Mr. Taylor offered to prove that Poe and Jefferson both carried chairs, if he were given 33 minutes in which to do so. This was not granted. In the most pathetic part where he was beseeching the support of his friends, one of the members leaning too far back in his chair suddenly was capsized. Taking advantage of the situation and of the man also, Mr. Steger cried: "Lo! (Low=[Mr.] Crawford) my enemy hath fallen!"[151]

Fearing a fate similar to the unfortunate enemy of Mr. Steger, the question was almost unanimously defeated, and the Society went on with its business.

The University's Centennial

The University of Virginia celebrated its centennial from May 31 to June 3, 1921. The celebration had been delayed from 1919 to 1921 because of "disturbed world conditions following the Great War."[152] The four days were filled by a monumental series of speeches from alumni and dignitaries from across the Commonwealth and the world. On the second day, academics from a great many universities around the world came as representatives of their institutions to honor Mr. Jefferson's University. Several of the delegates, more often than not the presidents of their respective universities, offered public remarks of greetings and congratulations. They participated in a grand procession on the Lawn, attended a reception at Carr's Hill, President Alderman's house, and witnessed numerous grand pageants and concerts. A plaque commemorating the University's sons who had died in World War I was unveiled on the Rotunda. On the fourth day of the celebration, the regular commencement exercises were held, a fitting conclusion to the celebrations.[153]

The Society's Centennial

By 1925, the Jefferson Society had geared up for its own centennial. The planning for the event, which was to be the grandest of all celebrations, began in 1924. A committee of the most established leaders of the Society was appointed: William P. Sandridge Jr., William D. Bouge, Charles L. Gleaves, Edward W. Gregory Jr., George P. Gunn, James D. Lovelace, and Thomas A. McEachern. Fred Quarles Jr. served as the chair. Quarles, along with Gleaves, Gunn, and McEachern, all would ultimately serve as president of the Society—evidence that the membership wanted to put its best foot forward for the celebration.

The celebration took place on November 18, 1925. In an almost unprecedented gesture, lectures at the University were suspended for the day to commemorate the occasion, and students crowded into the Cabell Hall auditorium to hear Alabama senator and former president of the Jefferson Society Oscar W. Underwood give the keynote address. Quarles, who by then had been elected president of the Society, and Alderman joined in the speech making.[154] Underwood spoke of Jefferson's legacy and of how his theories of government held relevance even a century later:

Mr. Jefferson proclaimed live truths in government as no other man in all history has done; the only regret I have is that often in our government we find merely the lip service to the truth of those great principles he taught and gave to us, and not the actualities in legislation and in government.

I know of no greater truth that he gave to you than that the men of your Society who have occupied commanding places have followed and buckled to themselves as an armor of success—that is, that the government governs least, governs best—the government governs best, governs least.[155]

FIGURE 19. Jefferson Society members in 1924. Image courtesy of the Albert and Shirley Small Special Collections Library at the University of Virginia, University of Virginia Visual History Collection, U.Va. Prints and Photographs File, RG-30/1/10.011, Print 09135.

Underwood moved on to discuss a few contemporary issues, including the need for cloture in the Senate, arguing that Jefferson would have supported it as a sound principle. He believed the Treaty of Versailles, which Underwood himself moved to ratify unconditionally, would have been ratified had there been cloture in the Senate.

The Centennial Celebration concluded with a banquet in Madison Hall, attended by Underwood, Alderman, and several other notable Jefferson Society alumni. Alderman offered a toast to the Society's future prosperity: "I hope those of this great University of 2,000 will see that you are carrying, and have carried forward for a century, a great constructive piece of the teaching in the University, which has passed out into the nation and the world."[156]

In 1925 the record of the Jefferson Society certainly spoke for itself—and for the transcendence of the University of Virginia's oldest student organization—which in its first century had managed to maintain a position of prominence in University life, had accrued an incredible roll of famous alumni, survived the Civil War and World War I, and had adapted to major changes in the character of the University and college life, all while maintaining its basic essence. While the Jefferson Society of 1925 was certainly different than it was in 1850 or even in 1880 when Woodrow Wilson served as its president, after one hundred years, the Society still inhabited a special place in the University of Virginia community, and in many ways continued to represent the best the University had to offer.

CHAPTER SIX

Change and Continuity in the Jefferson Society

1925–1960

When classes resumed after the Centennial Celebration and the Jefferson Society entered its second hundred years, significant headwinds bore down on its continued success. Having both survived and prospered in spite of significant competition for student time and interest, the Society would confront a host of new challenges over the next twenty years, including rapid growth at the University, prevailing student apathy to formalized political and intellectual discourse, and the austerity of the Great Depression. These pressures were not unique to the Jefferson Society, but the Society leadership responded to them in ways that ensured the survival of Virginia's oldest student organization while many other groups fell by the wayside. The Society adapted and changed both internally and in its interactions with the wider community to remain relevant in the face of far-reaching change at the University and in higher education. During the 1930s, the Society charted the course that would guide it through the Great Depression, World War II, and into the 1950s as a markedly different, but no less significant, institution at the University of Virginia.

This period of rapid change began almost immediately after the Society's Centennial. Enrollment and new construction at the University spiked in the late 1920s and 1930s, spurred by economic prosperity, philanthropic support, and the popularization of college education following World War I. After the death of Edwin Alderman in 1931, the new University president John Lloyd Newcomb initiated a sustained building campaign on the Grounds. The construction of new facilities such as Alderman Library and dorms for first-year students on Monroe Hill allowed the student population to balloon from 500 in 1904 to nearly 3,000 by 1937.[1] At first blush, a growing student body would imply a larger group of potential members for the Society to draw upon, but the prevailing trends of mass higher education behind this expansion meant that many of these new students lacked interest in the strictly regimented intellectual discourse that the Society had on offer. Instead, as Thelin notes, beginning in the 1920s, the "college man" was drawn increasingly to "hedonistic behavior" focused around drinking, including "homecoming celebrations, commencement week reunions, proms, year-round fraternity gatherings . . . bathtub gin, speakeasies," and gambling.[2] The situation at the University of Virginia reflected this national trend, and the *Virginia Spectator* (previously the *Virginia University Magazine*, renamed in 1927) lamented the lack of interest in the activities of literary societies: "intellectual things have lost their appeal . . . the unheeding student is overemphasizing dispensable activities."[3] The Society envisioned by Woodrow Wilson, one that rigorously schooled its members in the practice of debate and public affairs, was out of sync with the expectations and desires of this new, rapidly growing generation of students.

Coupled with the shift away from formalized intellectual pursuits outside of classes, another factor, this one particular to the University of Virginia, was at work: a vociferous aversion among students to any type of showmanship or individual accomplishment. This "supercilious indifference" was referred to as not "sticking one's neck out."[4] Virginius Dabney, in *Mr. Jefferson's University: A History*, which picks up where Philip Alexander Bruce's five-volume history of the University leaves off, explains that this fear on the part of students "seemed to cause near-paralysis when an effort was made to get the students to act affirmatively for the good of the university or to even answer a question in class," as "anyone who replied to a question addressed by the professor to the class as a whole was widely regarded as a show-off."[5] Students went so far as to wear prep school or varsity letter sweaters inside out so as to avoid any semblance of showmanship. This climate did not bode well for the Jefferson Society, where stirring oratory, skillful and incisive debate, and ultracompetitive political contests had long been vehicles for students to assert their superiority or demonstrate their skill and knowledge. The pressure to avoid "sticking one's neck out" and taking a stand on any particular issue likely contributed to the *Spectator*'s conclusion in 1928 that "the art of debate was never more scorned in the University than it is today."[6]

External Pressures

The combined effect of these factors on the University's literary societies was debilitating. The *Spectator* noted in 1927 that the day for literary societies "seems to be gone and with its demise Washington and Jefferson have faded into the background . . . no longer are the vital affairs of the University solved within their halls."[7] Indeed, the author's prediction had already been partially borne out: the Washington Society, the counterpart to the Jefferson Society for almost a century, effectively folded that year. In a sad tribute to one of the University's longest standing institutions, the *Spectator* recorded a visit to Washington Hall: "Within it is found dust, broken chairs, and a few weathered remnants to suggest its one time use . . . at the present time there is no trace of an organization to merit the worn slab above the door."[8] There were several attempts to revive the Washington Society throughout the 1930s, but none were successful for more than a few months.[9] The Jefferson Society, though it managed to continue meeting regularly, struggled to combat declining interest and relevance. It was described as a body whose "scanty, lackadaisical" membership simply shifted "the cud of contemplation from one side of their mouths to the other."[10]

The onset of the Great Depression only compounded these challenges. Though the University of Virginia fared far better than many other institutions of higher learning, some of which had to pay their professors in scrip or temporarily suspend salaries altogether, the Depression did restrict the finances and activities of both the University and the Jefferson Society.[11] The Virginia General Assembly imposed a ten percent across-the-board cut to the University's appropriation in 1932 and an additional cut of the same magnitude immediately after John Lloyd Newcomb officially assumed the University presidency in 1933. As a result, Newcomb was forced to cut salaries of all University employees by twenty percent and squeeze as many efficiencies as possible out of the annual budget. Dabney notes that, with the onset and deepening of the Depression, "austerity was the rule throughout the University."[12]

A similar state of penury prevailed in the Jefferson Society. The organization that once charged an exorbitant initiation fee of ten dollars during the antebellum period now regularly had less than five dollars on hand altogether.[13] While the Society remained solvent throughout the Depression, questions of cost and fiscal feasibility were regularly debated in planning events.[14] The treasurer was forced to constantly hound members to pay their dues in order to meet the Society's outstanding obligations. He used any recourse available to collect from delinquent members, including insisting on dues payments as "a prerequisite for the right of suffrage" in Society elections. This method was effective, but it was met with derision by some members who saw it as a "poll tax."[15] The cash-strapped state of the Society and similar student organizations likely contributed to the failure of the myriad attempts to revive the Washington Society or create a similar second literary organization.[16]

It was against this backdrop that the Society leadership sought to adapt once again to the changing environment. To remain both an attractive activity for students and a prominent organization on Grounds, the Jefferson Society once again had to reevaluate how it engaged the University community. After the Society ceased hosting their elaborate Final and Intermediate Celebrations and lost the prerogative to select the student orators for major University events, it became increasingly insular, focusing its efforts on formalized training in debate and oratory among its members. As the *Spectator* noted, however, this was not the tenor of discourse preferred by most students at the University; rather, "the day of the bull session is upon us, and in order to enjoy a group meeting everyone must talk rapidly and uproariously on a different subject."[17] The Society leadership needed to change the fundamental character of their meetings to accommodate this new desire to engage in unfettered, free-flowing discourse. They did so in 1935 with the passage of a new constitution and by-laws specifically providing for "forum sessions" in the place of traditional Society meetings.[18] These new meetings took place biweekly, with the intervening weeks' meetings reserved for the traditional conduct of Jefferson Society business, including electing officers and new members and internal Society debate and oratory.

Forum sessions revitalized Society meetings by opening the doors of Jefferson Hall to engage the University community on a variety of important issues. Each forum session was prescribed to proceed as follows: "a speaker, not necessarily a member of the Society, shall be invited to address the members and guests. At the conclusion of the address, two members of the Society, taking opposing views of the subject presented, shall open discussion, which shall be considered an integral part of the program."[19] After these two Society members framed the issue under consideration, discussion was thrown open to the room for all present to engage in a thorough bull session on the topic.[20] The first series of forum sessions in 1935–1936 focused on issues of both University and national importance, touching on topics as diverse as the new dorms for first-year students, the construction of Alderman Library, the need for a farmer-labor party, the power of judicial review, and "a stormy session . . . upon the question of admittance of negroes to the University."[21] This last question was "precipitated by the refusal of the University administration to admit Alice Hunt Jackson," a black woman who had applied to the graduate school but was ultimately denied.[22] Similar forum sessions continued throughout the decade with political, educational, and literary issues and even musical performances as themes.

The Society's historian in 1936, Werner Janney, offered some insight into the rationale for creating forum sessions:

The new Constitution is a radical . . . departure from the ancient and quite honorable traditions of the Society. It provides for the abolishment of the old classical program of debates and oratory in favor of a system of "forum" or open discussion meetings . . . It was felt—and the steady decline of the Society during the past few years seemed to sustain the feeling—that students were no longer interested in the type of material which the Society had to offer, and that the trend at present seemed to be toward the discussion type of program.[23]

Clearly then, the Society recognized the external threat of diminishing student interest and increased insularity and adapted accordingly. Although not universally well attended, the forum sessions were generally regarded as a success. They reintegrated the Society into the ongoing discourse among students and faculty at the University while maintaining its traditional precepts of free expression and intellectual engagement. In his farewell speech to the Society in the final term of 1937, President George Tabor remarked that the "institution of the forum is one of the outstanding monuments in the progress of Jeff in the past few years . . . Jeff has contributed much to the intellectual development . . . of a large percentage of the student body . . . it has been a medium of collective student expression."[24]

The Society used this position as a conduit of student expression to encourage dialogue on critical issues facing the student body. Janney, who became president of the Society in 1936, noted there was a need among the student body for "various other activities" that could be met by the

Society. Hence, it stuck "its collective nose into a good many enterprises," many of which were "quite successful."[25] The Society sponsored numerous events outside of Jefferson Hall, sometimes alone or in conjunction with other organizations, including rallies, forums, speakers, and discussions that sought to mobilize the often indifferent student body to action. For example, in 1935, with war clouds gathering in Europe, the Jefferson Society, Madison Hall, and the National Students' League held a public antiwar rally in Cabell Hall.[26] The event drew such interest that President Newcomb cancelled classes for one hour so students could attend. Dabney recalls that at the event, "the Hall was packed with about one thousand students, and 'chaotic demonstrations' followed the declaration by Francis Franklin . . . that tens of thousands of students would 'take the Oxford Oath never to support the government of the United States in any war it may undertake.'"[27] By way of such events, the Jefferson Society continued to promote meaningful intellectual engagement, even in a larger University.

Internal Changes

Despite the success of forum sessions in repositioning the Society in the University community, it still needed to make internal changes to retain and enlarge its membership. While public events drew in prospective members—Werner Janney reported that "applications for membership immediately increased"—it would be the affairs and activities of the Society itself that would keep these new men coming to Jefferson Hall on Friday nights.[28] In the span of a few years, the Society introduced several innovations to its activities to ensure continued regular member interest, including a wholesale revision of the membership process, changes to the tenor and content of the regular biweekly members-only meetings, and the introduction of new special events to the Society social calendar. Many of the new practices and activities introduced during this period continue to define Society membership to this day.

The most important structural change to the Society was the introduction of a new class of membership—probationary members. Concerned that "too many men were being admitted into the membership of the Society who were only slightly interested, and, naturally, after a time dropped out of active participation," in 1935 the Society amended the constitution such that all new members would initially be elected as probationary members, to be eligible for election into regular membership at the completion of a full term, contingent upon their attendance at and interest in Jefferson Society meetings and activities. Probationaries (sometimes called probationers) were entitled the same rights and privileges of regular members, with the exception of voting in elections or holding office, and were expected to spend time learning about the Society and fulfilling certain requirements.[29] President Janney described the probationary period as "an intermediate state . . . during which new men may observe the Society and are in turn observed . . . if the new men and the Society agree as to their respective merits, he is elected to regular membership."[30] The addition of probationary membership also aligned the Society's process for vetting and selecting new members more closely with those of fraternities, whose new members (often referred to as "goats") would endure a pledge term before becoming full brothers.[31]

New members were also expected to deliver a speech before the Society during their time as probationaries. While not officially codified as a requirement for regular membership until much later, presenting an acceptable maiden speech, previously an expectation of new regular members, seemed universally understood as a prerequisite to successful completion of the probationary term. Such a presentation tested the probationary's oratorical talents, but more importantly it validated his dedication to the Society by requiring that he "stick his neck out" in front of the Hall. The topics of these speeches, which were initially assigned by the president, and later selected at the discretion of the probationary, ranged widely from "names of various sizes of a smoked cigarette" to "how pump priming would improve the sanitary conditions of the Country," and even why "one should not neck on his first date."[32] Sometimes probationaries were permitted to prepare at home and present their speeches in "finished form," while other times the Society demanded they speak extemporaneously.[33] Regardless of topic or level of preparation, the maiden speech was almost certainly a stressful event in the life of most probationaries, as it had to be deemed by the membership to be of acceptable quality. The minutes of 1940 recall a particularly anxious probationary member, George Watts, who "struggled to his feet," with "palms and other parts of his body wet" before finally delivering a speech of "pleasing conversational quality."[34] The concept of a maiden speech exists to this day in the Jefferson Society, although it is now far more formalized and known as a probationary presentation.

The "Society sessions" of this period, those conducted in the inter-

vening weeks between the open forum sessions, retained similar content
and character to the meetings of the past half century but with a few key
differences. Society members still held debates and oratorical contests,
listened to maiden speeches, and presented literary works.[35] But with the
failure of their longtime counterpart, the Washington Society, the Jefferson Society struggled to find an adequate replacement for intersociety
competitions. The Harrison Trophy debate was discontinued after the
Washington Society closed its doors in 1929, and the annual oratorical
contests and medal debates filled with Jefferson and Washington Society
men ceased as well.

Several organizations temporarily filled the void left by the Washington Society, most notably the American Student Union, a left-wing student organization of which several Jefferson Society men were also members.[36] The Society debated the ASU in 1938 on the topic, "Resolved, that
the University of Virginia should by the raising of entrance requirements
be made a retreat for intellectual aristocracy."[37] However, these debates
were not judged and were characterized by friendlier competition than
the former fierce contests with the Washington Society. As a result, during this period the Society largely supplied its own intellectual content
while infrequently competing with numerous short-term replacements
for their age-old rivals.

Furthermore, in contrast to the seriousness of Woodrow Wilson's Jefferson Hall, the tenor of Society meetings during this period was much
lighter. Members often poked fun at one another, recorded gently insult-
ing characterizations of their fellows in the meeting minutes, and presented humorous material. Maiden speeches about cigarettes and dating
were typical of some of the topics discussed. In 1939, the Society held a
"liar's contest" in which the winner was awarded a "medal which was a
miniature toilet on the end of a ribbon. It was pinned on his lapel so that
it might always be handy whenever he started to 'sling the shit.'"[38] Society members even composed and presented elaborate epic poems of the
goings-on of Jefferson Hall. These works, which touched on both humorous and serious topics, such as admitting women into the Society, were
cleverly written and remain enjoyable to read even today.[39] The Society
also evidently had quite a sweet tooth during this time, as the treasurer's
records include receipts for dozens upon dozens of blocks of ice cream,
in an assortment of flavors and ranging in size from one to five gallons,
purchased from Monticello Dairy as meeting refreshments.[40] One can

imagine Society members relaxing at the end of a long semester as they did at the close of their final meeting in 1937 with "a riotous feast on ice cream and cookies."[41]

New Activities

In parallel with these changes to the membership and meetings, the Society began hosting numerous new events and activities for its own enjoyment and edification outside of regular meetings. The most important of these were created in honor of the Society's most prominent alumni: Woodrow Wilson and Edgar Allan Poe. The Woodrow Wilson Memorial Banquet and Poe Night served two purposes: they brought the regular membership and visiting alumni together for an evening of fellowship and amusement while simultaneously remembering and paying tribute to these famous men. They also frequently featured speakers and guests of significant national acclaim, lending credibility to the Society in the eyes of the University community and further enhancing the prestige and benefits of membership.

The first Woodrow Wilson Memorial Banquet was an evening to remember. Hosted by the Society at the Monticello Hotel on May 18, 1936, the banquet began as a simple "get-together to acquaint new men with older members."[42] Kenneth Giniger, the member appointed to plan the event, had a different idea. He launched into a full-scale campaign to invite University faculty and administration, state and national public figures, and friends and family of President Wilson. As Society historian Werner Janney recorded, Mr. Giniger "deserves mention . . . as the most energetic committee-man to arrive on the scene in 111 years . . . [he] charged to the fore, and led the assault upon the entrenched University and nation. Inviting President Roosevelt was all in the day's work."[43] As the list of notable guests grew, the event began to receive substantial coverage in *College Topics* and around Charlottesville.[44] The excitement for the banquet grew to such a degree that the Society reversed its long-standing rule about female attendees at Society functions and published an announcement "that ladies will be welcomed at the dinner. This is the first time in the history of the Jefferson Society that ladies have been permitted to attend its dinner."[45]

The event itself went off smoothly and lived up to the anticipation of members and guests alike. Janney wrote that "eighty banqueters arrived, and the Jeff men needed spy glasses to see each other."[46] Mr. Giniger's

FIGURE 20. Jefferson Society members gather at an early iteration of the annual Woodrow Wilson Memorial Banquet. Wilson Day continues to be an important formal function on the Society calendar each year. Image courtesy of the Albert and Shirley Small Special Collections Library at the University of Virginia, University of Virginia Visual History Collection, U.Va. Prints and Photographs File, RG-30/1/10.011, Print 09120.

efforts combined with the continued reverence held for Woodrow Wilson as a national figure to draw significant numbers of noteworthy guests. In attendance as guest of honor was Mrs. Edith Bolling Wilson, the late president's wife. United States senators Tom Connally of Texas and William Dieterich of Illinois, University president John Lloyd Newcomb, and University professor of history Richard Heath Dabney (a close friend of Wilson) all honored Wilson with remarks.[47] Also in attendance were US senators Joseph Guffey of Pennsylvania, Rush Holt of West Virginia, and J. Hamilton Lewis of Illinois, US Supreme Court justice James C. McReynolds, and Virginia governor George C. Peery.[48] Janney noted glibly, "the Society had got national advertising and more than a little local prestige out of the affair."[49]

The highlight of the evening occurred after the dinner was over and the attendees had headed out into the Charlottesville night. A group of Society members volunteered to accompany Mrs. Wilson to Jefferson

Hall, where her husband had wielded the gavel as president of the Society almost sixty years before. Upon arrival, they decided to honor Mrs. Wilson for her contributions to the Society and the nation:

There being more than a quorum of members present, the president called the Society to order, and entertained a motion by Mr. Dieterich that Mrs. Edith Bolling Wilson (Mrs. Woodrow Wilson) be elected to Honorary Membership in the Jefferson Society. The motion was enthusiastically seconded, and so great an impression had Mrs. Wilson's charm and graciousness made upon the members of the Society, she was elected by acclamation. Mrs. Wilson expressed her appreciation of the Society's action and seemed sincerely touched by the tribute.[50]

With that, Edith Bolling Wilson became the first female member of any kind in the Society, even though a constitutional amendment barring women from becoming regular members had been adopted sixteen years earlier. After that night in 1936, the Society continued to host similar banquets sporadically until the outbreak of World War II. After the war, the banquet was reorganized and is still celebrated by the Society each fall as Wilson Day.

A similar, though less elaborate, event was held annually to honor Edgar Allan Poe. The Society had honored the poet with a banquet in 1908; in 1926 they began hosting Poe Night, marking the occasion with a discussion or reading of Poe's works by the membership, an exhibition of "Poe relics" in Jefferson Hall, and a speaker.[51] Professor Stringfellow Barr had the privilege of being the inaugural speaker, though in the years following it was more often than not the internationally known Poe scholar James Southall Wilson, who was invited to speak at the event at least a dozen times.[52] In his series of lectures, Wilson touched on such diverse topics as a reflection on Poe's influence on American literature ninety years after his death to Poe burlesquing his own detective stories.[53] The Society held a Poe Night of this variety for more than thirty years and continues to honor him with an annual Poe Reading Contest.

The Era of Machine Politics

While the Jefferson Society leadership worked diligently to adapt and expand the Society's activities during this period, another endeavor consumed an equal if not greater share of their intellectual passion—party politics. While always a place for budding statesmen to practice their future craft, Society business in the late 1920s and '30s was dominated by partisan strife, intense political maneuvering, and parliamentary chicanery. The power of political machines, pioneered by Woodrow Wilson and his allies in the late nineteenth century, reached its zenith in the years leading up to World War II. These organizations, typically tight-knit groups of friends and political allies united around a powerful leader, sought to seize and maintain control of the Society for successive generations. So integral were these groups to a regular member's identity in the Society at this time that Jeff-men were often referred to by their party affiliation; for example, a "Rosenbergerite" was a regular member who supported the party led by Coleman Rosenberger.[54] Despite almost continuous attempts by elder statesman of the Society to discourage purely partisan politics for "personal gain and selfish reasons" in favor of "the common good," factional rivalry "bubbled and boiled" throughout the decade.[55]

During this time of continuous political wrangling, two regular members stand out for the ardor and intensity of their rivalry. The first of these opponents was Robert M. Musselman, a recognized "power" at the University during the 1930s and '40s.[56] While pursuing three degrees over a decade as a student, Musselman held almost every position possible in the Jefferson Society, including president, vice-president, membership chair, program chair, and auditor of the books, the latter of which he held continuously for ten years.[57] He controlled a political machine that dominated Society elections throughout the late 1930s and early '40s, making him one of the most successful Society politicians to this day. Musselman's influence stretched beyond the walls of Jefferson Hall; he served on the Student Senate, as chair of the *Virginia Spectator* board (the newly renamed *University of Virginia Magazine*), and as editor of *College Topics* at various times throughout his student career.[58] And though his personal political views were left of center, he was very much a traditionalist leader on the Grounds.

Arrayed against Musselman and his machine was Coleman Rosenberger. A true foil to Musselman, Rosenberger was an influential left-wing intellectual at the University, and he led a faction composed of Jefferson Society members who also belonged to the "semi-radical" American Student Union.[59] While a separate organization in itself, Rosenberger sought to leverage his established base of support in the ASU to control the Jefferson Society. Unfortunately for him, a fair portion of the ASU men

FIGURE 21. Jefferson Hall and West Range in 1940. Image courtesy of the Albert and Shirley Small Special Collections Library at the University of Virginia, University of Virginia Visual History Collection, U.Va. Prints and Photographs File, RG-30/1/10.011, Print 01684.

"seemed to have other interests which were at least as important to them as Jeff," so Rosenberger was typically unable to mobilize his supporters to their fullest extent.[60] Outside of the Society, Rosenberger also enjoyed a significant degree of prestige on the Grounds, though in a different sense than Musselman. Highly regarded as a writer, he rose to prominence as both an editor and contributor to the *Spectator*.[61]

The conflict between these two political parties reached its crescendo in the 1937–1938 academic year. The uneventful election for Society president the preceding spring gave no indication of the storm that would begin the following fall: Musselman was elected essentially unopposed, with only the outgoing president, ineligible to serve due to his impending graduation, running against him as a joke.[62] Musselman filled his Executive Committee with allies, including his closest confidant, James Brewbaker, who he appointed Membership chair, parliamentarian, and chair of an ad hoc Committee on Constitutional Revision.[63] It seemed that the Musselman machine would sit comfortably atop the Society for the foreseeable future.

But as the University resumed classes in the fall, Rosenberger and his allies began to put plans into action with the aim of unseating the Musselmanites. They recruited more ASU members to join the Society as probationaries, bolstering their faction's presence in the Hall. Chief among these new recruits was Palmer Weber, a prominent but apparently "antagonistic" leader in the ASU who Warner Janney tells us was seen as "a storm venter wherever he went."[64] Simultaneously, Rosenberger and Robert Jacob, the secretary and Musselman's handpicked successor as president, developed a plot in which Jacob would turn on Musselman and hand the next election to Rosenberger's party. The plan was for Jacob and Rosenberger to run against each other for president until the last minute when Jacob would drop out. Musselman would be caught by surprise, and Rosenberger would assume the presidency unopposed. In return, Rosenberger would rally the ASU faction to support Jacob for election to the *Magazine* board against Eugene Caffey, the incumbent and a member of Musselman's party.[65]

Despite careful planning, Rosenberger's plan backfired. Musselman caught wind of Jacob's plan to defect "the afternoon before the election" and was able to convince his chief advisor, Brewbaker, to run for the presidency as his party's candidate.[66] On a cold night in December 1937, the Society gathered for the election, which descended into "a very stormy session," with the contest between Jacob and Caffey alone "lasting for more than an hour and a half" as both men's supporters argued vehemently on behalf of their candidate.[67] All of the elections that evening were extremely close, with that of Caffey and Jacob being decided by only one vote, but in the end all of Musselman's candidates were triumphant.[68]

Clearly frustrated at having almost been outsmarted by Rosenberger and betrayed by Jacob, Musselman sought to restore his unquestioned authority upon the resumption of classes in January 1938. He spearheaded a motion to expel his former friend Mr. Jacob from the Society for malfeasance in office while secretary.[69] This was quite a drastic action: motions to expel fellow members have been exceedingly rare in the Society's history, and the number of such motions known to have succeeded can be counted on one hand. Though the motion failed, it indicated that Musselman was prepared to use every tool at his disposal to regain the political upper hand.

It was from his new position as membership chair that Musselman truly reasserted himself. To undermine Rosenberger's support, he blocked the admission of additional ASU members into the Society and ensured that Palmer Weber, one of Rosenberger's chief allies, was denied regular membership and dropped from the Society's rolls as a probationary.[70] Enraged, "the A.S.U. members swore vengeance in the form that every probationer, except those who were decidedly on their side, would be voted against" for regular membership, a time-tested tactic dating back to the days of A. C. Carson and Murray McGuire.[71] They stated their intention to maintain this policy even if it would "wreck Jeff."[72]

Not willing to be outmaneuvered again, Musselman went on the offensive and called a secret special meeting of the Society for a Sunday evening. Admittance to this meeting was "by private invitation only"; Musselman skirted the constitutional requirement of posting notice of special meetings twenty-four hours in advance on two college bulletin boards by placing note-card-sized messages on the boards in the Mechanical and Chemistry Laboratories, which Janney noted were "the two most inconspicuous bulletin boards in the University."[73] The record of the meeting noted that by this method "the desired result was obtained—no one of the opposing faction saw the announcement," and with one vote over a quorum, Musselman and his allies advanced ten young Musselmanites from probationary into regular membership.[74] Rosenberger and his allies were furious and accused Musselman's machine of "stinking" politics at the subsequent meeting.[75] But with their embargo on election of regular members effectively broken, the ASU party lost its last hold on power in the Society, and the Musselman machine remained the hegemonic party in the Society for several terms to come.

The Society membership seemed well aware that they experienced an extraordinary year of partisan conflict, even in this traditionally political organization. Janney, the Society historian, presented his record of this clash of political leaders to the Society as a parody of Lewis Carroll's "The Walrus and the Carpenter."[76] Pasted in its entirety into the Society minute book and heavily footnoted with helpful details and explanations for future generations, it captures the spirit and vitality of political activity in the Hall during this period. And while Society politics have calmed since their heyday, Janney's witty recording of the contest between these two ardent young men remains enjoyable and illustrative.

The Coal-man and the Muscle-man
Were feeling of their oats;
They wept like anything to see
Such quantities of votes.
"If we could each one get them all,"
They said, "we'd turn our coats!"

"If seven A.S.U. ward-men
Should try for half a year,
Do you suppose," the Coal-man said,
"They'd all be mine, old dear?"
"I doubt it," said the Muscle-man,
And leered a bitter leer.

"Oh, Jeff-men, come and walk with us,"
The Coal-man did beseech;
"A pleasant walk, a pleasant talk,
A nice election speech!
Oh, I could do with more than four,
And give a hand to each!"

The elder Cohen looked at them,
And shook his loggerhead;
The elder Cohen took the floor,
Whence all but him had fled
Meaning to say he did not choose
To do as either said.

But four young Jeff-men hurried up,
And yet another four,
And thick and strong they came along,
And more and more and more,
All hopping through the membership
And scrambling for the shore

The Coal-man and the Muscle-man
Talked on a month or so,
And then they rested on some schemes

(Conveniently low)
And all the little Jeff-men stood
And oh! they waited so!

"The time has come," said Muscle-man
"To talk of many things—
Of Palmer Weber, A.S.U.,
And confidential rings
To put the Hall upon the rocks
By secret caballings!"

"It's time to talk," the Coal-man said,
"Of other things as well;
Of leading strings, and oiled machines
With purpose to expel,
And biased rulings from the chair
Just playing general hell!"

"But wait a bit," the Jeff-men cried,
"Before we have our chat;
When do we get our membership?—
We'd like to ask you flat!"
"You never will," the Coal-man said;
They thanked him much for that.

"It seems a shame," the Coal-man said,
"To play the boys such tricks
After we've proved that being fair
And catching votes don't mix."
"Don't blush so hard," said Muscle-man;
"It's simply politics!"

"Another vote," the Coal-man said,
"Is what I chiefly need;
A seat upon the Board, besides,
Is very good indeed!"
"Go to it kid!" said Muscle-man;
"I'm ready to proceed!"

"I weep for you," said Muscle-man,
"I deeply sympathize."
With sobs and tears he sorted out
Votes of the largest size,
Holding his Special Meeting
Before his streaming eyes.

"Oh, Muscle-man," the Coal-man said,
"We've had a pleasant run;
Shall we be counting offices?"
But answer came there none—
This wasn't odd, for Muscle-man
Had gobbled every one!   —WERNER L. JANNEY

The *Mag* before World War II

One of the Jefferson Society's most important ongoing contributions to the University community, the *University of Virginia Magazine* or the *Mag*, also underwent a series of changes during the prewar period, reinventing itself at least half a dozen times between 1925 and 1940. For the *Mag*, this period was characterized by continued tumult and sporadic mismanagement as it competed for student readership. The editors tried cosmetic changes, such as altering the size of the pages or introducing color illustrations and covers, as well as wholesale directional changes to the purpose of the publication. Constantly strapped for cash (it was hundreds of dollars in debt several times) and beset by competition from humorous magazines, all of these changes were desperate attempts to attract fresh subscribers and keep the publication afloat.[77] It folded briefly during the 1926–1927 academic year, but it was revived quickly under a new name, the *Virginia Spectator*. But these tactics could not sustain interest (and more importantly, subscriptions), and by the outset of the Great Depression in 1929, publication had been suspended yet again and did not resume until 1932.[78] The great irony is that in this period of erratic publication, those issues that were produced contained some of the highest quality material the magazine had ever produced.

Throughout this time, the Jefferson Society continued in its traditional corporate role of subsidizing the publication and electing a board of directors to oversee the editorial board. But as the *Spectator* foundered, the Society was consistently drawn more deeply into its affairs to bail it out, reorganize or reestablish it, or generally atone for the editors' blunders.[79] Despite these challenges, the magazine, like its parent, the Jefferson Society, remained a vital forum for student discourse, literature, and art throughout the late 1920s and 1930s.

One of the primary concerns of the editors and the Society itself was what exactly the fundamental purpose of the publication should be. As Thelin notes, this time period was "the golden age of student journalism and student writing," during which student newspapers and magazines, including "student humor magazines," all grew and flourished.[80] This was certainly the case at the University, as *College Topics*, the *University of Virginia Magazine*, and several humorous publications—examples include the *Cavalier*, *Virginia Reel*, and the satirical *Yellow Journal*—all occupied the crowded space of student publications and were producing their most distinctive content. The issue for the *Mag* then was not whether to publish but what—should its content be informative, literary, or humorous in nature? In 1925, it focused firmly on literary content, which its editors claimed was the most worthy subject matter for such a publication, but also acknowledged was the most challenging to produce:

College magazines they say, are nineteenth century products . . . out distanced by the dailies and humorous publications. Witness the subscription lists! . . . College publications fall naturally into three classes: the journalistic, the humorous, and . . . the literary. Let the cub dash into the office with a story that is news to the news editor, and the next day he breaks into print. The veriest Freshman culls a gem from the esoteric contents of a barbershop weekly and gets it by because the editors have neglected their tonsorial obligations. Let the same men direct their efforts for the first time toward the production of essays or plays, short stories or verse, and immediately they are face to face with a wall adamantine and insurmountable to the average collegian—a task involving patience and time.[81]

However, the very same editors acknowledged the pressures facing purely literary publications. They lamented that

the college literary publication . . . faces and fights both intra- and extra-mural competitors . . . there pours against the collegiate hearthstone an endless flood of weekly and monthly magazines whose title pages carry names of premier rank. And twentieth century advertising has made possible a selling price for which a college magazine could not be printed.[82]

These questions about the fundamental mission of the publication, in conjunction with a racial scandal in 1926, derailed this iteration of the *Magazine* and forced a reevaluation of its content and purpose. Race and miscegenation were taboo subjects at the University and across the South in the 1920s. University administrators and most students expected that such vulgar topics would not be even obliquely referred to in collegiate publications. As such, when *Magazine* editor-in-chief Gilmore Spencer directly confronted not one but both issues in his October 1926 short story entitled "Mulatto Flair," there was an immediate indignant uproar on the Grounds.[83] Spencer's story detailed the pathos of a University student who discovers the local girl he is engaged to marry is, unbeknownst to her, partially black. The student struggles with whether to break off the engagement with the woman he loves or to ignore cultural mores and potential social scorn by going through with the marriage. Well written and, in retrospect, an interesting critique of the absurdity of twentieth-century racism and antimiscegenation laws, the article nonetheless overstepped the popularly held conventions for polite discourse in the 1920s. Spencer probably did not help his case by inserting what appeared to be deliberately inflammatory language, like this description of the University's first students: "seventeen students when it was founded, and they all had negro concubines. Our worthy forefathers."[84] The final straw came when Spencer, apparently in an attempt to save his reputation in the face of the negative criticism the story was receiving, broke into the *College Topics* office and withdrew "from the 'Topics' copy basket a review of the initial issue of his magazine and [submitted] in its stead a review written by himself," which commented favorably on "Mulatto Flair."[85] None the wiser, *College Topics* published Spencer's spurious review, but the switch was soon discovered and Spencer confronted.

The response from University administrators and students to "Mulatto Flair" was both swift and harsh. The administration published a broadside against the story in *College Topics*, arguing that Spencer

had absolutely no right to publish this distasteful and vulgar story, and still less had he the right to mention the University's name in any connection with it.

To say that the editor has hurt the University hardly expresses the harm done by him. Already letters are pouring in to the President from alumni and others interested in the University, demanding if such crudity and filth are typical of a "degenerating student body." There are some subjects which are not discussed by gentlemen in public nor are they published in a magazine of an untarnished reputation . . . . Southern gentlemen rebel to a man at the disgusting theme of "Mulatto Flair," while all gentlemen view with the most pronounced disfavor the linking of Virginia's name with a filthy and coarse theme of miscegenation.[86]

The editorial board of the *Magazine* met in special session to demand Spencer's resignation as editor-in-chief, and he obliged.[87] The *Magazine* enjoyed a position of such prominence on the Grounds, however, that it was not enough for Spencer to be relieved of his duties as editor; soon thereafter he was forced to leave the University in shame.[88] The *Magazine* was so integral to the culture of the University that an affront to its reputation was tantamount to an offense against the University itself. The reorganized *Magazine* staff attempted to move past the scandal, saying in the future they would not include any material "which could possibly give offense to anyone," but the damage was already done, and the *Magazine* managed to release only one more issue before suspending publication for the first time in almost one hundred years.[89]

A discussion ensued almost immediately on the Grounds about the need to revive the *Magazine* or create a new one for the University. A committee of interested students argued that this new publication should not be solely literary in nature but should also include "all those fields which are of general interest to the students of the University . . . music, drama, history, politics, international affairs, athletics, as well as the purely literary."[90] Like the previous iteration, this new endeavor garnered the sponsorship of the Jefferson and Washington Societies, as well as the added support of the Raven Society. Each organization elected one member to the board of directors.[91] The new publication took the name *Virginia Spectator* and released its first issue in December 1927 with the promise that "the spirit of the new [magazine] veers sharply from that of the old; ideals previously ignored have been set in the heavens to guide its course."[92] These new ideals would include a thoroughgoing analysis of "matters political, social, economic, educational," while "abandoning no literary aspiration."[93] The first run of the *Spectator* was short-lived however: the demise of the Washington Society deprived it of one of its sponsors, and the onset of the Great Depression in 1929 forced the suspension of the magazine for the second time in three years.

In 1932, the Jefferson Society, now working alone, again set to the task of resurrecting the magazine. By this time sentiment had shifted dramatically as to what form the publication should take. In contrast to the "ultrasedate and intellectual journal . . . printed on 'butcher paper'" of the 1920s, the new magazine, still titled the *Virginia Spectator*, "had metamorphosed . . . into a much better-looking and livelier production . . . a slick-paper publication with prose, poetry, fiction, nonfiction, drawings, a colorful cover, and some color advertising."[94] Tacking away from its predecessor's focus on topics outside the University, the new editorial policy stated the *Spectator* would be "the magazine of the University of Virginia, not a review of national and international affairs."[95] Initially under the direction of Ben Belitt, who became a nationally renowned poet later in life, the new *Spectator* published student literature, pictures and descriptions of major events on the Grounds, student drawings, and occasional humor pieces.[96] In this format, it was substantially better equipped to compete for student subscription dollars. It would continue to be published in this form until the outbreak of World War II, proving it worthy of its unofficial mascot—the phoenix—a bird which is reborn anew each time it dies.

The University at War

The specter of another war in Europe had been looming over the University for almost a decade by December 1941. Students and faculty alike had taken note of Hitler's aggression in Europe and desperately hoped to avoid another conflict like the Great War. The Jefferson Society and other student organizations held peace rallies, some students signed the Oxford Oath to never fight in an armed conflict, while still others simply hoped the United States would remain neutral even if war did break out.[97] The topic was constantly discussed at the Jefferson Society, with numerous debates, maiden speeches, and guest speakers touching on the prospects for war.[98] President Franklin Roosevelt used his address to the University's graduating class in June 1940, delivered in the newly constructed Memorial Gymnasium dedicated to veterans of World War I, to denounce Italy's surprise attack on France in support of the German invasion. Editing his speech upon hearing the news, Roosevelt castigated

Italy with the famous line, "the hand that held the dagger has stuck it into the back of its neighbor."[99] He went on to say that the United States would

extend to the opponents of force the material resources of this nation; and, at the same time, we will harness and speed up the use of those resources in order that we ourselves . . . may have equipment and training equal to the task of any emergency and every defense.[100]

Though many signs pointed to war, almost a year and a half of peace would pass after Roosevelt's speech before America and the University would once again be drawn into a global conflict.

The surprise Japanese attack on Pearl Harbor hit the University "like a thunderclap."[101] Though prior to December 1941 the University had been taking slow steps to prepare for war—for example, building a new, advanced NROTC building on the Grounds—the pace of change skyrocketed almost immediately after Pearl Harbor.[102] As Thelin notes, across the country "the 'college spirit' had conceded priority to the 'win-the-war spirit'" as young men rushed to enlist, many leaving school without regard to finishing their degrees.[103] President Newcomb pleaded with students to remain and complete their studies, but his exhortations largely fell on deaf ears. Many of those who did remain at the University pursued accelerated degree programs while simultaneously completing military training as part of the NROTC or other units that formed on the Grounds.[104] By the summer of 1942, the University of Virginia was a school at war.

The University was shaken by significant changes during World War II, with student life hit especially hard. As the *Alumni Bulletin* reported, "few industrial plants have undergone a more complete conversion to war aims than the University of Virginia."[105] Enrollment dropped precipitously in all departments: it decreased by seventy percent in the College of Arts and Sciences and by almost sixty percent in most graduate programs. The Law School was hardest hit, dropping from a peak enrollment of 405 students in 1939–1940 to only forty-four in 1944–1945. Overall enrollment fell from over 3,000 prior to the war to about 1,300 in the mid 1940s.[106] Similarly, large numbers of faculty were called into wartime service as advisors, researchers, or medical professionals.[107] Many of those who remained saw their teaching loads increase or their research redirected to support war aims. For example, the University physics department played a significant role in researching nuclear technology and developing advanced guided missiles.[108]

The students who remained at the University during the war were significantly different from the Virginia gentlemen on the Grounds in the 1920s and '30s. Roughly seventy-five percent were in some type of military program, many of whom never planned on attending college and would not have done so without the war.[109] For example, students in the Navy's popular volunteer V-12 program were assembled at the University from institutions across Virginia and the Carolinas.[110] The few not actively serving in a military capacity were still affected by the war, conscripted as air-raid wardens, auxiliary fire wardens, airplane spotters, and to fill similar support roles or simply having to adapt to wartime exigencies such as gas rationing. As such, a large portion of the wartime student body had little connection to the old University or its institutions. Jennings Wagoner and Robert Baxter note that the university lost "one of the distinctive traits it had long enjoyed—having a student population largely familiar with and sympathetic to its traditions and atmosphere. The new population seemed less amenable to tradition and more egalitarian in its orientation."[111] Some of the new students were downright derisive toward the University they now attended. In *Weather or Not*, the independent yearbook of the Army Pre-Meteorological Corps, new members of the corps were urged to "refrain from slipping into the morbid category of UVA student, or, abhor the thought, Cavalier."[112] This change in student body makeup and mindset would not bode well for the Jefferson Society or its *Spectator*, two of the oldest traditions at the University.

The Jefferson Society during World War II suffered a sharp decline in membership and limited student interest. We know comparatively little about the Society's activities during the war, as one detailed minute book ends in 1942 and the next does not pick up until 1947. What we can glean from the sporadic extant minutes and *College Topics* articles shows an organization struggling to survive. From a regular membership of almost forty, complemented by roughly fifty probationaries in 1941, only about a dozen members appeared to be attending regularly by 1942.[113] The Society initially carried on with its regular activities, electing members to the board of the *Spectator*, hearing maiden speeches, and even debating whether to award a medal to "the most competent drill student in the University Volunteer Unit."[114] In spite of these attempts at normalcy, "the question of reorganization and discontinuation of meetings" hung over Jefferson Hall.

In December 1942, the Jefferson Society was finally forced to temporarily suspend activities. Ironically, this decision was brought on at least partially by an overzealous member who believed himself to be helping the Society cope with the realities of the wartime University. Terrence Mullins, elected president of the Society on December 4, 1942, proceeded to appoint himself chair of all committees, effectively giving him dictatorial power over the organization. He justified his decision with the argument that "the committee system was a good one but that it was designed originally for a larger group."[115] He was convinced that "the Society has lacked the leadership it needs . . . there can be no dictatorship, but there can be leadership," and he "hoped the Society would cooperate; if it did, the society could be made into something."[116] The regular membership did not share Mr. Mullins's conviction, and they swiftly moved for his impeachment. Mr. Mullins abandoned his post after "a brief remark" and left the Hall.[117] This collapse in leadership appears to have been a devastating blow to the already weakened Society; it closed its doors and did not meet again for almost a year, going the way of similar student organizations, such as the Student Senate, which voted itself out of existence just one month later.[118]

The Jefferson Society reorganized in late November 1943 and continued to meet throughout the remainder of the war. It elected three veteran members—William L. Yost, Robert W. Ayers, and Robert M. Musselman, still a regular member nearly ten years after his initial election as president—to guide the organization through this period. Though the Society remained small, it is a testament to the leadership of these men that it was able to meet at all. By continuing to meet and maintain a core of members, they ensured the Society would be better positioned for growth and prosperity after the war finally ended.

Like its parent organization, the *Virginia Spectator* also folded briefly during World War II. Continuing to publish into the winter of 1943, it was forced to suspend publication when its editor-in-chief was called up for military service.[119] Other student publications suffered alongside the *Spectator*. *College Topics* also considered shutting down operations but was able to continue publishing as a smaller paper for the duration of the conflict. Similarly, *Corks and Curls* faced staff, budget, and production cuts.[120] The *Spectator* was reborn in its prewar form in September 1944, but it would soon undergo another transformation and become a more modern, humorous work.[121]

The war's end was met with relief and joy across the nation. The promise of a return of both loved ones and a state of normalcy prompted wild celebrations on V-J Day. The *Spectator* described the scene when news of Japan's surrender reached the University:

Soon streams of local vehicles pulled out of cob-webbed garages and joined the cavalcade from Rugby Road; the parade was on! The Corner now swarmed with a roaring mob of celebrants . . . after a brief but powerful demonstration, the cavalcade returned to the University. . . . The Corner by this time had become impassable with a swarm of merry makers who would have made Mardi Gras seem dull, and here the various parades which had been touring the town merged into a final demonstration.[122]

When the celebrations ended, it was time for faculty and students to turn to the task of returning their University to peacetime operation. And though the 1950s would indeed usher in an era of relative stability and prosperity nationally, they would also bring many new students and another period of rapid change to both the University and the Jefferson Society.

The Postwar University

By the time the extant Jefferson Society minutes fully resume in 1947, the University of Virginia was a radically different place than when they stopped in 1942. The *Spectator* commented on the most obvious change: "the Lawns, Ranges, fraternity houses, and even the basement of Mad Hall are stuffed like a scarecrow with straw coming out of its ears."[123] The enormous influx of returning veterans almost immediately reversed the wartime enrollment dip, and by 1946 the student population exceeded its prewar numbers. Droves of new students necessitated an equally significant expansion of the University's physical plant, and President Colgate W. Darden, who assumed office upon the retirement of President Newcomb in 1947, initiated substantial building projects on the Grounds, including an enormous new student union building.[124] These changes to the University's physical and student composition were compounded by a shift in curriculum focus, begun during the war, away from traditional liberal arts and toward the sciences, math, and engineering.[125] Taken together, these changes dramatically altered the face of the University, its environment, and the experience of students.

The Servicemen's Readjustment Act, commonly referred to as the GI Bill, had tremendous impact on both the University and American higher education as a whole, but when it was passed in 1944, it was not certain precisely what that effect would be.[126] As Thelin notes, "few expected much of the government's college plan," which guaranteed "a year of education for 90 days' service, plus one month for each month of active duty, for a maximum of 48 months."[127] Most government and education officials believed GIs would forgo college to enter the workforce immediately.[128] Nothing could have been further from the truth, as returning servicemen eagerly seized on the opportunity to advance their education and future career prospects. In the fall of 1945 only 88,000 veterans had participated in the program, but by 1946 more than one million had enrolled, a number that would grow steadily to two million by 1950.[129] The effect of the GI Bill at the University was significant. By the fall of 1946, enrollment stood at 4,204, forty percent higher than the prewar peak of 1939–1940.[130] Two-thirds of these students were returning veterans.[131]

The new students who crowded onto the Grounds did not represent a return of the prewar Virginia gentlemen who had characterized the University in the 1920s and '30s. Instead, many were middle-class veterans, some with families, but almost all of them brought a seriousness of purpose to their studies that was diametrically opposed to the University's "gentleman's C" culture.[132] As Wagoner and Baxter note, "the diversity that marked the Grounds of the University of Virginia during the war did not disappear following V-E Day or V-J Day. Virginia and other universities had been democratized by the war."[133] By and large, these men matriculated at the University of Virginia to earn a degree and enter the workforce with advanced training in fields such as engineering or business.

Luckily for the Jefferson Society, "contrary to some accounts, it is not accurate to say that veterans had no interest in traditional campus activities."[134] Indeed, the growing student population and physical size of universities in the postwar period created a sense of impersonality which drove students into smaller groups over which they could exert control. Thelin argues that overstretched administrators were all too happy to cede some level of independence to students, "the best formal manifestation" of which "was the ability of the students to incorporate and then operate elaborate student associations."[135] The changes the Jefferson Society implemented in the 1930s, augmented in the immediate postwar era, put them in a strong position to grow and prosper in this different, larger University.

The Postwar Society

In the years following the end of World War II, the Jefferson Society continued and built upon its prewar plan of serving as a forum for and conduit of student opinion. The Society resumed its custom of hosting open forum sessions at which students and faculty could discuss specific issues of University or national relevance. In 1949, the Society held a meeting focused on the topic of compulsory health insurance in the United States, an issue that remains relevant and timely more than sixty years later.[136] Closer to home, the Society regularly discussed questions such as who the University should hire as a football coach and what liquor regulations should apply to students.[137]

To highlight these open sessions, the Society leadership often invited speakers of University or national repute to address the membership and its guests. Examples during this period included Senator Harry F. Byrd, University President Colgate W. Darden, and even reclusive author John Dos Passos, particularly notable as he was "known to avoid public appearances or radio broadcasts."[138] These speakers would often engage in lively question and answer sessions with the audience, and some would even stay and enjoy a drink with the Society members upon concluding their presentations.

It was William Faulkner's address to Jefferson Hall in 1957 that best captured the spirit and purpose of these open meetings. During his time as writer-in-residence at the University for the 1957–1958 school year, Faulkner spoke or read from his works at no less than thirty-six events, totaling over twenty-eight hours of public speaking.[139] As the *Cavalier Daily* reported, most of these appearances were marked by a "strained and formal air," likely consistent with Faulkner's stated view that he was at the University to be "the writer-in-residence, not the speaker in residence."[140] His presentation to the Society, however, was a completely different affair. In the midst of the small and intimate crowd of intellectuals in Jefferson Hall, Faulkner was relaxed and affable, even puffing on his trademark pipe as he spoke.[141] After reading a passage from his novel *The Town*, Faulkner engaged with the Society on "a conversational level" and treated the

FIGURE 22. Authors William Faulkner (center) and John Dos Passos (left) at a reception following a lecture Dos Passos gave for the Jefferson Society on April 12, 1957. Photograph by Ralph Thompson. Image courtesy of the Albert and Shirley Small Special Collections Library at the University of Virginia, Accession #11252.

audience to a presentation "of Faulkner the man," not just Faulkner the author.[142] Indeed, the conversation got so personal that the *Cavalier Daily* noted that the "colorful anecdotes from his career" with which Faulkner peppered his remarks were "not entirely reprintable" in a newspaper.[143] The Society was so enamored with Faulkner that they both elected him as an honorary member and petitioned the University to create a permanent, chaired faculty position for him as writer-in-residence.[144] Just as they had with Madison and Monroe 130 years earlier, Jefferson Society members continued to pay tribute to and associate themselves with the intellectual patriarchs of their time through induction as honorary members. Similarly, they continued working to alter and improve the University curriculum in the areas of literature and oratory.

The Society also sought to expand its engagement with the University community outside of its meetings, a practice that began with the student peace rallies of the 1930s. For example, in 1949 the Society hosted Virginia gubernatorial candidates for four successive weeks in April.[145] The events, held in the Cabell Hall auditorium, were widely publicized and heavily attended by both students and faculty.[146] Similarly, the Society invited both University students and those from nearby schools for a weekend discussion session on "the future of the negro in the South . . . considering educational, economic, sociological, and political aspects."[147] An initial decision to invite only white schools was quickly denounced as "silly" and reversed to open the weekend to traditionally black colleges.[148]

In addition to reviving its prewar activities, the Jefferson Society also inaugurated several new events and opportunities to engage with the University community. Perhaps most significant of these was the Moomaw Oratorical Contest. The Society had conducted its annual oratorical contest sporadically for the past decade, but without the financial means to offer a substantial prize (the gold medals originally awarded in the nineteenth century now proved too expensive), the events were weakly attended and did not generate the level of student interest shown in the past.[149] This changed in 1948 when Dr. Benjamin C. Moomaw, an 1899 graduate of the Medical School and Society alumnus, was invited to speak on his reminiscences of the Society at the turn of the century. After concluding his speech, Moomaw remained for the meeting, while the membership debated holding an oratorical contest open to all students. So impressed with the Society's continued dedication to oratory, Moomaw rose to speak at the meeting's end:

Dr. Moomaw was recognized and he proceeded to commend the Society on their fostering such upstanding projects as the oratorical contest. He capped his discussion by saying that he wanted to present the Society with a rotating cup or trophy to be awarded the Outstanding Orator annually. When the sudden proposal had had time to sink in the assembled members' minds, there occurred a spontaneous clapping that has rarely been heard in the Hall.[150]

Now backed by a notable benefactor, the Society's oratorical contest would once again become a coveted prize at the University for both members and nonmembers alike.

The first annual iteration of this new contest was held over three successive nights in May 1948. It proved to be a hard-fought battle with eighteen speakers, nine each speaking the first two nights and the best six competing in the final round at the Society meeting on Friday night.[151] In the end, Morris B. Brown took home the prize, an "onyx and gold-leaf framed rag print of the University before the Rotunda fire," with his speech on "Logistics."[152] It was later shortened to one night. Moomaw continued to attend the event each succeeding year, and in 1951 he announced that he would "establish an endowment fund for the continuation of the Oratory Contest after his death."[153] The annual Moomaw Oratorical Contest continues to be one of the Jefferson Society's most exciting and valuable contributions to the University community.

During this time the Society engaged more directly in University student politics. The power to nominate candidates for student government positions had typically been exercised by the two "political societies" on the Grounds, Lambda Pi and Skull and Keys. These bodies were typically filled from the ranks of the social fraternities, and while Jefferson Society men certainly rose to prominence in both groups, the Society as a rule did not directly participate in either one.[154] In the late 1950s, the Society chose a path of involvement in student politics more in line with its traditionally nonpartisan stance, when the members decided to hold a public debate among the student candidates for office.[155] In the *Cavalier Daily* (formerly *College Topics;* it changed its name in 1948), the Society stated its goal was to "provide the means by which students may make sound decisions concerning their representatives," while not passing judgment or stating opinions about any of the speakers.[156] This debate received significant media attention and was hailed as "an unprecedented forum" and "the first of its kind" in the history of University student government.[157] The event, which was also endorsed by both political societies, was moderated by Society president Benet Gellman and consisted of four-minute speeches by each candidate followed by questions from the audience.[158] It was of such significance that it was recorded and broadcast on the University's radio station, WUVA.[159] The Society leadership had found yet another successful way to engage the University beyond the walls of Jefferson Hall.

Postwar Membership

Despite the valiant efforts of the members who sustained the Society through the war, student participation had dropped precipitously during the conflict, and the active membership remained very small in the late 1940s. Meetings were repeatedly adjourned on account of low attendance, with the minutes recording on one particular occasion in 1946 that there were only "five members present—most deplorable."[160] By 1947 there were still only thirty-six regular members, and *College Topics* noted that despite its contributions of "immeasurable worth" to student life, the Society still had to go "abegging for active members."[161] There was nothing new here; the Society continuously needed to compete for student attention with the myriad social and intellectual groups on the ever-expanding Grounds of the University. In an effort to attract members, the Society once again reformed two crucial parts of its character: the membership and probationary processes and its social environment, both in and out of meetings.

Throughout the 1940s and '50s, the Society refined the new membership processes it had implemented in the immediate prewar period, bringing them in line with the practices of other major University organizations. Prospective members were to submit a written application describing their interest in the Society and then would meet for a brief discussion with several regular members before being considered for probationary membership.[162] While not yet a formal interview, this process did help to ensure that those students most interested and therefore most likely to become active regular members were identified and admitted. The Society was careful to stress that even with this more structured procedure there was no limit on the number of probationaries who could be accepted, and "it is by no means necessary that a student interested in joining the Society have any extensive background in debating or writing. For the Society exists 'for the purpose of debate and literary improvement.'"[163]

To ensure sufficient applicants, the Society advertised more heavily to prospective members. These advertisements often took the form of *Cavalier Daily* articles touting the value of membership in the Society or reports about its activities to entice students to apply. One such article in 1956 noted:

Jefferson Hall remains as the last place in the University where a student may seriously discuss a topic under orderly parliamentary procedure. Its active members range in age from the teens to the sixties and come from all departments of the University. As much as they are separated individually they all have one thing in common, a desire to improve themselves intellectually. It is this desire that has enabled the Jefferson Society to go into its one hundred and thirty-first year as strong as the day it was organized.[164]

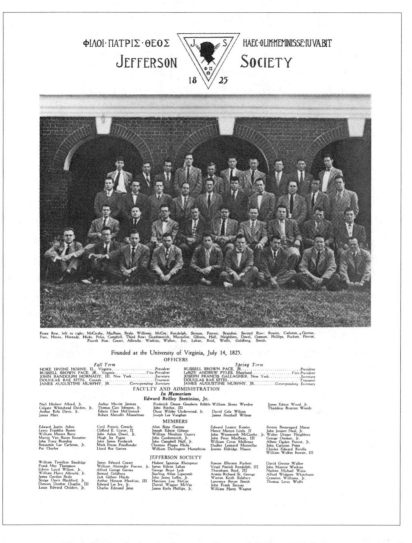

FIGURE 23. The Jefferson Society in the 1950 edition of *Corks and Curls*. Image courtesy of the Albert and Shirley Small Special Collections Library at the University of Virginia, *Corks and Curls* 62 (1950): 278.

The introduction of probationary membership in 1935 had moved the Society closer to the practice of social fraternities and other organizations with similar pledging periods. After the war, the probationary process was changed to admit "classes" of probationaries at fixed times during the academic year.[165] Previously, prospective probationaries were considered and accepted almost continuously, usually in small groups but sometimes one at a time. The introduction of classes fostered a greater sense of cohesion among the groups of probationaries who were admitted together, similar to a fraternity pledge class. These new members navigated the challenges of joining the Society together and even elected a probationary class chairman to represent them.[166] It also aligned the acceptance of new probationaries with both the semester-based calendar the University adopted in the 1948–1949 academic year and the recruitment process used by other University-wide social groups, indicating that commitment as a probationary member was on par with joining these other organizations.[167]

The membership preserved the lighter tenor of weekly meetings pioneered in the 1930s and relaxed the tone even further. With University culture becoming more liberal, topics that once would have been considered taboo were now discussed openly in Jefferson Hall. For example, in 1950, the Society hosted a "free love" night, which focused around a debate on whether "the practice of free love should be adopted by society."[168] The members in attendance were asked to fill out and eventually discuss surveys on their "sex experiences."[169] As might have been expected, this portion of the meeting was closed to all but members.

Beyond the sometimes risqué subject matter, meetings were made more jovial by the growing presence and consumption of alcohol in Jefferson Hall. While not yet the raucous atmosphere that would prevail in the late 1960s and '70s, beer and other libations began replacing the traditional cookies and ice cream as refreshments in the Hall. In 1947, an early mention of the soon to be ubiquitous beer keg in the Hall appears in the minutes, with a Mr. Russell suggesting that a keg "be in evidence at the Tuesday meeting," which was "very warmly received by the Society."[170] On the evening of the "free love" debate, the *Cavalier Daily* noted that "to ease any hot and parched throats worn dry by the fire of debate, a plentiful supply of foaming refreshment from Charlottesville's leading tea room, Carroll's, will be on hand."[171] Similarly, after each class of probationaries was inducted into the Society, the membership would typically break for beer "in honor of the initiation" and to offer congratulatory toasts to the new members.[172]

In addition to the lighter atmosphere of many regular meetings, the Society also began placing greater emphasis on—and dedicating more time to—probationary speeches. Evolving from the earlier maiden speeches, the probationary speech was now described as the "most important part of the probationary period," and offering a passing presentation became a *sine qua non* of being accepted as a regular member.[173] Significant time each week was dedicated to these speeches and the ensuing regular member critiques; sometimes seven or more probationaries would present in one evening.[174] If a probationary's speech was unacceptable to the Hall, they would typically be required to continue presenting, either that night or at a later time, until the regular membership was satisfied they had corrected the deficiencies of their original speech.[175] On the other side of the spectrum, beginning in the 1950s probationaries who gave exemplary speeches could be considered for the Best of Semester award, recognizing the probationary in each class who gave the most outstanding speech. Despite the importance and attention placed on these speeches, some members clearly would have preferred to spend less time on dry presentations and more on free love talks or enjoying themselves at the keg. In 1957, one frustrated secretary recorded that after the initial meeting program was concluded, "with a sigh of helpless resignation, the Hall settled back for its weekly dose of Probationary castor-oil."[176]

Society members also socialized more regularly outside of scheduled meetings during this period. Many of the long-running Society traditions that had been cancelled during the war, such as the Founder's Day Banquet, were revived. Other new, less formal activities were designed to capture the attention of the postwar University student. For example, in 1950, the Society sponsored a party for members and their dates at a cabin six miles from Charlottesville overlooking the Rivanna River.[177] The revelers were brought to the cabin by hay truck, and beer and other "liquid refreshments" were liberally provided.[178] The event was well publicized in the *Cavalier Daily*, at least partially to show prospective members the potential social advantages of joining the Society.

Amid the advertisements, membership drives, parties, probationary process changes, and sometimes veritable desperation for new members, one group of students was conspicuously absent from the Jefferson Society's efforts—women. Although women would not be admitted to the College of Arts and Sciences until 1970, female students had been enrolled in graduate and professional schools since 1920, at which time the Society voted to formally bar them from regular membership.[179] Numerous attempts to reverse this policy were undertaken throughout the 1940s and '50s, both from within the Society and from without. In 1949, a Mrs. Taliaferro applied to be a probationary member in direct contravention of the restriction on female membership. Her "case . . . was discussed by the Hall," but the membership eventually decided to uphold the ban with the provision that "Mrs. Taliaferro be informed of the Constitution's ruling against taking in women applicants."[180] The question also was raised and intensely debated in 1957, but once again the regular membership voted against lifting the constitutional bar.[181] Indeed, more than fifteen years would pass before the Society voted to admit women, becoming the last major student group on the Grounds to do so.

Its refusal to consider a large and growing portion of the student body for membership notwithstanding, the Society's efforts to rebuild itself after World War II were successful. The combination of external University engagement and internal reforms and adaptations increased the Society's appeal and prestige, bringing in countless new members. From the "deplorable" membership of five in 1946, the Society grew to more than one hundred regular members and fifty probationaries by 1954.[182] The Jefferson Society, like the *Spectator*, once again proved itself a phoenix, able to rise from the point of extinction brought on by war, reinvent itself, and thrive in the new and ever changing University.

The Postwar Magazine

Like its sponsor, the Jefferson Society, the *Virginia Spectator* also reorganized and grew in the postwar era. Forced to shutter operations due to wartime exigencies, the *Spectator* resumed publication in 1944 with a triumphant proclamation: "And so, patient reader, the *Spectator* rises from its ashes once again."[183] Despite the pomp, the operation remained small for several years, with the editorial board admitting they were forced to take "a somewhat radical deviation from a century-old editorial policy," as "wartime conditions having all but depleted the University's supply of literati, the harassed Board of Directors has been placed in the uncomfortable position of producing the magazine until conditions become more normal."[184] Gradually, however, the publication recovered and prospered. By 1947 the editorial board had grown to thirty-two strong, including editors for sports, photography, and literature.[185] From barely publishing one issue in 1944, the *Spectator* now put out seven high-quality magazines per year. Indeed, it gained such prominence on the Grounds that a Society member was moved to comment that "*Spectator* has become the University's magazine not the Hall's."[186]

As the University moved toward the 1950s, the *Spectator* began to change and adapt its content to the new student generation. Cognizant of its audience, the magazine continued its pivot from serious literary content to humorous collegiate satire. The editorial board boasted in 1949 that "the Openings issue . . . will have twice the usual number of jokes and cartoons," this due to the "increased demand from both students and various girls' schools." A publication once composed of original student literature and criticism now found its pages filled with jocular articles, color pictures of University events and parties, and illustrations in the style of the *New Yorker*. In 1956, the *Cavalier Daily* reflected on the cause of this change:

In 1944, as the war drew to a close and the veterans returned to the University, tired of battle and hungry to let off steam, the Spectator placed more and more emphasis on humor and added Rugby Road and Exchange Humor Sections . . . the current editorial policy was adapted wherein the Spectator attempts to both entertain and construct, to amuse and to provoke, to satisfy and to stimulate, to strike a balance between the old Spectator and the new.[187]

In a similar manner to the Jefferson Society itself, the *Spectator* continued tailoring its content to the tastes and demands of the current student generation in order to remain relevant and successful.

This new *Spectator* was met with enthusiasm and remained highly successful throughout the early 1950s. While continuing to struggle off and on with the problems typical of student publications—limited funding and high editorial turnover—the *Spectator* enjoyed a period of significant growth and prosperity. It increased both the frequency and size of its print runs, at points publishing biweekly and distributing hundreds of copies outside the Grounds of the University, especially to nearby women's colleges.[188] It became "quite a famous college publication," with national publications featuring reprints of its cartoons and other universities constantly writing to ask "how best to set up a magazine such as [the *Spectator*], inquiring into [its] methods of publishing, printing, and handling material."[189] Indeed, even editors at the *New Yorker*, the *Spectator*'s iconic role model, regularly reviewed its pages looking for promising young talent.[190]

But not everyone at the University was pleased with the *Spectator*'s burgeoning success. Critics in the student body and administration alike

often found its content too risqué and inappropriate for a collegiate publication. A disparaging editorial in the *Cavalier Daily* pronounced "that
the consistent emphasis on sex and drinking in this magazine shows a lack
of originality and independence of thought on the part of its contributors." The author went on to opine: "Let it be known that some of us at
Virginia have interests other than these and would sincerely like to see
a third subject introduced by the publication . . . glancing through the
September issue, one gets the impression that even our gas stations and
furniture stores are obsessed with the subject of sex."[191]

The contributors and editors of the *Spectator* did little to blunt these
criticisms; indeed, as the 1950s wore on they published increasingly
controversial material to the dismay of conservative members of the
University community. In 1953, an issue on the contentious question
of coeducation at the University was lambasted as tantamount to positioning the University "as a gang of nine year old boys who don't want
little girls in their club because it would destroy their reputation as 'he-
men.'"[192] A "Confederate issue" published in 1954, featuring cover art of
a triumphant Robert E. Lee posing with his foot on the defeated body of
Ulysses S. Grant, drew further condemnation. The issue contained satirical newspaper clippings celebrating a southern victory in the Civil War
and, according to a *Spectator* spokesman quoted in the *Cavalier Daily*,
advocated the "obvious supremacy of the South over the North."[193] In
1957, it published a "Jim Crow issue," which caused the editor-in-chief
to resign in disgust, stating that he "did not think it was the kind of thing
the magazine should print."[194] While the issue featured William Faulkner
as a moderator and sought to maintain a balanced stance on the issue of
integration by including arguments on both sides of the question, as was
the case with "Mulatto Flair" in the 1920s, simply raising the subject of
integration was viewed as incendiary.

The final straw came in late 1957 with the publication of an edition
modeled after the British humor magazine *Punch*. Entitled "Paunch," it
featured a litany of bawdy jokes and barely veiled sexual innuendos. University president Colgate Darden himself was lewdly lampooned in a full-
page cartoon as a scantily clad biblical Sampson pulling down the pillars
of student self-governance—the Inter-Fraternity Council and Student
Council. The *Cavalier Daily* dubbed the issue a "classic" and lauded it for
including "more jokes than ever printed before, including several full-
page cartoon illustrations."[195] Dabney notes that "the consensus among

the students, with few exceptions, seemed to be that the 'Paunch' issue was one of the best ever."[196]

Unfortunately for the *Spectator*, the University administration did not share these sentiments.[197] An unidentified senior faculty member contacted President Darden to complain that the content was obscene and not fit to be associated with the University.[198] Darden appointed a committee of four faculty members chaired by Dean of Women Roberta Gwathmey to investigate the allegation.[199] Though the committee stopped short of labeling the issue "obscene," it delivered the unanimous indictment that it discredited "the name of the University of Virginia," which the *Cavalier Daily* noted is "traditionally one of the most serious [charges] that can be leveled against . . . a publication."[200]

This damning accusation began a process that eventually forced the permanent suspension of the *Spectator*. President Darden submitted a letter condemning the publication's actions to the Board of Visitors, in which he accused the *Spectator* of "coarseness and vulgarity which are utterly out of keeping with the innate good taste which has distinguished the University of Virginia."[201] The board voted to endorse Darden's letter and eventually agreed to ban the *Spectator* permanently from publication.[202] Numerous attempts were made to revive the magazine shortly after this decision, including under the new title *Harlequin*, but the force of the administration's condemnation of the publication was too great to be overcome. After over a century of publication under various titles, the phoenixlike *Spectator* never again rose from the ashes as a student publication at the University of Virginia.

Shortly before the *Spectator*'s final demise, the Jefferson Society sought to remedy one of the major deficiencies raised by its critics—the total disappearance of any meaningful literary or intellectual content from its pages. In 1956, Alex Whitaker, a former *Spectator* editor, approached the Society to request their sponsorship of a second student publication. Like the *Magazine* and previous iterations of the *Spectator*, this new work was to be "strictly literary in nature," and its contents would include "short stories, informal essays, formal essays of criticism, book reviews of books of student interest, poetry, drama, music reviews, and critical papers in philosophy, foreign affairs, architecture, and English."[203] In April 1956, the new magazine published its first issue under the old title *University of Virginia Magazine* while also reverting to the simple, text-heavy format of the original *Magazine*. The first issue held true to its promise to focus on content of "a rather serious nature," including articles such as "The Impact of the West on the Middle East" and "JD Salinger, an Appraisal."[204]

While the new publication met with positive reviews by students, the new *Magazine* struggled financially. Immediately after the first issue, the editorial board released an appeal in the *Cavalier Daily* stating that "the *Magazine* is in need of financial support, and donations and subscriptions are welcomed."[205] While these financial difficulties eventually proved insurmountable, the new *Magazine* continued publishing quality literary content well into the 1960s, significantly longer than its ill-fated counterpart—the *Spectator* in its humorous form.

Conclusion

Just thirty-five years after its Centennial Celebration, the Jefferson Society had evolved into a new organization, fighting for a place on the stage at a larger, modernizing University. Hobbled by the penury of the Great Depression, then temporarily disbanded during World War II, the Society was forced to continually adapt and evolve, both internally and in its dealings with the University community, to remain relevant to each successive generation of students. Importantly, however, even amid the almost constant changes, the Society never lost sight of its original and ultimate purpose—to be a home for curious minds at the University seeking intellectual improvement. The ability to constantly revolutionize itself while remaining true to its core ideals ensured that the Jefferson Society thrived under these pressing challenges. Indeed, the Society found itself on its strongest footing in recent memory as it prepared to enter the raucous 1960s.

CHAPTER SEVEN

Finding a Place in the Beer-Keg Hall

1960–1980

The decade of the 1950s was a prosperous era of boom and technological progress, when the automobile reigned supreme and strength of the American family grew apace with consumer culture. The 1960s and 1970s brought protest and social unrest to the United States—African Americans and women clamored for civil rights, and the younger generation railed against the Vietnam War. At universities across the country, enrollment swelled with the first of the baby boomers, and institutions of higher learning raced to hire new faculty members, expand and create infrastructure, and break new ground in the study of science and technology. The idea of a "comprehensive university" took hold, and the trend toward professionalization of both education and in the faculty ranks that began in the early twentieth century came to fruition.[1]

The University of Virginia changed dramatically during this era. African American students began to attend the University in very small numbers in the 1950s and in larger numbers in the 1960s; by the late '60s and 1970s the school began actively working toward integration instead of gradual desegregation. Women entered the College of Arts and Sciences for the first time in 1970. Under the leadership of Rhodes Scholar Edgar F. Shannon, the fourth president of the University (1959–1974), the University of Virginia gained recognition for its academic rigor and the caliber of its scholarship. Spurred by the arrival of students from different cultural and socioeconomic backgrounds and by coeducation, the University began to shed its reputation as an institution devoted to maintaining social status—one where a gentleman's C was good enough to get by—and developed into a school that could offer a high-quality education to students willing to work hard.[2]

Frank Hereford took over for Edgar Shannon in 1974, serving as the fifth president of the University for eleven years before returning to teaching in 1985. The University continued to expand under Hereford, who led a major capital campaign that increased the University's endowment from $97 million to more than $280 million, allowing for the creation of almost two hundred new endowed professorships by 1993.[3] Under his leadership, the Office of African American Affairs was established in August 1976, and student protests in 1980 put pressure on his administration to recruit more African American faculty. By the end of his tenure in 1985, there were 1,198 African American students, representing almost 7% of the total student body. This diversity changed the fundamental character of the University of Virginia for the better, but issues of race continue to be crucial problems for the University to address. Access to the University and graduation rates for African American students, as well as the recruitment of African American faculty, remain areas where significant progress is needed.[4]

Together, Shannon and Hereford led the University of Virginia through a quarter of a century fraught with challenges, controversy, and unrest, but it was a time that also allowed for great change and improvement. In the words of John Casteen, who assumed the president's office in 1990:

As professor, faculty leader and provost, [Hereford] worked hand-in-glove with Edgar F. Shannon Jr., his predecessor as president, to conceive or imagine the University as it became in his time. As president, he continued building the graduate school, led with quiet courage in the work that created real diversity within the University and set the goal of making it the best public institution in America. He was a quiet, thoughtful, passionately principled man who knew right and wrong when he saw them and sided firmly with right.[5]

Desegregation, coeducation, the growth of research programs, the expansion of the Grounds beyond the Lawn and Jefferson's Academical Village to provide a supporting research infrastructure, and the bolstering of the modern endowment were all significant, pathbreaking changes that Shannon and Hereford saw to fruition.

By the 1960s the University of Virginia had begun to resemble what we know as a modern comprehensive university, complete with multiple schools, a mushrooming administrative structure, big-time athletics, dozens if not hundreds of student organizations, and a student body that numbered over 5,000 by 1960 and doubled that by 1970.[6] Growth at universities everywhere profoundly affected student life. Frederick Rudolph writes:

During all the years of university growth, the extracurriculum played a major role in sustaining collegiate values. The athletic teams, fraternities and social clubs, theater groups, newspapers, and magazines, all of these various enterprises not only allowed young undergraduates to emulate and prepare for life, but also provided them with experiences they knew to be profoundly human. Just as the extracurriculum in the collegiate era was a response to the sterility of the curriculum, in the university era it became a compensation for the one-sided intellectuality and the overwhelming impersonality of the official scheme of things.[7]

Long gone were the days when the Jefferson Society could expect to be the most important student organization, when the social elites of the University would automatically compete for its leadership positions, and when the Society played a central role in the affairs of the University simply by virtue of its history and well-regarded place on the Grounds. To continue to thrive, the Jefferson Society would have to adapt to the changing University environment yet again, just as it had with the arrival of fraternities and athletics at the turn of the century.

The Society's continued survival in the face of its declining political importance was due in no small part to its constant home close to the heart of the University: Jefferson Hall. Although the president of the Society no longer enjoyed the privilege of speaking to the whole University alongside dignitaries at Final Exercises or being the most recognizable student leader on the Grounds, the age-old meeting room on the West Range continued to offer an idyllic setting for students to engage with each other. Student leaders were drawn to the place where Woodrow Wilson had spent so much of his time as a young man, though most now came to enjoy discussion and the company of other members rather than to position themselves socially and politically. In the more diverse University community, the needs and expectations placed on students to be successful were changing, and a new premium was placed on interacting with intelligent, engaged students of varying backgrounds. By the 1970s, members came from all schools and all corners of the University and held as many views on politics, society, and the world as there were chairs to fill in Jefferson Hall. They debated with as much tenacity and skill as ever, and the Hall echoed with the voices of yet another generation of talented orators. The inclusion of members from all schools at the University stood in marked contrast to the way most other major student organizations operated by this time; law and medical students had all but disappeared from the ranks of fraternities, student publications, and athletic teams, which drew their membership almost exclusively from undergraduates beginning in the decades following World War II. The continued inclusion of graduate and professional students made the Jefferson Society unique in this respect.[8]

In 1961, the *Cavalier Daily* remarked of the Society, "Changing times have brought about a transition of her nature to that of a general discussion group, which she is today."[9] The Society had repositioned itself as a place where leaders from across the University could come to discuss and debate important topics and enjoy the company of other like-minded students. This was a departure from the days when political contests and social positioning were the primary factors that drove students to Jefferson Hall. A large number of other student organizations had emerged through which politically minded students could pursue their ambitions, such as Skull and Keys and Lambda Pi (both political societies that furnished platforms and candidates for major leadership positions in Student Council and individual schools). The Jefferson Society shifted its energies away from such pursuits and focused more on debate, literature, and wit—seeking to attract members who would contribute to lively and intellectual discussion.[10] The Society often played host to debates between candidates for Student Council, chair of the Honor Committee, and other positions, but it furnished candidates for those posts from among the membership with less frequency.[11]

In Jefferson Hall, students could find what was described as an "intellectual grab-bag" for their enjoyment and edification.[12] The Society established a regular series of guest speakers that was open to the public, drawing public figures and scholars to the Hall to share their knowledge with the membership and their guests. The Society invited speakers who, true to the oath taken by every member since the 1820s, represented a diversity of opinion and perspective and who might teach something not available in the regular classroom.

Speakers were one way that the Society maintained itself as a venue for discourse, but members themselves also debated timely issues including American foreign policy, voting rights, gender issues, and economic and trade policy. They followed and discussed current events, adjourning, for example, to Newcomb Hall on October 7, 1960, to watch the second televised presidential debate between John F. Kennedy and Richard Nixon—an unprecedented event in American political life and the field of debate.[13] It was now possible for the entire country to watch as two presidential candidates faced off, testing each other on the battlefield of debate, and the Society's members felt they should be engaged in the nation's political processes.

On a sadder note, not more than three years later, on November 22, 1963, "the Hall met briefly a few hours after President Kennedy had been assassinated and voted to send the following messages via telegram":

Mrs. John F. Kennedy, Washington:

Our heartfelt sympathy goes out to you and your children in this hour of great sadness. With the rest of the world we mourn the loss of the President, a great statesman, a great leader, a great man. May God be with you.

THE JEFFERSON SOCIETY, UNIVERSITY OF VIRGINIA

Lyndon B. Johnson, President of the United States, Washington:

As we mourn with the Nation and the world the tragic loss of John Fitzgerald Kennedy we pause to express our sincere confidence as you assume the grave responsibilities of the leadership of the Republic. May God grant you strength and courage in this hour.

THE JEFFERSON SOCIETY, UNIVERSITY OF VIRGINIA

The Hall adjourned immediately, the program for the evening having been canceled out of respect for the late President.[14]

Johnson acknowledged the Society's well wishes a few days later, promising to "cherish your prayers and support in the days ahead."[15]

As a forum for discussion, the Society enjoyed continued success, attracting more members than ever, even if they made up a smaller portion of the total student body. By the 1970s, the Society included members drawn from all corners of the University—including African Americans and women—a far cry from the plantocracy of the antebellum era and the Virginia social elite of the turn of the century.

"Don't Go Down to the Hall, My Son!"

Despite the characterization of the Society as a discussion group or forum, the Hall took on a distinctly social character in the mid to late twentieth century that often eclipsed any intellectualism or academic pursuit on the part of members. The minutes of each meeting portray a jovial scene, with members cracking jokes at each other's expense and stopping at nothing to gain the upper hand in a battle of wits and rhetoric within a group of worthy adversaries. Meetings lost much of the structure that had guided the proceedings in previous decades, and rigidly organized presentations and arguments gave way to more playful, informal, and witty banter.

After the evening's program, if one was scheduled, members came and went as they pleased, stopping by for a drink and a quick debate or heckling whoever was making an announcement (which was more often than not the treasurer pleading futilely with everyone to pay their dues or suffer some uncertain but surely dire consequence). It was the president's job to try to bring some semblance of order to bear on Friday evenings in the Hall, wailing upon his desk with the gavel in an effort to gain everyone's attention, and it fell to the secretary to chronicle this chaos in the minutes.

In jest, the Society made the decision to stipulate that meetings should begin at 7:29 p.m. so that members might actually arrive by 7:30, when meetings in those years were supposed to begin. At one point, even after the 7:29 time had been enshrined in the constitution, a joking "Mr. T. Harry moved that we begin meetings at 7:29—to help with attendance. It was now 10:30 and most of the members had arrived and voted down this absurd effort toward efficiency and responsibility."[16] In reality, meetings began whenever the president arrived and really got down to business when the vice president finally came in with a guest speaker in tow. Suffice it to say that every Friday meetings began "at the usual, though well past the appointed, hour."[17] The bizarre hour of 7:29 remains the appointed time for meetings to this day, disregarded with more or less impunity.

Meeting minutes often made light of the Sisyphean task of bringing the Hall to order on time. "Mr. Friedman's little wooden anvil first quailed under the solemn blows of the gavel at exactly 7:29 . . . plus 10 minutes, more or less."[18] Sometimes neither the president nor the vice president were present to make the call to order, and some opportunistic lower officer might boldly seize the chair. On May 12, 1961, for example,

Neither the President nor the Vice-President had arrived by 7:45, and the Secretary saw the situation as his chance of the year. With a cry of "Now I am Caesar!", he pounced upon the gavel, and began pounding with it noisily. Nothing happened. In uncomprehending disbelief, he hammered more vigorously. But it was no use—the members were too busy trying to get some beer to take any notice. Directly, the President arrived, and Mr. Henderson, his eyes wet with tears, yielded the gavel in bewildered resignation and went back to his dusty books. Thus ended the Beer-Hall Putsch, 1961.[19]

There were any number of reasons that it might have been a bit difficult to get going: guest speakers rarely arrived on time, and on April 22, 1960, the president arrived only to find that "Mr. Abraham . . . had thoughtfully locked up the secretary's books, safe from the Society, lest some fool scribble in them."[20]

In theory, the first order of business was to read and approve the minutes from the previous meeting. The secretary would take the lectern for a playful retelling of what had transpired the previous Friday, at least according to him. The president was frequently cast as a tyrant ruling with an iron fist over goodly members of the Hall, and the protagonist and leader more often than not, by sheer coincidence, was the secretary himself. The meeting of October 23, 1964, opened to the following scene:

Following the call to order by Mr. Ewers, the roll and minutes were read and accepted with some totally unjustified reservations. In a crass display of naked and arbitrary power, our self-styled Caesar otherwise known as Lathan the Terrible dared to order certain passages of the minutes stricken from the record. Temporarily overwhelmed by such dark and ominous forces of despotic dictatorship, this writer has vowed to persevere until more enlightened forces have restored the equilibrium of justice.[21]

Conniving members would deftly outmaneuver each other with dazzling displays of parliamentary procedure (in the most fast-and-loose sense of the term), and the Society seemed to mock its own tradition of using committees to conduct its business. Alongside the now long-standing bodies like the Program and Membership committees, to which the president could make appointments, the Society created and maintained committees on more trivial matters, some of which conducted their business over a short span of weeks. The Society's Onion Dip Commission looked into the troubling lack of tasty cream dip at the 1972 midsummers meeting, a project that lasted for the entire fall semester.[22] Members were quite attentive to the committee's investigation and report about this very troubling issue. A few years earlier, the Society's Committee on Un-Jeffersonian Activities had conducted a thorough witch hunt to uncover those Society members secretly harboring unpatriotic thoughts against the University's founder and the Society's namesake.[23] True to the example set by Senator McCarthy, everyone eventually came under suspicion.

The good humor of meetings was fueled in part by alcohol. In place of ice cream from Monticello Dairy, a keg of beer started to make regular appearances in the back corner of the Hall, and it seemed to be a more popular subject of attention for the membership than whoever happened to be speaking at the lectern. The customary keg, along with the members' antics, earned this generation of the Hall the nickname in some circles of the "Beer and Bullshit Society." A new leadership position was introduced, one that came to rival the responsibility of the president: the Keeper of the Keg, whose task it was to ensure that a fresh keg (or two) made its way to the Hall each week. The keeper was the last position elected each semester, and the minutes from the spring 1972 elections tell us that:

Only a fool would have refused nomination to the final, and most important office in the Society, that of the Keeper of the Keg. Probationaries ought early to be instructed in the significance of this duty. Candidates for the keepership are a select and elite breed—longer of tooth than most, stouter of heart than any, morally and physically well-suited to bear the raiments of office with grace and dignity.[24]

Failure in this important duty spelled nothing short of disaster for the Society, which depended on the keg to fuel their debates well into the early morning hours. Meeting recesses turned into beer breaks, and the meetings concluded in striking harmony with the moment the keg was pronounced to have run dry.[25] This scene was immortalized in the verse of Secretary Joseph Freeman, who composed a ballad in 1963 that became known as the "Ode to Jefferson Hall":

"Don't go down to the Hall, my son!"
So pleaded the gray-haired dame,
"Stay away from the Jeff Hall crowd, dear boy,
You'll never be the same."

"Fear not, dear mother," the youth replied,
"There's naught to fear on ole West Range.
The Devil shan't turn me from righteous paths
I promise my ways won't change."

So this fair haired youth put his rep tie on
And polished his weejuns bright,
He kissed his mother's faded cheek
And walked out on that fateful night.

For yards around the Hall's bright lights
Filled the rain-swept night with cheer.
As our proud young lad neared Jefferson Hall
He heard the unmistakable gurgling of beer.

The smell of tobacco and the fragrance of brew
Nearly knocked the lad off his feet
Then someone gave him a brim-full cup
And pushed him into a seat.

Then young Southern gentlemen, charming and neat,
Filled the air with speech and invective.
Their flair for discourse without getting hoarse
Left our youth very reflective.

Occasionally Yankees were allowed to squawk
In spite of their unfortunate birth.

This generosity on the part of the Hall
Impressed the lad of its worth.

But then the wild talk started to fly,
Talk of hard liquor and Madison women;
With the third, then the fourth, then the fifth
Cup of beer, the boy's innocent head went spinning.

It would take too long to recount the rest,
But virtue did not win.
That lad's long walk from his home to the Hall
Was the journey from purity to sin.

So now he's caught in the insidious web,
He's enslaved by the spell of the Hall,
And each Friday night as her son staggers off,
The mother will make this sad call:

"Don't go down to the Hall, my son!
Don't go!" cries the grey-haired dame;
"Stay away from the Jeff Hall crowd, my son;
You'll never be the same."
                                        —JOSEPH FREEMAN[26]

By the mid-1970s, the humor in the Society had risen to new levels, particularly in the secretary's minutes. In the place of carefully recorded transcriptions of the proceedings, the minutes from Friday nights in the Hall grew increasingly outlandish, and they sought more and more to entertain rather than bear any resemblance to what actually transpired during the meeting. Seemingly every week, the minutes became more elaborate as secretaries yearned to keep the Hall entertained, morphing into parodies of popular literary tropes, with Society members cast in key roles. Each meeting followed a different story, and the minutes took a different form, whether as an epic poem, a Greek tragedy, a letter from James Madison to Thomas Jefferson, a suite of Mother Goose nursery rhymes, a sports telecast, an Ian Fleming tale of James Bond, or, in what was perhaps the pièce de résistance from this time period, a screenplay parody of *Gone with the Wind*, aptly called "a cinematic extravaganza in 4½ Acts."[27]

One can imagine the cheers of Society members at a secretary's perfectly constructed joke, or the hisses coming from a member smarting after being hit with a fresh insult. Secretaries were no longer meant to record the proceedings; instead, they were rather like a flaneur, making their way through the Society and entertaining the members with tales of their own absurdity each week. Roy Alson, the secretary in spring 1973, offered some parting thoughts at the end of his term:

Were I able to counsel some as yet unborn scribe of the society, I would say to him: if you really want successful minutes, write then in verse. Poetry—or rather, doggerel,—is greatly appreciated in the Hall. An audience that likes rhymes is ideal for the harried Secretary. As long as your metre isn't atrocious and the end words of most lines rhyme, nobody really cares what you put in between. Consider yourself blessed if you can sing.[28]

As one might imagine, the minutes have contained very little in the way of substantive information ever since, as the scales tipped toward inside jokes and gossip.

Members of the Hall enjoyed great camaraderie, which translated to new traditions and renewed interest in some old ones, like the Founder's Day Banquet. In conjunction with Founder's Day, the Society began to make an annual pilgrimage at dawn to Jefferson's home, Monticello, on the morning of April 13, the founder's birthday. Harrison Bush led the first Dawn Pilgrimage in 1968, and Society members laid a wreath at Jefferson's grave, as they have every year since.[29] Another new tradition developed sometime before 1970, when a mailbox was affixed to the door of Jefferson Hall into which members (or anyone else, for that matter) could place resolutions for debate. The contents of the so-called Black Box would then be read out during each meeting, providing even more fodder for beer-fueled banter.[30]

Room 7, West Lawn

To enhance the social environment of the Hall during this time, in 1964 the Society applied for and received permission to reserve Room 7, West Lawn—the room in which the Society was founded—for a Society member to live in each year. While the resident of 7 West Lawn had been a Society member more often than not out of respect for the room's historical significance, institutionalizing the arrangement meant that Room

7 became another place where Society members could gather, converse, and carouse.

The minutes show that the Society's historian, William T. Walker, first proposed on October 2, 1964, that the Society ask the University "that Number 7 West Lawn be designated as the founding room of The Jefferson Society and be reserved for a member of the Society who in all aspects meets the University requirements for Lawn residence."[31] On November 13, 1964, Walker happily reported to the Society that Room 7 was theirs.[32] The Society soon created a "selection committee" composed of the combined executive committees from the fall and spring semesters for the purpose of choosing the resident each year.[33]

This deceptively simple arrangement with the administration was the single most important provision made for the Society since the Board of Visitors awarded it the use of Hotel C, West Range, in 1837, ensuring that the Society would always have a home. Within a few years, the Society had created a great deal of lore around Room 7, and the historic room hummed with activity on a weekly basis. It became popular for Society members to gather there and drink whisky sours before meetings on Friday afternoons. Resident Kevin Twomey, along with a few other Society mainstays, decided to enshrine the custom in a Seven Sours Sippers Society, which they styled a "lasting yet curiously tenuous association of friends and fellows."[34] Sippers, as these informal gatherings are still known today, gave members an opportunity to socialize before formal meetings and extended life in the Society outside of Jefferson Hall. The tongue-in-cheek Seven Sours Sippers constitution captures the spirit of these often jovial get-togethers. They promoted "convivial congregation; cogitation and divertissement upon issues and items of occasional interest."[35] Sippers could be called to good order by a quorum of just "one (1) member in good standing" enjoying a cold sour in view of the idyllic Lawn.[36] Room 7 has since become the location of many of the Society's social functions, including champagne toasts after formal events, tailgates, lawn games, and a "smoker"—an event held each semester and open to prospective new members. Society members, particularly those chosen for the honor of living in Room 7, feel a special connection to the room where the Society was founded centuries earlier, and many recall fond memories of conversations there lasting late into the night and amusing scenes of their fellow members' antics after a few drinks.

The resident of 7 West Lawn has also come to be an important leader for the Society, particularly for those aspects of the organization that extend beyond the meetings, debates, and speeches of Friday evenings. Lawn residents are recognized leaders in the University community generally, and accordingly the Room 7 resident often collaborates with the administration on special projects or serves as an ambassador for the Society to the public. Today, the Room 7 resident also manages the use and upkeep of Jefferson Hall and works as a liaison to the Society's alumni.

When the right to select a resident for Room 7 was first granted to the Society, rooms on the Lawn were not as highly sought after as they are today—students preferred the modern amenities available in dorms or apartments in surrounding Charlottesville neighborhoods. Since then, however, living in a room on the Lawn has become increasingly desirable and selection for the privilege is dramatically more competitive. Students see living on the Lawn as a great honor—a chance to experience the best that the University of Virginia has to offer, while also sharing Jefferson's Academical Village and all that it stands for with their peers, community members, and visitors. Only undergraduate students in their final year of study may apply to live in a room on the Lawn, and their applications are reviewed by a selection committee made up of leaders from the graduating class. Only three other organizations are afforded the privilege of a reserved room for one of their members, all of which were founded at the University: 46 East Lawn is reserved for a member of Kappa Sigma Fraternity, 17 West Lawn for a member of Trigon Engineering Fraternity, and 47 West Range for a member of Pi Kappa Alpha Fraternity. One other room—37 West Lawn—is reserved for the chair of the Honor Committee.

Because of the competitive nature of the Lawn room assignments, the Jefferson Society no longer enjoys complete control over selecting who lives in Room 7. In 2004, the Society was restricted to electing a resident from those members of the Society who were selected to live on the Lawn through the open application process or nominating a suitable candidate should no member be selected.[37] This helps to ensure that a truly deserving candidate is selected for the room, and the Society typically has several excellent choices. In 1986 the Society endowed Room 7 with an anonymous contribution of $1,000.[38] Bolstered by the collective financial support of the Society and its alumni in the years since, the housing fee for the room is furnished in full by the Society for the resident. And in 1982, the Society placed a soapstone in front of the door to Room 7 in commemoration of the Society's founding there 157 years earlier.

"State U"

Even in the 1960s, the Society and its membership in some ways must have felt more at home in the "Old University." The University was growing and changing more rapidly than it ever had before, but the Society remained ensconced in its traditional homes of Jefferson Hall and Room 7, in the nineteenth-century world of the Academical Village. It should come as little surprise, then, that the Society took an active stance against the expansion of the student body and the "State U-ism" that they perceived to come along with it.[39] They had earlier opposed the construction of New Cabell Hall, a massive classroom building that brackets Old Cabell Hall at the base of the Lawn, completed in 1952, as well as Newcomb Hall, a large student activities building completed in 1958, jokingly referred to by students as the "Ping-Pong Palace" or "Mama Newc's" for its dining and catering operations. These buildings, which could accommodate thousands of students, were anathema to the stately but modest Rotunda, the picturesque Lawn, and the intimate setting of the pavilions and Lawn rooms. The Stanford White buildings capping the south end of the Lawn, built in 1897, were integrated seamlessly into the Academical Village, but traditionalists struggled to come to terms with these more modern additions.[40]

Many students, and, it seems, particularly those in the Jefferson Society, opposed the expansion of the student body and new building projects throughout the 1960s and 1970s because they felt these changes threatened the distinctive character of the University, Jefferson's plan for holistic education through direct interaction with faculty, and, in particular, the student-run honor system. They feared that if the University grew too large, it would become indistinguishable from other large state schools, lose touch with its history and traditions, and become a drab, formulaic educational institution, too big to offer the kind of experience that students had come to cherish. The *University of Virginia Magazine* published an article to this effect in 1967, fearing "the vital character of the University [might] be lost."[41]

One instance captures the sentiments of the Society particularly well. On March 25, 1971, the membership directed Society president Thomas Rawles Jones Jr. to send a letter to University president Edgar Shannon, expressing to him "concern about the University's future growth."[42] He wrote:

Every member of this organization recognizes, I think, that the University of Virginia must continue to increase its enrollment in order to fulfill its responsibilities to the State of Virginia . . . [but] there is much which is worthy of preservation as the Old University gives way to the New. We have received the benefits of an environment which allows close student-teacher relationships, and which promotes the sense of community and the kinds of extracurricular activities that make "education" much more than a formal learning experience. We believe that this kind of environment can be and should be preserved as the University expands.[43]

The antiexpansionist sentiment reached a fever pitch a few months later when students began to stage protests to limit enrollment growth. The Student Council had created a Committee on Growth that had been working with the administration to find a solution to the issue, but by October the committee members were dissatisfied with the progress and began calling for more drastic action, particularly as more students came to believe that the administration itself was driving expansion, rather than external forces. Led by its president, Tom Collier, the Student Council planned protests for October 19 with the aim of demonstrating the strain that additional students would place on the physical facilities of the University.[44] President Shannon pleaded with Collier and other student leaders to cancel their plans, promising that the Board of Visitors and the administration would work diligently to address their concerns and expressing his fear that the protest would hinder efforts to secure state support for the University. This failed to deter Collier and his supporters, and the protest continued the following evening, with an estimated 1,500 students congregating on the Lawn.[45]

In one respect, the student body's resistance to expansion can be explained simply as nostalgia for a time gone by, for a University closer to Jefferson's vision, and a golden age of fondly remembered traditions. The transition had come into stark relief as African American students, followed soon after by female students, arrived on the Grounds. But for the Society in particular, there was another, perhaps more compelling, explanation: with each additional student, the Jefferson Society occupied a smaller proportion of the student ethos. Unable to grow along with the student body in the same way that athletics or the fraternity system could by simply adding another sport or another chapter complete with its own letters and chapter house, the Society remained tied to the Old University in ways that these institutions did not. Many of the things that students feared would be lost in expansion were the very things that had helped the Society build its prestige and notoriety.

The Restoration Ball

The Society's nostalgia and reverence for the Old University was put to good use in at least one important way in the 1960s, when it spearheaded the efforts to bring attention to the Rotunda, which was in dire need of renovation. Following the disastrous fire of 1895, the University had enlisted the services of the world-renowned architectural firm McKim, Mead, White to rebuild the Rotunda. Instead of following Jefferson's designs exactly, Stanford White reconceived the interior, entirely eliminating the third floor. Far from recklessly disregarding Jefferson's vision for the Rotunda as the secular centerpiece of his Academical Village, however, White's redesign increased the Rotunda's capacity as a library, creating a larger Dome Room with floor-to-ceiling shelving and a larger circulation desk made possible by the space freed up by eliminating the third floor.

But when Alderman Library—the large Public Works Administration project that became the University's main library—opened in 1938, the bulk of the collection was moved out of the Rotunda and across the street to the new facility.[46] The Rotunda still stood in all its splendor at the head of the Lawn, but it was no longer the beating heart of the Grounds. Fewer students had reason to enter the building, and most of the space was given over to offices, or worse, simply left unused.

After World War II, the University community began pushing for a restoration of the Rotunda that would befit its place in the Academical Village. A small-scale model of Jefferson's Rotunda was built for visitors to view in 1956, and President Colgate Darden began actively pursuing financial support for the project. Shannon took up the effort when he succeeded Darden, at one point writing to a donor: "the Rotunda was throughout the 19th century the most functional of our buildings. Today it is a hollow shell. Its interior is worse than unsightly. . . . We must restore it."[47]

Mary Hall Betts, the Rotunda hostess (and one of the most enduring personages at the University in the twentieth century) was another driving force behind the call for restoration, which had gained momentum by the beginning of the 1960s. "I've been the hostess for 14 years, and I've

FIGURE 24. The third annual Restoration Ball, held on May 15, 1965. In its early years, the Restoration Ball was held in the Dome Room of the Rotunda, re-creating the formal balls hosted by the Society in the antebellum era. Image courtesy of the Albert and Shirley Small Special Collections Library at the University of Virginia, University of Virginia Visual History Collection, U.Va. Prints and Photographs File, RG-30/1/10.011, Print 05870.

been on a crusade for the restoration. The Rotunda as it is now is just a temporary office building," she told the *Richmond Times Dispatch,* advocating for the cause.[48] Betts also happened to be an advisor to the newly formed University Guide Service, a student group that to this day showcases the Grounds to visitors and prospective students.[49] Betts recognized the potential for student involvement to spur interest and support for the restoration. She had always been passionate about sharing the history of the University with students, and the Guides were no exception. She also knew that the Dome Room had often been the setting of elaborate balls and galas for the University and its students—and that bringing people back to the Rotunda could inspire interest in having it restored. And so, as Mary Hall Betts sat around the table "with student guides over old lithographs which showed formal dances in the Dome Room," the Restoration Ball was born.[50] Who would be best to help them host a formal evening in the Rotunda? The very organization that had hosted many of the galas depicted in the lithographs—the Jefferson Society.[51]

Together, the Jefferson Society and the University Guide Service hosted the first Restoration Ball in 1963. It was immediately a smashing success, so much so that it turned into an annual event, and the name "Restoration Ball" became recognizable to all University of Virginia students: "The black-tie affair in the historic Rotunda is held each year to promote interest in the project of returning that building to the original designs of Thomas Jefferson."[52] The ball did not seek to raise the full amount required to finance the effort in and of itself, but rather to promote interest in the restoration project and inspire alumni and community members to support it.[53] In its early years the ball attracted more than 400 guests, and tickets for students sold out faster and faster every year.[54] It became so popular that in 1973, the ball sold out mere minutes after the tickets went on sale.[55] It was a good thing the Ball attracted that much attention, because once concrete plans were put in place in 1967, the cost of the restoration was expected to exceed $1.2 million.[56]

The accounts of the Restoration Ball are just as vibrant as those depicting the Jefferson Society Final Celebrations from the nineteenth century. Newspapers gushed about the scene set for the evening: "Magnolia and candlelight will re-create an old-South atmosphere in the Rotunda on the night of the Ball."[57] Descriptions of the atmosphere harkened back to Final Celebrations in the Rotunda:

Gaiety and laughter are recorded in the old Rotunda walls: "Hither came the belles . . . whose beauty, charm, and wit were . . . celebrated throughout the Southern States. The several tiers of galleries and alcoves on the floor were packed with excited spectators . . . enjoying the brilliance and animation of the splendid scene," reports an account of the times. The Restoration Ball is a re-creation of that era for one brief evening.[58]

As they arrived dressed to the nines, guests were transported to a world apart for their evening in the Rotunda:

As guests near the Rotunda on the night of the ball they pass a small garden lighted by candles and highlighted by a fountain with floating magnolia blossoms. The Rotunda's marble steps are lighted by flaming torches and topped by the portico that is transformed into a formal ante-room by drapery and lush paintings.

A garland of cedar and pine with antique tassels forms a perfect frame over the south door. Inside the Rotunda, the main floor has been transformed into a dramatic ballroom. 6-foot gilt candlelabra [*sic*] and classical urns containing arrangements of flowers and greenery add charm to the dome room.

Between dances, young ladies in long gowns and their formally-attired escorts walk along the three balconies that encircle the main floor. Here golden swags hang between Corinthian capitals of the 12 columns and more than 200 candles line the railing. Rosettes of magnolia leaves complete the decorations on the balconies."[59]

In just a few short years, the Restoration Ball had grown to be one of the most popular events for students and a highlight of the social calendar each spring. It was a celebration of everything the Old University stood for, of Jefferson's architectural achievements, and of the students' love for their school.

By 1969 there was concern, expressed in part by the Society of the Purple Shadows, one of the University's many secret societies, that the pomp and circumstance of the Restoration Ball was overshadowing the deeper purpose of why the event was being held in the first place. The year 1969 was the 150th anniversary of the founding of the University of Virginia, and plans for the ball were especially grand, as befit the occasion. Betts felt that the more festive the occasion, the more effective it would be at inspiring enthusiasm for the restoration. She wrote in reply to the Society of the Purple Shadows:

The lengthening shadow of Thomas Jefferson projects itself into 1969, the 150th anniversary of the founding of the University of Virginia—thus the reason for the University Guide Service and the Jefferson Literary and Debating Society bending their efforts toward making this year's Rotunda Restoration Ball a very special festive occasion. Ever striving to continue interest in restoring the Rotunda to Mr. Jefferson's original design, such conscientious efforts should reflect rather than overshadow the real purpose of the Rotunda Restoration Ball.[60]

The following year, ongoing student strikes in protest of the Vietnam War threatened to cancel the ball. In response to the May 3 shootings at Kent State University, an estimated 1,500 students converged on the Rotunda and then moved across University Avenue to Carr's Hill to condemn the shootings. They demanded that classes be cancelled and urged President Shannon to come out in support of ending the war. Shannon, who was perceived as weak by many of the protesters, refused to comply with their demands and requested a state police presence on the Grounds. The unrest continued for several days, disrupting traffic as students blocked cars from passing until they "honked for peace."[61]

On May 9, the night of the Restoration Ball, contrary to President Shannon's wishes, police arrested sixty-seven students in the midst of a chaotic protest. Downing Smith, a student at the time, recalled that on the night of the ball, a

> crowd was blocking the intersection of Rugby and University and not letting cars pass until they honked for peace. The police who were running out of patience told the crowd to disperse. When they didn't, they started arresting everybody and herded them into a moving van. Just about this time the Restoration Ball was letting out of the Rotunda so they arrested lots of people in evening gowns and tux[es].[62]

The next day, Shannon changed course in a move that may well have saved the University from further violence—and his own reputation in the process. He took to the steps of the Rotunda where students in formal attire had fled from the police the night before and addressed more than 4,000 students and staff, siding with the students and urging President Nixon to end the war. The incident became known as the "May Days." Shannon endured harsh criticism from state leaders for his actions, but his decision earned him the enduring respect of the students and faculty, who rewarded him with a standing ovation at Final Exercises that year.[63]

Ultimately, the restoration of the Rotunda took roughly three years to complete and cost the University and the Commonwealth of Virginia almost $2 million.[64] It rendered the Rotunda a replica of Jefferson's original design, as close to the particular details as was practical. The second or main public floor in Stanford White's design was retrofitted to include oval rooms on the east and west sides of the building, as well as a smaller one to the north. These rooms flank an elegant central hallway with curved staircases ascending to the Dome Room above and to the ground floor below. The Dome Room, which is formed by the re-creation of a third floor, featured Jefferson's double Corinthian columns encircling a formal assembly room flanked by artfully concealed library shelves.[65] The restoration brought back the oval rooms for the formal functions of the University president and Board of Visitors, as well as some classes, and also made it easier to use the Rotunda for dinners, events, meetings, and lectures, bringing more students back into contact with the building and restoring its place at the heart of the University.

The Tenth Restoration Ball, held in 1973, was meant to be the last, because construction on the Rotunda was slated to begin that June following Final Exercises. Headlines for the event read "Final Restoration Ball Set" and "Saturday Night Ends a Tradition." Demand to attend the event was so great that it was rescheduled from March to May to take advantage of warmer weather and accommodate more guests in the outdoor space around the Rotunda.[66] But the formal festivities each spring had become so popular that the Jefferson Society and the University Guide Service could not help but continue the efforts, and the ball resumed again the next year.[67] Since then, students have donned ball gowns and tuxedoes to attend to the Restoration Ball every spring. With the Rotunda restoration complete, the proceeds of the ball have been used over the years to contribute to various projects around the Grounds, such as the construction of a courtyard outside of Clemons Library.[68]

In 2010, the University announced that the Rotunda would need to undergo yet another comprehensive restoration, slated to cost in excess of $51 million. The marble capitals on the exterior porticos were crumbling, the roof needed replacing, and the interior plumbing and electrical systems were out of date.[69] In 2011, the Jefferson Society took over from the Guide Service as the sole host of the Restoration Ball and elevated the profile of the event to contribute to the newly launched Jeffersonian Grounds Initiative and the Heart of the Grounds capital campaign.[70] The festivities moved from Alumni Hall, where they had been held for some years, to a large outdoor tent (sometimes outside Peabody Hall across from West Range and sometimes in the McIntire Amphitheater) to accommodate even more guests. Since the move, and with renewed enthusiasm and support on the part of students, the Restoration Ball has substantially benefited the most recent renovation of the Rotunda, raising thousands in ticket sales and attracting sizeable donations from the Seven Society and private philanthropists.[71] The 50th Restoration Ball, hosted in April 2013, attracted over one thousand guests.

Integration and Coeducation for the Society

It was in the midst of the intensifying debate over the expansion of the University that the Society was faced with the question of integration and then, not more than ten years later, the question of coeducation. These were not questions that the Society proactively sought to resolve, and in the case of coeducation, the Society for a time stubbornly resisted change. In some ways these issues were thrust upon the Society by changes in the larger University, for no African American or woman could expect to join the Society without first being a student. But in both cases, once admitted to the University, African Americans and women actively sought membership, forcing the Society's leadership to make a decision. In both cases, the particular applicants had a decisive impact on the ultimate outcome.

The integration and coeducation of the Jefferson Society differ in several key respects. For one, by the time each question was resolved, there was far less history at the University with African American students than there was with women. The Society integrated in 1963, the first African American students having arrived on the Grounds only thirteen years prior, and only in considerable numbers two or three years earlier. This meant that when the Society was faced with the question of whether or not to admit an African American member, it had not yet developed a firm position on the matter. Before the Society became coeducational in 1972, female students had been at the University in some capacity for almost a century. Accordingly, the Society had adopted a long-standing ban on female members that would have to be lifted before any woman could be considered, and a large portion of the membership resisted this change, even in the face of significant pressure from the rest of the University. In both cases, debate raged over these important decisions that would forever alter the character of the Society, leading it to become one of the first major student organizations to integrate, but one of the last to become coeducational.

The Society Integrates: Wesley Harris Joins the Hall

The Jim Crow South was a brutal, hostile environment for African Americans. Almost everywhere, they encountered businesses open only to whites and segregated restaurants and public buildings. Degrading experiences were the norm—whites spat at blacks and swore at them while passing in the streets. Throughout the South, African Americans were not allowed to enroll at the same educational institutions as whites, depriving them of valuable opportunities for advancement and self-improvement. Protests aimed at spurring progress heightened tensions between whites and blacks and sparked violence in the name of white supremacy. The violence reached a flashpoint when fourteen-year-old Emmett Till was brutally beaten, castrated, and shot for whistling at a white woman in Mississippi on August 28, 1955, just as the University of Virginia's undergraduate population was desegregated for the first time.

Yet even as discrimination, tension, and violence reigned, there was cause for hope. Just over a year before Till was murdered, on May 17, 1954, the Supreme Court handed down its decision in the landmark case *Brown v. Board of Education*, outlawing segregation in America's public schools and ordering schools to integrate. African American men and women immediately pushed to attend formerly all-white universities and colleges across the nation that had once been closed to them, particularly in the South.

The first African American student enrolled at the University of Virginia in 1950 was Gregory Swanson, who entered the Law School. Because of the reigning jurisprudential principle of "separate but equal," the University could not avoid admitting African Americans to graduate and professional schools, such as law, medicine, and education, when no alternative existed at institutions that served black students. Then, in 1955, three brave students—Robert Bland, George Harris, and Theodore Thomas—arrived on the Grounds to pursue their studies and desegregate the undergraduate population. All three entered the School of Engineering, and when they arrived, they had to contend with the character of the prestigious, historically white University that for generations had attracted the social and political elite of Virginia. Unsurprisingly, faculty and students alike did not take kindly to the idea of black students at Mr. Jefferson's University.[72] Alienated from their classmates, Bland, Harris, and Thomas studied and socialized together. Bland and Harris were roommates and Thomas was "right down the hall" in his own single dorm room.[73] Participating in the same organizations and activities as their white counterparts was out of the question. They found a home, however, in the black community of Charlottesville, which welcomed the three pathbreaking students into their homes, churches, and social events. Charlottesville blacks were proud that black men were finally attending the University. At the end of the first year, Harris and Thomas withdrew and transferred to other universities. Bland stayed and as a result was the only African American to graduate in the class of 1959.[74]

For the rest of the 1950s, a small number of African American students came to the University of Virginia—less than ten each year. They were

brave young men who decided to attend for the academics or for principle, instead of matriculating at a historically black college. But despite
the ruling in *Brown v. Board of Education*, black students were still not
allowed to attend the College of Arts and Sciences, the largest and oldest
school at the University of Virginia. African American students broke that
barrier when Leroy Willis was allowed to enter the college in 1960 as a
transfer from the Engineering School. The same year, Virginius Thornton
became the first black graduate student to enter a doctoral program at the
University.

At roughly the same time, the University came under new leadership.
After twelve years at the helm, Darden passed the reins to Shannon. Darden
had been vocally resistant to desegregation, believing strongly that black
students had no place at a prestigious university like Virginia. He urged
Shannon to confront the question of race at the University very carefully,
for there was great fear that any move toward desegregation or encouragement of African American students to matriculate would draw the ire of
the state government and criticism from alumni, faculty, and students.

But Shannon candidly believed that African Americans had a rightful
place at the University and that it should be as welcoming as possible to
them. When many from the first classes of black students transferred to
other schools after bad experiences in Charlottesville, Shannon realized
that they were actively choosing not to attend and would continue to do
so without proactive change on the part of the University. He began working with his administration, the small but active Black Student Alliance,
and other student leaders to change the climate at the University and to
provide a caring and engaging home for black students, one he hoped
would encourage more African Americans to come to the Grounds. But
it took time for Shannon's efforts to lead to any improvement, and the
number of black students did not grow appreciably until the last years of
his presidency in the early to mid-1970s.

Given this environment, members of the Society likely realized they
would soon confront the question of integration, and it seems they faced
it with a lackluster trepidation—generally hostile to the idea, but somewhat disinterested without a particular case to argue over, as no African
American student had yet applied for membership. On March 18, 1960,
the secretary recorded: "At 10 of 11 it was decided to adjourn. Those who
wanted to remain and talk about niggers were free to do so."[75]

Meanwhile, the fervor of the civil rights movement escalated in the

1960s. On February 1, 1960, four students in Greensboro, North Carolina, staged a sit-in at the counter of Woolworth's department store; later that year, Congress passed the landmark Civil Rights Act. Meetings at Shaw University in Raleigh led to the organization of the Student Nonviolent Coordinating Committee, which went on to lead dozens of sit-ins and marches on the part of college students. The University of Virginia came alive with this spirit of activism. Students picketed places like Buddy's Restaurant on Emmett Street, the Holiday Inn, and other restaurants on the Corner because they would not serve blacks. Students marched on the Grounds in support of the march in Selma, Alabama, in 1965, and it seemed, in the words of one student of race history at the University of Virginia, that "the University was finally embracing chang[e], and [was] slowly detaching from the tradition that had made it so hostile an environment."[76]

One of the students participating in those protests was Wesley Harris, a young engineer from Richmond.

Harris was not even thinking about going to the University of Virginia . . . until his physics teacher, Eloise Bowles Washington, at Armstrong High School in Richmond pulled him aside and demanded that he should. "I was a black person, who was obviously black in appearance and I was extremely bright and would be successful at UVA," Harris recalled her telling him.[77]

Harris's view of the University of Virginia at the time was one that might be expected: that the institution was "small, elitist, racist, and probably very overrated," but nonetheless, Harris arrived in Charlottesville determined "to excel as a black scholar."[78]

He did just that. Harris studied aeronautical engineering and excelled in the classroom, though his experiences were varied: by his professors, "oftentimes he was ignored, by some he was welcomed." Some were, in his words, "straight out hard core racist." In his four years at the University of Virginia, he was the first student, black or white, to complete the engineering honors program, which allowed him to study on an individual basis with several faculty members, and he achieved Dean's List honors every semester.[79] He built deep relationships with several faculty members in engineering, one of whom was John Longley.

Harris recalled Longley, who "taught rhetoric in the School of Engineering," as a mentor during his University career. With Longley, who "pictured himself a disciple of William Faulkner," Harris said he "began to read writings in existentialism, and I became intrigued with Kierkegaard, with Faulkner himself and his writings, with Dostoyevsky, the Russian novelist, with Kafka, the Polish writer." And it was "with encouragement from Longley and interest on my part, I began to explore the possibility of joining the Jefferson Society."[80] Longley knew the Society well: he was invited to deliver an address, "Farewell to the Beats," in November 1960, and again in November 1963 on his recent book, *The Tragic Mask: A Study of Faulkner's Heroes*.[81]

For Harris, who had debated at Armstrong High School in Richmond, "the Jefferson Society was a choice, an option, a place where I thought I could add value, a place where I could be a citizen of the University, a citizen of the community, and participate in what I enjoyed: conversation, logic, structured conversation."[82] Of the members Harris encountered in Jefferson Hall, he met some he thought were very welcoming, but also some who questioned his motives, thinking he only wanted to join the Jefferson Society to prove a point, rather than "to be a citizen, to contribute, and to enjoy rigor, rhetoric, and conversation."[83]

Perhaps most importantly, Harris was an exceptionally well-qualified candidate to become the first African American member of the Society. A fortuitous accident of history gives us direct insight to the Society's decision to integrate and offer Harris membership. Scrawled in the margin of a draft budget from the semester Harris was elected to the Society is a set of sparse notes titled simply "Membership," which likely only survive because they were written on a financial document. They lay out a strikingly candid assessment of points in favor and against both integration and Harris himself. Whoever wrote the notes felt that Harris was "intelligent" and thought that his acceptance into both the University and the selective engineering honors program reflected well on his qualifications. But at the same time, a parenthetical acknowledged that many equally intelligent students were not in the Society. More crass were the points noted against Harris himself, which called his social activities "offensive," said he had a "bad personality," and questioned the desirability of him being "involved in racial issues."

The Society was also conscious of the "publicity" and potential "controversy" that integrating might bring upon the organization, particularly as a result of Harris's supposed "bad personality," his participation in civil rights activism, including sit-ins and strikes, and the fact that he did "not avoid controversy." There was concern that admitting Harris would turn reports on the Society into issues of color and that his membership would shift "emphasis off of what we are interested in." His "personal intentions" were also questioned, demanding that Harris be "put on the spot" to provide a "reason other than black" that he wanted to join the Society. The invective against Harris called him an "agitator," for which reason "he does not qualify."

Ultimately, the author of these notes was not sure if the "Society in which we live" was "ready for it." But indeed they were. Without allowing him to join the Society, it was "not possible for all to know him," and the membership decided that they should not "accept or reject" Harris merely "due to color," for the subtext of that logic was that "WH would be rejected." Wesley Harris was elected to probationary membership in spring 1963, becoming the first African American member of the Society in its nearly 150-year history.[84]

True to his mentor John Longley, who had encouraged him to join the Society, Harris delivered his probationary presentation on Kierkegaard and existentialism. Harris recalled that "the Jefferson Society was totally caught off guard, first of all that I was black, second that I was an engineer, and third that I was an engineer who knew something about … philosophy and literature."[85] He enjoyed conversations about classical music with some of the other members and attended every Friday meeting until he graduated in 1964.

Harris entered the Hall when one of the main attractions was the keg in the back corner, but he found the intellectual life of the Society to be stimulating and engaging and felt that the Society was a welcoming place to him, all things considered. Looking back:

The whole atmosphere was a bit different than it is now, having said that, there was conversation and everyone was appropriately prepared to engage. There was a period of relaxation and there was a keg of beer. In hindsight, reflecting on that, it did not hurt at all. Things never got out of control; everyone remained a gentleman. I don't remember any hostility resulting after we had a glass or a mug of beer. I would want to state that there was nothing unruly about that. No one reduced to calling names or anything like that, that was not a part of it.[86]

Outside of the Society, Harris was able to balance his activism with his academic pursuits; for him, "the national civil rights activities especially in the South [were] a motivating [f]actor or enabler that sustained or

provided me with extra incentive to achieve."[87] By his third year at the
University, Harris had become the chair of the Thomas Jefferson Chapter
of the Council on Human Relations, an interracial coalition of faculty
and students dedicated to actively addressing race issues at the University, and which sought to bring African American students to the University.[88]

Harris, in his capacity as chair of the council, was instrumental
in bringing Martin Luther King Jr. to the University to speak just five
months before his "I Have a Dream" speech. Dr. King arrived at the University alone, with no protection or handlers. Harris recalled: "To see him
up close, to shake his hand, to share a meal with him, just King himself,
alone and without an entourage—it was an important event in my life, a
cornerstone in my experience."[89] King addressed a capacity crowd of 900
students and faculty in Old Cabell Hall, speaking out against the jailing
of nonviolent protestors. Professor of history Paul Gaston recalled the
power of King's speech: "It was electric. The dynamism that the man suggested was impossible to believe unless you actually saw it."[90]

After King's address, a moment of fear highlighted how much progress
was yet to be made by the advocates of the civil rights movement. While
Harris and Professor Gaston were walking King to the motel on Emmet
Street where he would be staying the night, a loud noise rang out. Harris
immediately shielded King, pushing him up against a nearby wall. There
was no danger—the sound was nothing more than a car backfiring—but
it showed how tenuous progress was for African Americans. "Later in the
motel room, the group chuckled about the incident. Gaston recalls King
almost joking when he said, referring to the possibility of being shot, 'It's
going to happen to me sometime.'"[91]

These tense moments of King's visit cast in bold relief the hope African American students held for the future, relative to the hostile environment they still endured. Harris's accomplishments and involvement
in civil rights activism earned him a high profile among students at the
University (he was the second black student selected to live on the Lawn,
shortly after Leroy Willis became the first during the 1961–1962 academic
year), and he was the subject of intense racism and abuse as a result. White
students spit on him or threw lit cigarettes in his direction. "It was a time
that racism was in fashion . . . there was no way to misinterpret Wes Harris
as being anything other than a black person," he recalled. But beyond that,
he was a scholar, and after his graduation, Harris earned a doctoral degree

in chemical engineering from Princeton University before embarking on a prominent academic career in engineering.

Harris has returned to speak before the Society of two occasions, in 2005 and 2008, after many years away from the University. "As I grow older," he said, "the energy and the desire to return actually increases. Some of the sharpness of the experience begins to fade and the beauty and symmetry begins to appear . . . so it's good to return."[92] In 2008, Harris discussed diversity in the fields of science, technology, engineering, and math, issues of pioneering importance to him as associate provost for faculty equity at the Massachusetts Institute of Technology. Also the former chair of the Department of Aeronautics and Astronautics at MIT, Harris points to his studies at the University as a key factor in his success: "The essential piece of excellence and scholarship, I certainly picked that up, learned that, that was drilled into me, here [at the University of Virginia]."[93]

Decades after he left the University, Harris felt he had a home in the Society while a student, more so than other aspects of his student experience:

My return visits to the Society have been rewarding, warmly so. To be present when there are men and women of various backgrounds and different races, it was very refreshing to see that. It certainly gave me a sense of being at home. I can't say that in general about my experiences at the University, and retuning the Jefferson Society gave me a sense of having a foundation. Let me explain why I've come to this position: why go back to a reunion? I've had to ask myself that given my time on the Grounds. Well, you meet people, you develop friendships, you go to each other's weddings, you have telephone calls when you have children and you share it with your classmates, who you bonded with and who are true friends. You shake hands, you embrace when you see your classmates. That has never happened in my case. There has never been a wedding, a birth, or a death in which any members of the U.Va. Class of 1964 has invited Wes Harris. I'm a loner, I just don't exist, I'm invisible. But coming back to the Jefferson Society and seeing the difference, I've began to think that maybe it wasn't all a barren wasteland, maybe there is some substance that's still there. That's how it comes into perspective.[94]

A Golden Opportunity for Coeducation

Less than ten years after Wesley Harris first walked through the doors of Jefferson Hall, another major change would come to the Society: coeducation. By 1970, women had been at the University for decades but were marginalized and confined to the nursing, education, and graduate programs. Phyllis Leffler, prominent scholar of University history, explains in her seminal article on the subject, "Mr. Jefferson's University: Women in the Village!" that gender history at the University began years before formal coeducation of the undergraduate student body:

A common refrain frequently accepted without qualification to this day, is that women first came to the university in 1970. This myth reflects the fact that women were entitled to matriculate in the undergraduate College of Arts and Sciences on a non-exceptional basis with men in that year. With their entry, the nature of the university was forced to change, and with time, women would become a central part of the "academical village," making up a majority of students in recent years. The year 1970 thus marked a very significant turning point. Before that date, however, more than 15,000 women earned professional, graduate, and undergraduate degrees, and an equal or greater number earned diplomas or degrees in nursing. Others accessed the university through summer programs at which they often made up a majority.[95]

In fact, women first came to the University in the 1880s for summer educational institutes, though they could not earn academic credit for their studies. In 1901, the University began to offer a hospital-based nurses' training program, which granted "diplomas" to thousands of nurses, but the program was not recognized as an academic division of the University, just a part of the hospital. Significant numbers of women enrolled: in the 1920s, the program had about ninety students each year; ten years later in 1930 there were 153 enrolled nursing students.[96]

Women gained a major foothold in the University in 1920 when the Board of Visitors officially accepted white women into graduate and professional programs: law, medicine, the Graduate School of Arts and Sciences, and the School of Education. Women who enrolled in these programs were the first to earn full degrees conferred by the University.[97] The admission of women to degree programs, even on this limited basis, caused significant controversy at Mr. Jefferson's University, and it came only at the conclusion of protracted, heated debate involving administrators, alumni, legislators, and students. There were several attempts in Richmond to pass a bill through the state legislature allowing women to enroll as undergraduates in a separate college adjacent to the University of Virginia, by way of "coordinate education." This model, pioneered by partnerships like Barnard College and Columbia University, had become a popular solution to offer higher education to women. Classroom instruction remained segregated by gender, but otherwise men and women utilized shared facilities, resources, and faculty.[98]

But many saw coordinate education as merely a step along the way to full coeducation, and in a sense these forces antagonistic to coeducation won the day. According to Leffler, for them, permitting the "decision to admit women to graduate programs was a defensive move—a measure to hold back the floodgates of full coeducation. By restricting women to programs for which few would qualify, coeducation might be contained and made less of a threat to the character of the southern, male, largely aristocratic university."[99]

Although institutions of higher learning across the United States had been educating women in varying capacities for a century and a half, the inclusion of women came more slowly in the South than in the North or West. The more conservative mentality of the South, informed by lingering Victorian notions of "separate spheres" and the desire to preserve a patriarchal social order following the Civil War, prevented women from enjoying educational opportunities similar to those available in the North until a generation later. [100]

In the particular case of the University of Virginia, the debate over coeducation

was often framed in ideological terms related to Jeffersonian and southern values. A primary focus was on Jefferson's original intentions for the university, especially in terms of how aristocratic or democratic he wished it to be. Students and alumni regularly invoked Jefferson's name in their defense of the male-centered University.[101]

Murray McGuire—who, after winning the Society's Final presidency in 1893 by way of a boxing match, had become a respected leader of the alumni—was vitriolic in his opposition to coeducation. He claimed that allowing women would destroy the honor system and student government:

the University of Virginia is a man's university. It was founded as a men's university, and it has obtained a high position as such. Its history, its traditions, its system of government are all founded on the teaching of men and for the teaching of men and the association of men with men. The University is a little world of its own where young men find themselves, grow and develop amid surroundings that inculcate manliness and men's high ideals.[102]

After women were admitted to graduate programs in 1920, little progress was made until almost fifty years later. The number of women at the University increased fairly dramatically during World War II while men were deployed overseas (in the final year of the war they made up 18 percent of the student body), but they were still largely confined to nursing and education programs, and by most accounts felt isolated and unwelcome.[103] Excluded from traditional organizations and activities at the University, women responded by creating associations of their own: chapters of Chi Omega and Kappa Delta sororities were founded in 1927 and 1932, respectively. A Dean of Women was created to support the female student population, and a "co-ed room" on West Range provided a place for women to socialize and eat meals. Mary Washington College became the coordinate women's college of the University in 1944, but its location more than seventy miles away from Charlottesville in Fredericksburg meant that its academic connection to the Grounds was largely perfunctory.[104]

By the 1960s, coeducation was clearly on the horizon, but many male students continued to resist the idea until the very last. Again they brought the honor system into the argument. Leffler writes:

Even as full coeducation loomed, many male students continued to resist the full inclusion of women. Some felt that the Honor Code would fail if women were admitted. In 1967, the student newspaper, the *Cavalier Daily*, carried an article claiming "women have no honor, only deception." As studies were compiled to determine the effect of admitting women in full measure to the undergraduate College of Arts and Sciences, the Honor Committee published its own report in 1969: "Our principal and final conclusion is that it is not in the best interest of the honor system to make the University of Virginia coeducational."[105]

Despite these and other protestations, in 1969 federal courts mandated that the University become fully coeducational within three years. The first full class of women, including 350 first-year students, entered the College of Arts and Sciences the next fall, in 1970. With full coeducation came the inevitable question of whether or not student organizations would also become coeducational. Many did so immediately and with little discomposure, as women in the first class were tenacious about pursuing extracurricular opportunities. Those with longer history and more immutable traditions, like the Jefferson Society, however, were more reluctant to offer membership to women, even when they demanded to be let in.[106]

Women had walked through the doors of Jefferson Hall before, just never as members. Local women had flocked to the Hall to hear silver-tongued orators like Woodrow Wilson deliver speeches, and young ladies had often been invited as dates to Society functions like the Founder's Day Celebration. Even before formal undergraduate coeducation occurred in 1970, women had tried to join the Jefferson Society as nursing or education students, but their efforts were quickly rebuffed by the membership. The Society made its position clear: in early 1920, the minutes record a discussion of whether or not to allow women to join, presumably in conjunction with the Board of Visitors' recent decision to admit women to graduate programs. This discussion prompted an amendment to the Society's constitution specifying that only male students were eligible for membership. In reality, it is unlikely that any woman would have been seriously considered for membership before 1970 on account of their isolated status at the fringe of the University, but the amended language leaves no room for ambiguity about the sentiments of the membership.[107] The existence of a constitutional barrier meant that interested women would have to negotiate a change to the rules before they could even be considered for membership.

Once admitted to the college, however, women pursued membership directly, asking to be interviewed and considered despite the prohibition on female members in the constitution. From inside the Society, certain members advocated for lifting the ban on female members. Amendments were frequently proposed, and at the beginning of each semester "the long-awaited and . . . well prepared-for, debate on the amendment to co-educate the Hall" would surface. Debate on the subject at the February 12, 1971, meeting raged until 6:00 a.m. the next morning.[108] Supporters of coeducation employed numerous creative strategies, including attempting to first lower the threshold for amending the constitution before removing the ban, or at the very least offering a "sense of the Hall resolution" in favor of coeducation.[109]

Even with these tactics, the amendment failed repeatedly, and the

Society seemingly remained steadfast in its desire to remain all-male. A notice was posted outside Jefferson Hall just before the Society began to conduct interviews, warning women who sought to be included:

At present, the constitution of the Jefferson Literary and Debating Society specifies that only male students who have completed one semester at the University are eligible for probationary membership. Therefore, the membership committee cannot at this time consider the applications of any female students. You are welcome to stay and be interviewed if you are a female and are interested in the Jefferson Society, but it will be purely an academic exercise—your application will not be considered for probationary membership.

This Friday night, the membership of the Jefferson Society will vote, as it has for the past several semesters, on whether to eliminate the prohibition of female members from our constitution. If this change passes, measures will be taken to permit the entrance of coed members as soon as feasible.[110]

As the announcement indicated, despite the persistent efforts to change the constitution, for the moment Jefferson Hall remained the exclusive province of men. It is interesting, however, that women were allowed to interview given the prohibition on their membership. This meant that should the ban be lifted they could be immediately considered, but it was also probably a source of misogynistic pleasure for some members to interview women they felt to be undeserving or inferior, confident that the female candidates' efforts would be futile while the bar remained in place.

One of the women who applied for membership in the Society was Barbara Sugarman. She interviewed in the fall of 1971 and was denied on the grounds of her sex. She tried again in February 1972, this time threatening to bring suit against the Society for discrimination if her application was denied. She felt that "the Society is being very close-minded . . . they are relegating women to the position that Blacks held at the University ten years ago." Her threats brought some of the conversation into the open. Alex Simon, who was staunchly opposed to coeducation, told the Cavalier Daily, "The Hall has a dual function to serve as a debating society and a gentleman's club." He continued, "the induction of women would completely alter the atmosphere of the Hall. The introduction of women would cause the male members to try to pick up the female members of

PLATE 1. Portrait of Thomas Jefferson, by Thomas Sully (oil on canvas, 1821).
The portrait is owned by the Jefferson Society and hangs in the Rotunda.
Image courtesy of the Jefferson Society.

PLATE 2. Edgar Allan Poe's signature, clipped from the minute book of the Jefferson Society. Image courtesy of the Albert and Shirley Small Special Collections Library at the University of Virginia and the Jefferson Society, Accession #1018-k.

PLATE 3. The Best Orator Medal for the session of 1890–1891, awarded to Henry Louis Smith. One side is inscribed with the Greek letters of the Jefferson Society and Smith's name; the opposite features an engraved depiction of the Rotunda. Image courtesy of the Albert and Shirley Small Special Collections Library at the University of Virginia, Accession #15491.

PLATE 4. The Best Debater Medal for the session of
1867–1868, awarded to Alexander Pope Humphrey. One side
is inscribed with Humphrey's name; the opposite features an
engraved scene of the Lawn. Image courtesy of the Albert
and Shirley Small Special Collections Library at the
University of Virginia, Accession #9853.

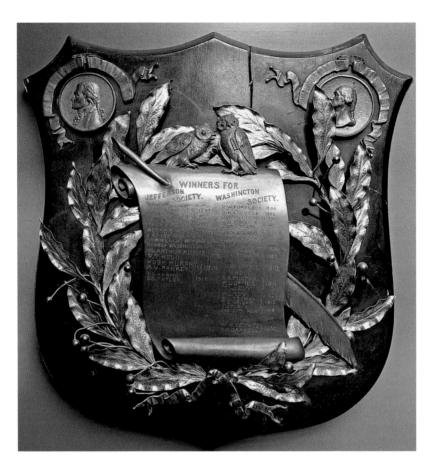

PLATE 5. The James A. Harrison Trophy, awarded to the winner of an annual debate between the Jefferson Society and the Washington Society. Image courtesy of the Jefferson Society.

PLATE 6. By the turn of the century, the cover designs for the *University of Virginia Magazine* had become increasingly elaborate, taking advantage of color printing and a burgeoning artistic community at the University. Image courtesy of the Albert and Shirley Small Special Collections Library at the University of Virginia, *University of Virginia Magazine* 62, no. 7 (April 1912).

THE VIRGINIA SPECTATOR

. C, NO. 1 ᴄᵂʰᵒˡᵉ ᵛᵒˡ. 185   PUBLISHED AT THE UNIVERSITY OF VIRGINIA   SEPT. 1938

EST. 1838

OCT 13 38

SPECTATOR AS PHOENIX: 100 YEARS

THE AMERICAN STUDENT UNION   COLLEGE TOPICS: AN OPPORTUNITY
M. F. MAURY OSBORNE   WILLIAM MAURY MOORE

JEFF, VIRGINIA, AND THE FUTURE
JOHN E. MANAHAN

POETRY   *REVIEWS*   *ARTICLES*   *HUMOR*

20 Cents   Centennial Year $1.00 A Year

PLATE 7. In 1938, the cover of the *Virginia Spectator* commemorated the magazine's 100th anniversary, likening its many names and forms to a phoenix. Image courtesy of the Albert and Shirley Small Special Collections Library at the University of Virginia, *Virginia Spectator* C, no. 1 (September 1938).

PLATE 8. Throughout its life, the magazine vigorously supported the cultivation of the literary arts at the University as well as a distinctively southern body of literature. The editorial staff relished the appointment of William Faulkner as writer-in-residence in 1957, which they commemorated with a special issue. Image courtesy of the Albert and Shirley Small Special Collections Library at the University of Virginia, *Virginia Spectator* 118, no. 8 (April 1957).

The Virginia Spectator

Integration Articles by
SARAH P. BOYLE
E. B. HENDERSON

Segregation Articles by
FLOYD FLEMING
JOHN KASPER

Moderation by
WILLIAM FAULKNER

The Jim Crow Issue   25 cents

PLATE 9. The magazine was frequently prone to controversy. The "Jim Crow" issue attracted the ire of the Board of Visitors and resulted in the resignation of the editor-in-chief, almost spelling the end for the embattled publication. Image courtesy of the Albert and Shirley Small Special Collections Library at the University of Virginia, *Virginia Spectator* 118, no. 9 (May 1957).

PLATE 10.
Dr. Wesley Harris, the first
African American member
of the Jefferson Society.
Image courtesy of Domi-
nick Reuter.

PLATE 11.
Judge Barbara Golden
Lynn, the first female
member of the Jefferson
Society. Image courtesy of
Judge Barbara Lynn.

PLATE 12. Room 7, West
Lawn, where the Jefferson
Society was founded on
July 14, 1825. The Society
has selected the resident of
Room 7 from amongst the
membership each year
since 1964. Image courtesy
of the Jefferson Society.

PLATE 13. The exterior of Jefferson Hall, Hotel C, West Range, the meeting place of the Jefferson Society since 1837. Image courtesy of the Jefferson Society.

PLATE 14. The interior of Jefferson Hall, Hotel C, West Range, the meeting place of the Jefferson Society since 1837. Image courtesy of the Jefferson Society.

PLATE 15. Dr. Terence Holt appeared as a guest speaker before the Jefferson Society on March 27, 2015. Image courtesy of the Jefferson Society.

the Hall."[111] Simon's somewhat ludicrous argument fell to the kind of brilliant riposte that only one man could provide:

In opposing the admission of Barbara Sugarman and other women to the Jefferson Society, Alex Simon claimed that "the introduction of women would cause the male members to try to pick up the female members of the Hall." Should Mrs. Sugarman be admitted to the Society, I would expect that Mr. Simon and the other members of his "gentleman's club" would have enough discretion to refrain from trying to pick up my wife.

ROBERT A. SUGARMAN (LAW 3)[112]

Coeducation, nonetheless, had its strong advocates within the Society. Mike Lynn was one of them, and he took a different tone with the newspaper: "besides the familiar issues of equality and giving women the same opportunities at the University that men have, there is another issue which is more practical," he said. "There is the important question of the survival of the Jefferson Society in the future. The society needs to take in the best possible members, and they are often women."[113]

As late as January 1972, three semesters after the first full class of women arrived on the Grounds, the Jefferson Society was among a small group of holdouts, apart from fraternities, that refused to become coeducational, which included Alpha Phi Omega (a service organization) and Omicron Delta Kappa (a leadership honor society). The intransigence was such that the Student Council urged their president, Tom Collier, to take action that would compel coeducation by denying use of University facilities to any organization that did not comply.[114] The Student Council devoted significant time to discussing how best to handle the situation, inviting administrators to participate in the conversation as well.[115] Pressure was mounting on the Society to admit women.

It took fortuitous circumstances for change to finally occur. In 1972, Mardi Gras fell on February 15, and several members of the Society had traveled to New Orleans for the weekend to take part in the revelry. Supporters of coeducation saw a golden opportunity when they looked around Jefferson Hall—they had enough votes to pass an amendment removing the word *male* from the constitution and allowing female students to join. The *Cavalier Daily* reported that the vote was 35-7 (well above the required three-fourths needed to pass an amendment) and that it had come after hours of debate for which less than half of the member-ship was present.[116]

In the early hours of that Saturday morning, the triumphant mem-bers posted an announcement: "By a vote of the Regular Membership of the Jefferson Society of the University of Virginia, taken this twelfth day of February, Nineteen-Hundred and Seventy-Two," article I, sec-tion 1 of the constitution had been changed to say that "all students in regular attendance at the University of Virginia who have completed at least one semester shall be eligible to Probationary Membership."[117] The announcement went on to say that "the effect of this amendment . . . is to extend the privilege of membership to all students at the University, without qualification as to sex. This amendment is adopted after years of deliberative consideration as reflecting the best tradition of the Soci-ety."[118] Although it took a full three semesters and a bit of opportunistic maneuvering for the Society to become coeducational after the Univer-sity fully opened its doors to women, there was a feeling that women had a rightful place in Jefferson Hall and in the debate and discourse that takes place within its walls. The Society's announcement put it most clearly: "The process whereby the Society has affirmed its dynamic concern for the future and stewardship of the rights of free speech has been in the best tradition, moreover, of free and open debate. No tyranny of ideology shall prevail where the collision of the minds in an atmosphere of decorum is sanctified in tradition."[119]

The Society elected its first female member that very night, from five who were under consideration: Barbara Golden, a history major from New York in the first class of women, had insisted on interviewing that semester (and several before that), and once the constitutional bar to her membership was removed, she was easily elected to probationary membership.[120] She had the support of her future husband, Mike Lynn, who was then vice president and who had helped lead the charge for the constitutional amendment.[121]

A debater in high school, Golden was looking for an outlet to continue her interest in public speaking while in college, and Lynn had brought her to several meetings, thinking she would enjoy watching the Soci-ety's debates. She was captivated by the spirit of the Hall and wanted to join almost immediately. She recalls "show[ing] up for interviews every semester, even though the Society had no intention of admitting me under the existing by-laws." Then Lynn seized the opportunity on the Friday night before Mardi Gras, and Golden was elected.[122] "'That no doubt cemented our relationship," remarked Lynn in a newspaper article profiling the couple in 2014.[123]

Now the chief judge of the US District Court for the Northern District of Texas, Barbara Golden Lynn remembers her time in the Jefferson Society fondly. She recalled,

My entire experience as an undergraduate at the University of Virginia was affected by my association with the Society . . . my experience with the Hall and members of the Hall was really one of the high points of my life. I learned a great deal here, I think I made a positive difference, and I treasure my memories of it.[124]

She excelled in the Society, winning the 25th Moomaw Oratorical Contest shortly after joining, delivering a speech entitled "The End of World War Two" on the bombing of Hiroshima and Nagasaki.[125] The next fall she served in the important position of probationary chair, helping new members navigate expectations and requirements as they joined the Society. She met with academic success at the University as well, and she was selected to be an Echols Scholar and a member of the prestigious, honorary Raven Society.[126] She continued trailblazing for women after graduating from the University, becoming the first female partner at a major Dallas law firm before being appointed to the federal bench by Bill Clinton in 1999.[127] Like Wesley Harris, Judge Lynn has returned to visit the Society on several occasions, sharing observations from her tenure as a judge.[128]

It did not take long for women to establish a strong presence in the Society. Lynn recalls being warmly welcomed by the Society's members after joining, and she found the Society full of "wonderful, intellectually stimulating public speakers and outstanding rhetoric[ians]."[129] An article marking the Society's 150th year in 1975 penned by Robin Lee Ackerman and James Guinivan pointed out that just three years after coeducation, "almost 15 women are either members or future members."[130] Women sought membership actively and fit naturally into the society. Ackerman and Guinivan wrote:

The admission of women to the Hall has done little to alter its character radically, since those who apply tend, quite naturally, to be those who are attracted by the Hall as it is. Therefore, any changes they have made have been subtle ones.

Barbara Golden . . . used to hope that admitting women would cause the men
to become better gentleman and the Hall thus to live up better to its self-image.
Most members would agree that this is what happened.[131]

Four years later the Society elected its first female president, Anne
Camper, in the fall semester of 1979.

The addition of African American and female members to the Society would forever alter the character of the organization. Many felt the
inclusion of women marked the beginning of a new era. Roy L. Alson, the
secretary during the spring of 1973, remarked in his final set of minutes
that most of those who could recall a time when the Society was all male
would graduate at the end of the semester:

> With this meeting, the "Old Hall" as it was known to many of us ceased, and
> while it was a time of sadness and nostalgia, for all election meetings in the
> spring are, it was also a time of hope, for the Hall is changing and growing. Do
> not mourn for the Old Hall, for it outlived its day. To survive, this Society must
> adapt, because if we do not, we stagnate. Stagnation and intelligent debate can-
> not coexist in the same room. To those who leave, we express our thanks for all
> you have given to the Society. We will indeed miss your presence on Fridays,
> but there is a spirit that lives on and in that spirit, we hope you will, as Mr.
> McRae said, ". . . return to drink from the cup served with cheer on the old west
> range." We await your return.[132]

The often bitter debates surrounding integration and coeducation had at
last been resolved, and new generations of members, African Americans
and women finally among them on equal footing, arrived ready to shape
the Society according to their own vision.

The University of Virginia Magazine Folds

Amid the celebrations of the Restoration Ball and the debates over integration and coeducation, one of the most venerable institutions associated with the Jefferson Society and the University quietly faded from existence, reinforcing the change in the character of the Society. Even as the
Society was successfully adapting to the growing, modern University, the
century-old *University of Virginia Magazine* failed to survive the changing
environment. It was racked with over $6,000 of debt in back fees to the

printers, and declining revenues spelled the end for the magazine, which finally ceased publication 1969.

Since its humorous counterpart, the *Virginia Spectator*, had effectively shut down in 1958, the *University of Virginia Magazine* remained the lone literary publication for the University. The release of each issue, which came quarterly, was noted by the *Cavalier Daily*, and students were invited to purchase a copy in Newcomb Hall.[133] *UVM* even began releasing a Christmas issue in 1962 to fill the gap left by the lack of a holiday issue of the *Spectator*, and the Jefferson Society also continued to offer a prize for the best piece to appear in *UVM* in a given year.[134] But despite the time and energy devoted by so many to its continued success, students could not be persuaded to purchase enough copies to keep the publication afloat, and it went into irreversible debt.

The rapid broadening and professionalization of the University curriculum lessened student interest in literature and writing from what it had been just ten years earlier, and there was no way for a literary magazine to survive, even with the support of the Society. There was simply not enough interest among students to support a full-scale publication of literature and creative writing, and even more than one hundred years of history could not keep the *Mag* afloat. The Society valiantly tried to raise the money necessary to save it by hosting a Poe Ball in 1970, but even this event lost money and the Society was forced to discharge the debts over time.[135] The impact of the *Magazine* cannot be overstated, even as it faded from existence. By the end of the 1960s, the University of Virginia was recognized globally as a premier institution for the study of English literature and creative writing—a reputation placed in bold relief by the recent stays of William Faulkner and John Dos Passos as authors-in-residence. The *University of Virginia Magazine* had long provided an outlet for students to practice their literary talents, becoming a centerpiece of the literary culture at the University of Virginia.

The Society continued its interest in promoting the literary arts, and on at least one occasion tried to bring a student magazine back to the Grounds. Spurred by the efforts of two successive presidents, Charles Sharp and Stephen Jordan, the Society briefly revived the *Virginia Spectator* in the early 1990s.[136] With Peter Soderquist as the first editor, the first issue of the resurrected publication was released in the fall of 1990.[137] But, as always, the *Mag* suffered from lack of financial support, and the effort lasted for only a few semesters.[138] The *Jefferson Society Journal* (sometimes known simply as the *Jefferson Journal*) a newsletter for alumni that began publication in 1980, is now the only somewhat regular publication of the Society.

1975: The Society's Sesquicentennial

Despite closing the book on the *Mag*, there was much cause for celebration at the 150th anniversary of the Jefferson Society's founding in 1975. The sesquicentennial celebrations were not quite as grand as those marking the centennial—classes stayed in session throughout the revelry, while President Alderman had cancelled them fifty years earlier. But the festivities suited the ways in which the Society had changed since then. The series of events that marked the occasion over Founder's Day weekend, from April 11 through April 13, were a mixture of heartfelt retrospective and lighthearted, tongue-in-cheek celebration. The annual Founder's Day Dinner, which the Society had been hosting since 1908, was held in the Clark Hall Mural Room (the Rotunda was still under construction).[139] At the event, Society leaders Robin Lee Ackerman and James Guinivan recalled the "heyday of such societies . . . in the nineteenth century, when, according to the Southern Agrarian poet John Gould Fletcher, 'what took the place of athletics in the older schools of the South were literary and debating societies.'"[140] But the Jefferson Society could still claim a place at the University of Virginia, where even after 150 years students continued to flock to Jefferson Hall.

The Society lampooned its storied history during the sesquicentennial year with two humorous debates: one, "Resolved: That the Patrick Henry Society is Rowdy and Vulgar, and Not a True Representation of the Literary and Debating Talents of University Gentlemen," and another debate in which one side argued "that the University needs a more serious debating society founded on the principles of Thomas Jefferson," with the other side "arguing that the 'beer and bullshit' society is all the University really wants."[141] On a more serious note, the Society also traveled to engage both the Whig-Clio Society at Princeton and the Douglas Southall Freeman Society at the University of Richmond in competitive debates.[142]

After 150 years, the Society remained a lively and important facet of student life at the University of Virginia, though changed by the passage of time. Whether attracted to the Society's history, or to Jefferson Hall as a place to meet and engage with their peers from across the Grounds, more students joined the Jefferson Society every semester, including Student Council presidents, athletes, fraternity men, and the best speakers and debaters the University could call its own. To their ranks were added women and African American students, who earned the right to call themselves members of the Jefferson Society soon after the University accepted them as students. The Society they joined had left behind the political gamesmanship and gentlemanly ritual of years past to focus on creating a vibrant forum for discussion every Friday evening. And after working for more than a century to foster the literary culture of the University by sponsoring efforts like the *University of Virginia Magazine* and the *Virginia Spectator*, the Society turned its attention to finding new ways to give back to the University, such as the Restoration Ball. The Jefferson Society continued to develop into an intellectual organization for college students in the following decades, by heightening the already rigorous standards expected of both members and applicants and by hosting speakers and debates aimed at broadening intellectual pursuits outside of the classroom.

CHAPTER EIGHT

The Society Today

An Intellectual Organization in the Modern Age

Over the past forty years, the Jefferson Society has solidified its reputation as an intellectual organization for students in the modern age; at the same time the University of Virginia has bolstered its own prestige among colleges and universities. Following the tumultuous decades of the 1960s and '70s, the University's record of academic excellence, particularly in English literature, world languages, science, and the humanities, gained worldwide recognition.

Beginning in the late twentieth and continuing into the twenty-first century, higher education has grown increasingly competitive as universities fight to attract the best students, the most-qualified faculty, and the largest philanthropic donations. This "arms race," as some commentators have called it, has driven universities to invest monumental resources into building state-of-the-art facilities, while treating students as savvy consumers seeking utility from their college education rather than a life-shaping experience. The rise in popularity of college rankings, epitomized by those published annually in *U.S. News & World Report*, exemplifies this thirst for information and hyperawareness of reputation on the part of prospective students.[1] The University of Virginia has performed well in national rankings since they first appeared in 1983, climbing into the top twenty-five and remaining there ever since. The success and notoriety of the University's two marquee professional schools, the School of Law and the Darden School of Business, helped solidify the University's strong reputation. While the University had long been recognized as a prestigious institution, in part because of its rich history, it was only in the latter half of the twentieth century that it achieved true global excellence and reach.

In addition to its academic prestige, the University of Virginia also attracted national notoriety for being a major party school in the 1970s and early '80s. "Easters," a raucous weekend full of "beer-soaked gatherings that drew thousands of people from out of town, filling Madison Bowl and forcing the closure of Rugby Road," earned an infamous reputation for being the biggest and best college party on the East Coast.[2] The uncontrolled drinking and partying, which began as a series of tame tea parties and balls at the turn of the century, led *Playboy* magazine to rank the University as the number one party school in the country in 1974, an accolade of a very different stripe than those the school was earning for academics. The burning of a "junked" automobile became an annual fixture at Easters that same year. After numerous attempts to keep things under control, the administration was forced to take action, first moving the event to a more controlled location before permanently cancelling it in 1982. The University of Virginia had matured into a modern college, complete with a stellar academic reputation and a raucous fun streak.

The Jefferson Society occupied a somewhat different place at the University during this period of sometimes wild partying. Although the keg still made a weekly appearance in the back corner of the Hall, the Society was busy holding "debates on controversial topics, such as withdrawal from the United Nations, the imposition of excess-profits taxes on oil companies, and American policy on Indochina."[3] According to the Society, "these debates are held to provide a forum for members to present and defend their views, not to put the Society on record on either side. The debate itself, not the final vote, is the most important thing."[4] In the last quarter of the twentieth century, the Society had once again turned its attention to the spirited pursuit of debate and oratory as a vehicle for testing ideas and exploring issues of the day. Debate captured most of the Society's attention, and the topics for discussion were limitless. The membership deliberately kept the floor of Jefferson Hall open to all ideas and perspectives: "As a corollary to these principles, the Society traditionally refuses to take official stands on controversial political topics, preferring instead to remain an impartial forum for all views."[5] The Society had welcomed diverse perspectives since its inception—recall Merritt Robinson's abolitionist speech at the 1832 Intermediate Celebration—but not taking stances on debate topics was a departure from the days when the Society openly advocated a particular side of certain issues, as in the case

FIGURE 25. Students gather to listen to a speaker in Jefferson Hall. Image courtesy of the Albert and Shirley Small Special Collections Library at the University of Virginia, University of Virginia Visual History Collection, U.Va. Prints and Photographs File, RG-30/1/10.011, Print 11672.

of its support of Virginia's secession or its opposition to the expansion of enrollment in the early 1970s.

To cement its place in the new intellectual pantheon of the University, the Society needed to accomplish several things. First, with enrollment now in excess of 17,000 students, the Society increased its selectivity and strengthened the requirements for membership, in part to attract the best and brightest students as new members. To do so, the Society implemented a more rigorous interview process, formalized and expanded the expectations of probationary members, committed itself to public service, and continued to take up intellectually challenging questions for debate. The Society devoted significant energy toward its Distinguished Speaker Series, bringing scholars, experts, and public figures to Jefferson Hall for the benefit of the membership and the wider University community alike. Finally, in 1979, several members of the Jefferson Society resurrected the long-dormant Washington Society to increase opportunities for debate on the Grounds, reviving the long-standing friendly rivalry between the two organizations. These changes helped the Jefferson Society mature into the intellectual forum it is for students today.

Selecting Members

After over a century of relying simply on the recommendation of existing members to find and vet new ones, the Society began conducting open interviews in the 1960s. At first they were perfunctory—conducted over the course of one or two days and lasting only a few minutes each. The Society advertised in the *Cavalier Daily* to reach potential members:

Membership interviews will be held by the Jefferson Society today and tomorrow between 3 p.m. and 5 p.m. in Jefferson Hall on West Range. Male students in all schools and departments of the University are invited to make application.

Although the interview will not as a rule last longer than five minutes, the applicant should anticipate a wait of up to a half hour. Those elected to membership must serve for one term as probationary members. Election to regular membership is based upon the quality of a speech made by the probationary, and in consideration of his attendance record.[6]

By the 1980s, membership interviews had become much more rigorous. Over the span of an entire week, Society members confronted potential probationaries for forty-five minutes to an hour in adversarial discussions, with teams of four members testing a candidate's skill in argument and knowledge of a set of topics the candidate selected. At the conclusion of the interview, each member of the panel evaluated the candidate's performance in writing before making a final recommendation of passage or failure. The panel's comments and recommendations were forwarded to the Membership Committee, who made a holistic evaluation of all the interviewees (which often numbered in the hundreds). The committee would then recommend a set of candidates for election to probationary membership, subject to the approval of the Society as a whole. This method of selecting new members remains largely unchanged to this day.

Performing well in an interview was sometimes insufficient to secure admission. The Society set a high bar for offering probationary membership, requiring the approval of four-fifths of the regular members present and voting for any individual to be elected. Even those who interviewed well sometimes failed to secure the requisite support for a variety of reasons. All membership deliberations were—and still are—conducted in strict secrecy, allowing for free discussion of the candidates without fear of retribution. Additionally, although this is no longer the case, by about 1960 undergraduate students in their first semester of study were ineligible to interview until they gained the benefit of more experience.[7] Success in this membership process proved to be quite difficult, and only a small portion of those who interviewed could expect to be elected to probationary membership. The selectivity of the modern Society caused it to be well regarded by students and faculty alike for the quality of the members ultimately selected through this rigorous process.

Probationary Presentations

The Society also raised its expectations of probationary members once elected. In 1977, Probationary chairman Charles Choyce focused his attention on the first presentation given by probationaries to the Society, taking it upon himself to make it a more important step in the process of joining the Society. New members had long been asked to give speeches early in their tenure, which were known for years as maiden speeches. These would typically be assigned to and delivered by a new member within the first few meetings of joining the Society, usually without notes and on a subject chosen at random by the president.[8] When the Society formalized the semester-long probationary process in the 1930s, delivering a speech was institutionalized as a requirement to move from probationary to regular membership. These speeches could be delivered on any topic of the probationary's choosing.

By the 1950s, the probationary presentation became central to membership in the Society, but the precise requirements remained somewhat vague. Choyce pushed the Society to standardize the criteria by which each presentation would be evaluated and to give probationary members greater flexibility in how they might fulfill the requirement. Choyce drew on the practice that originated in the 1910s at the urging of Professor Paul of appointing a member as "critic" to offer constructive feedback on the debates and speeches of the evening. While the president had intermittently appointed critics to review individual or groups of probationary speeches for decades, in September 1977 the Society began deliberately appointing a specific critic for each probationary presentation. The critic would discuss the quality of the presentation and recommend passage or failure, after which the Society would vote on the question. Failure meant the probationary would have to try again at a subsequent meeting.[9] The practice continues to this day.

The next year, Choyce proposed an even more important change to the probationary presentation. Until then, probationary members had only one type of presentation available to them—a speech. In 1978, the "Choyce Amendment" gave probationary members the option to read a piece of original literary work or argue one side of a debate instead of giving a speech in order to fulfill the presentation requirement. Charles English, who would later go on to be president and a Room 7 resident, was the first probationary to debate under this new system, for which he was honored as having given the best presentation of the semester.[10] Probationary members continue to enjoy the option of presenting a speech, but many opt to debate or to present a literary work, according to their preference.

At roughly the same time, probationaries became subject to a period of "questioning and heckling" at the conclusion of their presentation (or after the constructive portion of their debate) to test their ability to think on their feet and knowledge of their presentation topic.[11] Regular members gleefully shouted "Probationary!!" at the top of their lungs to get the attention of the poor student at the front of the room, often hurling at them some obscure question or point of contention. Frequently, the probationary barely had time to utter a few words in response before the yelling started again. In time, it became common practice to demand that, during the questioning and heckling, probationary members answer questions on "Hall facts," which might include a brief history of the Society, the names of specific famous and honorary members, the Society's Greek letters and Latin motto, and several other tidbits about the Society's traditions and culture. Probationary members are still subjected to this questioning, but by most accounts the intensity of the heckling has trailed off in favor of more discerning questions.[12]

In many respects, probationary presentations provide new members an opportunity to offer their first contribution to the intellectual life of the Society, delivering a focused presentation on a particular topic of interest or expertise. The importance of these presentations is highlighted by the fact that, in accordance with the Society's parliamentary custom, they are one of three instances that merit the undivided attention of everyone in the room, the others being a "point of Societal privilege" and a "swansong," the last speech a member gives before graduating. Probationaries devote substantial time to preparing their presentation, and they are judged to an exacting standard. Often probationaries are asked to present several times before they deliver what is judged to be a passing presentation, adding yet another challenging step to becoming a full member of the Society.

The Jefferson Society Distinguished Speaker Series

Building on the tradition of Final Celebrations, which had drawn such distinguished speakers as William Jennings Bryan, Grover Cleveland, and Teddy Roosevelt to the Grounds of the University of Virginia, in the 1960s and '70s the Jefferson Society moved to institutionalize its invitation of speakers by including them as regularly scheduled parts of its weekly meetings. The Society had, on occasion, invited speakers to meetings in the past, but many of these were University faculty or others who dealt with subjects of unique interest to the Society—Edgar Allan Poe, Woodrow Wilson, and professors who could expound on the art of public speaking and oratory or literature, for example.

Regularly inviting speakers to meetings was another way the Society deepened its intellectual, academic, and cultural contributions to the University community. Beginning in the 1960s, the Society heavily publicized its speakers and opened the events to the general public. The Society's vice president traditionally arranged the Speaker Series, sitting ex officio as the chair of the Society's Program Committee. Invited speakers were (and still are) meant to be reflective of the latest scholarship, the state of the arts and sciences, or the cutting edge of salient political issues. Speakers continue to be at the top of their fields, and taken as a whole, the subjects of their presentations have touched upon almost every imaginable discipline.

Since the series began, hundreds of distinguished speakers have graced Jefferson Hall with their presence, including politicians, authors, scientists, artists, journalists, and historians. Every University of Virginia president has spoken before the Society, as have many rectors of the Board of Visitors and countless faculty members, including football and basketball coaches. Among the most notable recent visitors have been Chief Justice William Rehnquist, US senators John Warner and George Allen, Virginia governor Jim Gilmore, then Georgia governor Jimmy Carter, Vermont governor and presidential candidate Howard Dean, Utah governor and presidential candidate Gary Johnson, Congressman Bob Barr, US senator and presidential candidate Gary Hart, Congressman Asa Hutchinson,

Colombian president Victor Mosquera Chaux, authors William Faulkner, Robert Frost, John Dos Passos, and Tom Clancy, Pulitzer Prize–winning journalists George Will and Bob Woodward, Peabody Prize–winning broadcaster Charlie Rose, political scientist John Mearshimer, Nobel Prize–winning economist Robert Solow, and Antarctic explorer Roald Amundsen.[13]

At times, speakers invited to address the Society have been controversial, and their presentations have spurred Society members to action. In the early part of the 1960s, the Society took a keen interest in African affairs, inviting a series of speakers that included American ambassadors to African countries, African ambassadors to the United States, officials from the Department of State, and several African political leaders.[14] In 1961, when the Society invited the South African ambassador to the United States, William Naude, to speak before the Hall, opponents of apartheid threatened to protest and disrupt the event.[15] President Shannon was supportive of the Society's desire to hear speakers expressing all points of view and wrote to the Society on the day the event was scheduled to take place:

The Department of State has advised the University that certain persons have threatened to demonstrate this evening, on the Grounds of the University, against a visiting speaker. . . . The purpose of these threats is to dissuade the members of the Jefferson Society from holding a meeting to hear their invited speaker, an ambassador accredited to the United States. Students at the University founded by Thomas Jefferson have the right to hear, without interference, the views of any invited guest. Also, any visitor to our grounds should be courteously received, whether he agrees or disagrees with the views of any other visitor. [16]

Shannon offered the protection of the University police so that the event could continue without incident. They were instructed to allow for peaceful picketing outside but not to permit vocal protests or indoor demonstration.

The next year, the Society invited Moise Tshombe, the controversial leader of the secessionist Katanga Province in the Democratic Republic of the Congo. Tshombe accepted the invitation, but the Department of State denied his request for a visa to travel to the United States. The stated reason for the denial was that his absence from the Congo "would jeopardize progress" toward unification under UN supervision. This was a euphemistic framing for American fears that the Soviet Union would use the unrest to gain a foothold in the heart of Africa and was prompted by an even more urgent desire to conceal American involvement in the crisis following the toppling of Prime Minister Patrice Lumumba and the installation of kleptocratic military dictator Colonel Joseph Mobutu.[17]

The denial of Tshombe's visa received national press attention, and many rose to the Society's defense, harshly criticizing the federal administration's perceived violation of the free exchange of ideas and information. One editorial in the *Richmond News Leader* even invited the administration to "take a nod" from the Jefferson Society, whose "atmosphere of free expression of opinion" was vastly preferable to the obfuscation of the State Department.[18]

The Society pressed the issue. The membership displayed such interest in learning about the situation in Katanga that, while continuing to advocate for Tshombe's visa with the State Department, it sought out another speaker on the subject, Michel Struelens, a representative of the province in the United States.[19] Struelens's speech questioned the accuracy of much of the information disseminated in the Western world about Katanga. The Society responded by sending two members, Samuel Garrison and Joseph Freeman, to Katanga over the next summer to conduct field observations and publish a report on the conditions. Garrison and Freeman spent time interviewing Congolese leaders and UN administrators before writing up a historical and political analysis of the situation.[20] The Society's attention, coupled with their travels and report, helped focus public scrutiny on the issue in the United States.

Another controversy arose in 2010 when former United States Justice Department legal consultant John Yoo spoke before the Society. Yoo was the primary author of a memo to President George W. Bush that defended the legality of "enhanced interrogation techniques," including waterboarding. Protesters gathered across the street from the event and several opponents of Yoo's point of view began shouting during his speech, disturbing the presentation for several minutes.[21] Despite negative reactions in the University community to these and other speakers, the Jefferson Society remains committed to providing an open forum in which all points of view are free to be expressed and stand or fall on their own merits.

These incidents of controversy illustrate the prominence of the Jefferson Society's Distinguished Speaker Series and its critical role in exposing the University community to a wide spectrum of opinion. Over the years it has gained a national reputation for being one of the best student-run lecture programs in the country. The University has had the privilege of hearing hundreds of speakers hosted by the Society, and the series continues to be one of the Society's most visible contributions to student life at the University.

The Return of the Washington Society

The year 1979 marked the return of the Jefferson Society's debating counterpart and sometime rival, the Washington Society, after an absence of nearly fifty years from the Grounds. Three members of the Jefferson Society—J. Mitchell Aberman, Stephen L. Huntoon, and Josh Henson—took the initiative to reestablish the Washington Society. They enlisted the help of a friend, Richard Nichols Randolph, who was not a Jefferson Society member, as the 1924 constitution of the Washington Society, in force when that group last met in 1929, still contained the exclusivity clause prohibiting any student from joining both groups. R. E. Heischmen, a member of the Washington Society prior to the Great Depression, initiated Randolph into the Washington Society over the phone. Randolph then dispensed with the exclusivity clause and inducted his three friends, and the Jefferson Society could once again enjoy the company of another literary society at the University.[22]

It may seem puzzling at first that members of the Jefferson Society were the driving force behind the revival of their rival organization. Five of the first members of the new Washington Society had served as officers of the Jefferson at one time or another—Huntoon and another early member, Jack Davis, as president.[23] But the resurrection of the Washington Society had distinct benefits for the Jefferson Society. Most importantly, the two organizations could attract more interest together than one could by itself—much like the Greek system as a whole is more attractive to students than a single fraternity or sorority could be without counterparts. Second, many of the old collaborative efforts between the two groups were also restored. And, of course, it meant that the two organizations could be rivals once again.

The University had long since repurposed Washington Hall (Hotel B, East Range), so the Washington Society resumed its meetings in Jefferson Hall on Thursday nights. Its membership wasted no time in rekindling their relationship with the Jefferson Society, aided by the dual membership of many of the early members. Under the leadership of Leslie Eliason, the fifth member and first female president of the Washington Society, the societies picked up many activities where they left off, before what Washington Society members call the "interregnum." The Harrison Cup debate resumed in 1981 after the two societies agreed to terms for how it should proceed.[24] Henson recalled:

To the surprise of many, the newly revived and younger Washington Society convincingly won the reactivated debate in 1981 by unanimous decision of the judges. It was the first debate following the revival of the society and the Washington Society wasted no time in publicly claiming to have won "every Harrison Trophy Debate held in the past 50 years."[25]

Debating had been central to the relationship between the Jefferson Society and the Washington Society before the interregnum, and it would continue to give life to their interactions in the present. Recall that not only had debates between the two societies attracted talent and crowds to match, but also together the two societies had controlled the selection of debaters to represent the University at competitions. Good debating was a mark of pride in the societies, as was wit:

Jack Davis and John Jebb were the first crossover members of the Jefferson Society to join Mickey Aberman, Josh Henson and Steve Huntoon to bolster the fledgling Wash in its early revival years. . . . It was a bragging right of sorts for these first five crossovers that the heavily negotiated agreement to revive the Harrison Debate between the societies in 1980 specifically prohibited each of the five by name from participating in the event. While these five dual members probably liked to view it as a sign of their debating skill, each was also known for an unusual sense of humor and admittedly both societies might have had reason to be concerned about what any of them might do in the debate, whatever side they were supposedly representing.[26]

The Smith Simpson Debate on Diplomacy

Just five years after the Harrison Cup resumed, another contest deepened the friendly rivalry between the two groups. Smith Simpson, a career Foreign Service officer and 1927 graduate of the University, endowed a debate on diplomacy with an initial donation of $1,500.[27] Simpson had written a notable report on the "deficiencies of students applying for the Foreign Service" in 1962, pointing out that American diplomats abroad were often asked cultural questions. Many of the students "could not name a single American painter, a single composer, a single philosopher," knowledge they would need to be successful diplomats.[28] In accordance with his desire to educate future diplomats, Simpson created a debate that focused on *diplomacy* rather than rote foreign policy or international affairs. To Simpson, foreign policy could easily be taught in class, but diplomacy— and the skills, knowledge, and way of thinking it required—had to be practiced.[29] Simpson established the debate with four purposes in mind: (1) to disseminate a clearer idea of diplomacy and how it contributes to the international peace process; (2) to promote an interest in debating, which has become a significant form of communicating ideas both nationally and internationally; (3) to dignify human discourse; and (4) to make a contribution to the intellectual and cultural life of the university community (thereby hopefully reducing the excessive glorification of sports).[30] The debate was first held in the Dome Room of the Rotunda in 1986. Represented by Wolfgang Drechsler and Rafael Madan, the Jefferson Society won the first contest, along with the next three. The Washington Society has since evened the score, and the Smith Simpson Debate remains hotly contested in the spring of each year.

The two societies added a third annual debate in the early 2000s on subjects with ethical considerations. Debates between the Jefferson Society and Washington Society, occurring with greater frequency and on more sophisticated subjects, give life to the rivalry between the two organizations and add yet another intellectual element to their character.

Controversy Strikes the Society

In the late 1980s and early 1990s, the Society endured a series of controversies related to the consumption of alcohol at meetings and sexism in the membership process. Taken together, they showed the darker side of the bourbon swilling, good-old-boy's-club nature bred into the history of the Jefferson Society. The Society long held a reputation for heavy drinking— the keg in the back corner was as powerful a draw to Jefferson Hall as the speeches, debates, and political skirmishes. The Society's drinking culture initially drew negative attention when one member, Martha Cole-man, concerned that the consumption of alcohol had become excessive, alerted the Virginia ABC (Alcoholic Beverage Control). Understandably, this drew negative press and administrative ire toward the Society and its activities.[31] Coleman's actions also did not sit well with several members, who saw them as an attack on their culture and traditions. One of the Society's leaders wondered "if the Hall and its keg can hold out forever against the Women's Temperance and Anti-Fun League."[32]

No serious consequences came out of the incident for the Society, but the cavalier attitude of some of the members in response foreshadowed more serious troubles to come. No more than six years later, in the spring of 1992, a female member of the Society, Jennifer Isbell, leveled serious allegations that members of the Society were behaving in a sexist man-ner toward women, creating a "hostile environment" for female proba-tionaries. Isbell claimed that the president, Christopher Martin, handed her an issue of Penthouse and told her to read it aloud at the February 14 meeting, which she felt amounted to sexual harassment. Isbell was then serving as correspondence secretary, a post she later resigned. Isbell's complaint was ultimately, in her words, "not a case against the Jefferson Society" but against Martin himself, but the Society was implicated nev-ertheless. Martin defended his actions, replying that he had not meant to harass Isbell; rather, he had only passed the magazine along to some-one standing near him in the midst of a discussion of an article featuring Board of Visitors member Patricia Kluge.[33] While the issue was ultimately resolved by mutual agreement and resulted in no formal action, Isbell's complaint and the very public discussion that followed brought to the forefront problems that were systemic in the Society at the time: two decades after they had been admitted, women still faced challenges in joining the Society and many did not feel welcome in Jefferson Hall.[34] The "hostile environment" Isbell described was very real; it resulted in large part from the power dynamic between the Society leadership and the rest of the membership, particularly probationary members. The need to change the culture in the Hall did not go unnoticed—and that May the Society elected as president Daniel Kirwin, who they hoped could lead a turn for the better.[35]

But less than a year later, another group of Society members came forward with more extensive complaints. Seven members of the self-styled "Committee for Constructive Reform" wrote a letter to University president John Casteen, Virginia governor Douglas Wilder, the University's Board of Visitors, and major media outlets alleging systematic and repeated violation of state law, University regulations, and the student code of conduct on the part of the Society. Writing with the goal of reforming and improving the Society, the authors of the letter, including a former president, James Feezel, accused Society members of "sexual assault, verbal harassment, and other conduct hostile to women."[36] They described a number of incidents in detail: one female member left a meeting abruptly after being told her probationary presentation had only been accepted because it was 3 a.m., she was cute, and she was wearing a short skirt. Another female member was greeted by a male member who said "nice tits."[37] The letter also made reference to Isbell's complaint from the previous year about *Penthouse* magazine. Heather White, another of the letter's authors, read the letter at the April 9, 1993, meeting of the Society, announcing her own resignation in the process. She revealed that she had been sexually harassed "by an officer of the society. She [had] decided not to report the incident because she was afraid that the conflict would keep her from being accepted as a regular member" and that she had later received no vindication from an internal investigation.[38]

The Committee for Constructive Reform felt these discrete incidents were products of an engrained culture in the Society that glorified sexual conquest. It had become customary to award a package of condoms to the regular member "who has 'scored' with the most probationary members," and the letter alleged women were consistently harassed and disrespected.[39] These allegations mounted on top of the rampant alcohol consumption during meetings, a good part of which, the committee claimed, was by those under the age of twenty-one. The committee urged the University administration to address these issues, believing the Society to be incapable of reforming itself from within.[40] In addition to the public letter, one member, Guinevere Christmann, filed a bill of compliance in Albemarle County Circuit Court, demanding the Society and its officers come into compliance with the terms of its agreement with the University as a student organization, which included guarantees of nondiscrimination on the basis of gender, race, religion, or sexual orientation.[41] No individual charges were filed against members, however.

The accusations threw the Society into a frenzy. Debate raged for hours that meeting and the next (and spilled over into the pages of the *Cavalier Daily* for months) about how best to address these issues.[42] Some professed to be "sickened" by the idea of sexual harassment, yet they felt that the inappropriate behavior of a few members should not reflect poorly on the organization as a whole.[43] Others believed that the prevailing culture in the Society brought out the worst in its members, condoning or even encouraging abusive behavior. Still others questioned why the committee had taken their complaints to the administration and the public instead of bringing them before the student Judiciary Committee, calling their choice a rebuke of student self-governance.[44] Committee member Brian Dally defended the choice. Citing the Society's unique situation within the University community resulting from its history and place in the Academical Village, he urged intervention from without because the hostile, sexist climate had become so entrenched.[45] The president, Dan Kirwin, insisted that change from within was still possible and that significant progress had been made since Isbell's complaints a year earlier. Nonetheless, the *Cavalier Daily* reported that many female members who stayed for the discussion on April 9 left because of sexist remarks that persisted from some members during the discussion.[46]

President Casteen responded to the allegations by ordering the Office of the Dean of Students and the University Police Department to investigate the Society's activities. The Committee for Constructive Reform met with the vice president for Student Affairs, Ernest Ern, and Chief of Police Michael Sheffield to review their concerns. The sentiment was that the Society had a long way to go to improve: "Society President Dan Kirwin has made some important efforts, but none of them have had a substantial effect, despite his good intentions," said Dally.[47] The committee hoped the Society would be placed under administrative control and supervision.

Ern selected a panel of four faculty members and two students to conduct the formal investigation and recommend sanctions or condemnation for the Society.[48] Ern himself undertook a review of the applications for membership and the written comments of interview panelists for the preceding three semesters, and "based on the record," he concluded "there is no evidence that the society has acted discriminatorily in accepting members on probationary status."[49] But the allegations contained in the committee's letter and pervasive problems with alcohol told a different story, and by mid-June the panel had recommended sanctions based on their investigation.

Ern informed the Society on June 23 that it would "lose all use of" and control over Jefferson Hall for the fall 1993 semester, the first time the Society had been without their home since 1837. The Society would also be required to create an ombudsman who could "provide an avenue for probationary members to seek assistance for any ways they might feel exploited by regular members, without retribution," as well as construct a plan for compliance with University policies regarding alcohol at all Society events, including those held in Room 7.[50]

The press coverage and administrative action resulting from these allegations brought the Jefferson Society to task. The Society's very survival was threatened, and it needed sound leadership to negotiate addressing these issues adequately while keeping the Society whole. Kirwin, nearing the end of two terms as president of the Society spanning the 1992–1993 academic year, continued as the Society's representative to the University and in any legal proceedings until the situation was resolved, even though his term was technically over.

To comply with the University's sanctions, the Society made several important and substantive changes to the constitution, in addition to continuing efforts to change the culture in the Hall. The Probationary Committee was charged with defining and circulating set and specific requirements for membership at the beginning of each semester, so that they might be understood and followed by all. A new position, the sergeant-at-arms, would ensure the Society practiced appropriate nondiscriminatory policies and followed all relevant laws. The keg was banished from Jefferson Hall. Finally, to reinforce the seriousness of the membership process, a penalty of expulsion for divulging details of membership proceedings was instituted.[51] Interim vice president of student affairs Robert T. Canevari and the University administration allowed the Society to return to Jefferson Hall in January 1994 after a full semester of exclusion.[52] Heather White characterized the measures taken by the University as "constructive."[53] These troubling events reinforce how even the most well intentioned of organizations can, without careful stewardship, be vulnerable to abuse. That the Society persisted and took necessary steps to improve its climate is a testament to its leadership and the dedication the membership felt toward its foundational principles.

The Society Today

Now almost two hundred years old, the Jefferson Society stands as a monument to the efforts of each successive student generation to create and sustain an institution where they could pursue their interests, learn from their peers, and shape their University experience.

From the earliest days, when the sons of elite southern planters practiced a social ritual designed to prepare them for political life, to the college men of the late nineteenth century who played at oratory and constitution making to advance their experience beyond the classroom, to the beer-guzzling humorists of the 1960s who prized a quick wit above all else, each year new students have made the Society their own—adding one more layer to its already rich, storied traditions.

The Society today bears the mark of the contributions of all of these students. Three times each year, the Society evokes the pomp and elegance of the old-time Final Celebrations by hosting formal affairs: the Founder's Day Banquet, the Wilson Day Banquet, and the Restoration Ball.

It is unlikely that students will ever again resort to boxing as a way to settle an election in the way Murray McGuire and Mallory Cannon did in 1893. Nonetheless, every semester the election for president of the Jefferson Society remains one of the most hotly contested and closely watched political contests among students, with hundreds of members turning out to vote and dozens of speeches offered in favor of the different candidates.

Jefferson Hall is a place of lively intellectual discourse for students from every corner of the University. Beginning with the rigorous interview process, members challenge themselves to consider new ideas through debate and conversation. Week in and week out, speakers at the cutting edge of their fields introduce new subjects and perspectives to students in the Hall or revisit old ones with fresh eyes. Following in the steps of Edgar Allan Poe and Thomas Nelson Page, poets and authors offer their original writing to a discerning audience, honing their craft and sharing their talents. In many ways, the Society became and remains the heart and soul of intellectual life outside the classroom at the University of Virginia; nowhere else do students from every school engage with one another intellectually as they can in Jefferson Hall.

But what is most enduring, most remarkable, about the Jefferson Society is the way it is woven into the very fabric of the University of Virginia. It is astonishing to consider how many of the University's favored sons and daughters and its most prominent alumni spent many of their student days in Jefferson Hall. A home for every generation of students, founded just weeks after the first of them arrived, no organization has been more central to student life than the Jefferson Society. Nor has any other organization defined so many of the contours of the University itself than the one that calls a small, unassuming hotel on West Range home—the only building at the University of Virginia named for its founder, Thomas Jefferson himself.

Afterword

The Fate of Literary Societies

Thomas Harding's monograph *College Literary Societies* concludes in 1876. He writes of the demise of literary societies across the country: "Between 1866 and 1876 the literary societies of most northern colleges declined rapidly as students developed new interests—athletics, social fraternities, and music and dramatic clubs, as well as the liberalization of the curriculum," while those at southern colleges and universities struggled to revive after the Civil War and never attained their former vitality.[1] Harding is wrong to give up on literary societies so easily. While it is true that they are undoubtedly less central to student life today than they once were, the preceding pages emphatically refute Harding's misapprehension that literary societies have become irrelevant to modern higher education.

In addition to the competition mentioned above, Harding offers four reasons for the decline of literary societies:

First, debating and public speaking activities became part of the curriculum, thereby depriving the literary society of its justification for existence.

Second, the college or university administration assumed responsibility for the annual commencement activities, including the expense of securing well-known speakers . . . .

Third, other student groups assumed responsibility for editing or publishing the college magazines, which were often started by the literary societies.

Finally, most of the society libraries were absorbed by the college or university.[2]

All of these things came to pass in one way or another at the University of Virginia. The Jefferson Society, rather than succumbing to irrelevance, continually reinvented itself, finding new ways to capture the hearts and minds of each generation of students and giving back to the University community continuously through a variety of activities. Interest and participation in literary societies was great enough to sustain two such organizations when the Washington Society was resurrected in 1979. Still alive and well in the twenty-first century, both organizations have memberships numbering in the hundreds.

There are dozens of literary societies thriving at other universities as well, mostly on the East Coast, some with histories as rich and storied as the Jefferson Society. Recognizing that literary societies might benefit from support and networking, several of those still in existence organized to form the Association of American College Literary Societies. Organized in 1978, the AACLS was formed "to protect the twenty-five remaining literary and debating societies in the United States and to promote the formation of new societies."[3] By joining the AACLS, the Jefferson Society hoped it could help strengthen the community of collegiate literary societies and further the ideals of intellectual curiosity and the power of debate.[4]

The AACLS initiated a series of congresses for representatives of the different societies to gather, which the Jefferson Society hosted at the University of Virginia on at least a few occasions.[5] While it was relatively short-lived, the association helped build lasting relationships between literary and debating societies at other colleges and universities that have endured. The Jefferson Society hosts regular events and visits with the Georgetown Philodemic Society, the Dialectic and Philanthropic Societies at the University of North Carolina Chapel Hill, the American Whig-Cliosophic Society at Princeton, and the Demosthenian Literary Society at the University of Georgia, to name a few.

Although each is distinct and practices its own traditions, these societies and others like them are key facets of student life at their respective institutions, woven into their fabric, often from the earliest days. So long as students continue to value defining their own enterprises, the perspective gained by hearing differing opinions, and honing their skills in debate and public speaking, there will be a place for literary and debating societies at colleges and universities across the country.

On to Three Centuries

The meticulous minutes, voluminous correspondence, and considerable library of publications that gave life to this book tell a remarkable story.

The compelling stories, enduring contributions, and unique characters chronicled here speak for themselves as a testament to the awesome impact the Jefferson Society has had on the University of Virginia and every generation of its students. Every aspect of the Society has been shaped, at least in some small way, by the thousands upon thousands of students who have walked through the doors of Jefferson Hall and left a legacy behind for us to find. That is perhaps what is most powerful about the Society—that it can be shaped into a new image by each passing generation of students, all the while maintaining its distinctive historical character, and that every student who ever called it home has a different reason for why it holds a special place in their heart.

In 2025, the Jefferson Society will celebrate its 200th anniversary. A third century will bring new students, new projects, and new memories:

We cannot mold the Hall as masters of a material thing. But we can influence its development from within as a spiritual thing. In this sense we are all somewhat pioneers in an experiment which I hope will never be finished—and which has given us a history for which we have to take no backseat to any other collegiate society in the nation. We are continually in a new age, and yet we are in the same age, able to maintain proper and useful ties with the past. You can only influence the Hall's development if you recognize and respect it as a thing of the spirit.

—R. TAYLOR HOSKINS, MAY 14, 1965[6]

Famous Members of the Jefferson Society

PRESIDENTS OF THE UNITED STATES OF AMERICA
Thomas Woodrow Wilson
James Madison*
James Monroe*

FIRST LADIES OF THE UNITED STATES
Edith Bolling Galt Wilson*

PRIME MINISTERS OF THE UNITED KINGDOM
Margaret H. Thatcher, Baroness Thatcher*

SPEAKERS OF THE UNITED STATES HOUSE OF REPRESENTATIVES
Robert Mercer Taliaferro Hunter

UNITED STATES SENATORS
Oscar W. Underwood, Senate Minority Leader, Alabama
Hugh Scott, Senate Minority Leader, Pennsylvania
Robert Mercer Taliaferro Hunter, Virginia
John S. Barbour Jr., Virginia
Willis P. Bocock, Virginia
William Cabell Bruce, Maryland
Harry F. Byrd Jr., Virginia
Clement C. Clay, Alabama
Charles Allen Culberson, Texas
John Warwick Daniel, Virginia
Charles J. Faulkner, West Virginia

*Indicates an honorary member.

John W. Stevenson, Kentucky

Claude A. Swanson, Virginia

Robert Toombs, Georgia

Louis Wigfall, Texas

John Sharp Williams, Mississippi

Eugene J. McCarthy, Minnesota*

James Monroe, Virginia*

MEMBERS OF THE UNITED STATES HOUSE OF REPRESENTATIVES

Oscar W. Underwood, House Majority Leader, Alabama

John Sharp Williams, House Minority Leader, Mississippi

James Lindsay Almond Jr., Virginia

John S. Barbour Jr., Virginia

Garland Hale "Andy" Barr IV, Kentucky

Thomas H. Bayly, Virginia

Richard L. T. Beale, Virginia

William Waters Boyce, South Carolina

William Henry Brockenbrough, Florida

John S. Caskie, Virginia

John Critcher, Virginia

Colgate W. Darden, Virginia

Wharton J. Green, North Carolina

Robert Mercer Taliaferro Hunter, Virginia

Joseph Chappell Hutcheson, Texas

Thomas W. Ligon, Maryland

Augustus Maxwell, Florida

Richard Parker, Virginia

William Ballard Preston, Virginia

Roger A. Pryor, Virginia

Hugh Scott, Pennsylvania

James Alexander Seddon, Virginia

John W. Stevenson, Kentucky

Alexander H. H. Stuart, Virginia

Claude A. Swanson, Virginia

Robert A. Thompson, Virginia

Robert Toombs, Georgia

John Randolph Tucker, Virginia

William L. Wilson, West Virginia
James Madison, Virginia*
Eugene J. McCarthy, Minnesota*

GOVERNORS
James Lindsay Almond Jr., Virginia
Charles Allen Culberson, Texas
Colgate W. Darden, Virginia
James Gilmore III, Virginia
Albertis Sydney Harrison, Virginia
Frederick W. M. Holliday, Virginia
Thomas W. Ligon, Maryland
Richard I. Manning III, South Carolina
John W. Stevenson, Kentucky
Claude A. Swanson, Virginia
Thomas H. Watts, Alabama
Thomas Woodrow Wilson, New Jersey
James Monroe, Virginia*

MEMBERS OF THE UNITED STATES CABINET
William Ballard Preston, Secretary of the Navy
Edward R. Stettinius Jr., Secretary of State and First Ambassador to the United
    Nations
Alexander H. H. Stuart, Secretary of the Interior
Claude A. Swanson, Secretary of the Navy
William L. Wilson, Postmaster General
James Madison, Secretary of State*
James Monroe, Secretary of State and Secretary of War*

NOTABLE JURISTS
James Lindsay Almond Jr., Judge of the United States Court of Appeals for the
    Federal Circuit
John W. Brockenbrough, Judge, Federal District Court
William Daniel, Judge of the Supreme Court of Virginia
Samuel J. Douglas, Judge of the Supreme Court of Florida
James Keith, Chief Justice of the Supreme Court of Virginia
George H. Lee, Judge of the Supreme Court of Virginia

Daniel B. Lucas, Chief Justice of the Supreme Court of West Virginia

Barbara M. Lynn, Judge, Federal District Court, First Female Member of the
Society

Richard Morris, Associate Justice, Supreme Court of Texas

William B. Napton, Judge of the Supreme Court of Missouri

William J. Robertson, Judge of the Supreme Court of Virginia

James Madison, Father of the Constitution and Bill of Rights*

Gilbert du Motier, Marquis de Lafayette, author of the Declaration of the
Rights of Man and Citizen*

Gordon Slynn, Baron Slynn of Hadley, European Court of Justice*

OFFICIALS OF THE CONFEDERATE STATES OF AMERICA

John B. Baldwin, Confederate House of Representatives from Virginia

William Waters Boyce, Confederate House of Representatives from South
Carolina

John W. Brockenbrough, Confederate House of Representatives from Virginia

Clement Clay, Confederate Senate from Alabama

Muscoe R. H. Garnett, Confederate House of Representatives from Virginia

Thomas S. Gholson, Confederate House of Representatives from Virginia

James P. Holcombe, Confederate House of Representatives from Virginia

Frederick W. M. Holliday, Confederate House of Representatives from Virginia

Robert Mercer Taliaferro Hunter, Secretary of State of the Confederate States
of America, Confederate Senate from Virginia

Augustus Maxwell, Confederate Senate from Florida

William Ballard Preston, Confederate Senate from Virginia

Roger A. Pryor, Confederate House of Representatives from Virginia

George W. Randolph, Secretary of War of the Confederate States of America

James Alexander Seddon, Secretary of War of the Confederate States of
America

Robert Toombs, Secretary of State of the Confederate States of America

Thomas H. Watts, Attorney General of the Confederate States of America

NOTABLE ACADEMICS

John Stewart Bryan, President of the College of William and Mary

John T. Casteen III, President of the University of Virginia, President of the
University of Connecticut

Charles W. Dabney, President of the University of Cincinnati, President of the University of Tennessee

Colgate W. Darden, President of the University of Virginia

James H. French, President of Concord University

Wesley Harris, Associate Provost, Massachusetts Institute of Technology, First African American Member of the Society

Tiberius G. Jones, President of the University of Richmond

Benjamin B. Minor, President of the University of Missouri

Robert Saunders Jr., President of the College of William and Mary

Charles E. Taylor, President of Wake Forest University

Lyon Gardiner Tyler, President of the College of William and Mary

Thomas Woodrow Wilson, President of Princeton University

William L. Wilson, President of Washington and Lee University

Edwin A. Alderman, President of the University of Virginia, Tulane, and University of North Carolina*

Paul B. Barringer, President of Virginia Polytechnic Institute*

Ernest Campbell Mead, Professor Emeritus of Music, Recipient Thomas Jefferson Award*

John L. Newcomb, President of the University of Virginia*

Edgar F. Shannon, President of the University of Virginia*

NOTABLE LITERARY FIGURES

Philip Alexander Bruce, noted Virginia historian

William Cabell Bruce, Pulitzer Prize–winning author

Joseph Bryan, Editor, *Richmond Times Dispatch*

Virginius Dabney, Pulitzer Prize–winning author

W. S. Gilman, Editor, *Richmond Whig*

Armistead C. Gordon, noted southern author

James Hay Jr., author of "The Honor Men"

Thomas Nelson Page, noted southern author

Edgar Allan Poe

William F. Ritchie, Editor, *Richmond Inquirer*

John R. Thompson, Editor, *Southern Literary Messenger*

James S. Wilson, Founder and Editor, *Virginia Quarterly Review*

William Faulkner*

George Will, Pulitzer Prize–winning author and journalist

Presidents of the Jefferson Society

The compilation of this appendix represents the first-ever complete listing of the students who served as Jefferson Society president. The listing is organized chronologically by academic year. Major changes in the length of terms should be noted, first from shorter terms (usually six weeks) to three terms per year in 1880, and then to semester-long terms in 1946. Complete names are given where available, and ambiguity in spelling reflects the most legible source. It is also worth noting that although it is a popularly held belief that, according to tradition, presidents of the Jefferson Society do not succeed themselves in office, five presidents have served two terms in a row: Robert Whitehead in 1918–1919, Herbert C. Pollock in 1932–1933, Werner L. Janney in 1935–1936, Robert W. Ayers in 1943–1944, Robert M. Musselman in 1944–1945, and Daniel T. Kirwin in 1992–1993.

1825–1826
John H. Lee
Mann A. Page
George W. Lewis
John W. Brockenbrough
John B. Magruder
Chapman Johnson
1826–1827
Edgar Mason
A. B. Mason
Chapman Johnson
S. A. Townes
1827–1828
Chapman Johnson
W. C. Swan
Alexander H. H. Stuart
James L. Green

John Willis
R. H. Brown
1828–1829
R. T. Luckett
B. T. Moseley
Thomas H. Bayly
Robert M. Saunders
Thomas M. Jackson
Robert Toombs
1829–1830
George P. Beirne
Henry Tutwiler
George E. Tabb
William B. Napleton
1830–1831
Robert M. Saunders
Alexander Moseley

Socrates Maupin

J. W. Wimbish

Benjamin F. Randolph

1831–1832

William H. Brockenbrough

Socrates Maupin

Charles Randolph

Thomas Semmes

Fairfax Catlett

1832–1833

Thomas Semmes

Willis P. Bocock

James L. Cabell

Richard Parker

William D. Hodges

1833–1834

William H. Brockenbrough

William Frazier

William Marten

Aaron Lindsey

E. Taliaferro

1834–1835

Robert C. Stanard

James H. Davis

G. W. Goode

O. N. Ogden

G. W. Trueheart

1835–1836

James H. Davis

G. W. Goode

J. Browning

Richard Morris

M. Carleton

1836–1837

John W. Harris

R. H. Bayly

John F. Wickham

W. C. Gray

1837–1838

Peter K. Skinner

Benjamin B. Minor

J. Critcher

William Old

T. J. Hungerford

R. L. T. Beale

1838–1839

Clement C. Clay

R. A. Johnson

J. Critcher

J. A. Strother

1839–1840

J. D. Bracey

Joseph D. Shields

T. H. Watts

R. B. Gooch

J. H. Oliver

1840–1841

John S. Caskie

A. E. Maxwell

C. E. Parkhill

James F. Jones

Robert L. Dabney

1841–1842

J. H. Parkhill

J. R. Mosby

J. F. Bullitt

G. W. Brent

Edmund Randolph

1842–1843

John C. Rutherford

William M. Cooke

J. F. Kunkel

1843–1844

William M. Cooke

Thomas George

Tiberius G. Jones

1844–1845
  William C. Rivers Jr.
  W. H. R. Workman
  Roscoe B. Heath
1845–1846
  Frederick W. Page
  Lewis Minor Coleman
  Robert J. Morrison
1846–1847
  Edmund W. Caskie
  Fendall Gregory
  V. E. Shepherd
1847–1848
  Charles S. Venable
  W. L. T. Fleshman
  W. B. Woolridge
1848–1849
  Frederick W. Page
  M. Green Peyton
  John A. Broadus
1849–1850
  Edward Warren
  Richard V. Gaines
  Richard H. Baker
1850–1851
  Henry Taylor
  James Cochran
  W. L. Moody
  T. A. T. Reilly
  Hunter C. Pope
  John D. Pennybacker
1851–1852
  H. B. Davenport
  Joseph Vanmeter
  Robert A. Caskie
  James A. Latane (Resigned)
  Joseph H. Vanmeter
  John L. Scott
  George L. Gordon

1852–1853
  J. W. Hutcheson
  John Y. Gholson
  Alexander L. Nelson
  William J. Martin
  Charles T. Friend
  James William Morgan
1853–1854
  James A. Latane
  Charles M. Blackford
  Philip M. Ambler
  George E. Dennis
  J. A. Ware
  William Roane Aylett
1854–1855
  Charles Grattan
  Thomas L. Yancey
  R. J. Ambler
  Henry Mason Mathews
  P. C. Dozier
  James Taylor Jones
1855–1856
  Robert W. Hunter
  Henry Mason Mathews
  Claud E. Earle
  Charles Norvell
  Powell Harrison
  Creswell Garlington
1856–1857
  William N. McDonald
  Augustus W. Cockrell
  Joseph Edwin Cox Jr.
  Samuel G. Compton
  John M. Martin
  Edward C. Preston
1857–1858
  Charles L. C. Minor
  Charles M. Massie

William Elliott

William T. Haskell

Lancelot M. Blackford

William G. Field

1858–1859

M. Lewis Randolph

Thomas R. Price Jr.

William P. DuBose

Bennett Taylor

E. Holmes Boyd

W. Moultrie Dwight

1859–1860

Richard M. Venable

Edward C. Anderson Jr.

Robert M. T. Hunter Jr.

Blake L. Woodson

John Lawson

P. J. Glover

The Jefferson Society and the Washington Society met together as the University Literary Society in 1861. No record of that period survives. The Jefferson Society resumed meeting at the beginning of the 1863–1864 school year.

1863–1864

H. A. Atkinson

Gratz Cohen

B. H. Berry

Robert Frazer

William A. Anderson

Everett W. Early

1864–1865

C. E. Rivers

William M. Taliaferro

William C. Holmes

Frank Q. Moore

George B. Finch

Everett W. Early

1865–1866

Thomas R. Joynes

William A. Anderson

John W. Daniel

John T. Rogers

Everett W. Early

William W. Scott

1866–1867

incomplete records

W. W. Foote, Final President

1867–1868

Harry Burnett

Joseph Bryan

Ian D. Portis

W. H. Clofton

C. T. Ellerby

J. B. Gant

1868–1869

incomplete records

Shepherd Barclay, Final President

1869–1870

A. Carey Estes

J. H. Wilson

Peter Francisco Pescud

S. P. Dendy

1870–1871

J. R. Leuheart

W. C. Bower

J. B. Healy

J. W. E. Horne

A. W. Hamilton

G. C. Hume

1871–1872
  Jas. B. Green
  A. T. McCalley
  F. Marrion
  J. E. Churchill
  M. Summerell
  Moses L. Wicks
1872–1873
  McCleod Kasey
  W. R. McKenny
  B. C. Wicks
1873–1874
  Frederick F. Reese
  no known record
  Frederick F. Reese
1874–1875
  E. P. Cole
  T. A. Seddon
  Lyon G. Tyler
  R. M. Hughes
  Mathew W. Ransom
  Benjamin Fitzpatrick
1875–1876
  Eppa Hunton III
  B. S. Downing
  B. S. Johnson
  A. P. Thom
  Lyon G. Tyler
  H. H. Downing
1876–1877
  J. A. Watts
  Robert M. Hughes
  Gordon Robertson
  Charles Dabney
  J. Allen Southall
1877–1878
  T. Ellett
  J. A. Watts

  H. W. Hobson
  Frank Glasgow
  L. W. Gunther, Jr.
1878–1879
  Wyndham R. Meredith
  H. D. Higgins
  C. P. Courad
  G. W. Morris
  George D. Fawcett
1879–1880
  Braxton D. Gibson
  Benjamin L. Abney
  John B. Adger
  W. P. Roberts
1880–1881
  T. Woodrow Wilson
  Walter S. Lefvere
  Floyd Hughes
1881–1882
  Charles W. Kent
  E. W. Saunders
  William Corcoran Eustis
1882–1883
  William P. Trent
  Dudley DuBose
  J. Hunter Pendleton
1883–1884
  Oscar W. Underwood
  R. W. Mallett
  Jefferson Randolph Anderson
1884–1885
  M. Selden Macon
  Francis R. Lassiter
  R. C. Taylor
1885–1886
  H. D. Flood
  E. M. Moore
  Francis R. Lassiter

1886–1887
George Wayne Anderson
Robert R. LaMonte
George Wayne Anderson
1887–1888
T. W. Russell
John H. Boogher
W. J. H. Bohannon
1888–1889
Joseph H. Kelly
Joseph B. Dunn
George Gordon Battle
1889–1890
Edwin L. Gibson
Joseph W. Chinn
Raleigh C. Minor
1890–1891
Thomas L. Waters
Thomas J. Randolph
R. Spratt Cockrell
1891–1892
Robert S. Radford
John M. Pierce
J. Gordon Leake
1892–1893
Hugh S. Cumming
Powell C. Fauntleroy
Murray Mason McGuire
1893–1894
William Gardner Peterkin
Hampson Gary
Joseph A. Massie
1894–1895
Matthias Mahorner Tunis
George N. Wise
Hollins N. Randolph
1895–1896
J. Mercer Garnett

George C. Moomaw
George Nelms Wise
1896–1897
Henry Alexis Hopkins
Charles Wesley Miller
Walter Tansill Oliver
1897–1898
John Archer Cocke
Joseph Crenshaw Taylor
Charles Weston Miller
1898–1899
Archer McLain Graham
Edward Reinhold Rogers
Joseph Crenshaw Taylor
1899–1900
Warren Stuart
S. Ernest Bradshaw
W. T. Shannonhouse
1900–1901
E. Preston Dargan
George Floyd Rogers
J. L. Heard
1901–1902
C. R. Williams
James M. Mason
James Hay Jr.
1902–1903
J. S. Barron
J. Littleton Jones
C. R. Williams
1903–1904
J. B. Swartwout
J. A. Ritter
J. Ashley Williams
1904–1905
W. T. Basket
F. Ashbury Rern
John Shishmanian

1905–1906
George Arthur Paddock
Frank Roswell Rogers
W. Brockenbrough Lamb

1906–1907
H. E. D. Wilson
A. H. Foreman
John J. Luck

1907–1908
Allen J. Saville
W. L. Davidson
Herbert M. Peck

1908–1909
L. M. Robinnette
Paul Micou
W. Bruce Buford

1909–1910
W. G. Dearing
W. W. Douglas
Stanley M. Cleveland

1910–1911
Morton L. Wallerstein
W. T. Tabb
J. O. Beaty

1911–1912
D. H. Ramsey
J. B. Frazier Jr.
Decatur H. Rogers

1912–1913
Oscar W. Underwood Jr.
P. P. Holmes
William Arthur Adams

1913–1914
Robert Barton Jr.
Louis H. Milsaps
W. W. Woods

1914–1915
Christian Talbot Steger

John Hugh Murphy
A. V. Pankey

1915–1916
Harry Lee Carter
Eugene S. Williams
E. B. Harper

1916–1917
F. S. Harmon
John Parker Jr.
John E. McCall

1917–1918
D. C. Wilson
S. J. Hart
Robert Whitehead

1918–1919
Robert Whitehead
Ellsworth Wiltshire
W. Irving Matthews

1919–1920
Robert Button
Gordon B. Ambler
Frank Martin Lemon

1920–1921
F. W. Davies
T. D. Hopkins
F. D. G. Ribble

1921–1922
Bernard P. Chamberlain
J. A. Dean
F. B. Fite Jr.

1922–1923
J. C. Sherwood
Thomas Mumford Boyd
Curtis Simpson

1923–1924
J. A. Tyler
O. A. Kirkman Jr.
Raymond B. Pinchbeck

1924–1925
W. P. Sandridge
E. W. Gregory Jr.
C. L. Gleaves

1925–1926
F. H. Quarles Jr.
J. T. McEachern Jr.
E. H. Copenhaver Jr.

1926–1927
G. T. Gwathmey Jr.
Horace A. Teass
George B. Gunn

1927–1928
L. A. Daffan Gilmer
Albertis S. Harrison Jr.
C. F. Williamson

1928–1929
R. W. Church
W. S. Weedon
Earl N. Evans

1929–1930
Edward S. Gwathmey
Baldwin C. Burnam
Edward R. Baird

1930–1931
Henry Emerson Biggs
John C. Wyllie
Thomas K. Tindale

1931–1932
S. Douglas Shackleford Jr.
Joseph O. Reither Jr.
Thomas G. Shufflebarger

1932–1933
George C. Seward
Herbert C. Pollock
Herbert C. Pollock

1933–1934
William S. Mundy Jr.

S. R. Wallace Jr.
J. Winfree Smith

1934–1935
Edwin C. McClintock
John A. Watts
W. J. Gold

1935–1936
George L. Tabor
William J. Dieterich
Werner L. Janney

1936–1937
Werner L. Janney
James M. Brewbaker
Russell B. Stevens

1937–1938
Robert M. Mussleman
James M. Brewbaker
Eugene M. Caffey

1938–1939
John E. Manahan
Ralph D. Alley
Frank W. Shaffer

1939–1940
Kernon D. Hitchings
Hunter Hughes
Sykes Scherman

1940–1941
Elmer L. Kelly
Jesse William Levy
Eugene Van Ness Goetchius

1941–1942
Edward G. Lewis
William Turner Brown Jr.
Eugene Van Ness Goetchius

1942–1943
A. Rutherfoord Holmes
Terence Mullins
World War II hiatus

1943–1944
World War II hiatus
William L. Yost
Robert W. Ayers

1944–1945
Robert W. Ayers
Robert M. Musselman
Robert M. Musselman

1945–1946
Kenwyn Nelson
Allen B. Ashby

1946–1947
W. F. Lyle
Charles Stevens Russell

1947–1948
Robert Harold Lund
David W. Kindleberger

1948–1949
Stephen Dawson Carnes Jr.
Benjamin Leo Carleton Jr.

1949–1950
Hoke Irvine Horne II
Russell Brown Pace Jr.

1950–1951
William W. Rowan III
John J. Loflin Jr

1951–1952
Gene B. Burns
Robert Coe

1952–1953
Archer Jones
Jay Gladstone Weinberg

1953–1954
John Ritchie
John Pluenneke

1954–1955
Dave Lyle
Joe Hughes

1955–1956
William F. Whalen
Norman S. Karpf

1956–1957
George Bryson Thomas Jr.
Benet D. Gellman

1957–1958
William W. Purkey
John Moore

1958–1959
William R. Bruce
Joseph Weeks

1959–1960
Herman S. Moorman
Leslie H. Friedman

1960–1961
W. Nathaniel Howell
James W. Jones

1961–1962
Richard Clemens
Michael A. Hoover

1962–1963
J. Marshall Coleman
Andrew Francis

1963–1964
John E. Via
James G. Pastorius Jr.

1964–1965
Lathan M. Ewers Jr.
Michael A. Hoover

1965–1966
H. Judd Herndon
James B. Massey III

1966–1967
Nicholas W. Jones
Gary Carlson

1967–1968
Samuel P. Cargill Jr.
Ronald L. Smallwood

1968–1969
Kevin M. Twomey
Harrison Bush

1969–1970
Walter J. Camp
Walker L. Chandler

1970–1971
Clifford R. Weckstein
Thomas R. Jones Jr.

1971–1972
Peter E. Gillespie
Robert Rust

1972–1973
Howard T. Macrae Jr.
William P. Zink

1973–1974
Richard W. Walter Jr.
James L. Alexander

1974–1975
James M. Guinivan
Resse C. Lenheiser

1975–1976
Michael A. Partridge
Michael Shortly

1976–1977
John C. Harrison
Harold Segroves

1977–1978
Steven L. Huntoon
John F. Jebb

1978–1979
Resse C. Lenheiser
Steven P. Frantz

1979–1980
Anne B. Camper
L. Jackson Davis II

1980–1981
James R. Davis
Robert R. Dively

1981–1982
William B. Baker
Marcus A. Manos

1982–1983
Karl W. Saur
Charles M. English

1983–1984
Rafael A. Madan
Jane E. Beard

1984–1985
Wesley G. Marshall
Rafael A. Madan

1985–1986
John S. Vishneski III
Treadwell Ruml III

1986–1987
Joshua Sharf
Elizabeth Bartolo

1987–1988
Marcus A. Manos
Matthew W. Levin

1988–1989
Jonathan M. Miller
David J. Burger

1989–1990
Dennis E. Logue Jr.
Charles Sharp

1990–1991
Stephen Jordan
Satinder S. Gill

1991–1992
James T. Feezel
Christopher W. Martin

1992–1993
Daniel T. Kirwin
Daniel T. Kirwin

1993–1994
Michael K. Pullen
George Y. Banks III

1994–1995
    Edgar B. Hatrick IV
    Mark Staton
1995–1996
    Sean C. Serpe
    Judson True
1996–1997
    Christopher P. Bonavia
    E. Stewart Jeffries
1997–1998
    Arun Rao
    Bill Sanderson
1998–1999
    Scott Barclay *(resigned)*
    John Buford
    Samuel Waxman
1999–2000
    Brooke Brower
    Jonathan E. Carr
2000–2001
    Daniel E. Grunberger
    Mazen M. Basrawi
2001–2002
    Brian Boyle
    Mohsin Raza Syed
2002–2003
    Nathaniel S. Adams
    Richard B. Carroll
2003–2004
    Aaron N. Silverman
    Peter M. Milligan
2004–2005
    Donald P. Brownlee
    Peter P. Gelzinis IV
2005–2006
    James L. Kennedy
    Michael J. McDuffie

2006–2007
    Katie R. Bray
    Christopher Riggs
2007–2008
    Assaf Sternberg
    Douglas M. Hillebrandt
2008–2009
    Paul Harper
    Ashton Gilmore
2009–2010
    Katie Croghan
    Tyler Criste
2010–2011
    Emma King *(resigned)*
    Katie R. Bray
    Fredrick W. Eberstadt
2011–2012
    Keenan W. Davis
    Marie Connor
2012–2013
    Owen W. Gallogly
    Audrey Birner
2013–2014
    Thomas L. Howard III
    Henry McCulloch Cline
2014–2015
    Patrick P. Greco
    Kathryn Anne Kingsbury
2015–2016
    Brianna Hogan
    Henry T. Knight II
2016–2017
    Austin Owen
    John Hayes Chellman

Winners of the Benjamin C. Moomaw Oratorical Contest

1948	Morris B. Brown	1976	John C. Harrison
1949	Vernon L. Bounds	1977	Josh Henson
1950	Samuel Goldberg	1978	Peter T. Canning
1951	Harold W. Laubscher	1979	Alberto R. Coll
1952	Paul C. Worthington	1980	Adam Mars-Jones
1953	John R. Weathley	1981	Thaddeus R. Maciag
1954	William Parsons	1982	Kevin F. Brady
1955	Mohammed Khaishgi	1983	Jeffrey Divack
1956	Alfred T. DeMaria	1984	Mary Froestch
1957	Wayne Lustig	1985	James Grubbs
1958	Brereton C. Jones	1986	Treadwell Ruml II
1959	Robert Montague III	1987	James Grubbs
1960	Kenneth Ringle	1988	John S. Vishneski III
1961	Robert Montague III	1989	Treadwell Ruml II
1962	James Apple	1990	Mark W. Hertzog
1963	Lathan M. Ewers Jr.	1991	James T. Feezell
1964	Stephen G. Johnakin	1992	B. Daniel Blatt
1965	H. Judd Herndon Jr.	1993	Simon H. Bloom
1966	John W. Hay Jr.	1994	James E. Connelly
1967	*unknown*	1995	James E. Connelly
1968	Edward Sledge	1996	Jason A. Johnson
1969	Clifford R. Weckstein	1997	Xin Quang Le
1970	Dennis Unkovic	1998	Trent Teti
1971	Peter E. Gillespie	1999	Sandra F. Beasley
1972	Barbara Golden Lynn	2000	Dennis E. Logue Jr.
1973	F. Timothy Nagler	2001	Zubin Talib
1974	Resse C. Lenheiser	2002	Syed Sami Ulah Shah
1975	Richard W. Walter Jr.	2003	Khuram Hussain

2004	Benjamin D. Mitchell	*2011*	Lauren Simenauer
2005	Sandy Alexander	*2012*	Roraig Finney
2006	Noah P. Sullivan	*2013*	Ashley Stevenson
2007	Sara Tisdale	*2014*	Leah Jane Gunn
2008	Prasan Ulluwishewa	*2015*	Jordan Carson
2009	Matthew Waring	*2016*	Andrew Kaiser
2010	Eric S. Kay		

Constitution of the Jefferson Society, 1837

Order of Proceedings

1. Roll call.
2. Nomination, election and initiation of members.
3. Reading the minutes of last meeting.
4. Reading the essay, or delivery of the oration.
5. The debate.
6. The selection of a question.
7. Reports of Committees.
8. Motions and resolutions.
9. Election of Essayist or Orator.
10. Election of Officers.
11. Consideration of unfinished business.
12. Report of the Secretary.
13. Roll call.

The Initiation of Members

The President shall request the gentleman to rise after which, the Secretary shall read,

The undersigned students of the University of Virginia, holding it to be true, that opinions, springing out of solitary observation and reflection, are seldom, in the first instance, correct; that the faculties of the mind are excited by collision; that friendships are cemented, errors corrected and sound principles established by society and intercourse; and, especially in a country where all are free to profess and by argument maintain their opinions, that the powers of debate should be sedulously cultivated, have, therefore, associated themselves under the name of THE EFFERSON SOCIETY OF THE UNIVERSITY OF VIRGINIA

In becoming members of this society they mutually pledge themselves to conform to its regulations and to cherish its prosperity. In testimony whereof they have hereunto affixed their names.

After the gentleman shall have signed the Constitution, the President shall again request him to rise, and read, as follows:

Sir, You have been informed of the nature of our society, and of the obligations which rest upon its members. You have voluntarily entered into the bonds of our union. As one of the duties incident to the chair, I have, in the name of the society, to lay you under the most solemn injunctions not to divulge any of its proceedings, or, anything which may occur within its walls.

It only remains for me to declare you a member of the Jefferson Society.

Article I

The style of this society shall be THE JEFFERSON SOCIETY OF THE UNIVERSITY OF VIRGINIA.

Article II

The officers of the society shall consist of a President, Vice President, Secretary, Assistant Secretary, Librarian and Treasurer.

Article III

Duties of the Officers

§ I. PRESIDENT. It shall be the duty of the President to preside at all meetings of the society; to take the vote on all questions decided "viva voce," and to declare the result; to announce the number of votes given each candidate for any office; to appoint committees; to appoint officers pro tempore; and to call meetings of the society whenever it shall be necessary.

He shall construe the constitution; and decide all questions of order.

He shall keep a book, in which any member of the Society may record a question for discussion; from these questions he shall select three to be submitted to the choice of the House; if he find no suitable questions recorded, it shall be his duty to supply the deficiency.

The Secretary shall report to the President any member who shall not have paid his fines eight weeks after the day they were imposed, whose duty it shall then be to apprise the member of such neglect; and, if no adequate excuse be rendered within two weeks thereafter, to pronounce upon him in the presence of the society, a sentence of expulsion.

§ II. VICE PRESIDENT. In the absence of the President, it shall be the duty of the Vice President to exercise the powers and perform the duties of that officer.

It shall be his duty to report to the society any officer for neglect of duty.

He shall, after the adjournment of the society, assume the functions of President and investigate such cases of disorder, as the President may have reported; or, as may have attracted his own attention during the session of the society. From his decision, no appeal shall be made.

§ III. SECRETARY. It shall be the duty of the Secretary to keep a neat and attested record of the proceedings of the society; to call the roll at the opening and adjournment of each meeting; and to read the proceedings of each meeting.

He shall preserve the paper and documents of the society; shall deliver a list of all fines assessed, within one week after their assessment, to the Treasurer for collection; shall record all motions passed, with the names of the movers; also, the names and number of those composing committees; shall read all communications addressed to the society; and write such letters as it may direct.

§ IV. ASSISTANT SECRETARY. It shall be the duty of the Assistant Secretary to aid the Secretary in the discharge of his official duties; to discharge those duties in his absence; to compile all laws passed during his term of service; to embody in the constitution any amendments to the same, which may, from time to time, be adopted; and to see that the Hall be properly prepared before each meeting of the society.

§ V. TREASURER. It shall be the duty of the Treasurer to keep a correct account of the receipts and expenditures of the society; to make all disbursements; to collect all dues; to exhibit at each meeting of the society a statement of the amount due, from each member; and to report to the President the name of any member who shall have not paid his fines within eight weeks after the day upon which they were imposed.

§ VI. LIBRARIAN. It shall be the duty of the Librarian to preserve all books, periodicals, and other literary publications belonging to the society; to give them to members applying for them, and to enter their names in a book; to estimate the amount of injury done to any book and hand the same within one week after its assessment, to the Treasurer, for collection; to keep a catalogue of the books; to make known any donations which may be made, together with the names of the donors; to call in, at the expiration of his term of service, all books, periodicals, &c, to return them to their proper places for the inspection of the Vice President; to report the loss of any book, periodical, &c, with the name of the borrower; and to make a detailed report of the condition of the library, at the expiration of his term of service.

Article IV

Election of Officers, &c.

§ I. When the President shall announce the election of officers to be in order, nominations shall be made, and the Secretary shall call the roll and each member declare the candidate of his choice. The majority of the votes shall determine the election.

§ II. A member shall be elected at each meeting of the society, who shall, as he may choose, read an essay, or deliver an oration, two weeks from the day of his election.

§ III. Any student of the University may be proposed for admission to membership, at any regular meeting of the society. Applicants for membership shall be elected 'viva voce;' and three fourths of the votes given shall be necessary to elect.

§ IV. The society may also elect any gentleman an honorary member, whose literary attainments shall entitle him to the honor. Three fourths of the members present shall be necessary to elect.

Article V

The Debate

§ I. The members of the society shall be divided, alphabetically, into four classes, one of which shall debate at each regular meeting of the society. The class of debaters shall be read out, by the Secretary, at the meeting but one, preceding that on which it is to debate; and the President, after the selection of the question, shall name one on each side, to open the debate.

§ II. The opinion of the House shall be taken upon the merits of the question by calling the roll, when the number of votes, for each side shall be noted by the Secretary, and read by the President to the society.

§ III. No gentleman shall address the House more than twice, without the consent of the President; nor more than three times, upon any condition.

Article VI

Fines

§ I. The roll shall be called at the opening and adjournment of each meeting of the society; and members shall be fined 12 ½ cents for absence at either roll call.

§ II. If any one, appointed to open the debate, fail to do so, he shall be fined fifty cents; and if any other member of the class of debaters fail to debate, he shall be fined twenty five cents.

§ III. Any member, refusing to take an office given him by the society, or the President; or, after his election, resigning it before the time of service shall have expired; or failing to perform the duty attending any honour conferred upon him, shall be fined one dollar.

§ IV. If the Secretary, Assistant Secretary, Treasurer, or Librarian, be reported for neglect of duty, the Vice President shall impose upon him a fine of fifty cents.

§ V. If any member detain a book from the library longer than one week, he shall be fined five cents, for every day, beyond that time.

§ VI. If any member lose a book, belonging to the society, he shall pay the value of that book; and if the book lost belong to a set of volumes, he shall pay the value of the whole set, the value to be assessed by the Librarian.

§ VII. If a committee fail to report at the proper time, each member of the committee shall be fined fifty cents.

§ VIII. Any member shall be deemed guilty of disorder, who shall by hissing, clapping, laughing aloud, or any other unnecessary noise whatever, interrupt the President, or any member while speaking; or, refuse to take his seat when ordered by the President; or, withdraw from the Hall, without the permission of the President; or, pass between the President and any member addressing the chair; or, address the President without rising from his seat; or, persist in motions, resolutions or remarks which have been pronounced to be out of order. It shall likewise be considered disorder, for any member to second a motion without rising from his chair; or to read any book, pamphlet or periodical, in the Hall, unless in conjunction with the regular business.

Article VII

The President shall have power to appoint a Secretary, an Assistant Secretary, Librarian and Treasurer, every five weeks throughout his term of service.

Article VIII

Any student of the University, who at the time of leaving college, may be a member of this society shall be considered an honorary member---entitled to attend its meetings, and to engage in its enterprises, at discretion.

Article IX

The President and Vice President shall be elected for a term of ten weeks.

Article X

In case of a dissolution of this society the library shall be presented to the University; and any other disposition of it, in that event, will be regarded as a violation of good faith and honorable feeling.

BYE LAWS

I. Amendments to propositions to amend the constitution shall not be required to lie on the table one week; and no resolution shall be considered, unless it be in writing, and the mover specify the article of the constitution, if any, affected thereby.

II. The President, Secretary, Assistant Secretary, Librarian and Treasurer are exempted from all but official duties.

III. No officer of the society shall be permitted to make a verbal report; but all nominations shall be made viva voce.

IV. Any member who shall have withdrawn from the society may re-enter by paying fifty cents into the Treasury.

V. No gentleman shall speak more than twice on any motion or resolution.

VI. Any gentleman may attend a meeting of the society, with the consent of any one of the officers, provided, however, that no student be thus admitted.

VII. No member shall be allowed to withdraw from the society until he shall have paid all the fines which he may have incurred whilst a member.

VIII. Any gentleman, who may be elected a member of the society, shall pay into the treasury one dollar, within eight weeks after the day of admission.

IX. The Secretary shall have printed, annually, two hundred copies of the Constitution and these Bye Laws and shall present each member with a copy on the day of his initiation.

Constitution and Bye Laws of JS, Charlottesville, James Alexander, Printer, 1838, U.Va.

Constitution of the Jefferson Society, 1860

Form of Initiation

The President shall request the candidate to arise, and the Secretary read to him as follows:

"The undersigned, Students at the University of Virginia, holding it to be true that opinions springing out of solitary observation and reflection are seldom, in the first instance, correct; that the faculties of the mind are excited by collision; that friendships are cemented, errors corrected, and sound principles established by society and intercourse, and especially in a country where all are free to profess and, by argument, to maintain their opinions; that the powers of debate should be sedulously cultivated—have therefore associated themselves under the name of the JEFFERSON SOCIETY OF THE UNIVERSITY OF VIRGINIA. In becoming members of this Society they mutually pledge themselves to conform to its regulations and to cherish its prosperity. In testimony whereof they have hereunto affixed their names."

The Constitution is then signed.

After the candidate shall have signed the Constitution, the President shall again request him to arise, and shall read to him as follows:

"SIR: You have been informed of the nature of our Society, and of the obligations which rest upon its members; you have voluntarily entered into the bonds of our union, and, as one of the duties incident to the Chair, I have, in the name of the Society, to lay you under the most solemn injunctions to obey the laws; uphold the Constitution; to observe all propriety as a member and a gentleman; to advance, by strict adherence to duty, the welfare of the Society; to preserve its honor; cherish its prosperity, and to promote its ends to the best of your ability.

"I now declare you a member of the Jefferson Society, and welcome you to the bonds of our union."

Article I

This Society shall be styled the JEFFERSON SOCIETY OF THE UNIVERSITY OF VIRGINIA.

Article II

Sec. 1. The officers shall be a President, Vice-President, Secretary, Treasurer, and Assistant Treasurer.

Sec. 2. The President and Vice-President shall be elected every six weeks, and the Treasurer every three months; but the Secretary and Assistant Secretary shall be appointed by the President.

Article III

The Society shall be composed of Regular, Irregular, and Honorary Members.

Article IV

Sec. 1. At each second regular meeting in January a member shall be elected to deliver an Anniversary Oration on the thirteenth day of April following, and at the same time another shall be elected to read the Declaration of Independence.

Sec. 2. At each first regular meeting in April a member shall be elected to deliver a Valedictory Oration at the close of the session.

Sec. 3. At the first regular meeting in each month a member shall be elected to deliver an Oration before the Society one month thereafter, and at this time shall be extended no ease beyond one week.

Article V

Sec. 1. All motions and resolutions which affect the Constitution shall be in writing, and shall lie upon the table one week before they can be acted upon.

A vote of *two-thirds* of the whole Society shall be necessary to change the Constitution, either in whole or in part, but a majority of those present may suspend, alter, or amend the Rules hereto annexed.

Article VI

Resolutions in regard to the *Virginia University Magazine*:

Sec. 1. That the Jefferson Society unite with her sister Literary Societies in sustaining a Literary Magazine, to be issued monthly during the session, and that the title of this periodical be the *Virginia University Magazine*.

Sec. 2. That an editor be elected on the part of this Society to serve for a term of three months.

Sec. 3. That the Jefferson Society appropriate its quota for the purchase of a Prize Medal, to be awarded to the author of the best contribution to the *Magazine* during an entire session, and that the prize be presented on the occasion of the delivery of the Oration before the three Literary Societies; or, in default of such, on the night of the final celebration of that Society, which may be preferred by the successful competitor.

Article VII

Resolutions in regard to the DEBATER'S MEDAL:

Sec. 1. That the Medal be given by this Society, at the close of each session, to its *best* DEBATER.

Sec. 2. That at the last regular meeting in May of each year an election shall be held for the *best* DEBATER; that no nomination be made, a majority being necessary for a choice. After the first ballot, if no choice be made, the candidate who has the least number of votes shall be dropped and so on until a majority of votes are cast for one member, who shall then be declared elected.

Sec. 3. That the Medal thus awarded be publicly presented by the President of the Society to the successful candidate on the night of its final celebration.

Sec. 4. That the medal be of GOLD and cost FIFTY DOLLARS.

Sec. 5. That the form of the Medal be circular, and its diameter not less than one inch and three-quarters, and that it bear on its face, enclosed in a wreath of laurel, "PRESENTED BY THE JEFFERSON SOCIETY TO ------ AS THEIR BEST DEBATER, SESSION 18-." Under the wreath the Greek letters, "ΦΠΘ." On the reverse, a representation of the University of Virginia, surmounted by the Coat of Arms of Virginia beneath the motto of the Society, "HAEC OLIM MEMINISSE JUVABIT," and around it the words, "UNIVERSITY OF VIRGINIA, June 28th, 18--."

BY-LAWS

I.

No one shall be a *Regular Member* of this Society who is not a student of the University of Virginia, or who is a member of any other Literary or Debating Society at said University.

II.

Irregular Members shall consist of those who, having been members of this Society regularly, have left the institution without having joined any other Literary Society at the University, and have discharged all their dues.

III.

Honorary Members shall consist of such eminent persons as the Society shall deem worthy of membership. And all Honorary and Irregular Members shall have the privilege of attending the meetings of the Society, and of participating in the discussion of the questions, but shall not be allowed to vote (except on the question debated), nor to hold any office in the Society.

IV.

The nomination, election, and initiation of members shall be at regular meetings only. The vote shall be taken *viva voce, three-fourths* of the members present being necessary to elect; and any member who withdraws from the Society shall, in order to renew his connection therewith pay the treasury the sum of two dollars and a half.

V.

Each Regular Member shall pay to the treasury *ten dollars* initiation fee, and the annual tax of *two dollars and a half* every subsequent year that he is a member; and no member of this Society shall be allowed to vote or hold office whose initiation fee is due, or the amount of whose fines unpaid amount to *two dollars and a half*. It being herein provided that all initiation fees are due on and after the day two weeks from the members signing the Constitution.

VI. – DUTIES OF OFFICERS

The President shall preside over all meetings of the Society, preserve order and decorum, and appoint committees and officers *pro tempore*. He shall construe the Constitution and Rules, and decide all questions of order *subject to an appeal*. He shall give notice of all elections at least one week before they are to take place, and convene the members whenever, in his opinion, the good of the Society requires it.

VII.

In all cases of election by the Society, the President shall vote. In other cases, he shall not vote unless the Society shall be equally divided, or unless his vote, if given to the minority, will make the division equal, and in case of such equal division the question shall be lost.

VIII.

The Vice-President shall preside in the absence of the President. He shall report all cases of disorder and neglect of duty at the same meeting at which they occur or come to his knowledge. He shall record them, with the prescribed fines annexed in a book to be provided for that purpose. *Excuses for fines* imposed by the Vice-President shall be made to him at the meeting following that on which they were imposed, and no excuses made after that time shall be considered valid unless the delay was due to an unavoidable absence. The Vice-President shall have it at his discretion to decide whether an excuse is valid. An appeal from the decision of the Vice-President shall require a vote of two-thirds to sustain it.

IX.

The Secretary shall record and read the proceedings, conduct the correspondence, and carefully preserve all records and documents of the Society.

X.

1. It shall be the duty of the Treasurer to report to the Society at each regular meeting a list of all the fines and fees due. All such fees shall be considered due after two weeks membership, and all fines from the time incurred. He shall also be required, at the end of each presidential term, to report to the Society its exact financial condition.

2. The report of the Treasurer, the approval or disapproval of the Committee, and the Society's action upon the same shall be transcribed in the Minutes.

3. During the term of his office the Treasurer shall be excused from all Society duties save that of attendance on its meetings.

4. There shall be appointed by each President, at the beginning of his term, a Finance Committee, consisting of three members, whose duty it shall be to inspect and approve all bills before payment, and at the end of each presidential term to examine the Treasurer accounts, and report the condition of the same to the Society.

5. Every Treasurer, after serving a full term of three months, shall have optional attendance on the meetings of the Society for six months.

XI.

The Assistant Secretary shall perform the duties of the Secretary in his absence: call the roll and read the names of the Debaters; and, also, at the close of each meeting he shall read the names of those composing the class which is to debate at the next meeting; he shall also aid the Secretary in taking the vote by ballot;

he shall also, at the close of each meeting, read over the names of the absentees from both roll-calls, and furnish the Vice-President with a list of such absentees after the adjournment.

XII.—ELECTIONS

The Officers, Orators, Editors, and Reader of the Declaration of Independence shall be elected by ballot—a majority of the votes cast being necessary to elect. All other votes shall be taken *viva voce*, provided that in the election for Orators and Reader two weeks membership be super-added to the requisitions of the Treasury clause for voters.

XIII.

At each ballot, if no choice be made, the candidate who has received the lowest number shall be dropped, and in no case after the first ballot shall a nomination be made.

XIV.

When only one candidate is nominated for any office the President may, after a considerable time, put the vote to the Society *viva voce*; but no motion shall be in order to declare a candidate elected by acclamation without the consent of the President.

XV.— QUESTIONS AND DEBATES

The members arranged alphabetically shall be divided into six classes if there be more than *sixty* members; into four classes if less than sixty—one of which shall debate at every regular meeting.

XVI.

The President shall, at the time of selection, appoint from the proper class one member on the affirmative and one on the negative to open the debate, and when the debate is ordered the Assistant Secretary shall, after the question has been read, call the names of those appointed to open the debate, and then the remainder of the class. This being done, the president shall announce the question open for general debate.

XVII.

At the close of the debate the vote of the Society shall be taken on the merits of the question by calling the roll, and the result announced to the Society by the

President. No member shall be allowed to address the Society more than twice at the same meeting on the same subject without the consent of the Society, and no one shall be allowed to speak more than thirty minutes at any one time, except the members appointed to open the debate, who shall be allowed to speak three times.

XVIII.—QUESTION COMMITTEE

Sec. 1. Each President, on the opening of his term, shall appoint *five* members, who shall constitute a Standing Committee on Questions.

Sec. 2. This Committee shall, at each regular meeting, offer four questions, from which one shall be selected by a *viva voce* vote of the Society.

Sec. 3. This Committee shall meet every Saturday evening fifteen minutes before the meeting of the Society, for the selection of Questions.

XIX.—FINES

The roll shall be called at the opening and adjournment of each meeting, and members shall be fined *ten cents* for each absence, and each member failing to debate the question when his name is called, shall be fined *Twenty-five cents.*— But if the member appointed to open the debate in the affirmative or negative fails to do so, he shall be fined FIFTY CENTS. Any member who shall be absent from the Society when his class is called upon to debate, shall be fined for not debating unless he is excused for his absence.

XX.

Any member who fails to perform the duty of any honor conferred upon him, except in case of having resigned, shall be fined ONE DOLLAR.

XXI.

Every officer who fails to perform his official duty shall be fined FIFTY CENTS, and each member of every Committee who fails to make a report within two weeks after its appointment, shall be fined TWENTY-FIVE cents, unless the time for such report is deferred by consent of the Society.

XXII.

Any member shall be deemed guilty of disorder who shall, by hissing, clapping, laughing aloud, or by any unnecessary noise, interrupt the President or any member while speaking, or shall withdraw from the hall without permission from the Vice-President or address the President without rising from his seat, or persist in motions, resolutions or remarks which have been pronounced out of order. It shall also be deemed disorder for any member to read any paper, book, pamphlet, or periodical in the hall, unless, in connection with the regular business, to engage in conversation while a member is speaking, to leave the hall for more than twenty minutes, while the Society is in session, or to pass between the chair and a member who is speaking. And for each offense herein enumerated he shall be fined the sum of TWENTY-FIVE CENTS.

XXIII.

If any member shall leave the hall while another is speaking, without permission, he shall be fined FIFTY CENTS.

XXIV.—ADJOURNMENT

A motion for adjournment shall always be in order, but to adjourn the Society before the regular business shall have been transacted shall require a vote of two-thirds of the members present, and no member voting for the adjournment shall be allowed to move it again during the same meeting.

XXV.—RESIGNATIONS

All resignations shall be in writing, and shall not be accepted unless accompanied with a written certificate of the Treasurer, that all dues are paid or transferred by permission.

XXVI.—ABSENCE OF PRESIDENT AND VICE PRESIDENT

In the absence of the President and Vice-President, a member shall be called to the Chair who shall perform the duties incident to that office.

XVII.—QUORUM

Fifteen members shall form a quorum and no business shall be transacted unless a quorum is present.

XXVIII.—PRIVILEGED QUESTIONS

When a question is under debate, no motion shall be raised but—
    To adjourn.
    To lay on the table.
    For the previous question.
    To postpone indefinitely.
    To postpone to a certain day.

To amend an amendment or to amend which of several motions shall have precedence in the order they stand arranged.

XXIX.—PREVIOUS QUESTIONS

The previous question shall be of this form, viz: "Shall the main question be now put?" and on it there shall be no debate.

XXX.—QUESTIONS OF ORDER

Any member may call another to order, but such member can only be ruled out of order by the Chair. Either party may appeal from the decision. When no appeal is made, the member speaking shall immediately desist from his course of remark. When an appeal is made he shall yield until it is decided, being entitled to it again after the decision, conforming his remarks thereto. If the President is doubtful in a point of order, he may take the sense of the Society.

XXXI.—MOTIONS

No motion shall be debated until the same shall be seconded, and when the motion shall be made and seconded, it shall be reduced to writing, if desired by the President, or any member.

XXXII.—CALLS OF AYES AND NOES

When ayes and noes shall be called for by any *two* of the members present, the President shall direct the Assistant Secretary to call the roll, and after the decision is announced from the Chair, no member shall be permitted to vote under any circumstances whatever.

XXXIII.—PARLIAMENTARY PRACTICE

The rules of Parliamentary Practice comprised in "JEFFERSON'S MANUAL" shall govern the Society in all cases to which they can apply, and when they are not inconsistent with the Constitution and Rules.

XXXIV.—VOTE ON QUESTION

On a regular question for debate, a motion for the previous question or call for the vote shall not be in order before half past ten, and any one violating this law shall be fined fifty cents. But if all debate cease before that time, the President shall put the question to the Society.

XXXV.—TIME OF MEETING

The regular meeting of the Society shall be on Saturday, at seven o'clock P.M., from October to April, and at half-past seven from April to June.

XXXVI.—FINES REPEALED

Fines may be repealed by a vote of two-thirds of the members present.

XXXVII.

Any member calling on another regular member shall be fined ONE DOLLAR.

XXXVIII.—SUCH RECENT ENACTMENTS AS AFFECT THE CONSTITUTION

It was resolved that such changes should be made in the Constitution as may be found necessary in regard to the final celebration. Page 101 of Minutes.

XXXIX.—EVERETT MEDAL

Whereas, by gift of the Hon. Edward Everett, a fund yielding an annual interest of about $30 is held jointly by the Jefferson and Washington Societies. Be it therefore

1. Resolved, That we can in no better way acknowledge our sense of the generosity of the giver, than by encouraging a department of literature in conjunction with his name, to which he has specially devoted his talents, and which he has shown most worthy of cultivation.

2. That, in accordance with the wishes of Edward Everett the annual interest of this fund be devoted to the purchase of a Medal, which shall be awarded as a prize for the best biographical essay on an American citizen, written by a student of this University.

3. That the Committee of award be composed of such members of the Faculty as may be chosen annually by the Societies.

4. That the medal be called the Everett Medal.

XL.—ELIGIBLE PERSONS

1. Resolved, That all meetings of the Jefferson Society, whether called or regular, are intended for the sole and exclusive use of its members—Regular, Irregular, and Honorary.

2. That hereafter it shall be unlawful for any gentleman to introduce into the Hall any person not a member, during the whole or any part of a meeting of the Society.

XLI.—SCHOLARSHIP OF THE JEFFERSON SOCIETY

Whereas, experience has shown that the annual accruing income of the Jefferson Society is sufficient beyond the incidental expenses for the education and maintenance of a student at the University. Be it therefore

1. Resolved, That the Society hereby institute a scholarship in the University of Virginia as a testimonial of abilities and worth, with an annual appropriation of $250, to be paid quarterly to such a student of fair character and capacity as may be deemed most in want of assistance.

2. That the sum shall be placed in the hands of the Proctor by the Treasurer of the Society upon the election of the said incumbent.

3. That the election shall take place at the last meeting in May of the present year, and of each succeeding year hereafter.

4. That a committee of five, to be designated by ballot, shall be chosen at least three weeks before the election, to whom all nominations shall be referred, and no nomination shall be acted upon until approved by that Committee, nor unless made one week before the election.

5. From the nominations approved of by this Committee, the Society shall elect one upon whom the scholarship shall be conferred.

6. That the benefit of this scholarship is intended to be confined exclusively to Academical Students, and shall be extended during *two scholastic years*.

7. If said incumbent shall prove himself to be unworthy of the confidence reposed in him, he shall be impeached and removed by order of the Society.

8. That a committee of five be appointed this night (May 21st, 1859,) to receive nominations to be presented to the Society for election at our next regular meeting.

9. As it is designed that this scholarship shall be a testimonial of abilities and worth, it is prescribed to the committee and recommended to the Society at large, that they be vigilant in conferring the honor on those only whose real merits warrant it.

Constitution and Bye Laws of JS, Charlottesville, 1860, LVA.

Constitution of the Jefferson Society, 1880

Form of Initiation

The President shall request the initiate (or initiates) to come forward and sign the Constitution, and shall then read to him (or them) the following:

Sir—(or Sirs)—You have voluntarily become a member (or members) of the Jefferson Society, and I have, in its name, to lay you under the most solemn injunctions to obey and uphold its Constitution, to observe all propriety as a member and a gentleman; and to advance, by strict adherence to duty, the welfare of our organization.

Preamble

We, the members of the Jefferson Society of the University of Virginia, in order to form a more perfect organization, provide for our common improvement in the art of debate, promote general culture amongst ourselves and those around us, and drill ourselves in all those exercises which strengthen for the free duties of citizenship, do ordain and establish this Constitution for our government.

Article I

Membership

Sec. 1. Only students in regular attendance upon one or more of the schools of the University of Virginia and not members of any other similar organization in this institution shall be eligible as regular members of the Society.

Sec. 2. The duties and privileges of regular membership in this Society, once assumed, can be renounced only by resignation, under the conditions and in accordance with the rules hereinafter set forth, and by the final termination of a member's connection with the University of Virginia as a student.

Sec. 3. All the privileges of membership, except that of voting on Society business, shall be extended to alumni of the University of Virginia who have been members of the Society.

Sec. 4. The privilege of attendance upon the meetings of the Society shall be accorded to its honorary members, to regular members of the Washington Society of the University of Virginia, and to none others except by a special resolution agreed to by a vote of two-thirds of the members present.

Sec. 5. To the privileges and dignity of honorary membership this Society may elect such eminent persons as it may deem worthy of its courtesy.

Sec. 6. For the election of regular members of this Society a vote of two-thirds of the members present at any regular meeting shall be required.

Sec. 7. For the election of honorary members of this Society a vote of four-fifths of the members present at any regular meeting shall be required.

Article II
Outline of Government

Sec. 1. The executive government of this Society shall be vested in a President, a Vice-President, a Treasurer, a Committee of Ways and Means, a Committee of Conference, a Judicial Council, a Final Committee, and a Question Committee.

Sec. 2. The President shall be elected by a majority of the members present at a regular meeting of the Society to serve for a term of three months.

Sec. 3. The Vice-President shall be chosen in the same manner and for the same term as the President.

Sec. 4. The Treasurer shall be elected in the same manner as the President, to serve during the academic session.

Sec. 5. The Committee of Ways and Means shall consist of the Vice-President, as chairman *ex-officio*, and of two other members appointed by the President to serve during a presidential term.

Sec. 6. The Committee of Conference shall consist of five members appointed by the President to serve during the academic year.

Sec. 7. The Judicial Council shall consist of the President, the Vice-President and the Treasurer.

Sec. 8. The Final Committee shall be appointed by the President in February of each year, to serve during the remainder of the academic session, and shall consist of two members from the State of Virginia and one member from each of the other States represented in the Society; but in no case shall it consist of less than ten members.

Sec. 9. The Question Committee shall consist of two members appointed by the President to serve six weeks.

Sec. 10. The President shall appoint, to serve during his term of office, a Secretary and an Assistant Secretary; and shall appoint monthly a Sergeant-at-Arms.

Article III

Duties of Officers

Sec. 1. *The President.*—The President shall preside over all meetings of the Society and of the Judicial Council, to preserve order and decorum; shall construe and enforce the Constitution and By-Laws of the Society and the rules of practice, subject always to an appeal to the Society itself; shall appoint the Secretary, the Assistant Secretary, the Sergeant-at-Arms, the non-official members of the Committee of Ways and Means, the Committee of Conference, the Final Committee, the Question Committee, all special committees ordered by the Society, and all officers *pro tempore*; and perform all other duties usually pertaining to his office. It shall be his duty to convene the Society whenever requested to do so by a writing signed by *five* regular members. He shall have no vote save a casting vote. It shall be his privilege to take part in any of the regular debates of the Society, after having called the Vice-President to the chair *pro tempore*.

Sec. 2. *The Vice-President.*—The Vice-President shall be *ex-officio* chairman of the Committee of Ways and Means and member of the Judicial Council. In the absence of the President, he shall occupy the chair and exercise all the functions of presiding officer.

Sec. 3. *The Treasurer.*—The Treasurer shall receive and take charge of all the funds of the Society, keeping, in a book provided for the purpose, a careful and minute account of all receipts and disbursements, which account he shall submit to the Committee of Ways and Means at their regular meetings. He shall make no disbursements except such as shall have been approved by the Committee of Ways and Means and reported by that Committee to the Society. He shall report at each regular meeting of the Society a list of all fines imposed within the two preceding weeks, with the cause and date thereof, and an account of all moneys received and paid out since his last report, with receipted bills for all payments exceeding one dollar. His reports must be submitted in writing, in a book provided for the purpose, and shall, after adoption, be filed, together with all accompanying receipts, with the Secretary. He shall also submit at the end of each presidential term a full and exact written report of the financial condition of the Society which report he shall leave with the Committee of Ways and Means to be incorporated in their next regular report to the Society.

Sec. 4. *The Secretary.*—The Secretary shall keep a careful record of the proceedings of the Society; shall conduct its correspondence; shall carefully preserve all its records and all documents that may be entrusted to his care; shall transcribe, in a book kept for the purpose, all amendments and additions to this Constitution and to the By-Laws of the Society; shall read the appointments for debate; and shall perform all the duties naturally incident to the office of recording and corresponding Secretary.

Sec. 5. *The Assistant Secretary.*—The Assistant Secretary shall perform the duties of the Secretary in the absence of the latter: shall call the roll; shall keep an alphabetical list of the members of the Society, from which he shall, at each regular meeting, furnish the Secretary with the list of the appointments for debate for the third ensuing meeting; shall aid the Secretary, when no tellers are appointed, in taking the vote by ballot; and shall, at the close of each meeting, furnish the Treasurer with a list of the absentees from each roll-call.

Sec. 6. *The Sergeant-at-Arms.*—It shall be the duty of the Sergeant-at-Arms to see that no person enter the Hall of the Society during its meetings who is not privileged to be present by the provisions of this Constitution contained in Secs. II and III of Article I; to see that the Hall is suitably prepared for the meetings of the Society, and is left in proper condition after adjournment; to note all cases of disorder and neglect of duty, recording them, with the prescribed fines annexed, in a book to be provided for the purpose, reading them at the close of the meeting during which they have been incurred, and transmitting a list of them to the Treasurer immediately upon adjournment; and to act as the President's ministerial officer in enforcing order. He may, with the consent of the President, appoint, when necessary, one or more temporary assistants to aid in enforcing order.

Article IV

Duties of Committees

Sec. 1. *The Committee of Ways and Means.*—The Committee of Ways and Means shall meet in the Hall of the Society every Saturday evening immediately after the adjournment of the Judicial Council. It shall be their duty carefully to audit and examine at these their regular meetings, the accounts of the Treasurer; to act upon all bills presented by him and upon all disbursements which he shall report as necessary or expedient; to attend to the supplying of all necessaries for the Hall, and to the furnishing, heating and repairing of the Hall; and to act as executive committee of the Society in carrying out all business not entrusted to any other committee. It shall, further, be their duty to report to the Society, at each regular meeting, upon the condition of the Treasurer's accounts, and upon all outlays by them deemed advisable; and no disbursements ordered by them shall be made by the Treasurer unless and until their report upon such orders shall have been adopted by the Society.

Sec. 2. *The Committee of Conference.*—It shall be the duty of the Committee of Conference to act in conjunction with similar committees appointed by the

Washington Society, upon all matters, regular and incidental, requiring the joint action of the two Societies.

Sec. 3. *The Judicial Council.*—The Judicial Council shall meet in the Hall of the Society every Saturday evening immediately after the adjournment of the Society. It shall be their duty to hear and act upon all excuses for fines and upon all offers of resignation of membership; and they shall hear no excuses for fines which have been standing for more than two weeks, saving in the case of members who have been unable to submit their excuses within that time on account of sickness or in absence from the University. From their decisions an appeal shall in all cases lie to the Society itself. It shall be the duty of the Treasurer to embody the action of the Judicial Council in his weekly reports to the Society.

Sec. 4. *The Final Committee.*—The Final Committee shall take entire charge of all matters that concern the Final Celebration of this Society.

Sec. 5. *The Question Committee.*—It shall be the duty of the Question Committee to submit at each meeting of the Society two questions for the regular debates three weeks thereafter; and after the submission of their report it shall be the privilege of any member to propose a question to be voted on, if seconded by any member of the Society, along with those offered by the Committee.

Article V
Regular Exercises

Sec. 1. From an alphabetically arranged roll of the members of the Society, which it shall be the duty of the Assistant Secretary to prepare, the Secretary shall divide the members of the Society into six classes containing as nearly as possible an equal number of members; and these classes shall be appointed for debate in regular order.

Sec. 2. Each question for regular debate shall be selected, from the questions submitted as hereinbefore provided, by the class which is to debate it; and a majority of the members thereof who are present when choice should be made, shall have power to select. In case of a tie, the President shall have the casting vote. In case of a failure to choose in the part of the class, the choice shall be left to the Society.

Sec. 3. After the discussion by the regularly appointed debaters, the question shall be open to the house for debate. During the discussion thereof a motion for the previous question or a call for a vote shall not be in order before half-past ten o'clock. At the close of the regular debate, the vote of the Society shall be taken by yeas and nays upon the question.

Sec. 4. At the first regular meeting of the Society in each month, except June, a member shall be elected to deliver an oration before the Society one month thereafter.

Article VI
The Medal

Sec. 1. At the close of each session two medals, ranking respectively as first and second, shall be given by the Society to the two best debaters. But whenever there are but two contestants no second medal shall be given.

Sec. 2. These medalists shall be chosen by a committee of three members of the Faculty of the University of Virginia who shall be elected by the Society at its first regular meeting in November of each year.

Sec. 3. At the first regular meeting in April and at the first regular meeting in May respectively there shall be a debate to be participated in only by the contestants for the medals; and at these meetings the aforesaid committee of the Faculty shall sit as judges.

Sec. 4. The decision of the Electoral Committee, which shall be final, shall be rendered within one week after the May debate.

Sec. 5. After the last regular meeting in February the contestants for the medals shall meet to select a question for their first debate. After this first debate they shall choose a question for their second debate.

Sec. 6. The medals thus awarded shall be publicly presented by the President of the Society to the successful contestants on the night of the Final Celebration of the Society, when each of the medalists shall deliver an oration.

Sec. 7. The form of the first medal, which shall be of gold and of the value of fifty dollars, shall be circular, its diameter not less than one inch and three-quarters. It shall bear on its face, enclosed in a wreath of laurel, PRESENTED BY THE JEFFERSON SOCIETY TO ------ AS THEIR BEST DEBATER, SESSION 18-. Underneath this inscription there shall be a representation of the University of Virginia, surmounted by the coat of-arms of Virginia beneath the motto of the Society, HAEC OLIM MEMINISSE JUVABIT; and, following the circumference, the words, UNIVERSITY OF VIRGINIA, JUNE (OR JULY)-, 18-.

Article VII
The Magazine

Sec. 1. There shall be at least eight numbers of the Magazine issued during each collegiate year, of which the first shall be published in October.

Sec. 2. The editors of the Magazine shall be six in number. Of these, three shall represent the Jefferson and three the Washington Society. They shall be elected annually, the Jefferson Society making choice of her representatives at the regular meeting of the Society in January of each year. Of the corps of editors thus chosen by the two Societies, five shall have charge of the literary department of the Magazine and the sixth of its financial and other business; and the election of this business editor shall fall alternatively to the two Societies. If, at any time, the Jefferson Society have not her full complement of editors, the Society shall, after due notice, proceed to complete it by election.

Sec. 3. The literary editors of the Magazine shall, in January of each year, select from their own number an editor-in-chief; and if at any time the office of editor-in-chief become vacant, it shall be their duty immediately to fill it by election. The editor-in-chief shall have entire control over both the literary and business management of the Magazine. He shall have power to allot their work to the other editors and to accept or reject all articles offered for publication.

Sec. 4. When requested to do so, the editors shall preserve strict secrecy as to the authorship of contributions; and no contributions shall be accepted for publication in the Magazine which has previously appeared in print.

Sec. 5. The business editor shall have control, under the editor-in-chief, of all business matters connected with the Magazine, such as its financial management, its subscription lists, its advertising department, and the mailing and distribution of its issues. He shall, at the end of each three months of his term of office, make to each Society, through its Secretary, a report, exhibiting the exact condition of the Magazine as regards the concerns under his management.

Sec. 6. No member shall be eligible for the position of literary editor of the Magazine who has not had at least one prose article of his own composition accepted for publication in the Magazine.

Sec. 7.—*The Magazine Medal*—This Society shall at the beginning of each session, through its Committee of Conference, join with the Washington Society in choosing a committee of three members of the Faculty of the University of Virginia to select the best literary production contributed to the Magazine during the session by a member of either Society; and to this number the two Societies shall jointly award a gold medal of the value of fifty dollars. This medal shall be publicly presented by the Chairman of the aforesaid committee of the Faculty at the Final celebration of that Society to which the recipient of the medal may belong.

Article VIII
Rules of Election
Sec. 1. No one shall be entitled to vote for any officer of this Society or for

any editor of the Magazine unless he shall have been a member of this Society for two weeks previous to the election.

Sec. 2. No member who is indebted to the treasury of the Society shall be qualified to vote for the Final President or Vice President, or be eligible for either of those offices.

Sec. 3. No member may be Final President or Vice-President or Medalist of this Society unless previous to election (or previous to his appearing before the electoral committee of the Faculty, in the case of the Medalist) he shall have spoken on at least two separate occasions before the Society, either as monthly orator or on a question chosen for regular debate.

Article IX
The Badge

Sec. 1. The badge of this Society shall be of gold in the shape of a scroll, three-quarters of an inch wide. On its face shall be engraven the following: U. V. JEFF. SOC., two pens crossed, 1825, and the initial letters of the three Greek words "Φιλοι, Πατρις, θεος."

Article X
Resignation of Membership

Whenever any member wishes to resign he shall signify his desire in writing to the Judicial Council, stating his reasons, and, upon obtaining the acquiescence of the Council and paying all his dues to the Society, may be permitted to withdraw. If the consent is withheld, he shall have the privilege of appeal to the Society.

Article XI
Changes in Constitution and By-Laws

Sec. 1. All motions and resolutions affecting the Constitution or By-Laws of this Society and all resolutions proposing appropriations of Society funds shall be submitted in writing and pass through three readings and a Committee of the Whole; and not more than two readings shall be taken at one sitting of the Society.

Sec. 2. A vote of two-thirds (2/3) of the regular members of the Society shall be necessary to amend this Constitution; but a vote of two-thirds (2/3) of the members present at any regular meeting shall be sufficient to amend the By-Laws.

Sec. 3. Two-thirds (2/3) of the members present at any meeting of the

Society may, by a single vote, suspend, for that sitting, any provision of the By-Laws.

BY-LAWS

Article I

Meetings

Sec. 1. This Society shall meet every Saturday evening during the session at seven o'clock P.M., from October to April, and at half-past seven from April to June.

Sec. 2. If, after having been properly requested to do so, the President fails to call a meeting of the Society, a quorum of members may convene it, after having given twenty four hours' notice of the time at which the meeting is to take place, and of the purpose for which it is called. Notice posted upon four of the college bulletin-boards shall be sufficient.

Sec. 3. Option attendance on the meetings of the Society shall be allowed to all applicants for degrees and to members living one mile from college at the discretion of the Judicial Committee.

Article II

Members Excused from Duty

Sec. 1. Members of less than two weeks standing shall be excused from all duties except attendance on the meetings of the Society.

Sec. 2. Members shall be excused from all duties for one week before and four days after each of their examinations.

Article III

Dues and Fines

Sec. 1. Each member shall pay to the treasury of the Society *Ten Dollars* initiation fee, and an annual tax of two dollars and a half every subsequent session that he is a regular member.

Sec. 2. The roll shall be called at the opening and the close of each meeting, and members shall be fined twenty-five cents for unexcused absence from each roll-call.

Sec. 3. Each member failing to debate the question upon which he has been regularly appointed shall be fined fifty cents.

Sec. 4. Every officer and every member of a committee who fails promptly to perform his official duty shall be fined *one dollar*.

Sec. 5. Any member elected monthly orator who fails to perform his duty as such shall be fined *one dollar.*

Sec. 6. Any member guilty of disorder shall be fined twenty-five cents, the Sergeant-at-Arms being judge of what constitutes disorder.

Sec. 7. *Special Fines—*

(1) For passing between President and member speaking, twenty-five cents.

(2) Leaving the Hall without permission, twenty-five cents.

(3) Persisting in resolutions, motions, or remarks ruled out of order, fifty cents.

(4) Absence from Hall on leave for more than twenty minutes during meeting, twenty-five cents.

Article IV

Debate

Sec. 1. It shall be the duty of the Secretary to re-arrange, from time to time, the classes for debate with a view to keeping the numbers in the several classes as nearly as possible equal. He shall also separate each class into two divisions, one division consisting of the first, third, fifth, &c., on the roll of the class, the other, of the second, fourth, sixth, &c.

Sec. 2. *Manner of Choosing Question for Regular Debate.*—The President shall call upon the Secretary to read the questions which have been submitted in accordance with Article IV, Sec. 5 of the Constitution, and, after the reading of each question, shall inquire if it is seconded by any member of the class appointed to debate the question which may be chosen. He shall then take the vote of the said class upon each question thus seconded. The first of these questions which shall receive the votes of a majority of the class he shall declare chosen. If none of them is chosen by the class, the selection of a question shall fall to the House.

Sec. 3. After the choice of question the Secretary shall read in alphabetical order the names of the members of the class which is to debate the question chosen. He shall then give the privilege of the choice of sides to each member of the class in succession until one declares his preference. The side thus chosen shall be debated by the division to which the member making choice belongs.

Sec. 4. Each member of the class appointed for debate shall, at the meeting for which he is appointed, have the privilege of speaking twice upon the questions chosen. The Secretary shall call upon the appointed debaters in order, naming alternatively those allotted to the affirmative and those allotted to the negative. In this order he shall twice call upon each appointed debater.

Sec. 5. Members not regularly appointed to debate shall have the privilege of speaking twice on each regular question after its discussion has been thrown open to the house; on all other questions also each member shall be allowed to speak twice.

Article V
Quorum
One third of the members of the Society shall constitute a quorum for the transaction of all business.

Article VI
Order of Business

1. First Roll-Call.
2. Reading and adoption of minutes of last meeting.
3. Installation of officers.
4. Nomination, election and initiation of new members.
5. Election of officers.
6. Monthly Oration.
7. Debate.
8. Report of Question Committee and choice of question.
9. Announcement of class to debate and determination of sides.
10. Treasurer's report.
11. Reports of committees, Ways, Means, Conference, etc.
12. Extraordinary and unfinished business.
13. Motions and resolutions.
14. Reading of class to debate within one, two, and three weeks, with announcement of sides and questions.
15. Notices of elections.
16. Report of Sergeant-at-Arms.
17. Second Roll-Call.
18. Adjournment.

Article VII
Miscellaneous Business
Sec. 1. All motions and resolutions must be submitted in writing, in a blank

book provided for the purpose and kept at the desk of the Secretary. They must be signed by the movers and read by the Secretary in the order in which they are submitted.

Sec. 2. The President shall give notice of every election at least one week before it is to take place.

Sec. 3. To adjourn the Society before the regular business has been transacted shall require a vote of two-thirds of the members present; and no member who has voted for adjournment shall be allowed to move it again during the same meeting.

Sec. 4. *Call for Yeas and Nays*—At the request of *five* members the vote shall be taken by *yeas* and *nays*.

Sec. 5. The rules of parliamentary practice as set forth in "Robert's Rules of Order" shall govern the proceedings of this Society in all cases in which they are not inconsistent with its Constitution and By-Laws.

Sec. 6. Any student of the University who was a member of this Society previous to the session of 1880–81, but is not now one, may reconstitute himself an active member by signing the Constitution and subjecting himself to the payment of the annual tax.

Sec. 7. Blank books shall be provided by the Treasurer for the reports of each of the standing committees, of the Secretary, of the Treasurer, and for all other uses called for by the Constitution or By-Laws.

Sec. 8. At the meeting in April, at which the first medal debate takes place, and immediately prior to the debate, Article VI of the Constitution shall be read by the President to the Electoral Committee of the Faculty.

Article VIII

Previous Acts not Herein Contained
All motions and resolutions affecting the Constitution and By-Laws of this Society previously passed, and not herein contained, shall be and are hereby *repealed*.

Constitution and By-Laws of the Jefferson Society of the University of Virginia, Founded 1825, Charlottesville, Charlottesville Chronicle Print, 1881, U.Va.

Constitution of the Jefferson Society, 2015

Preamble

We, the members of the Jefferson Literary and Debating Society at the University of Virginia, in order to form a more permanent organization, provide for our common improvement in debate, promote general culture amongst ourselves and those around us, and drill ourselves in all exercises which strengthen us for the free duties of citizenship, do ordain and establish this Constitution for our government, and pledge ourselves in its support.

Article I

Membership

Section 1. Non-Discrimination.

The Jefferson Literary and Debating Society does not discriminate in its membership or membership policies based on age, citizenship, color, disability, gender, race, religion, national origin, political affiliation, sexual orientation or status as a disabled Veteran or Veteran of the Vietnam era.

Section 2.

A. REGULAR MEMBERSHIP.

All students in regular enrollment at the University of Virginia who have demonstrated by attendance and participation during a probationary period of not less than one academic semester that they are worthy of Regular Membership in the Society in accordance with its purposes as set forth in the Preamble to the Constitution, who have presented an acceptable Probationary presentation as set forth in Article VI of the Bylaws, and no other person, shall be eligible for Regular Membership in the Society. Candidates presented to the Society by the Membership Committee and receiving votes of four-fifths of the regular Members of the Society present and voting shall be deemed duly elected as Regular Members of the Society; provided that in every case, four-fifths of the votes cast shall be at least one-third of the Regular Membership in good standing at the time. The failure of a candidate so presented to receive a four-fifths affirmative vote shall result in his being dropped from membership in the Society, unless he shall be continued as a Probationary Member by specific action taken at the same meeting, approved by four-fifths of those voting.

B. PROBATIONARY MEMBERSHIP.

All students in regular enrollment at the University of Virginia shall be eligible for Probationary Membership of this Society. Candidates for Probationary Membership shall make written application to the Society, furnishing such information as the Membership Committee may desire. The Membership Committee shall make a non-binding report. The affirmative vote of four-fifths of the Members in good standing present and voting shall be required to elect a candidate to Probationary Membership. Probationary Members shall have all the rights and privileges of the Hall, except those of holding office, voting for Officers of the Society, voting upon the adoption of amendments to the Constitution and the Bylaws, voting on the passage of Probationary presentations, and voting upon the election of candidates for Probationary Membership and of Probationary Members into Regular Membership.

C. ASSOCIATE MEMBERS.

When a Regular Member of the Society ends his regular enrollment at the University of Virginia, he shall become an Associate Member of the Society. When an Associate Member returns to regular enrollment at the University of Virginia, he may regain Regular Membership after re-signing the Roll. The Executive Committee, subject to review by the Society, shall have the power to rule on any case where reasonable doubt exists as to a person's status as an Associate Member. When a Member of the Society who has paid Regular Member dues for two semesters shall so request in writing, he shall become an Associate Member. Associate Members of the Society shall have all the privileges of Regular Members except that they may not hold office, or have any share or interest in the property or possessions of the Society. Associate Members may vote only after paying dues in the amount established for Regular Members, or a onetime fee of equal to four times this amount as established at the time of payment, or a one-time fee of two-hundred dollars paid prior to August 23, 2011; after which they shall have the vote on all questions except those upon the election of Officers, the amendment of the Constitution and of the Bylaws, and the consideration of candidates for Probationary, Regular, and Honorary Membership.

D. HONORARY MEMBERS.

Honorary Membership shall be reserved for those who are not students at the University of Virginia and who have rendered signal service to the Society. Honorary Members shall be elected by the signed approval of four-fifths of the Regular Members in good standing. Honorary Members must sign the Roll.

Section 3. Secrecy.

The consideration of candidates for Regular, Probationary, and Honorary Membership shall be in sessions closed to all but Regular and Associate Members. No member shall divulge the proceedings of the closed sessions to non-members. Violations of the aforementioned constitute grounds for expulsion as well as any other sanction the Society deems appropriate.

Section 4. Initiation of Members.

Initiation into Probationary and Regular Membership shall be conducted according to the ritual adopted by the Society, except that the following shall always be included in initiation of Regular Members:

> I, _____, a student at the University of Virginia, holding it to be true that opinions springing out of solitary observation and reflection are seldom, in first instance, correct; that the faculties of the mind are excited by collision; that friendships are cemented, errors corrected, and sound principles established by society and intercourse, and especially in a country where all are free to profess and , by argument, maintain their opinions; that the powers of debate should be sedulously cultivated—therefore associate myself with the Jefferson Society at the University of Virginia. In becoming a member of the Society, I pledge myself to conform to is regulations and cherish its prosperity. [In testimony whereof, I have hereunto affixed my name.]

After initiation, the initiated Probationary or Regular Member shall sign the Probationary or Regular Member Roll, respectively.

Section 5. Expulsion from Membership and Resignation.

A. EXPULSION BY VOTE.

Any Member shall be subject to expulsion from the Society for any cause deemed sufficient by the Society, provided that in every case due notice and opportunity for defense shall have been given to the offending Members, and that two-thirds of the Regular Membership shall vote for expulsion.

B. RESIGNATION.

The resignation from the Society of any Members shall be made in writing to the Secretary and shall be effective one week after its receipt. Resignation of the Secretary will be made in writing to the President and Historian of the Society.

Article II

Officers and Elections

Section 1. Eligibility.

All Regular Members in good standing who are full time students at the University of Virginia, as defined by the University Registrar, may hold office. All Regular Members in good standing may vote in all elections of officers. There shall be no absentee ballots.

Section 2. Elective Officers, Their Terms and Duties.

The elective Officers of the Society shall be a President, a Vice President, a Secretary, a Treasurer, an Historian, and a Keeper. No Member shall hold more than one of these offices at one time.

A. PRESIDENT.

The President shall be elected at the last regular meeting of the Society in each semester and shall hold office until the installation of his successor. The President shall preside over all the meetings of the Society, shall preserve order and decorum, shall construe and enforce the Constitution and Bylaws of the Society, shall appoint the Committees of the Society as provided for in the Bylaws, and all other officers pro tempore, and shall perform all the other duties pertaining to his office.

B. VICE PRESIDENT.

The Vice President shall be elected at the last regular meeting of the Society in each semester and shall hold office until the installation of his successor. He shall serve as the Chairman of the Program Committee and in the absence of the President he shall occupy the chair and exercise all functions of the presiding officer.

C. SECRETARY.

The Secretary shall be elected at the last regular meeting of the Society in each semester and shall hold office until the installation of his successor. He shall call the Roll and keep a record of all absentees, shall carefully preserve an account of the proceedings of the Society and all its records and documents that may be entrusted to him, shall transcribe in a book kept for that purpose all amendments to this Constitution and to the Bylaws of the Society, and shall perform all other duties incident to the office of recording secretary.

D. TREASURER.

The Treasurer shall be elected at the last regular meeting of the Society in each semester and shall hold office until the installation of his successor. The Treasurer shall collect and take charge of all funds of the Society. He shall make no disbursement unless directly authorized by the Executive Committee, and shall not make authorized disbursements exceeding the sum of fifty dollars, unless directly authorized to do so by the Society. The Treasurer shall keep, in a book provided for the purpose, a careful and minute account of all receipts collected and disbursements made by him for the Society. This book shall be open at all times to the inspection of any Member of the Society at all reasonable times, and it shall be transmitted to the Executive Committee for auditing at times provided for in the Bylaws of the Society. The Treasurer shall at every meeting of the Society report to the President the names of, and object to the assignment of the floor to, all Members who are subject to the provisions of the Bylaws with reference to failure to pay any fees, dues, fines, or assessments.

E. HISTORIAN.

The Historian shall be elected at the last regular meeting of the Society in the spring semester and shall hold office until the election of his successor. The Historian shall prepare a chronicle of the activities of the Society during his session in office and shall submit this chronicle to the society at the last regular meeting of the Society in the spring semester. The Historian shall arrange and host the annual Moomaw Oratorical Contest, the Wilson Banquet, and the Founder's Day Banquet. The Historian, being the sole officer to serve for the full academic term, shall, on the C.I.O. Agreement, be the primary signatory of the Society; his signature shall have the full consent, force, and effect of the Society with respect to the C.I.O. Agreement, barring a vote to the contrary by the Society, preventing the aforementioned signature.

F. KEEPER.

The Keeper shall be elected at the last regular meeting of the Society in each semester and shall hold office until the installation of his successor. The Keeper shall perform all duties consistent with the historical significance of his office.

Section 3. Appointed Officers, Their Terms and Duties.

A. PROBATIONARY CHAIRMAN.

The President shall appoint a Probationary Chairman, whose duty it shall be to chair the sessions of the Probationary Committee, to act as intermediary between the Regular and Probationary Members, and to schedule, supervise, and present Probationary presentations. He and the Probationary Committee shall discuss the topic, content, and procedure of the presentation with the Probationary Members as well as determine, at the beginning of each semester, the requirements for membership, and consult the Executive Committee when formulating these standards.

B. MEMBERSHIP CHAIRMAN.

The President shall appoint a Membership Chairman, whose duty it shall be to chair the sessions of the Membership Committee, to present the candidates for Probationary and Regular Membership to the Society, to report the candidate recommendations of the Committee to the Society and shall report to the Executive Committee any breaches of the Society's non-discrimination policy.

C. WAYS AND MEANS CHAIRMAN.

The President shall appoint a Ways and Means Chairman, whose duty it shall be to chair the meetings of the Ways and Means Committee and to execute the traditional responsibilities of his office.

D. PARLIAMENTARIAN.

The President may appoint a Parliamentarian, whose duty it shall be to advise the President as to parliamentary procedure at his request or that of any Regular Member, as defined in the Bylaws, and to advise the President in matters of construction of this Constitution and of the Bylaws of the Society.

E. PEN AND INK CHAIRMAN.

The President shall appoint a Pen and Ink Chairman, whose duty it shall be to chair the meetings of the Pen and Ink Committee, to publish and disseminate the Jefferson Journal, and to carry out other responsibilities which may be assigned by the Society.

F. SERGEANT-AT-ARMS.

The President shall appoint a Sergeant-at-Arms, whose duty it shall be to prevent, in the best of his power, the violation of Federal, State, and local penal statutes at the meetings of the Society, to report all infractions of said statutes to the Executive Committee, and to enlist the aid of the General Membership or any public official in performing his duties. It shall be within the power of the Sergeant-at-Arms to bar from meetings any person determined by him to be in violation of said statutes at that time, within a standard of reasonable sensibility.

G. DEBATE AND ORATORY CHAIRMAN.

The President shall appoint a Debate and Oratory Chairman, whose duty it shall be to chair the meetings of the Debate and Oratory Committee and to carry out other responsibilities which may be assigned by the Society.

H. PUBLIC SERVICES CHAIRMAN.

The President shall appoint a Public Services Chairman, whose duty it shall be to chair the meetings of the Public Services Committee and to promote the Society's good standing in the Community.

I. ALUMNI RELATIONS CHAIRMAN.

The President shall appoint an Alumni Relations Chairman whose duty it shall be to maintain contact with Alumni, promote all relevant events to Alumni, and organize in conjunction with the Executive Committee opportunities for charitable giving to the Society.

Section 4. Electoral Procedure.

The election of Officers of the Society shall be by secret written ballot which shall be collected and counted by two tellers appointed and assisted by the President. A simple majority of the votes cast, a quorum being present, shall be sufficient to elect. If this majority be not obtained on the first ballot, the candidate with the least number of votes shall be dropped, and the Society shall proceed to another ballot. This process shall be continued until one candidate shall have obtained a majority of the votes cast. The result of the election shall then be transmitted by the tellers in writing to the President, who shall announce the result to the floor. Ample opportunity shall be allowed for a demand for a recount, after which the ballots shall be destroyed by the tellers. There shall be no further balloting for that office.

Section 5. Installation of Officers.

The retiring President shall administer the following oath (or affirmation) to his successor before relinquishing to him the office of President:

Do you solemnly swear (or affirm) upon your honor, and in the presence of this Society, that you will faithfully execute the duties of the office to which you have been elected?

The new President shall then administer the same oath (or affirmation) to each of the other newly elected officers.

Section 6. Vacancies.

Should a vacancy occur in any of the elected offices of the Society, such a vacancy shall be filled by the Society not later than the next meeting following the formal announcement of such a vacancy.

Section 7. Discipline and Resignation of Officers.

Any elected Officer of the Society shall be subject to removal from office for neglect of duty, misconduct in office, or for any cause deemed sufficient by the Society; provided that in every case due opportunity for defense shall be given. For such removal, a three-fourths vote of the Regular Members in good standing present and voting shall be necessary; provided that in every case, three-fourths of the votes cast shall be a majority of the Regular Membership in good standing at the time. The President shall have the power to remove any appointive officer, for cause deemed by him sufficient. Resignation from an office in the Society shall be made in writing to the President. Resignation from the office of President shall be made in writing to the Vice President and to the Secretary.

Section 8. Corporate Officers.

Whatever Board of Directors or Board of Governors may be required by law and the charter of incorporation of this society, whensoever the Society shall be incorporated, shall consist of all the elective officers of this Society. The President of the Society shall be the President of the Board; the Treasurer of the Society shall be the Treasurer of the Board; each elective officer of the Society shall fill a corresponding office on the Board; whenever such corresponding office shall exist.

Article III

Powers of the Society

Section 1. Powers.

The Society shall have the power to:

(A) perform all functions reasonably consistent with its purposes as set forth in the preamble to the Constitution.

(B) provide for the open expression of the collective opinion of the Society.

(C) levy duties and assessments and to contract loans.

(D) provide general rules under which officers and members may be sanctioned for failure to perform their duties.

Section 2. Bylaws and Amendments.

A. BYLAWS.

Bylaws not contrary to the Constitution shall become part of the governing rules of the Society when they have been submitted in writing to the Secretary, have been read at two regular meetings of the Society, and have then been passed by two-thirds of all Regular Members in good standing present and voting, provided that the number of Regular Members voting constitutes at least one-half of the Regular Membership in good standing.

B. AMENDMENTS.

Amendments to, and revisions of, this Constitution shall become effective, and this Constitution shall be by them altered or revised, when such amendments or revisions have been submitted in writing to the Secretary, have been read at two consecutive regular meetings of the Society, and have then been passed by an affirmative vote of three-fourths of the Regular Members in good standing present, provided that the number of Regular Members voting constitutes at least one-half of the Regular Membership in good standing.

BY-LAWS

Article I

Meetings, Quorum, and Good Standing, Signing of the Roll

Section 1. Meetings.

A. REGULAR MEETINGS.

The Society shall meet regularly each week during the academic year on a set evening at a convenient hour; the day of the meeting shall be selected by a two-thirds vote of the Regular Members. The day of the meeting during the week shall be subject to change, or a meeting may be canceled, by a two-thirds vote of the Executive Committee, subject to the approval of the Regular Membership. Unless otherwise decided by the Society in accordance with this section, the Society shall meet at 7:29 p.m. on Fridays when classes are in session in the

College of Arts and Sciences of the University of Virginia in the Fall and Spring semesters.

B. SPECIAL MEETINGS.

A special meeting may be called by the President at any time he deems it necessary. It shall also be the duty of the President to call a special meeting when requested in writing to do so by five Regular Members. If the President fails to call a special meeting when so requested, a quorum of Regular Members may call a special meeting. Notice of a special meeting shall be posted plainly in front of the Society's Hall at least forty-eight hours before the designated time for the special meeting. The notice shall state the following: the date, time, and place of the special meeting; the purpose of the special meeting; and by whose authority the special meeting was called. The notice shall remain posted until the time designated for the special meeting.

Section 2. Quorum.

A. NUMBER.

One fourth of the Regular Members in good standing of the Society shall constitute a quorum for the transaction of all business, unless otherwise provided in the Constitution of the Society, provided that the Regular Membership in good standing be thirty or less; but when the Regular Membership is above that number, one-fifth of such Membership shall constitute a quorum.

B. GOOD STANDING.

Membership in Good Standing shall be construed as follows:

(1) A Member shall be computed in the total Membership in Good Standing immediately upon signing the minute book of the Society, in accordance with Article I, Section 3, of these Bylaws. Such "signing of the Roll" should take place at the first meeting attended of each academic semester. Only such Members as have signed the minute book shall be considered Members in Good Standing for the ensuing semester, and shall have privileges of membership as stated in Article 1, Section 1 of the Constitution.

(2) All members must pay any fees, dues, fines, or penalties in accordance with Article 2 of the By-Laws in order to be considered a Member in Good Standing. Failure to meet this obligation shall result in the loss of all privileges of membership, at which point the negligent member shall be discounted in the determination of quorum.

C. RECORD OF MEMBERS IN GOOD STANDING.

The Secretary of the Society shall keep a record of all Regular Members and shall report the total Regular Membership in good standing to the President or presiding officer at such times as there is a call for a quorum by a Regular Member in good standing.

Section 3. Signing of the Roll.

At the first meeting attended of each academic semester, each Member of the Society should sign his name in the minute book of the Society, together with the State of his residence and the date of such signing; all persons elected to Membership in the Society shall likewise sign this Roll. The Roll shall be so kept as to keep the lists of Probationary and Regular Members separate. At the head of each such Roll shall be inscribed that part of the initiation ritual required by Article I, Section 2, of the Constitution.

Article II

Dues, Fines, and Penalties

Section 1. Dues and Fees.

A. DUES.

Probationary and Regular Members shall pay dues of sixty dollars per semester. Failure to pay dues before the adjournment of the third meeting of the semester shall result in an additional fee of ten dollars being added to Regular Member dues, making them seventy dollars after such time. Failure of a Probationary Member to pay dues before the adjournment of the third meeting of his Probationary Membership shall result in an additional fee of ten dollars being added to Probationary Member dues. Associate Members shall be exempt from all fees and dues, but not from fines and assessments; Associate Members may pay Regular Member dues or a one time fee of equal to four times this amount as established at the time of payment, or a one-time fee of two-hundred dollars paid prior to August 23, 2011, to earn the additional privileges in Article I, Section 2, Paragraph C, of the Constitution.

B. FEES.

The Society may levy additional fees, by a two-thirds vote, to cover any operating deficit or extraordinary expense in a given semester.

C. SHINGLE FEES.

Probationary Members shall pay a shingle fee of five dollars at the time of their dues payment so that they may be presented with a certificate of membership upon successful crossover into Regular Membership.

Section 2. Fines and Penalties.

A. FAILURE TO MAKE PAYMENT.

Any Member shall automatically lose the privileges of his Membership, including the privileges of the floor, for failure to pay any fees, dues, or fines by the prescribed time. In the absence of payment or appeal within two weeks thereafter, the name of the Member shall be stricken from the Roll at the discretion of the Executive Committee. In the event that a Regular Member fails to pay his dues during two consecutive semesters, he shall be subject to expulsion. The Treasurer shall be responsible for notifying any Member who fails to pay his dues that, upon the next semester of delinquency, the Member's name will be stricken from the roll and the Member shall lose his Good Standing. Membership may be reinstated through payment of exactly double the dues of the present semester or, in special circumstances, by petition of the Executive Committee.

B. PENALTY FOR ABSENCE.

It shall be the duty of the Secretary to Report to the Executive Committee the absence of any Member from two-thirds of the semester's meetings of the Society.

C. MEMBERS IN GOOD STANDING.

Any Member not subject to any fee, due, fine, or penalty under this article shall be deemed a Member in Good Standing provided that the Member has signed the roll in accordance with Article 1, Section 2, Paragraph B of the By-Laws.

Article III

Committees

Section 1. Standing Committees.

A. NUMBER AND DESIGNATION.

There shall be the following Standing Committees:

(1) Program Committee.
(2) Executive Committee.
(3) Membership Committee.
(4) Appropriations Committee.
(5) Ways and Means Committee.
(6) Historical Committee.

(7) Pen and Ink Committee.

(8) Probationary Committee.

(9) Public Services Committee.

(10) Restoration Ball Committee.

(11) Debate and Oratory Committee.

(12) Alumni Relations Committee.

B. PROGRAM COMMITTEE.

The Vice President shall be Chairman of the Program Committee. The President shall appoint at least two other members. It shall be the duty of the Committee to arrange a suitable program for the meetings of the Society. Each program shall be announced at least one week before the time at which it is to be presented. In the arrangement of the program, the Committee shall be guided by their own discretion and by the purposes of the Society, expressed in the Preamble to the Constitution. Upon objection to any program, it may be changed by a majority vote of those present when the program is announced.

C. EXECUTIVE COMMITTEE.

The Executive Committee shall be composed of the President, the Vice President, the Secretary, the Treasurer, the Historian, the Chairman of Membership, Probationary, Ways and Means, Pen and Ink, Debate and Oratory, and Public Services Committees, the Keeper, and the Society's Resident of Room Seven, West Lawn. Besides performing the duties elsewhere delegated to it, this Committee shall act as an advisory body and shall consider all matters of interest to the Society. It shall have the power to bring upon the floor measures which it believes the Society should consider. Its functions, however, should not conflict with those of other regular committees. The Executive Committee of the Fall semester (those who hold office at the end of the semester), and the Spring semester (those who hold office at the time of the selection) shall select the Society's Resident of Room Seven, West Lawn.

D. MEMBERSHIP COMMITTEE.

The Membership Committee shall be composed of five members elected by the President. The membership committee shall have the goal of publicizing the Society to the University community and encouraging all members of the community to take an interest in the Jefferson Literary and Debating Society. It shall be the duty of this Committee to investigate such men and women as it has reason to think are interested in literary society membership and who would enrich the Society by their participation, to receive applications for Probationary Membership, and to arrange for each applicant to be interviewed by a panel of Regular and Associate Members. No applicant shall be interviewed more than once each semester for each class of Probationary Members. The Membership Committee shall consider the advice of such panels, and will present in a non-binding report at the next business meeting of the Society the names of those men and women whom it recommends for such Membership. The reports of the Membership Committee, including both majority and minority reports in the case of a division, shall be endorsed on each application, and the application placed in the hands of the Historian to be kept among the records of the Society. It shall also be the duty of the Committee to consider the eligibility of each Probationary Member for Regular Membership, and to report at an appropriate meeting of the Society its recommendations as to his candidacy not later than one semester after the date of his signing of the Probationary Roll. The meetings of the Membership Committee shall be closed and proceedings shall be held confidential. It shall be the duty of the Membership Committee to prevent, to the best of its powers, any violation of the Society's nondiscrimination policies, to report all infractions of said policies to the Executive Committee, and to enlist the aid of the General Membership in performing these duties.

E. APPROPRIATIONS COMMITTEE.

The Appropriations Committee shall consist of five members, one of whom shall be the Treasurer of the Society; no other member of the Executive Committee shall be a member of this Committee. The four remaining members shall be elected by the Society at the final regular meeting of the semester to serve for the semester immediately following and may only be removed by a vote of the Society.

F. WAYS AND MEANS COMMITTEE.

The Ways and Means Committee shall be composed of three members, appointed by the President. The Committee shall provide for the Society's social events, including a Probationary party and a faculty cocktail party each semester.

G. HISTORICAL COMMITTEE.

The Historical Committee shall be composed of six members, one of whom shall be the Historian of the Society; the other members shall be appointed by the President. The Historian of the Society shall always be Chairman of this Committee. One member of this Committee shall be known as the Scribe, whose duties it shall be to maintain the Society's computer files and web site, which shall include a current copy of the Constitution, Bylaws, Standing Rules, Ball Committee Constitutions, and other such records as the Society may require. Another member of this committee shall be known as the Illuminator, whose responsibility it shall be to maintain a pictorial record of the semester's events. The additional members of this Committee shall otherwise assist the Historian in the fulfillment of his duties. This Committee shall plan and make all necessary arrangements for the Benjamin C. Moomaw contest to be held annually during the Spring. Such arrangements shall include the selection of judges and the distribution of appropriate publicity materials. This Committee shall plan and make all necessary arrangements for the annual Wilson and Founder's Day Banquets, as well as be responsible for planning and executing the annual Edgar Allan Poe reading contest.

H. PEN AND INK COMMITTEE.

The Pen and Ink Committee shall be composed of four members, appointed by the President. It shall be the duty of this Committee to publish The Jefferson Journal, to make necessary arrangements for the Society's literary contests, and to assist the Society in facilitating literary presentations and discussions.

I. PROBATIONARY COMMITTEE.

The Probationary Committee shall be composed of at least five members, appointed by the President. The Probationary Committee shall discuss the topic, content, and procedure of the Probationary presentation with the Probationary members.

J. PUBLIC SERVICES COMMITTEE.

The Public Services Committee shall consist of five members, including a chairman, all appointed by the President. The Committee shall be responsible for Society scholarships and for activities authorized by the Society to promote the Society's good standing in the Community.

K. RESTORATION BALL COMMITTEE.

The Restoration Ball Chairman shall be elected at the last regular meeting of the Society in the spring semester and shall hold office until the election of his successor. The Restoration Chairman will lead the University of Virginia student initiative to restore and preserve the Rotunda. The President shall appoint the remaining five members of the Restoration Committee, which will be responsible for the logistics and budget of the Restoration Ball (Event Planning), engagement with other student organizations for co-sponsorship to cover the full costs of the event (Co-Sponsorship), marketing the Restoration Ball to the University community (University Outreach), and alumni relations and fundraising related to the Restoration Campaign (Alumni Engagement).

L. DEBATE AND ORATORY COMMITTEE.

The Debate and Oratory Committee shall be composed of three members, appointed by the President, one of whom shall be the Debate and Oratory Chairman. The duties of this committee shall include: arranging for the annual Smith-Simpson Debate on Diplomacy and all other inter-collegiate debates and competitions. This Committee shall plan and make all necessary arrangements for the Great Orators of History contest. The Committee may assist the Society in facilitating debate and oratory during its regular meetings.

M. ALUMNI RELATIONS COMMITTEE.

The Alumni Relations Committee shall consist of three members appointed by the President, one of whom shall be the Alumni Relations Chairman. The duties of this committee shall be to maintain contact with Alumni, promote all relevant events to Alumni, and organize in conjunction with the Executive Committee opportunities for charitable giving to the Society.

N. EX-OFFICIO MEMBERS OF COMMITTEES.

The President of the Society shall be ex officio a member of all Committees. There shall be no other ex-officio members appointed or named. Ex-officio members shall have no vote.

Section 2. Other Committees.

The President, or, in his absence, the Chairman, shall appoint such other committees as he shall see fit, and such as are authorized by the Society.

Section 3. Removal.

Any member of an appointive committee may be removed by the President from his office for neglect of duty, or for any other cause deemed sufficient.

Article IV

Orders of Business

Section 1. Regular Meetings.

The following shall be the order of business at each regular meeting.

(A) Induction of New Members.

(B) Reading of the Minutes.

(C) Roll Call.

(D) Presentation and Discussion of Scholarly and Literary Works and the Delivery of Oratorical Addresses.

(E) Announcement of the Program.

(F) Reports of the Committees.

(G) Report of the Treasurer.

(H) Extraordinary and Unfinished Business.

(I) New Business, Motions, and Resolutions.

(J) Probationary Presentations.

(K) Adjournment.

When deemed appropriate by the President, the program and/or presentation of Probationary presentations may precede any or all of the other portions of the order of business. In any other case this order of business may be suspended at any meeting by a two-thirds vote of those regular members in good standing present and voting.

Section 2. Elections Meetings.

For the last meeting of each academic semester, the following shall be the order of business, subject to change by a two-thirds vote of those regular members in good standing present and voting:

(A) Induction of New Members.

(B) Reading of the Minutes.

(C) Roll Call.

(D) Reading of the Historian's Chronicle (Spring Semester).

(E) Report of the Treasurer.

(F) Extraordinary and Unfinished Business.

(G) Election of the President.

(H) Induction of the President-Elect.

(I) Election of the Vice President.

(J) Election of the Secretary.

(K) Election of the Treasurer.

(L) Election of the Appropriations Committee.

(M) Election of the Historian (Spring Semester only, except in the case of a vacancy).

(N) Induction of the Vice President-Elect, the Secretary-Elect, the Treasurer-Elect and the Historian-Elect.

(O) Reports of Committees.

(P) New Business, Motions, Resolutions.

(Q) Election and Induction of the Keeper.

(R) Adjournment.

The procedure for the election of officers shall be as follows:

1. Each candidate shall have a total of 15 minutes consisting of one 8-minute period and one 7-minute period.

2. The order in which candidates shall proceed shall be determined by agreement among the candidates. In the absence of agreement, the order shall be determined by lot. The same order shall apply to both periods allotted to the candidates.

3. Each candidate's 8-minute period may be utilized at his discretion and may consist of any combination of speeches, including a candidate speech.

4. Once all of the candidates have completed their 8-minute periods, each candidate shall inform the chair as to the manner in which he wishes to allocate his 7-minute period, as well as appoint a representative to observe the counting of the ballots as provided by Article II, Section 4 of the Constitution.

5. The chair shall administer the 7-minute period in accordance with the candidate's instructions.

Article V.

Finances

Section 1. Reports of the Treasurer.

At the first meeting in each Presidential term, the Treasurer shall submit a written report, which shall be read before the Society, and, if accepted, be spread on the minutes. At the last meeting of each session he shall report the financial standing of the Society and the names of all Members who have not paid their dues, which report is also to be spread upon the minutes and to be re-read at the first meeting of the succeeding session.

Section 2. Audit.

Between the sixth and the eighth meeting of the semester and at the end of each semester, the accounts of the Treasurer are to be audited under the discretion of the Executive Committee, and the books, vouchers, etc., are to be turned over to the Historian for safe keeping.

Section 3. Funds of the Society.

No Member of the Society, acting in any capacity, may obligate the funds of the Society without the express authorization of the Treasurer, acting within his power to make disbursements. The Society shall honor all obligations legally incurred in its name by its Members, but must assess against any Member any amount to which he obligates the funds of the Society without approval, unless the disbursement is subsequently ratified by the Society.

Article VI

Probationary Presentations

Section 1. Probationary Presentations.

A. REQUIREMENT.

Each Probationary Member shall present a probationary presentation to the Regular Membership. Acceptance of such presentation shall be a prerequisite to Regular Membership.

B. PROCEDURE.

The probationary presentation requirement may be satisfied by completing any one of the following:

(1) A probationary speech of nine minutes in length, and presented according to the following procedure:

   (A) Uninterrupted constructive speaking: five minutes, with a light tap of the gavel at four minutes.

   (B) Constructive speaking subject to questioning and heckling, by the Regular and Associate Membership: three minutes.

   (C) Uninterrupted summary: one minute.

(2) A debate against a Regular or Associate Member according to the following procedure:

   (A) If the Probationary Member wishes to utilize the debate procedure, he should contact the Probationary Chairman at least one calendar day prior to the presentation, indicating that he wishes to debate. The Probationary Chairman shall attempt to secure a volunteer from the Regular or Associate Membership to debate the Probationary Member. Volunteers may debate only once on the same resolution each semester.

(B) Debates shall proceed in the following manner:

   (i) The volunteer from the Regular or Associate Membership shall speak in favor of the resolution for four minutes of uninterrupted constructive speaking, being warned that the three-minute mark by a light tap of the gavel.

   (ii) The Probationary Member will speak extemporaneously in opposition to the arguments of the regular Member and the resolution for four minutes of uninterrupted constructive speaking, also being warned at the three-minute mark by a light tap of the gavel.

   (iii) There shall be two minutes of questioning and heckling of the Probationary Member by the Regular and Associate Membership.

   (iv) Two minutes of rebuttal speaking by the volunteer Member, addressing arguments raised in the Probationary Member's constructive speech.

   (v) Two minutes of rebuttal speaking by the Probationary Member, addressing arguments raised in the volunteer Member's constructive speech. The Probationary Member may not bring any prepared materials to the debate, but he may refer to notes taken while the volunteer Member is speaking. The chairman will cite rules of procedure (i) through (v) for a probationary debate listed in Article VI, Section 2, Paragraph B, Subsection (2) of the Bylaws immediately prior to such debate.

(3) A literary presentation according to the following procedure:

   (A) The probationary member shall read an original cohesive work of fiction or poetry under a single title, of at least six but no more than twenty minutes

   (B) There shall be at least one, and at the Chair's discretion, up to five minutes of questioning and heckling of the Probationary Member by the Regular and Associate membership.

C. CRITIQUE.

Prior to the beginning of a probationary presentation, the President shall appoint a critic from the Regular or Associate Membership. The critic shall listen to the presentation and observe the speaker carefully and at the conclusion of the presentation shall render a constructive critique; the critique shall also recommend to the Regular Membership that the presentation be accepted or rejected.

D. LIMITATION ON FURTHER CRITIQUES.

Critiques of probationary presentations shall be limited to the initial critique; followed by five speakers, each of whom shall be limited to five minutes total time, except where debate is extended by a two-thirds vote of the Regular members in good standing present and voting. The speaker making the initial critique, or any other speaker at the time of the debate on the probationary presentation, may recommend that the presentation be recorded as passing with distinction. A presentation shall be deemed to have passed with distinction if the recommendation is not objected to, at the time it is made, by any Regular or Associate Member. A presentation that has passed with distinction shall be considered for all appropriate awards at the end of the semester. A presentation that has passed without a dissenting vote shall not be deemed to have passed with distinction unless the other requirements of this paragraph have been met.

E. VOTE ON ACCEPTANCE.

Following the critique and any pertinent discussion, the Regular Membership shall vote on the question: Shall the presentation be accepted? A majority of two-thirds of those voting, a quorum being present, shall be required for the acceptance of a probationary presentation.

F. VOTE COUNT.

If the presentation is rejected, the vote count shall be revealed by the President upon request of any Regular Member or of the Probationary Speaker.

G. REPEAT PRESENTATIONS.

The rejection of a probationary presentation shall be without prejudice. Another presentation on the same or different topic may be made during the semester, as scheduled by the Probationary Chairman.

H. FAILURE TO PRESENT A PROBATIONARY PRESENTATION.

Unexcused failure to present a probationary presentation at such time as is scheduled by the Probationary Chairman shall bar the Probationary Member involved from making any probationary presentation that semester.

I. SUBJECT.

Probationary Presentation shall be upon any subject capable of stimulating the intellect.

J. DISCUSSION OF TOPIC.

Upon a showing, during or following a probationary presentation but prior to the vote on acceptance of such presentation, that the Probationary Member involved did not discuss his topic and probationary presentation with the Probationary Chairman, the President, at his discretion, may require that the Probationary Member give his presentation at a later date and after he has so discussed it with the Probationary Chairman.

Article VII

Presentation from the Membership

Section 1. Membership Speeches.

No Member shall be required to make any speech, dramatic presentation, debate or reading to retain his or her active membership privileges.

A. PRESENTATIONS.

Should a Member of the Society desire to make a speech, debate, or presentation to enlighten, excite, or generally edify the Society, he or she may use, but is not limited to, the following motions to structure his or her presentation:

(1) Motion to Present a Topic. This motion grants a member three minutes for an extemporaneous or prepared speech. Two minutes of questioning, serious or otherwise, from the membership is to follow, with a conclusion from the member which should last no longer than one minute. Should the membership be so inclined, the Chair may recognize up to three members to respond to the topic for a time no greater than two and one half minutes.

(2) Motion to Challenge. A member may make this motion to incite debate with another member, by challenging that member with a resolution. The parameters of debate are as follows: Four minutes for the affirmative argument; four minutes for the negative; a two-minute rebuttal from the affirmative, then a two-minute rebuttal from the negative. Should members be so inclined, the Chair may recognize no more than three members to speak for no more than two and one half minutes regarding the debate.

(3) Motion for a Presentation. This motion grants a member as much time as he or she may consume in making a presentation.

B. MOTIONS.

All above motions shall be made as unanimous consent requests of the following form: Mr./Madam President (Chairman/Chairwoman), I request unanimous consent for [Name of Motion].

Article VIII
Badges and Shingles
Section 1. The Badge.
The Badge of the Society shall be of gold, triangular in shape, pointing down, approximately five-eighths of an inch to a side. It shall have upon its face two quills crossed, upon which, facing to the left, shall be a profile of Thomas Jefferson. In the corners at the top shall be: On the left side the Letter "J," and on the right side the letter "S." At the bottom shall be the Greek letters Phi Pi Theta.

Section 2. Shingles.
A certificate of membership, of suitable size and design, shall, after being designed and printed by the Membership Committee, be presented by the Executive Committee to all Regular Members as soon as practicable following their initiation into Regular Membership. The Membership Committee shall be required, after each semester, to provide one such shingle to each Regular Member from the Probationary Class of the previous semester.

Section 3. Certificates of Merit.
A distinct certificate of merit may be presented by the Executive Committee to any Member who shall have evidenced outstanding participation in or service to the Society. Such certificates shall be awarded at the discretion of the Executive Committee and the President, at such times as they shall deem suitable.

Article IX
Rules of Order
The rules contained in Robert's Rules of Order, latest edition, shall govern the Society in all cases in which they are applicable and in which they are not inconsistent with the Constitution and the Bylaws of the Society.

Notes

ABBREVIATIONS USED IN THE NOTES

In citing works in the notes, short titles have been used for works frequently cited. These are identified by the following abbreviations:

BOV Minutes of the Board of Visitors at the University of Virginia, Albert and Shirley Small Special Collections Library, University of Virginia, Charlottesville, VA.

Bruce Philip Alexander Bruce, *History of the University of Virginia, 1819–1919: The Lengthened Shadow of One Man*, 5 vols. (New York: Macmillan, 1920).

Faculty Minutes Minutes of the Faculty at the University of Virginia, Albert and Shirley Small Special Collections Library, University of Virginia, Charlottesville, VA.

JS Jefferson Literary and Debating Society at the University of Virginia.

JS Archives Archives of the Jefferson Literary and Debating Society, Alderman Library, University of Virginia, Charlottesville, VA.

LVA Library of Virginia, Richmond, VA.

Papers of WW Arthur S. Link, ed., *The Papers of Woodrow Wilson*, 69 vols. (Princeton, NJ: Princeton University Press, 1966–1994).

U.Va. Albert and Shirley Small Special Collections Library, University of Virginia, Charlottesville, VA.

VHS Virginia Historical Society, Richmond, VA.

The extant minutes of the Jefferson Society are incomplete. All minutes prior to 1875 were destroyed in the Rotunda Fire of October 27, 1895. The vast bulk of extant minutes are preserved in handwritten bound minute books that were used until they became full, before being placed in the Society's archives. There are a few years for which meeting notes taken by the secretary have been preserved, but no formal minutes are extant. After 1987, minutes were kept on loose paper and remain unbound. Beginning in 1998, minutes have been uploaded weekly to the Society's website. Fourteen years of minutes are missing from the years following the Rotunda Fire.

EXTANT MINUTE BOOKS OR MINUTES	MISSING MINUTES	EXTANT MEETING NOTES
1875–1894	Fall 1923	1825–1874
1894–1905	1941–1946	1926–1935
1905–1918	Spring 1963	1952–1956
1919–1925		1969
1925		
1935–1942		
1947–1951		
1957–1962		
1963–1966		
1967–1968		
1970–1971		
1971–1974		
1974–1983		
Spring 1986		
Fall 1986		
1987–1997		
1998–present		

The documentary record of magazines published by the Jefferson Society is quite complex and confusing. As a general rule, the magazine is cited using the name under which it was published.

The *Virginia University Magazine* underwent several changes to its numbering system. Issues are cited using the "New Series" designation that begins in October 1857 with vol. I, no. 1, of the *Virginia University Magazine*. In October 1882, the editors began also numbering issues under the "Old Series," which began in October 1837 and recognized the *Collegian* and other earlier student magazines as part of the same series. For the next four years, however, the masthead read "Old Series—Vol. XLIV," while the New Series continued to be updated. Then, in 1886, the editors caught the error, but updated the volume numbers in both series, thus causing the New Series notation to be incorrect by four volumes. This subsequent error was not corrected until 1894, though many extant copies of the *Virginia University Magazine* have been corrected by hand. *Society Ties* cites in the New Series as if these errors never occurred, using the true volume number and accurate date.

Then, beginning in October 1922, the editors dropped the New Series designation, and issues appeared with only one serial number. Accordingly, from October 1922 onward, *Society Ties* cites the volume number under which the issue was published, following any changes the editors made in numbering scheme.

In 1927, the editors renamed the magazine the *Virginia Spectator* but continued to serialize uninterrupted. Publication ceased for a short time in the 1930s and resumed under the name *University of Virginia Magazine* in 1932. It was again changed back to the *Virginia Spectator* in 1937, at which point the editors briefly restarted numbering with volume 1, number 1, before resuming the Old Series with a commemorative volume C beginning in September 1938. They continued numbering under the Old Series until the *Virginia Spectator* was banned in 1958.

With the revival of the *University of Virginia Magazine* in April 1956, the editors chose to begin numbering volumes again at volume 1, number 1, to differentiate from the *Virginia Spectator* while the two publications appeared side by side. Finally, in February 1962 the editors of the *University of Virginia Magazine* returned yet again to Old Series.

INTRODUCTION

1. James McLachlan, "'The Choice of Hercules': American Student Societies in the Early Nineteenth Century," in Lawrence Stone, ed., *The University in Society* (Princeton, NJ: Princeton University Press, 1974), 472.

2. Timothy J. Williams, *Intellectual Manhood: University, Self, and Society in the Antebellum South* (Chapel Hill, NC: University of North Carolina Press, 2015), 20.

3. Speech to the Patrick Henry Society, Robert Mercer Taliaferro Hunter Papers, 1826–1860, Accession #6662, U.Va.

CHAPTER ONE

1. Constitution and By-Laws of JS, 1837 (James Alexander, 1838), in Garnett Family Papers, 1812–1913, Accession #38-45-b, U.Va.

2. *Bruce I*, 267.

3. See "A Bill for the More General Diffusion of Knowledge," *The Papers of Thomas Jefferson Digital Edition*, ed. Barbara B. Oberg and J. Jefferson Looney (Charlottesville: University of Virginia Press, Rotunda, 2008–2015).

4. Charles Coleman Wall, "Student Life at the University of Virginia, 1825–1861" (PhD diss., University of Virginia, 1978), 4.

5. Thomas Jefferson to Joseph C. Cabell, Dec. 28, 1822, *Founders Early Access* (Charlottesville: University of Virginia Press, Rotunda, 2008–2015). This letter is also reproduced in an excellent little volume of letters relating to the founding and early days of the Univer-

sity of Virginia: N. F. Cabell, ed., *Early History of the University of Virginia as Contained in the Letters of Thomas Jefferson and Joseph C. Cabell* (Richmond, VA, 1856), 260.

6. Thomas Jefferson to John Adams, Oct. 28, 1813, *The Papers of Thomas Jefferson Digital Edition.*

7. Thomas Jefferson to Joseph C. Cabell, Jan. 22, 1820, *Founders Early Access.*

8. Thomas Jefferson to Benjamin Henry Latrobe, June 12, 1817, *The Papers of Thomas Jefferson Digital Edition.* This letter began a long correspondence between Jefferson and Latrobe in which the two collaborated to design the layout of the University of Virginia.

9. Wall, "Student Life at the University of Virginia, 1825–1861," 6.

10. Ibid.

11. Virginius Dabney, *Mr. Jefferson's University: A History* (Charlottesville: University of Virginia Press, 1981), 6–7.

12. *Bruce* II, 298–299.

13. Wall, "Student Life at the University of Virginia, 1825–1861," 91–92.

14. Ibid.

15. John R. Thelin, *A History of American Higher Education* (Baltimore, MD: Johns Hopkins University Press, 2011), 66.

16. Thomas Spencer Harding, *College Literary Societies: Their Contribution to Higher Education in the United States, 1815–1876* (New York: Pageant Press International, 1971), 1.

17. Ibid.

18. Ibid., 22. On the societies at Princeton, see Charles Williams, *The Cliosophic Society, Princeton University: A Study of Its History* (Princeton, NJ: Princeton University Press, 1916); and J. Jefferson Looney, *Nurseries of Letters and Republicanism: A Brief History of the American Whig–Cliosophic Society and Its Predecessors, 1765–1941* (Princeton, NJ: American Whig–Cliosophic Society, 1996). On the societies at the University of North Carolina, see "The Literary Societies," in Kemp Plummer Battle, *History of the University of North Carolina*, vol. 1 (Raleigh, NC: Edwards & Broughton Printing Company, 1912), 72–85, 565–569; and John E. Giles, *The Phi Society: 155 Years of Contribution to the Carolina Way of Life, 1795–1949* (Oct. 29, 1949), http://diphi.web.unc.edu/files/2012/03/giles-1949.pdf.

19. On the Oxford Union, see David Walter, *The Oxford Union: Playground of Power* (London: Macdonald, 1984); and Fiona Graham, *Playing at Politics: An Ethnography of the Oxford Union* (Edinburgh: Dunedin Academic Press, 2005).

20. *Catalogue of the Jefferson Society* (Richmond, VA: MacFarlane and Fergusson, 1854), U.Va.

    The Jefferson Society published two editions of a "catalogue," first in 1854 and again in 1859. These documents detail much of what we know about the first days of the Society. They include a brief history of the Society and a roll of the members through their respective dates of publication. The committees that published them would have had access to minute books, roll books, and other early documents of the Society. As a result, there is little reason to doubt the information they provide, even though it is nearly impossible to independently verify it.

    Jefferson Society members kept copies of these catalogues and made notations in them, labeling famous members or counting votes with a plus or minus sign next to each member from a particular session. Less than twenty copies of these rare documents survive in research libraries, and each one tells a slightly different story.

21. *Catalogue of the Jefferson Society*, 1854; "The Early Days of the Jefferson Society," *University of Virginia Magazine* 42, no. 4 (Jan. 1899): 180.

22. *Catalogue of the Jefferson Society*, 1854.

23. See, for example, Constitution and By-Laws of JS, 1837; the minutes and several news reports of this time period and later tell the story of debates lasting long into the night.

24. *Bruce* II, 357.

25. Constitution and By-Laws of JS, 1837, "Initiation of Members."

26. *Catalogue of the Jefferson Society*, 1854.

27. Ibid.

28. The 1837 Constitution is the oldest surviving constitution of the Jefferson Society. It is preserved in a bound volume of University of Virginia documents and remembrances belonging to the Garnett family. It is likely very similar to the original 1825 Constitution.

29. Harding, *College Literary Societies*, 40–41.

30. Ibid., 55–83, 104–115.

31. *Bruce* III, 102; "The Origin and History of the Jefferson Literary Society," *University of Virginia Magazine* 42, no. 7 (Apr. and May 1899): 332.

32. *Bruce* II, 358.

33. *Catalogue of the Jefferson Society*, 1854.

34. Ibid.

35. Ibid.

36. Ibid.

37. Ibid.

38. Wall, "Student Life at the University of Virginia, 1825–1861," 269.

39. Ibid., 317n8.

40. *Catalogue of the Jefferson Society*, 1854.

41. William Raimond Baird, *American College Fraternities* (New York: James T. Brown, 1920), 5–11.

42. Harding, *College Literary Societies*, 38–40, 91; Charles Frederick Irons, "Public Men and Public Universities" (master's thesis, University of Virginia, 1999), 37.

43. Irons, "Public Men and Public Universities," 10.

44. Ibid., 35.

45. "The Origin and History of the Jefferson Literary Society," 332.

46. Edgar Mason, J. W. Brockenbrough, and Robert Saunders, Committee of JS, to Thomas Jefferson, Aug. 11, 1825, *Founders Early Access*. The original is in the possession of the Missouri Historical Society.

47. Thomas Jefferson to Edgar Mason, J. W. Brockenbrough, and Robert Saunders, Committee of JS, Aug. 12, 1825, *Founders Early Access*. The original is in the possession of the Missouri Historical Society.

48. Richard B. Bernstein, *Thomas Jefferson* (Oxford, UK: Oxford University Press, 2003), 118.

49. John Willis, Thomas S. Gholson, and R. Howerton, Committee of JS, to James Madison, May 5, 1827, *Founders Early Access*. The original is in the possession of the Library of Congress, and docketed by James Madison: "May 5. postmarked 17. 1827."

50. BOV, July 18, 1827, 173.

51. *Richmond Enquirer,* Sept. 6, 1825, LVA.

52. Ibid.

53. *Bruce* II, 356.

54. Irons, "Public Men and Public Universities," 36–37.

55. Arthur Hobson Quinn, *Edgar Allan Poe: A Critical Biography* (New York: Appleton-Century-Crofts, Inc., 1941), 99–100.

56. Miles George to E. V. Valentine, May 18, 1880; ibid., 107.

57. Edwin A. Alderman, "Edgar Allan Poe and the University of Virginia," *Virginia Quarterly Review* 1, no. 1 (Spring 1925): 79.

58. John Shelton Patton, *Jefferson, Cabell, and the University of Virginia* (Washington, DC: Neal Publishing Company, 1906), 92–94.

59. Report and documents respecting the University of Virginia, University of Virginia, Board of Visitors, LD5662, U.Va.; Quinn, *Edgar Allan Poe: A Critical Biography,* 99.

60. John Henry Ingram, *Edgar Allan Poe: His Life, Letters, and Opinions* (London: John Hogg, Paternoster Row, 1880), 52.

61. Ibid., 47.

62. William Wertenbaker, "Edgar A. Poe," *Virginia University Magazine* 7, nos. 2–3 (Nov. and Dec. 1868): 114–117.

63. Alderman, "Edgar Allan Poe and the University of Virginia," 80.

64. James A. Harrison, *Life and Letters of Edgar Allan Poe,* vol. 1 (New York: Thomas Y. Cromwell and Co., 1902), 40.

65. Quinn, *Edgar Allan Poe: A Critical Biography,* 109–112.

66. "The Early Days of the Jefferson Society," *Virginia University Magazine* 10, no. 3 (Dec. 1871): 159.

67. *Catalogue of the Jefferson Society,* 1854.

68. "The Early Days of the Jefferson Society," 159.

69. Edgar Allan Poe's signature is now housed in the Albert and Shirley Small Special Collections Library at the University of Virginia as Edgar Allan Poe, Minutes and Signature, 1826, Accession #1018-k, U.Va. The only reason Poe's signature as secretary survived the Rotunda Fire of 1895 was because Blackford stole it.

70. Letter from John Willis, in William F. Gill, *The Life of Edgar Allan Poe* (New York: D. Appleton & Co., 1877), 36.

71. Ibid.

72. Harrison, *Life and Letters of Edgar Allan Poe,* vol. 1, 43.

73. Ingram, *Edgar Allan Poe: His Life, Letters, and Opinions,* 48.

74. See "A Tale of the Ragged Mountains," in Edgar Allan Poe, *Poetry and Tales* (New York: Literary Classics of the United States, 1984), 655–665.

75. George W. Spotswood to John Allan, May 1, 1827, in Quinn, *Edgar Allan Poe: A Critical Biography,* 111–113; *Richmond Standard,* May 7, 1881, LVA.

76. *Bruce* III, 214.

77. Minutes of JS, Dec. 12, 1908, Minute Book of JS 1905–1918, JS Archives, 101.

78. Alderman, "Edgar Allan Poe and the University of Virginia," 84.

79. Ibid.

80. Report and documents respecting the University of Virginia, University of Virginia, Board of Visitors, LD5662, U.Va.

81. Rebecca Lomax to R. M. T. Hunter, Mar. 27, 1826, Box 21, Garnett Family Papers, 1812–1913, Accession #38-45-b, U.Va.

82. Marion Mills Miller, *Great Debates in American History,* vol. 6, *The Civil War* (New York: Current Literature Publishing Company, 1913), 55.

CHAPTER TWO

1. Charles Coleman Wall, "Student Life at the University of Virginia, 1825–1861" (PhD diss., University of Virginia, 1978), 25.

2. Thomas Jefferson to James Breckenridge, Feb. 15, 1821, *Founders Early Access* (Charlottesville: University of Virginia Press, Rotunda, 2008–2015).

3. Lorri Glover, *Southern Sons: Becoming Men in the New Nation* (Baltimore, MD: Johns Hopkins University Press, 2007), 83.

4. John R. Thelin, *A History of American Higher Education* (Baltimore, MD: Johns Hopkins University Press, 2011), 52, 63.

5. Glover, *Southern Sons,* 9.

6. Wall, "Student Life at the University of Virginia, 1825–1861," 66.

7. Ibid., 48.

8. Glover, *Southern Sons,* 27, 51.

9. Richard McIlwaine, *Memories of Three Score Years and Ten* (Washington, DC: Neal Publishing Company, 1908), 73.

10. Frederick Rudolph, *The American College and University: A History* (Athens, GA: University of Georgia Press, 1962), 59, 65.

11. Glover, *Southern Sons,* 104.

12. Faculty Minutes, vol. VI, Mar. 2, 1839.

13. Faculty Minutes, vol. III, Feb. 25, 1833.

14. Report of the Faculty Committee for General Purposes to the Board of Visitors, in Faculty Minutes, vol. I, Sept. 9, 1826.

15. Wall, "Student Life at the University of Virginia, 1825–1861," 183.

16. Glover, *Southern Sons,* 105. As Glover remarks, younger men participated in duels with far less frequency than their fathers, simply because there was more at stake for a younger man. For students at the University of Virginia, the traditional image of two men with dueling pistols would have been rare and shocking to see. Instead, just the challenge to a duel or a fistfight would have been sufficient to settle "affairs of honor" between students. Conspicuously absent from most sources that mention duels at the University of Virginia is mention of their conduct or outcome.

17. Bertram Wyatt-Brown, *The Shaping of Southern Culture: Honor, Grace, and War: 1760s–1880s* (Chapel Hill, NC: University of North Carolina Press, 2001), 62.

18. Wharton J. Green, *Recollections and Reflections: An Autobiography of a Half-Century and More* (Raleigh, NC: Edwards and Broughton Printing Company, 1906), 96.

19. Faculty Minutes, vol. IV, Apr. 19 and 23 and May 16 and 20, 1836; Wall, "Student Life at the University of Virginia, 1825–1861," 89.

20. Student Diary of Charles Ellis Jr., Mar. 10–June 25, 1835, Charles Ellis, Diary and Letters,

1834–1836, Accession #8745, U.Va., 61.

21. Constitution and By-Laws of JS, 1837.

22. Rudolph, *The American College and University*, 87.

23. Ibid., 88.

24. Ibid., 89.

25. Thelin, *A History of American Higher Education*, 94.

26. Ibid.

27. Timothy J. Williams, *Intellectual Manhood: University, Self, and Society in the Antebellum South* (Chapel Hill, NC: University of North Carolina Press, 2015), 9, 12–13.

28. Rudolph, *The American College and University*, 136; Thelin, *A History of American Higher Education*, 63–65.

29. Wall, "Student Life at the University of Virginia, 1825–1861," 145.

30. Ibid., 146.

31. Glover, *Southern Sons*, 58.

32. Williams, *Intellectual Manhood*, 75.

33. Albert Howell to Morton B. Howell, Oct. 20, 1850, and Nov. 4, 1850, Morton Boyte Howell Correspondence, 1851-60, Accession #8463, U.Va.

34. Valedictory Speech to the Jefferson Society, 1854, Papers of the Aylett Family, 1851–1896, Accession #110, U.Va.

35. Kenneth S. Greenberg, *Masters and Statesmen: The Political Culture of American Slavery* (Baltimore, MD: Johns Hopkins University Press, 1985), 12.

36. Glover, *Southern Sons*, 98.

37. Thomas H. Malone and John H. Moore, ed., "The Old Dominion through Student Eyes, 1852–1855: The Reminiscences of Thomas Hill Malone," *Virginia Magazine of History and Biography* 71, no. 3 (July 1963): 307–308.

38. Lancelot Minor Blackford, "The University from 1855 to 1860," *Corks and Curls* 3 (1890): 26–29.

39. Ibid.

40. Constitution and By-Laws of JS, 1837. The oath remains the same to this day. It is also worth mentioning that Glover, in *Southern Sons*, comments on the importance of the networks of acquaintants students acquired. She writes: "Beginning career men also relied on their own networks of friend and business connections to promote professional distinctions" (p. 161). While the term *network* is perhaps a bit anachronistic, the members of the Jefferson Society no doubt formed lasting connections that would benefit them greatly in business, politics, and even marriage. Some of the fruits of these relationships will show forth in later chapters of this work.

41. Green, *Recollections and Reflections*, 103–105.

42. Ibid.

43. Charles S. Venable, "Student Life at the University in 1845," *Corks and Curls* 3 (1890): 36.

44. Ibid.

45. Ibid., 37.

46. Student Diary of Charles Ellis Jr., 41.

47. Ibid.

48. Valedictory Speech to the Jefferson Society, 1854.

49. John Shelton Patton, *Jefferson, Cabell, and the University of Virginia* (Washington, DC: Neal Publishing Company, 1906), 46.

50. BOV, vol. II, July 18, 1831, 46.

51. Patton, *Jefferson, Cabell, and the University of Virginia*, 46.

52. Faculty Minutes, vol. V, Sept. 13, 1837.

53. *Bruce* II, 359; *Bruce* III, 171.

54. *Bruce* III, 173–174; *Bruce* IV, 87. When the renovations to Washington Hall were completed in 1869, the interior space created was larger than Jefferson Hall. As a result, the two societies, if they were meeting together for some special purpose, as they often did after the Civil War, would usually choose Washington Hall. When the Washington Society folded for the second time at the onset of the Great Depression in 1929, the University retook control of Washington Hall. It is now occupied by the Office of Equal Opportunity Programs.

55. Williams, *Intellectual Manhood*, 101–109; Thomas Spencer Harding, *College Literary Societies: Their Contribution to Higher Education in the United States, 1815–1876* (New York: Pageant Press International, 1971), 108. See also Maurice C. York, "The Dialectic and Philanthropic Societies' Contributions to the Library of the University of North Carolina, 1886–1906," *North Carolina Historical Review* 59, no. 4 (Oct. 1982): 327–353. The story of the collaboration between the Dialectic and Philanthropic Societies is extraordinary and interesting. It is worth noting that the vast majority of books in the holdings of the University of North Carolina at Chapel Hill still feature book plates that read "Endowed by the Dialectic and Philanthropic Societies."

56. Constitution and By-Laws of JS, 1837.

57. Student Diary of Charles Ellis Jr., 101.

58. Irons, "Public Men and Public Universities," 40.

59. *Bruce* III, 102.

60. Fiske Kimball, "The Life Portraits of Jefferson and Their Replicas," *Proceedings of the American Philosophical Society* 88, no. 6 (Dec. 1944): 527–529, in particular 529n115.

61. BOV, Nov. 27, 1923.

62. Minutes of JS, Sept. 29, 1923, Minute Book of JS 1919–1925, JS Archives, 277.

63. In July 1989, the Sully portrait belonging to the Jefferson Society was appraised at $250,000, and in May 1997, it was appraised at $500,000. Both appraisals were conducted by Peter Rathborne, the former director of American paintings and sculpture at Sotheby's. It was most recently appraised at $600,000 in January 2013 by Elizabeth Goldberg of Sotheby's. Jasper Honn, Vice President, Sotheby's, to Suzanne Folley, Curator, Bayly Art Museum, July 28, 1989, JS Archives; Elizabeth F. Byrns, Vice President, Sotheby's, to Jean Lancaster Collier, Registrar, Bayly Art Museum, May 22, 1997, JS Archives; Melannie Chard, Vice President, Sotheby's, to Audrey Birner, Jan. 23, 2013, JS Archives.

64. Constitution and By-Laws of JS, 1837.

65. See, for example, Speech of RMT Hunter to a UVa Society, Papers of the Hunter Family, 1788–1873, Accession #7093-ae, UVa.; Robert Garlick Hill Kean Speech, Kean Family Papers, 1859–1951, Accession #1331-c, UVa.; Green, *Recollections and Reflections*, 103–106.

66. Williams, *Intellectual Manhood*, 176.

67. Ibid., 197.

68. Student Diary of Charles Ellis Jr., 135.

69. *Bruce* III, 176.

70. Student Diary of Charles Ellis Jr., 135.

71. Student Diary of Robert Garlick Hill Kean, Kean Family Papers, 1859–1951, Accession #1331-c, UVa.

72. Harding, *College Literary Societies*, 192–215.

73. "Editor's Table," *The Collegian* 1, no. 9 (June 1839): 346.

74. Faculty Minutes, vol. VIII, Dec. 14, 1858.

75. Addendum to Jefferson Society CIO Agreement, Revised June 1, 1993, JS Archives.

76. *Bruce* III, 173.

77. *Bruce* II, 359.

78. "Collegiana," *Virginia University Magazine* 2, no. 6 (June 1859): 289. Here the magazine gave a schedule of Final Celebrations that was typical for the antebellum years and illustrates a normal agenda for finals: Monday, July 26 at 7:30—Columbian Society; Tuesday, July 27 at 7:30—Washington Society; Wednesday, July 28 at 11 am—Society of Alumni; Wednesday, July 28 at 7:30—Jefferson Society.

79. "Collegiana," *Virginia University Magazine* 13, no. 1 (Oct. 1874): 89.

80. "Collegiana," *Virginia University Magazine* 12, no. 1 (Oct. 1873): 50.

81. "Editor's Table," *Jefferson Monument Magazine* 1, no. 8 (May 1850): 264.

82. *Bruce* III, 172.

83. "Editor's Table," *Virginia University Magazine* 2, no. 5 (May 1858): 237.

84. *Bruce* III, 172–173.

85. Blackford, "The University from 1855 to 1860," 27. The Debater's Medal was awarded in the selection above to John Sharp Williams, a future senator. See "Collegiana," *Virginia University Magazine* 12, no. 1 (Oct. 1873): 50.

86. Blackford, "The University from 1855 to 1860," 27.

87. Patton, *Jefferson, Cabell, and the University of Virginia*, 373.

88. *Jefferson Monument Magazine* 2, no. 7 (Apr. 1851): 264.

89. The nomenclature surrounding the "Anniversary Celebration," "Intermediate Celebration," and "Founder's Day" is complex and confusing. They all mean essentially the same thing. The term *anniversary* denotes the anniversary of Jefferson's birth, while the term *intermediate* denotes the intermediate term of the academic year, about when an anniversary celebration would have taken place. The term Founder's Day is more modern and did not come into widespread use until the twentieth century. Some of the Society's past chroniclers have used the term *Founder's Day* to describe all of the events since 1832, out of simplicity and to use a term Society members (their only true intended audience) would recognize. To use *Founder's Day* to describe anything before 1908, however, obscures the evolution of the event.

90. *Bruce* II, 358.

91. *Bruce* II, 358.

92. Wall, "Student Life at the University of Virginia, 1825–1861," 138.

93. "Editor's Table," *The Collegian* 1, no. 9 (June 1839): 346–347.

94. Blackford, "The University from 1855 to 1860," 28.

95. Ibid.

96. Ibid.

97. Harding, *College Literary Societies*, 59.

98. Wall, "Student Life at the University of Virginia, 1825–1861," 141.

99. Ibid., 141n13. There were a number of other inconsequential efforts: "The first student literary magazine was the *Chameleon,* a weekly which began publication in the spring of 1831. Relying on the heavy usage of reprinted articles, it did not survive beyond 1831. The *University Magazine* appeared as a monthly in the second half of the 1848–1849 session, and was succeeded in the fall of 1849 by the *Jefferson Monument Magazine.*" See also *Bruce* II, 350–353; *Bruce* III, 106–111; and Patton, *Jefferson, Cabell, and the University,* 254–259. Bruce incorrectly suggests that the *University Magazine* was the precursor to the *University Literary Magazine,* which began publication in the 1856–1857 session and was subsequently renamed the *Virginia University Magazine* in February 1858.

100. "Editor's Table," *Collegian* 1, no. 10 (July 1839): 395.

101. "Prospectus," *Jefferson Monument Magazine* 1, no. 1 (Oct. 1849): obverse.

102. "To Our Subscribers," *Jefferson Monument Magazine* 2, no. 1 (Oct. 1850): 31.

103. "Collegiana," *Virginia University Magazine* 11, no. 3 (Dec. 1872): 154.

104. At least one attempt has been made since to revive a magazine published by the Jefferson Society, but to no avail. A magazine of the same title also continues to be published by the U.Va. Alumni Association, through no connection to either the Society or the original publication.

105. "Editor's Table: Address to the Literary Association," *The Collegian* 4, no. 1 (Oct. 1841): 31.

106. "Collegiana," *Virginia University Magazine* 8, no. 6 (Mar. 1870): 37.

107. Wall, "Student Life at the University of Virginia, 1825–1861," 144.

108. "Drinks and How They are Made," *Virginia University Magazine* 7, no. 2–3 (Nov. and Dec. 1868): 95–99.

109. "Mensalia," *Virginia University Magazine* 1, no. 6 (June 1857): 258.

110. "Collegiana," *Virginia University Magazine* 3, no. 1 (Oct. 1858): 33.

111. "Collegiana," *Virginia University Magazine* 1, no. 9 (Nov. 1857): 424.

112. "Editor's Table," *Virginia University Magazine* 4, no. 7 (Apr. 1860): 389.

113. "Editorial," *Jefferson Monument Magazine* 2, no. 3 (Dec. 1850): 95.

114. Ibid.

115. Minute book of the Washington Society, 1859–68, Papers of the Washington Literary Society and Debating Union, 1859–1924, Accession #1780-a, U.Va., 19.

116. Wall, "Student Life at the University of Virginia, 1825–1861," 136.

117. John Robson, ed., *Baird's Manual of American College Fraternities,* 18th ed. (Menasha, WI: G. Banta Co., 1968), 2.

118. John M. Strother to Morton B. Howell, May 4, 1860, Morton Boyte Howell Correspondence, 1851–60, Accession #8463, U.Va.

119. Addendum to Jefferson Society CIO Agreement, Revised June 1, 1993, JS Archives.

120. Ibid.

121. "Mensalia," *Virginia University Magazine* 1, no. 7 (Oct. 1857): 334.

122. Williams, *Intellectual Manhood,* 39.

123. Minute Book of the Washington Society, 1859–68.

124. Peter S. Carmichael, *The Last Generation: Young Virginians in Peace, War, and Reunion* (Chapel Hill, NC: University of North Carolina Press, 2005), 79–82.

125. "Another Cane for Mr. Brooks," *Richmond Enquirer*, May 30, 1856, LVA.

126. Ibid.

127. Preston S. Brooks to J. H. Brooks, May 23, 1856, in Chauncey Samuel Boucher, "South Carolina and the South on the Eve of Secession, 1852 to 1860," *Washington University Studies* 6, no. 2 (Apr. 1919): 115.

128. Wall, "Student Life at the University of Virginia, 1825–1861," 282.

129. Ervin L. Jordan Jr., *Charlottesville and the University of Virginia in the Civil War* (Lynchburg, VA: H. E. Howard, 1988), 24–25.

130. *Bruce* III, 285.

CHAPTER THREE

1. Ervin L. Jordan Jr., *Charlottesville and the University of Virginia in the Civil War* (Lynchburg, VA: H. E. Howard, 1988), 10.

2. Richmond Enquirer, Dec. 29, 1855, LVA.

3. Jordan, *Charlottesville and the University of Virginia in the Civil War*, 10.

4. Ibid., 14.

5. Daniel W. Voorhees, An address delivered before the literary societies of the University of Virginia, July 4, 1860 (Richmond, VA: West and Johnston, 1861), U.Va.

6. John Shelton Patton, *Jefferson, Cabell, and the University of Virginia* (Washington, DC: Neal Publishing Company, 1906), 252; *Albany Law Journal* 6 (1872): 49–50.

7. Patton, *Jefferson, Cabell, and the University of Virginia*, 252.

8. Ibid.

9. Randolph H. McKim, *A Soldier's Recollections: Leaves from the Diary of a Young Confederate* (New York: Longmans, Green, and Co., 1910), 1.

10. Ibid.

11. Ibid.

12. Journals of the Chairman of the Faculty, 1827–1864, Mar. 16, 1861, RG-19/1/2.041, U.Va. Writing in 1910, McKim's memory seems to have been only slightly inaccurate; the journal of the faculty places the incident on March 16.

13. Jordan, *Charlottesville and the University of Virginia in the Civil War*, 18.

14. Patton, *Jefferson, Cabell, and the University of Virginia*, 252. Page made the motion on April 25, 1861.

15. Joint Committee of the Jefferson Society and Washington Society to John Letcher, May 10, 1861, JS Archives. Photocopy of original, LVA.

16. Jordan, *Charlottesville and the University of Virginia in the Civil War*, 14.

17. Ibid., 24–25.

18. Journals of the Chairman of the Faculty, 1827–1864, Apr. 17, 1861, RG-19/1/2.041, U.Va.

19. Jordan, *Charlottesville and the University of Virginia in the Civil War*, 26.

20. Ibid., 32.

21. Ibid., 22–23.

22. *Bruce* III, 332–334.

23. Jordan, *Charlottesville and the University of Virginia in the Civil War*, 47.

24. Patton, *Jefferson, Cabell, and the University of Virginia*, 249.

25. Gratz Cohen to Miriam Cohen [?], Nov. 26, 1863, in the Miriam Gratz Moses Cohen Papers #2639, Southern Historical Collection, Wilson Library, University of North Carolina at Chapel Hill.

26. John Lipscomb Johnson, *The University Memorial: Biographical Sketches of the University of Virginia Alumni Who Fell in the Confederate War* (Baltimore, MD: Turnbull Brothers, 1871), 705–707.

27. Gratz Cohen to Miriam Cohen [?], Dec. 6, 1863, in the Miriam Gratz Moses Cohen Papers #2639, Southern Historical Collection, Wilson Library, University of North Carolina at Chapel Hill.

28. Adam Goodheart, *1861: The Civil War Awakening* (New York: Alfred A. Knopf, 2011), 77.

29. See Peter S. Carmichael, *The Last Generation: Young Virginians in Peace, War, and Reunion* (Chapel Hill, NC: University of North Carolina Press, 2005).

30. Patton, *Jefferson, Cabell, and the University of Virginia*, 220n1.

31. Jordan, *Charlottesville and the University of Virginia in the Civil War*, 102.

32. Statistics regarding the casualties of the Civil War vary widely. These are taken from Gary W. Gallagher, *The Confederate War* (Cambridge, MA: Harvard University Press, 1999).

33. Frederick Rudolph, *The American College and University: A History* (Athens, GA: University of Georgia Press, 1962), 242.

34. Ibid., 244.

35. Virginius Dabney, *Mr. Jefferson's University: A History* (Charlottesville, VA: University of Virginia Press, 1981), 26–28; John R. Thelin, *A History of American Higher Education* (Baltimore, MD: Johns Hopkins University Press, 2011), 74–75; Rudolph, *The American College and University: A History*, 244.

36. Jordan, *Charlottesville and the University of Virginia in the Civil War*, 98.

37. Socrates Maupin to James Alexander Seddon, Oct. 18, 1864, Socrates Maupin Papers, 1853–1870, Accession #2769, U.Va.

38. Jordan, *Charlottesville and the University of Virginia in the Civil War*, 105.

39. "Collegiana," *Virginia University Magazine* 12, no. 1 (Oct. 1873): 49.

40. Ibid., 50.

41. "Collegiana," *Virginia University Magazine* 9, no. 6 (Mar. 1871): 343.

42. "Collegiana," *Virginia University Magazine* 12, no. 6 (Mar. 1873): 338.

43. "Editors' Table," *Virginia University Magazine* 9, no. 5 (Feb. 1871): 36.

44. "Collegiana," *Virginia University Magazine* 8, no. 1 (Oct. 1869): 38.

45. "Editor's Table," *Virginia University Magazine* 8, no. 7 (Apr. 1870): 46.

46. Constitution and By-Laws of JS, 1837.

47. "Collegiana," *Virginia University Magazine* 9, no. 2 (Nov. 1870): 101.

48. "Editor's Drawer," *Virginia University Magazine* 7, no. 5–6 (Feb. and Mar. 1869): 290.

49. "Editor's Table," *Virginia University Magazine* 7, no. 1 (Oct. 1868): 46.

50. "Collegiana," *Virginia University Magazine* 8, no. 1 (Oct. 1869): 39.

51. Minutes of JS, Dec. 23, 1875, Minute Book of the JS 1875–1896, JS Archives, 5–7.

52. "Editor's Drawer," *Virginia University Magazine* 7, no. 5–6 (Feb. and Mar. 1869): 294.

53. "Collegiana," *Virginia University Magazine* 7, no. 3 (Dec. 1869): 36.

54. Minutes of JS, Nov. 23, 1878, Minute Book of JS 1875–1896, JS Archives, 71.

55. "Collegiana," *Virginia University Magazine* 10, no. 3 (Dec. 1871): 163.

56. Minutes of JS, Dec. 18, 1875, Minute Book of JS 1875–1894, JS Archives, 5.

57. Minute Book of JS 1875–1894, JS Archives, i.

58. Minutes of JS, Feb. 12, 1876, Minute Book of JS 1875–1896, JS Archives, 11.

59. Minutes of JS, Oct. 20, 1877, Minute Book of JS 1875–1896, JS Archives, 41.

60. "Collegiana," *Virginia University Magazine* 9, no. 6 (Mar. 1871): 343.

61. "Collegiana," *Virginia University Magazine* 12, no. 3 (Dec. 1873): 189.

62. "Collegiana," *Virginia University Magazine* 13, no. 6 (Mar. 1875): 362.

63. "Editors' Table," *Virginia University Magazine* 9, no. 3 (Dec. 1870): 159.

64. One example of these periodic surveys of organizations appears in "Collegiana," *Virginia University Magazine* 7, no. 4 (Jan. 1869): 186. "Clubs. There are 15 secret societies in college, and their respective numbers are about as follows: Chi Phi, 16; Delta Psi, 16; S.A.E., 12; D.K.E., 12; Phi Kappa Psi, 12; Beta Theta Pi, 11; Zeta Psi, 10; Sigma Chi, 10; Mystic Seven, 7; Phi Gamma Delta, 8; Kappa Phi Lambda, 8; Alpha Tau Omega, 7; Chi Psi, 7; Pi Kappa Alpha, 6; and lastly, and we are compelled to say least, the 'Sons of Confucius' have but four members."

65. "Editor's Table," *Virginia University Magazine* 7, no. 1 (Oct. 1868): 48.

CHAPTER FOUR

1. Edward Younger, "Woodrow Wilson: The Making of a Leader," *Virginia Magazine of History and Biography* 64, no. 4 (Oct. 1956): 392.

2. Woodrow Wilson to Ellen Axson, Oct. 30, 1883, in Ray Stannard Baker, *Woodrow Wilson, Life and Letters*, vol. 1, *Youth, 1856–1890* (Garden City, NY: Doubleday, Page and Co., 1927), 109.

3. *Papers of WW*, vol. 1, *1856–1880*, 663n2.

4. Virginius Dabney, *Mr. Jefferson's University* (Charlottesville, VA: University of Virginia Press, 1981), 24–25.

5. *Papers of WW*, vol. 1, *1856–1880*, 663n2.

6. Archibald W. Patterson, *Personal Recollections of Woodrow Wilson and Some Reflections upon His Life and Character* (Richmond, VA: Whittet and Shepperson, 1929), 19.

7. Ibid., 12.

8. Ibid.

9. Ibid.

10. Ibid., 7.

11. Ibid.

12. Younger, "Woodrow Wilson: The Making of a Leader," 392–393.

13. Patterson, *Personal Recollections of Woodrow Wilson*, 8.

14. Minutes of the Eumenean Society, May 23, 1874, *Papers of WW*, vol. 1, *1856–1880*, 51.

15. *Papers of WW*, vol. 1, *1856–1880*, 56n1.

16. Baker, *Woodrow Wilson, Life and Letters*, vol. 1, 123.

17. Minutes of the Eumenean Society, May 9, 1874, *Papers of WW*, vol. 1, *1856–1880*, 49.

18. Minutes of the Eumenean Society, Oct. 4, 1873, *Papers of WW*, vol. 1, *1856–1880*, 31.

19. Younger, "Woodrow Wilson: The Making of a Leader," 392; Patterson, *Personal Recollections of Woodrow Wilson*, 7.

20. Janet Woodrow Wilson to Woodrow Wilson, Nov. 6, 1879, *Papers of WW*, vol. 1, *1856–1880*, 580.

21. Minutes of the American Whig Society, Sept. 24, 1875, *Papers of WW*, vol. 1, *1856–1880*, 75.

22. Minutes of the American Whig Society, Oct. 29, 1875, *Papers of WW*, vol. 1, *1856–1880*, 78.

23. Younger, "Woodrow Wilson: The Making of a Leader," 391.

24. Ibid; minutes of the American Whig Society, Oct. 21, 1877, *Papers of WW*, vol. 1, *1856–1880*, 292.

25. Report of the Committee on Hall Improvement, from the minutes of the American Whig Society, Nov. 9, 1877, and minutes of the American Whig Society, June 7, 1878, *Papers of WW*, vol. 1, *1856–1880*, 316, 380.

26. *Papers of WW*, vol. 1, *1856–1880*, 130.

27. Younger, "Woodrow Wilson: The Making of a Leader," 391.

28. Ibid; minutes of the Liberal Debating Club, Sept. 22, 1877, *Papers of WW*, vol. 1, *1856–1880*, 292.

29. Shorthand diary of Woodrow Wilson, Mar. 20, 1877, *Papers of WW*, vol. 1, *1856–1880*, 253.

30. "Editorial Elections," *The Princetonian* 2 (Feb. 21, 1878), *Papers of WW*, vol. 1, *1856–1880*, 360.

31. "College Meeting," *The Princetonian* 3 (Oct. 24, 1878), *Papers of WW*, vol. 1, *1856–1880*, 423.

32. Arthur S. Link, *Wilson: The Road to the White House* (Princeton, NJ: Princeton University Press, 1947), 6–11.

33. *Papers of WW*, vol. 1, 1856–1880, 576n1; Patterson, *Personal Recollections of Woodrow Wilson*, 6.

34. Minutes of JS, Oct. 18, 1879, *Papers of WW*, vol. 1, *1856–1880*, 576.

35. Constitution and By-Laws of JS, 1860 (Peyton and Southall, 1860), By-Laws Sec. IV, LVA, 9.

36. Constitution and By-Laws of JS, 1860, By-Laws Sec. IV, 9.

37. Patterson, *Personal Recollections of Woodrow Wilson*, 9.

38. Ibid.

39. Ibid.

40. Woodrow Wilson to Charles Andrew Talcott, Dec. 31, 1879, *Papers of WW*, vol. 1, *1856–1880*, 591; Younger, "Woodrow Wilson: The Making of a Leader," 392.

41. Patterson, *Personal Recollections of Woodrow Wilson*, 9.

42. Ibid., 8.

43. Ibid.

44. Constitution and By-Laws of JS, 1860, By-Laws Sec. IX, 10.

45. Minutes of JS, Nov. 22, 1879, *Papers of WW*, vol. 1, *1856–1880*, 587.

46. Patterson, *Personal Recollections of Woodrow Wilson*, 8.

47. Ibid.

48. Ibid.

49. Baker, *Woodrow Wilson, Life and Letters*, vol. 1, 113.

50. Ibid.

51. Minutes of JS, Oct. 9, 1880, *Papers of WW*, vol. 1, *1856–1880*, 683.

52. Ibid.

53. See James P. C. Southall, *In the Days of My Youth: When I Was a Student at the University of Virginia, 1888–1893* (Chapel Hill, NC: University of North Carolina Press, 1947).

54. Addendum to Jefferson Society CIO Agreement, Revised June 1, 1993, JS Archives.

55. Minutes of JS, Oct. 9, 1880, *Papers of WW*, vol. 1, *1856–1880*, 683.

56. Minutes of JS, Oct. 16, 1880, *Papers of WW*, vol. 1, *1856–1880*, 685, for example.

57. Minutes of JS, Oct. 23, 1880, *Papers of WW*, vol. 1, *1856–1880*, 686.

58. Ibid.

59. Ibid.

60. Minutes of JS, Dec. 11, 1880, *Papers of WW*, vol. 1, *1856–1880*, 703.

61. See, for example, *Virginia University Magazine* 20, no. 2 (Nov. 1880), 65.

62. Newspaper report of Wilson's Final oration, *Richmond Daily Dispatch*, July 1, 1880, *Papers of WW*, vol. 1, *1856–1880*, 661–663.

63. Baker, *Woodrow Wilson, Life and Letters*, vol. 1, 124.

64. *Papers of WW*, vol. 1, *1856–1880*, 688.

65. Ibid.

66. Constitution and By-Laws of JS, 1860, Constitution Article VI, 6.

67. *Papers of WW*, vol. 1, *1856–1880*, 688–689.

68. See Constitution and By-Laws of JS, 1880, Article II, *Papers of WW*, vol. 1, *1856–1880*, 691, as compared with Constitution and By-Laws of JS, 1860, Constitution Article II, 5.

69. *Papers of WW*, vol. 1, *1856–1880*, 688.

70. Constitution and By-Laws of JS, 1860, By-Laws Sec. I, 8.

71. Constitution and By-Laws of JS, 1880, Article I, Sec. 1, *Papers of WW*, vol. 1, *1856–1880*, 690.

72. See Constitution and By-Laws of JS, 1860; and Constitution and By-Laws of JS, 1880, *Papers of WW*, vol. 1, *1856–1880*, 688–699.

73. *Papers of WW*, vol. 1, *1856–1880*, 688.

74. Constitution and By-Laws of JS, 1880, Article V, Sec. 3, *Papers of WW*, vol. 1, *1856–1880*, 694.

75. Ibid.

76. Ibid.

77. Ibid., Article VIII, Sec. 3, 696.

78. *Papers of WW*, vol. 1, *1856–1880*, 689.

79. Patterson, *Personal Recollections of Woodrow Wilson*, 8.

80. Newspaper report of Wilson's Final oration, *Richmond Daily Dispatch*, July 1, 1880, *Papers of WW*, vol. 1, *1856–1880*, 662.

81. Ibid.; Constitution and By-Laws of JS, 1880, Preamble, *Papers of WW*, vol. 1, *1856–1880* (1966), 690.

82. *Papers of WW*, vol. 1, *1856–1880*, 688.

83. See Constitution and By-Laws of JS, 1860.

84. Constitution and By-Laws of JS, 1880, Article IV, *Papers of WW*, vol. 1, *1856–1880*, 693.

85. See Woodrow Wilson, "On Cabinet Government," *International Review* 6 (Aug. 1879): 146–163.

86. *Papers of WW*, vol. 1, *1856–1880*, 688–689.

87. Constitution and By-Laws of JS, 1880, Article II, Sec. 1, *Papers of WW*, vol. 1, *1856–1880*, 691.

88. *Papers of WW*, vol. 1, *1856–1880*, 689.

89. Ibid.

90. Constitution and By-Laws of JS, 1860, Constitution Article VI, Sec. 2, 6.

91. Constitution and By-Laws of JS, 1880, Article VII, *Papers of WW*, vol. 1, *1856–1880*, 695.

92. Ibid.

93. *Papers of WW*, vol. 1, *1856–1880*, 689.

94. Constitution and By-Laws of JS, 1860, Constitution Article VII, 6–7.

95. Patterson, *Personal Recollections of Woodrow Wilson*, 16.

96. Minutes of JS, Dec. 11, 1880, *Papers of WW*, vol. 1, *1856–1880*, 700.

97. Constitution and By-Laws of JS, 1880, Article VI, Sec. 1, *Papers of WW*, vol. 1, *1856–1880*, 894.

98. Woodrow Wilson to Richard Heath Dabney, Feb. 1, 1881, *Papers of WW*, vol. 1, *1856–1880*, 17.

99. Patterson, *Personal Recollections of Woodrow Wilson*, 8.

100. Minutes of JS, Oct. 25, 1879, *Papers of WW*, vol. 1, *1856–1880*, 578.

101. Patterson, *Personal Recollections of Woodrow Wilson*, 8.

102. Woodrow Wilson to Robert Bridges, Feb. 25, 1880, *Papers of WW*, vol. 1, *1856–1880*, 603.

103. Ibid.

104. Minutes of JS, Mar. 6, 1880, *Papers of WW*, vol. 1, *1856–1880*, 608.

105. Woodrow Wilson, "John Bright, a Biographical Essay," *Virginia University Magazine* 19, no. 6 (Mar. 1880): 367–370.

106. Ibid., 367.

107. Ibid., 368.

108. Ibid., 368–369.

109. William Cabell Bruce, *Recollections* (Baltimore, MD: King Brothers, 1936), 69.

110. Patterson, *Personal Recollections of Woodrow Wilson*, 19.

111. "Collegiana," *Virginia University Magazine* 19, no. 7 (Apr. 1880): 445–450.

112. Patterson, *Personal Recollections of Woodrow Wilson*, 15.

113. "Collegiana," *Virginia University Magazine* 19, no. 7 (Apr. 1880): 446.

114. Patterson, *Personal Recollections of Woodrow Wilson*, 15.

115. Ibid.

116. Ibid.

117. Ibid.

118. *Papers of WW*, vol. 1, *1856–1880*, 652.

119. Bruce, *Recollections*, 75.

120. Ibid., 80.

121. "Collegiana," *Virginia University Magazine* 20, no. 2 (Oct. 1880): 51.

122. Ibid.

123. Woodrow Wilson to Cordell Hull, Sept. 12, 1922, *Papers of WW*, vol. 68, *1922–1924*, 134–135.

124. Newspaper report of Wilson's Final oration, *Richmond Daily Dispatch*, July 1, 1880, *Papers of WW*, vol. 1, *1856–1880*, 661.

125. Ibid., 663.

126. "Collegiana," *Virginia University Magazine* 20, no. 4 (Jan. 1881): 250.

127. Newspaper report of Wilson's Final oration, *Richmond Daily Dispatch,* July 1, 1880, *Papers of WW,* vol. 1, *1856–1880,* 663.

128. Janet Woodrow Wilson to Woodrow Wilson, Dec. 14, 1880, and Joseph R. Wilson to Woodrow Wilson, undated, *Papers of WW,* vol. 1, *1856–1880,* 701, for example.

129. Woodrow Wilson to Richard Heath Dabney, Feb. 1, 1881, *Papers of WW,* vol. 2, *1881–1884,* 17.

130. "Collegiana," *Virginia University Magazine* 20, no. 4 (Jan. 1881): 250.

131. Woodrow Wilson to Richard Heath Dabney, Feb. 1, 1881, *Papers of WW,* vol. 2, *1881–1884,* 17.

132. Newspaper report of Wilson's Final oration, *Richmond Daily Dispatch,* July 1, 1880, *Papers of WW,* vol. 1, *1856–1880,* 661–663.

133. Ibid., 662.

CHAPTER FIVE

1. "Editorial," *Virginia University Magazine* 31, no. 3 (Dec. 1891): 210.

2. "Editorial," *Virginia University Magazine* 30, no. 2 (Dec. 1890): 151–152.

3. "Editorial," *Virginia University Magazine* 31, no. 4 (Jan. 1892): 285.

4. Ibid., 283.

5. *Bruce* IV, 90.

6. James P. C. Southall, *In the Days of My Youth: When I Was a Student at the University of Virginia, 1888–1893* (Chapel Hill, NC: University of North Carolina Press, 1947), 184.

7. Ibid., 185.

8. *College Topics* clippings, Jefferson Society Papers, 1892–1893, RG-23/50/2.051, U.Va.

9. Southall, *In the Days of My Youth,* 186.

10. Ibid., 186–187.

11. Judgment of the Committee, Jefferson Society Papers, 1892–1893, RG-23/50/2.051, U.Va. The lengthy briefs filed on behalf of McGuire are also included in this file, preserved by James Southall.

12. Daniel A. Clark, *Creating the College Man: American Mass Magazines and Middle-Class Manhood, 1890–1915* (Madison, WI: University of Wisconsin, 2010), 183.

13. John R. Thelin, *A History of American Higher Education* (Baltimore, MD: Johns Hopkins University Press, 2011), 103, 127, 154; Frederick Rudolph, *The American College and University: A History* (Athens, GA: University of Georgia Press, 1962), 272.

14. *Bruce* IV, 93–94.

15. *Bruce* IV, 333; Minutes of JS, Nov. 26, 1896, and Nov. 23, 1901, Minute Book of JS 1894–1905, JS Archives, 184, 422.

16. *Bruce* IV, 334.

17. *Bruce* IV, 90–91.

18. Minutes of JS, Oct. 5, 1895, Minute Book of JS 1894–1905, JS Archives 68.

19. Minutes of JS, Jan. 4, 1896, Minute Book of JS 1894–1905, JS Archives, 102.

20. See Morgan P. Robinson, *The Burning of the Rotunda* (Charlottesville, VA: Michie Company, 1905).

21. John T. Thorton to Rosalie Thorton, Oct. 27, 1895, U.Va.

22. Minutes of JS, Special Meeting, Oct. 27, 1895, Minute Book of JS 1905–1918, JS Archives.

23. Clark, *Creating the College Man*, 5.

24. Thelin, *A History of American Higher Education*, 156.

25. Clark, *Creating the College Man*, 6.

26. Thelin, *A History of American Higher Education*, 155.

27. Ibid., 117.

28. Rudolph, *The American College and University: A History*, 189.

29. For an excellent, detailed account of Alderman's career, see Dumas Malone, *Edwin A. Alderman: A Biography* (Garden City, NY: Doubleday, Doran & Co., 1940).

30. James M. Becker, "Education and the Southern Aristocracy: The Southern Education Movement, 1881–1913" (master's thesis, University of North Carolina at Chapel Hill, 1972), 17.

31. Ibid., 90, 94.

32. Ibid., 5. See also Michael Dennis, "Reforming the Academical Village: Edwin A. Alderman and the University of Virginia, 1904–1915," *The Virginia Magazine of History and Biography* 105, no. 1 (Winter, 1997): 53–86.

33. Becker, "Education and the Southern Aristocracy," 98.

34. Minutes of JS, Oct. 1, 1904, Minute Book of JS 1894–1905, JS Archives, 522.

35. Ibid.

36. See, for example, Minutes of JS, Oct. 25, 1913, Minute Book of JS 1905–1918, JS Archives, 359.

37. *Bruce* IV, 109–110; Coy Barefoot, *The Corner: A History of Student Life at the University of Virginia* (Charlottesville, VA: Alumni Association of the University of Virginia), 29, 94.

38. *Bruce* IV, 94.

39. Ibid.

40. "Collegiana," *Virginia University Magazine* 26, no. 5 (Feb. 1887): 374; "Y.M.C.A. Notes," *Virginia University Magazine* 26, no. 6 (Mar. 1887): 456–458.

41. Barefoot, *The Corner*, 107, 108.

42. *Bruce* IV, 94.

43. See *Bruce* IV, 336–337. Alumni were key drivers in the efforts to build chapter houses for fraternities. See, for example, correspondence between John Hampden Chamberlayne Bagby, Thomas Longstreet Wood, and others related to fund-raising and construction of a house for Delta Kappa Epsilon in Bagby Family Papers, 1824–1960, MSS1 B1463 b, Part 9, Section 154, VHS.

44. *Bruce* IV, 97–98.

45. "Collegiana," *Virginia University Magazine* 23, no. 1 (Oct. 1883): 50.

46. *Bruce* IV, 97–98.

47. *Bruce* IV, 101, 341–342; *Corks and Curls*, 1890–1925. The membership rosters of all of these clubs, including the ribbon societies, appeared annually in *Corks and Curls*, the University's yearbook beginning in the 1880s. As might be expected, there was much overlap in the membership as the student body of the University was still relatively small. As a matter of note, fraternities were traditionally listed in the order of their chapter's founding in *Corks and Curls*.

48. Barefoot, *The Corner*, 94.

49. Virginius Dabney, *Mr. Jefferson's University: A History* (Charlottesville, VA: University of Virginia Press, 1981), 36.

50. Clark, *Creating the College Man*, 113.

51. Minutes of JS, Apr. 30, 1904, Minute Book of JS 1894–1905, JS Archives, 509.

52. Rudolph, *The American College and University: A History*, 273–293, 374.

53. Barefoot, *The Corner*, 79; John Shelton Patton, *Jefferson, Cabell, and the University of Virginia* (Washington, DC: Neal Publishing Company, 1906), 260. Dabney puts the founding of the GAA in 1892, but that is likely incorrect, given their control of *College Topics* prior to that date.

54. Thelin, *A History of American Higher Education*, 178.

55. See, for example, on the Temperance Union: "The Student's Union," *Virginia University Magazine* 23, no. 3 (Dec. 1883): 145; "Temperance in the University," *Virginia University Magazine* 26, no. 1 (Oct. 1886): 42–44; on the YMCA: "Y.M.C.A. Notes," *Virginia University Magazine* 26, no. 6 (Mar. 1887): 456–458; and on fraternities: "Collegiana," *Virginia University Magazine* 22, no. 7 (Apr. 1883): 450; and "Fraternities," *Virginia University Magazine* 23, no. 7 (Apr. 1884): 425–428.

56. The *Magenta*, later called the *Crimson* at Harvard; the *Princetonian* at Princeton.

57. "Editor's Table," *Virginia University Magazine* 22, no. 5 (Feb. 1883): 327.

58. "Communication," *Virginia University Magazine* 29, no. 2 (Jan. 1889): 155.

59. Ibid.

60. Ibid.

61. "Editor's Table," *Virginia University Magazine* 22, no. 4 (Jan. 1883): 259.

62. *Virginia University Magazine* 26, no. 6 (Mar. 1887): 436.

63. "Communication," *Virginia University Magazine* 29, no. 2 (Jan. 1889): 155.

64. Patton, *Jefferson, Cabell, and the University of Virginia*, 259–260.

65. Ibid.

66. Ibid.

67. "Collegiana," *Virginia University Magazine* 29, no. 4 (Jan. 1890): 329.

68. "Editorial," *Virginia University Magazine* 30, no. 1 (Oct. 1890): 66.

69. "Collegiana," *Virginia University Magazine* 24, no. 9 (June 1885): 575.

70. "Editorial," *Virginia University Magazine* 31, no. 4 (Jan. 1892): 280.

71. "Collegiana," *Virginia University Magazine* 29, no. 4 (Jan. 1890): 317.

72. Charles W. Kent, "The Magazine's Higher Mission," *Virginia University Magazine* 33, no. 3 (Dec. 1893): 95.

73. Thomas Nelson Page, "From the Pen of Edgar Allan Poe," *Virginia University Magazine* 30, no. 5 (Mar. 1891): 331–333.

74. "Editorial," *Virginia University Magazine* 30, no. 5 (Mar. 1891): 383.

75. See "Arcade Echoes: A Review," *Virginia University Magazine* 30, no. 2 (Dec. 1890): 141; Thomas Longstreet Wood, ed., *Arcade Echoes: Selected Poems from the University of Virginia Magazine, 1856–1890* (Charlottesville, VA: A. C. Brechin, 1894).

76. "Editorial," *Virginia University Magazine* 33, no. 4 (Jan. 1894): 183. Wood was also the editor of *Arcade Echoes*.

77. "Editorial," *Virginia University Magazine* 35, no. 8–9 (May and June 1896): 457. For the precise terms of the Harrison Translation Medal and the Harrison Trophy, see "Edito-

rial," *Virginia University Magazine* 35, no. 4 (Jan. 1896): 252.

78. "Editorial," *Virginia University Magazine* 36, no. 1 (Oct. 1896): 42.

79. "Editorial," *Virginia University Magazine* 37, no. 1 (Oct. 1897): 46.

80. "Editorial," *Virginia University Magazine* 38, no. 3 (Dec. 1898): 144.

81. Minutes of JS, Jan. 9, 1897, and Feb. 20, 1897, Minute Book of the JS 1894–1905, JS Archives, 203–204, 216; Minutes of JS from the U.Va. Chapel, June 15, 1897, Minute Book of JS 1894–1905, JS Archives, 245.

82. Southall, *In the Days of My Youth*, 88.

83. Thelin, *A History of American Higher Education*, 163–164.

84. Ibid.

85. Minutes of JS, Mar. 1, 1902, Minute Book JS 1894–1905, JS Archives, 433.

86. Minutes of JS, Dec. 7, 1912, Minute Book of JS 1905–1918, JS Archives, 321.

87. "Editor's Table," *Virginia University Magazine* 27, no. 1 (Oct. 1887): 66.

88. Minutes of JS, Oct. 30, 1897, Minute Book of JS 1894–1905, JS Archives, 259. Maiden speeches were a precursor to modern-day probationary presentations but should not be taken as equivalent. The format varied, but maiden speeches were typically delivered impromptu on a topic the chair selected, and while they were judged for quality and delivery, they were not subjected to the same detailed scrutiny that probationary presentations would later receive.

89. Minutes of JS, Oct. 30, 1897, Minute Book of JS 1894–1905, JS Archives, 259.

90. Minutes of JS, Sept. 23, 1899, and Oct. 26, 1901, Minute Book of JS 1894–1905, JS Archives, 337, 421.

91. Minutes of JS, May 21, 1904, Minute Book of JS 1894–1905, JS Archives, 513.

92. Karl W. Saur, "A History of the Jefferson Society," Feb. 5, 1982, JS Archives.

93. Minutes of JS, May 8, 1909, and May 15, 1909, Minute Book of JS 1905–1918, JS Archives, 142.

94. Report of the Membership Committee, May 12, 1917, JS Archives.

95. Saur, "A History of the Jefferson Society."

96. The eleven names that appear on the plaque are Leroy Howard Clapp, Thomas William Cumming, William Alexander Fleet, Peter Puryear Holmes, Walter Klioh Knight, John Lyon, Stephen Patrick McGroarty, Farrell Dabney Moomaw Jr., Daniel Glovis Moomaw, Wyatt Rushton, and Frank Leslie Young.

97. Minutes of JS, Dec. 4, 1897, Minute Book of JS 1894–1905, JS Archives, 266.

98. Minutes of JS, Apr. 9, 1910, Minute Book of JS 1905–1918, JS Archives, 194.

99. Minutes of JS, Oct. 31, 1903, Minute Book of JS 1894–1905, JS Archives, 484.

100. Ibid., 485.

101. Minutes of JS, Dec. 9, 1899, Minute Book of JS 1894–1905, JS Archives, 347.

102. Minutes of JS, Sept. 2, 1895, Minute Book of JS 1894–1905, JS Archives, 65.

103. F. S. Harmon, President's Report, Fall 1916, JS Archives.

104. The collection of letters may be found under John Randolph St. John, Correspondence Regarding Portraits for the Jefferson Society, 1905, Accession #1018-h, U.Va.

105. John W. Daniel to John Randolph St. John, May 17, 1905, in John Randolph St. John, Correspondence Regarding Portraits for the Jefferson Society, 1905, Accession #1018-h, U.Va.

106. Minutes of JS, Oct. 7, 1911, Minute Book of JS 1905–1918, JS Archives, 251.

107. Congressman Oscar W. Underwood to D. Hiden Ramsey, President JS, entered into the Minutes of JS, Oct. 31, 1911, Minute Book of JS 1905–1918, JS Archives, 250.

108. Senator Claude A. Swanson to D. Hiden Ramsey, President JS, entered into the Minutes of JS, Oct. 28, 1911, Minute Book of JS 1905–1918, JS Archives, 252.

109. Resolution to Honor Woodrow Wilson, entered into the Minutes of JS, Nov. 4, 1916, Minute Book of JS 1905–1918, 247, JS Archives, 252.

110. Minutes of JS, Mar. 27, 1897, Minute Book of JS, 1894–1905, JS Archives, 227.

111. Minutes of JS, Dec. 13, 1902, Minute Book of JS 1894–1905, JS Archives, 461.

112. Minutes of JS, Nov. 24, 1897, Minute Book of JS 1894–1905, JS Archives, 265.

113. Minutes of JS, Jan. 19, 26, Feb. 9, and Mar. 27, 1895, Minute Book of Jefferson Society 1894–1905, JS Archives, 35, 36, 38, 227.

114. Minutes of JS, Oct. 31, 1908, Minute Book of JS 1905–1918, JS Archives, 96; Dabney, *Mr. Jefferson's University*, 101. Paul would remain active until he retired on account of poor health in 1936.

115. Minutes of JS, Feb. 24, 1912, Minute Book of JS 1905–1918, JS Archives, 285; C. W. Paul to H. W. Hackley, entered into the Minutes of JS, Feb. 29, 1912, Minute Book of JS, 1905–1918, JS Archives.

116. Minutes of JS, Feb. 13, 1909, Minute Book of JS 1905–1918, JS Archives, 121.

117. Minutes of JS, Oct. 26, 1895, Minute Book of JS 1894–1905, JS Archives, 73.

118. Minutes of JS, Feb. 15, 1896, Minute Book of JS 1894–1905, JS Archives, 122.

119. Harrison Cup Program, entered into the Minutes of JS, May 1, 1896, Minute Book of JS 1894–1905, JS Archives, 140.

120. Minutes of JS, June 12, 1897, Minute Book of JS 1894–1905, JS Archives, 244.

121. The original Harrison Trophy is a handsome plaque featuring profiles of both Washington and Jefferson and a scroll encircled by a laurel and transected by a quill. It is engraved with the names of the winners arranged in columns under the heading of their respective societies. The plaque resided in the hall of the year's victor until the next debate, and it was used from 1896 to 1913, when the Washington Society column filled to capacity. One of the winners from that year, W. W. Koontz, kept the trophy, and it was discovered in the attic of one of his relatives in May 2012, along with a cup awarded in place of the trophy when Koontz won the contest again the next year. Tyler Slack to the Washington Society, May 11, 2012, JS Archives.

122. "Editorial," *Virginia University Magazine* 31, no. 5 (Feb. 1892): 365.

123. *Bruce* V, 240–241.

124. *Bruce* V, 241.

125. Minutes of JS, Jan. 17, 1914, Minute Book of JS 1894–1905, JS Archives, 377.

126. "Collegiana," *Virginia University Magazine* 27, no. 3 (Dec. 1887): 202.

127. "Memorabilia," *Virginia University Magazine* 30, no. 4 (Feb. 1891): 322.

128. Letter from L. R. Hamberlin, Southern Interstate Oratorical Association, to Jefferson Society and Washington Society, Dec. 2, 1896, JS Archives.

129. Minutes of JS, Oct. 31, 1908, Minute Book of JS 1905–1918, JS Archives, 96.

130. Minutes of JS, Oct. 2, 1909, Minute Book of JS, 1905–1918, JS Archives, 153.

131. Minutes of JS, Nov. 9, 1895, Minute Book of JS 1894–1905, JS Archives, 77; "Editorial," *Virginia University Magazine* 41, no. 4 (Jan. 1902): 241.

132. Minutes of JS, Jan. 18, 1902, Minute Book of JS 1894–1905, JS Archives, 426; James S. Baron to Charles T. Reese, Feb. 7, 1938, JS Archives.

133. Expenses of the University Debating Team Incident to the Debate with Pennsylvania, in Minutes of JS, Apr. 3, 1903, Minute Book of JS 1894–1905, JS Archives, 473; Minutes of JS, May 9, 1904, Minute Book of JS 1894–1905, JS Archives, 510. It was long believed that this photograph pictured Woodrow Wilson and his friend Richard Heath Dabney. The true identities of the individuals were supplied in a 1938 letter from James S. Baron, one of the debaters, but the error somehow persisted. In 1903, J. W. Ayres, J. S. Baron, and W. Parrish were selected by a committee of the faculty as the debaters to go to the University of Pennsylvania, and R. B. Wood was selected as an alternate. Baron successfully identified the other three individuals in the picture and added, on the question of "Resolved, that employers are justified in refusing to treat with labor unions, a majority of whose members are unincorporated," that "Virginia was fortunate enough to win the debate." Associate Justice Edward White of the Supreme Court served as one of the judges. See John N. Fishburne, J. H. Lindsay, and Charles W. Kent to R. H. Keren, entered into the minutes of JS, Mar. 7, 1903, Minute Book of JS 1894–1905, JS Archives, 470; James S. Baron to Charles T. Reese, Feb. 7, 1938, JS Archives.

134. "Intercollegiana," *Virginia University Magazine* 23, no. 1 (Oct. 1883): 63.

135. F. S. Harmon, President's Report, Fall 1916, JS Archives.

136. *Bulletin of the Virginia High School Literary League*, vol. 1, no. 1 (1914), VHS.

137. Ibid.; Minutes of JS, Nov. 29, 1913, and Dec. 13, 1913, Minute Book of JS 1905–1918, JS Archives, 371.

138. *Bulletin of the Virginia High School Literary League*, vol. 1, no. 1 (1914), VHS.

139. Ibid.

140. VHSL Handbook, 6. Available online: http://www.vhsl.org/doc/upload/pub -handbook-2011-123.pdf, accessed June 1, 2012.

141. Minutes of JS, Sept. 30, 1899, Minute Book of JS 1894–1905, JS Archives, 339.

142. See Charles W. Kent, ed., *The Unveiling of the Bust of Edgar Allan Poe in the Library of the University of Virginia* (Lynchburg, VA: J. P. Bell and Company, 1901).

143. Minutes of JS, Dec. 12, 1908, Minute Book of JS 1905–1918, JS Archives, 101.

144. Ibid., 106.

145. "Jeff Society Honors Poe," newspaper clipping enclosed in the Minute Book of JS 1905–1918, JS Archives.

146. "Letter from William A, Poe to JS," entered into the Minutes of JS, Jan. 11, 1909, Minute Book of JS 1905–1918, JS Archives, 107.

147. Minutes of JS, Nov. 15, 1904, Minute Book of JS 1895–1905, JS Archives, 534.

148. Saur, "A History of the Jefferson Society."

149. Minutes of JS, Oct. 22, 1898, Minute Book of JS 1894–1905, JS Archives, 306.

150. Minutes of JS, Feb. 13, 1915, Minute Book of JS 1905–1918, JS Archives, 450.

151. Ibid., 451.

152. John Calvin Metcalf, *The Centennial of the University of Virginia, 1819–1921: The Proceedings of the Centenary Celebration, May 31 to June 3, 1921* (New York: G. P. Putman's Sons, 1922), xv.

153. Metcalf's book provides a comprehensive account of the celebrations, including text of

almost every speech that was given, rosters of the delegates who attended, the full script of the centennial pageant, and pictures from the event.

154. John Shelton Patton, "The Jefferson Literary Society: Its Centennial," *Corks and Curls* 38 (1926): 20.

155. Ibid., 22.

156. Ibid., 23.

CHAPTER SIX

1. Virginius Dabney, *Mr. Jefferson's University: A History* (Charlottesville, VA: University of Virginia Press, 1981), 88, 132, 164, 185–186.

2. John R. Thelin, *A History of American Higher Education* (Baltimore, MD: Johns Hopkins University Press, 2011), 211.

3. "Editorial," *Virginia Spectator* 88, no. 1 (Dec. 1927): 16.

4. Dabney, *Mr. Jefferson's University*, 86.

5. Ibid.

6. "Editorial," *Virginia Spectator* 88, no. 2 (Jan. 1928): 48.

7. Randolph W. Church, "Why Literary Societies: A Critical Review of the Past, Present, and Future," *Virginia Spectator* 89, no. 4 (Jan. 1929): 189.

8. Ibid., 188.

9. See, for example, "Washington Society to Meet Bi-Monthly," *College Topics* 43, no. 60 (Apr. 11, 1932): 1; and David Carliner, "Laboratory Politics," *Virginia Spectator* 101, no. 1 (Sept. 1939): 10.

10. Church, "Why Literary Societies," 189.

11. Thelin, *A History of American Higher Education*, 252.

12. Dabney, *Mr. Jefferson's University*, 141.

13. Minutes of JS, May 28, 1937, Minute Book of JS 1935–1942, JS Archives, 92.

14. Minutes of JS, May 22, 1936, "Report of the Banquet Committee," Minute Book of JS 1935–1942, JS Archives, 29.

15. Minutes of JS, Mar. 5, 1937, Minute Book of JS 1935–1942, JS Archives, 67.

16. Such other societies included the short-lived Woodrow Wilson Society.

17. "Editorial," *Virginia Spectator* 89, no. 4 (Jan. 1929): 189–190.

18. By-Laws of JS, 1935, Article 1, Section 3, a, JS Archives.

19. Ibid.

20. See, for example, minutes of JS, Apr. 23, 1937, Minute Book of JS 1935–1942, JS Archives, 79.

21. Minutes of JS, May 22, 1936, Minute Book of JS 1935–1942, JS Archives, 15.

22. Ibid.

23. Ibid., 24.

24. Minutes of JS, May 28, 1937, Minute Book of JS 1935–1942, JS Archives, 103–104.

25. Werner L. Janney, "God Loves Jeff Men," *University of Virginia Magazine* 95, no. 1 (Sept. 1936): 12.

26. Dabney, *Mr. Jefferson's University*, 147.

27. Ibid.

28. Janney, "God Loves Jeff Men," 12.

29. Constitution of JS, 1935, Article 1, Section 1, a, JS Archives.

30. Janney, "God Loves Jeff Men," 28.

31. Dabney, *Mr. Jefferson's University*, 87.

32. Minutes of JS, Dec. 3, 1938, Minute Book of JS 1935–1942, JS Archives, 234.

33. Minutes of JS, Nov. 12, 1936, Minute Book of JS 1935–1942, JS Archives, 128.

34. Minutes of JS, Nov. 27, 1940, Minute Book of JS 1935–1942, JS Archives, 437.

35. The oratorical contest faded in and out of existence several times during this period due to a lack of funding and participation. See minutes of JS, Feb. 24, 1939, Minute Book of JS 1935–1942, JS Archives, 255, for an example of one of its revivals. It would not become a permanent annual program again until Dr. Benjamin C. Moomaw began to sponsor the contest in 1948.

36. Dabney, *Mr. Jefferson's University*, 226.

37. Minutes of JS, May 13, 1938, Minute Book of JS 1935–1942, JS Archives, 168.

38. Minutes of JS, Apr. 29, 1938, Minute Book of JS 1935–1942, JS Archives, 290.

39. See, for example, Warner Janney, "A Cantering Tale by Jeff Chaucer," minutes of JS, Feb. 29, 1937, Minute Book of JS 1935–1942, JS Archives, 61.

40. Receipt Book, 1936, JS Archives.

41. Minutes of JS, May 28, 1937, Minute Book of JS 1935–1942, JS Archives, 106.

42. "A History of the Jefferson Society of the University of Virginia for the Session, 1935–36," Minute Book of JS 1935–1942, JS Archives, 26.

43. Ibid.

44. See, for example "Many Outsiders Will Attend Jeff Banquet This Coming Monday," *College Topics* 47, no. 83 (May 12, 1936): 1–2.

45. "Wilson Dinner," *College Topics* 47, no. 84 (May 14, 1936): 1.

46. "A History of the Jefferson Society . . . for the Session, 1935–36," 26.

47. "Dieterich and Connally Laud Wilson at Memorial Banquet," *College Topics* 47, no. 86 (May 18, 1936): 1–2.

48. See, for example, "Many Outsiders Will Attend Jeff Banquet This Coming Monday."

49. "A History of the Jefferson Society . . . for the Session, 1935–36," 26.

50. Minutes of JS, May 18, 1936, Minute Book of JS 1935–1942, JS Archives, 22.

51. Minutes of JS, May 22, 1936, Minute Book of JS 1935–1942, JS Archives, 25.

52. "Literary Societies to Hold Poe Night," *College Topics* 38, no. 54 (Jan. 27, 1926): 1.

53. Minutes of JS, May 22, 1936, Minute Book of JS 1935–1942, JS Archives, 25; Minutes of JS, Jan. 27, 1939, Minute Book of JS 1935–1942, JS Archives, 248.

54. "History of the Session, 1937–38," Minute Book of JS 1935–1942, JS Archives, 185.

55. "Song of the Marching Jefferson," Minute Book of JS 1935–1942, JS Archives, 100; "For the Sake of Posterity or the Underlying Circumstances That Made a Special Meeting Imperative on February 6, 1938," JS Archives.

56. "History of the Session, 1937–38," 185.

57. Minutes of JS, Mar. 26, 1937, Minute Book of JS 1935–1942, JS Archives, 71.

58. "Meeting of Assembly Addressed by Wilkin on Function, Powers," *College Topics* 47, no. 10 (Oct. 9, 1936): 1; "*College Topics* Rewards Musselman with Post of Editor," *College Topics* 46, no. 50 (Apr. 5, 1935): 1.

59. "History of the Session, 1937–38," 182.

60. Ibid., 183.

61. See Coleman Rosenberger, "Spectator as Phoenix: 100 Years," *Virginia Spectator* 100, no. 1 (Sept. 1938): 6.

62. "Song of the Marching Jefferson."

63. Minutes of JS, Oct. 15, 1937, Minute Book of JS 1935–1942, JS Archives, 123.

64. "History of the Session, 1937–38," 185.

65. Ibid.

66. Ibid., 183.

67. Minutes of JS, Dec. 3, 1937, Minute Book of JS 1935–1942, JS Archives, 131.

68. "For the Sake of Posterity."

69. "History of the Session, 1937–38," 184. It remains unclear whether Mr. Jacob did commit the malfeasance of which he was accused (incorrectly dating a regular member's signing of the roll book to reestablish his voting rights), or whether it was simply a cover by Musselman to exact revenge. While it seems to have been established that the signature was dated incorrectly, it is unknown whether this was an intentional deception or simply a scrivener's error.

70. Minutes of JS, Jan. 7, 1937, Minute Book of JS 1935–1942, JS Archives, 136.

71. "For the Sake of Posterity."

72. "History of the Session, 1937–38," 185.

73. "For the Sake of Posterity."

74. Ibid.

75. Ibid.

76. Ibid.

77. "New Virginia Magazine to Make Appearance as Virginia Spectator," *College Topics* 39, no. 35 (Dec. 2, 1927): 1.

78. Rosenberger, "Spectator as Phoenix," 6.

79. "Societies Will Act to Revive Magazine," *College Topics* 39, no. 24 (Nov. 9, 1927): 1.

80. Thelin, *A History of American Higher Education*, 218.

81. "Editorial," *University of Virginia Magazine* 76, no. 1 (Oct. 1925): 31.

82. Ibid.

83. Gilmore Spencer, "Mulatto Flair," *University of Virginia Magazine* 87, no. 1 (Oct. 1926): 8; Dabney, *Mr. Jefferson's University*, 98.

84. Spencer, "Mulatto Flair," 8.

85. "The Magazine Review," *College Topics* 37, no. 5 (Oct. 15, 1926): 2.

86. "Magazine Vulgarity," *College Topics* 37, no. 6 (Oct. 19, 1926): 2.

87. "Virginia Magazine Staff Suffers Reorganization," *College Topics* 37, no. 5 (Oct. 15, 1926): 1.

88. Dabney, *Mr. Jefferson's University*, 98.

89. "Virginia Magazine Staff Suffers Reorganization," 1.

90. "Work Is Continued to Revive Magazine," *College Topics* 39, no. 22 (Nov. 4, 1927): 1.

91. "Societies Will Act to Revive Magazine," *College Topics* 39, no. 24 (Nov. 9, 1927): 1.

92. "Editorial," *Virginia Spectator* 88, no. 1 (Dec. 1927): 15.

93. Ibid.

94. Dabney, *Mr. Jefferson's University*, 181.

95. *Virginia Spectator* 93, no. 1 (Oct. 1934): 3.

96. "Ben Billet," Poetry Foundation, retrieved from http://www.poetryfoundation.org/bio/ben-belitt, accessed Mar. 15, 2015.

97. Dabney, *Mr. Jefferson's University*, 226.

98. See, for example, a discussion of sea power and its potential implications for the coming conflict; minutes of JS, Nov. 18, 1938, Minute Book of JS 1935–1942, JS Archives, 229.

99. Samuel Irving Rosenman, ed., *The Public Papers and Addresses of Franklin Delano Roosevelt*, 13 vols. (New York: Macmillan, 1938–1950), 9, 263–264; "The Hand That Held the Dagger: FDR Delivers Historic Speech in Mem Gym," *Virginia Magazine* (Summer 2013), retrieved from http://uvamagazine.org/articles/the_hand_that_held_the_dagger, accessed Mar. 17, 2015.

100. Ibid.

101. Dabney, *Mr. Jefferson's University*, 229.

102. Ibid.

103. Thelin, *A History of American Higher Education*, 257.

104. Jennings L. Wagoner Jr. and Robert L. Baxter Jr., "Higher Education Goes to War: The University of Virginia's Response to World War II," *Virginia Magazine of History and Biography* 100, no. 3 (July 1992): 404.

105. *Alumni Bulletin* 5 (Mar. 1943): 1.

106. William H. Wranek Jr., "University of Virginia War Program," 3, and "Enrollment Report Summaries," University of Virginia Office of Institutional Analysis, William H. Wranek Papers, Accession #6838, U.Va.

107. Wagoner and Baxter, "Higher Education Goes to War," 407.

108. Ibid., 408.

109. Dabney, *Mr. Jefferson's University*, 238.

110. Wagoner and Baxter, "Higher Education Goes to War," 413.

111. Ibid., 415.

112. *Weather or Not* 1, no. 2 (Oct. 18, 1943): 3–8.

113. "Roll for 1941–1942," Minute Book of JS 1935–1942, JS Archives, 552–555, as compared to minutes of JS, Dec. 4, 1942, loose pages, JS Archives.

114. Minutes of JS, Nov. 13, 1942, loose pages, JS Archives.

115. Minutes of JS, Dec. 4, 1942, loose pages, JS Archives.

116. Ibid.

117. Ibid.

118. "Jefferson Society Will Reorganize," *College Topics* 54, no. 17 (Nov. 25, 1943): 1; "Jeff Society States Plans for Nimbus," *College Topics* 54, no. 21 (Jan. 6, 1944): 1; "No Official Release Yet on Interim Committee," *College Topics* 54, no. 32 (Jan. 8, 1943): 1.

119. "Spectator Notice," *College Topics* 54, no. 48 (Feb. 17, 1943): 4.

120. Wagoner and Baxter, "Higher Education Goes to War," 423.

121. "Spectator to Appear Next Week," *College Topics* 55, no. 14 (Sept. 29, 1944): 1.

122. Charles S. Russell, "Victory Night and Its Implications," *Virginia Spectator* 107, no. 1 (Aug. 1945): 3.

123. "Vanguardia," *Virginia Spectator* 107, no. 3 (Jan. 1946): 1.

124. Dabney, *Mr. Jefferson's University*, 283.

125. Wagoner and Baxter, "Higher Education Goes to War," 408, 424–425.

126. Ibid, 427; Thelin, *A History of American Higher Education*, 263.

127. Thelin, *A History of American Higher Education*, 263; Edwin Kiester Jr., "The G.I. Bill May Be the Best Deal Ever Made by Uncle Sam," *Smithsonian* 25 (Nov. 1994): 128–139.

128. Thelin, *A History of American Higher Education*, 263.

129. Ibid.

130. Dabney, *Mr. Jefferson's University*, 249.

131. Ibid.

132. Thelin, *A History of American Higher Education*, 212.

133. Wagoner and Baxter, "Higher Education Goes to War," 427.

134. Thelin, *A History of American Higher Education*, 266.

135. Ibid, 307.

136. "Jefferson Society to Hold Debate Program Tonight," *College Topics* 56, no. 17 (Oct. 11, 1949): 1.

137. "Vital Topics Discussed by Jefferson Society," *College Topics* 40, no. 44 (Jan. 23, 1929): 1, 3.

138. "Dos Passos Speaks Tonight," *Cavalier Daily* 63, no. 119 (Apr. 12, 1957): 1.

139. For a rich resource regarding Faulkner's time as writer-in-residence at the University of Virginia, see William Faulkner, Frederick L. Gwynn, and Joseph Blotner, *Faulkner in the University: Class Conferences at the University of Virginia, 1957–1958* (Charlottesville, VA: University of Virginia Press, 1959).

140. William Faulkner to Professor A. B. Shepperson, Dec. 1, 1957, Faulkner Papers, Digitization #000003743_0062, U.Va.

141. "From Jefferson Hall," *Cavalier Daily* 63, no. 135 (May 17, 1957): 2.

142. Ibid.

143. Ibid.

144. Minutes of JS, Mar. 21, 1958, Minute Book of JS 1957–1962, JS Archives, 66.

145. Minutes of JS, Jan. 7, 1949, Minute Book of JS 1947–1951, JS Archives, 91.

146. "Gubernatorial Candidate Will Address University Audience at 8 Tonight," *College Topics* 55, no. 112 (Apr. 27, 1949): 1.

147. Minutes of JS, Nov. 3, 1940, Minute Book of JS 1935–1942, JS Archives, 224.

148. Ibid.; minutes of JS, Dec. 1, 1940, Minute Book of JS 1935–1942, JS Archives, 230.

149. "Jefferson Society and Oratory," *College Topics* 51, no. 68 (Apr. 17, 1940): 2.

150. Minutes of JS, Mar. 19, 1948, Minute Book of JS 1947–1951, JS Archives, 55.

151. "Brown, Dale, Pierce Win Second Contest," *College Topics* 54, no. 77 (May 7, 1948): 1.

152. "Jeff Society Sponsors Oratorical Contest," *College Topics* 54, no. 61 (Apr. 8, 1948): 1.

153. Minutes of JS, Apr. 20, 1951, Minute Book of JS 1947–1951, JS Archives, 259.

154. "Jefferson Society in Politics," *Cavalier Daily* 63, no. 87 (Mar. 12, 1957): 2.

155. Minutes of JS, Mar. 15, 1957, Minute Book of JS 1957–1962, JS Archives, 9–10.

156. "From Jefferson Hall," *Cavalier Daily* 63, no. 114 (Apr. 5, 1957): 2.

157. "College Council Candidates Take Platform Tonight," *Cavalier Daily* 63, no. 122 (Apr. 25, 1957): 1.

158. Ibid.

159. Ibid.

160. JS Meeting Notes, May 1, 1946, Rough Log 1945, JS Archives.

161. Minutes of JS, Sept. 26, 1947, Minute Book of JS 1947–1951, JS Archives, 3; "Activities and Student Indifference," *College Topics* 55, no. 113 (Apr. 28, 1949): 4.

162. Dave Gordon, "Jefferson Society Now Accepting Members; Has 127 Year History," *Cavalier Daily* 59, no. 46 (Dec. 11, 1952): 2.

163. Ibid.

164. Philip Kolvoord, "Jefferson Society Has 131-Year History," *Cavalier Daily* 63, no. 48 (Dec. 4, 1956): 2.

165. Gordon, "Jefferson Society Now Accepting Members," 2.

166. Minutes of JS, May 23, 1957, Minute Book of JS 1957–1962, JS Archives, 28.

167. Dabney, *Mr. Jefferson's University*, 328.

168. "Free Love Discussed at Jeff Meeting Tonight," *Cavalier Daily* 56, no. 79 (Mar. 3, 1950): 1.

169. Ibid.

170. Minutes of JS, Oct. 24, 1947, Minute Book of JS 1947–1951, JS Archives, 11.

171. "Free Love Discussed at Jeff Meeting Tonight," 1.

172. See, for example, minutes of JS, May 12, 1950, Minute Book of JS 1947–1951, JS Archives, 210.

173. Minutes of JS, Dec. 9, 1949, Minute Book of JS 1947–1951, JS Archives, 194.

174. See, for example, Minutes of JS, Dec. 10, 1949, Minute Book of JS 1947–1951, JS Archives, 89.

175. See, for example, Minutes of JS, Jan. 14, 1949, Minute Book of JS 1947–1951, JS Archives, 99–101.

176. Minutes of JS, Mar. 22, 1957, Minute Book of JS 1957–1962, JS Archives, 11.

177. "Jeff Society to Hold Party for Members," *Cavalier Daily* 56, no. 94 (Mar. 24, 1950): 1.

178. Minutes of JS, Mar. 10, 1950, Minute Book of JS 1947–1951, JS Archives, 204.

179. "Breaking and Making Tradition: Women at the University of Virginia," University of Virginia Library, retrieved from https://www.lib.virginia.edu/small/exhibits/women/ grad_profi.html, accessed Mar. 15, 2015.

180. Minutes of JS, Apr. 26, 1949, Minute Book of JS 1947–1951, JS Archives, 145.

181. Minutes of JS, May 3, 1957, Minute Book of JS 1957–1962, JS Archives, 19.

182. "Jefferson Society Holds Annual Elections Today," *Cavalier Daily* 60, no. 63 (Jan. 15, 1954): 1.

183. *Virginia Spectator* 107, no. 1 (Aug. 1945): 1.

184. Ibid.

185. *Virginia Spectator* 109, no. 3 (Dec. 1947): 1.

186. Minutes of JS, Mar. 2, 1951, Minute Book of JS 1947–1951, JS Archives, 246.

187. Jim Plowden-Wardlaw, "'Spectator' Was Once 'Serious Publication,'" *Cavalier Daily* 63, no. 54 (Dec. 12, 1956): 2.

188. Karl B. Knust Jr., "Spectator to Sparkle," *Cavalier Daily* 59, no. 2 (Sept. 19, 1952): 2.

189. Alexander Whitaker, "Former 'Spectator' Editor Defends Magazine," *Cavalier Daily* 64, no. 113 (May 1, 1958): 2.

190. Ibid.

191. Thomas Morgan, "Too Much Sex Found in Magazine," *Cavalier Daily* 60, no. 21 (Oct. 20, 1953): 2.

192. David J. Hatmaker, "Spectator Issue 'More Than Silly,'" *Cavalier Daily* 60, no. 42 (Nov. 25, 1953): 2.

193. "'Spectator' Claims Southern Victory in Weekend Issue," *Cavalier Daily* 61, no. 19 (Oct. 15, 1954): 1; see also *Virginia Spectator* 116, no. 1 (Oct. 1954).

194. Gordon Smith, "From Jefferson Hall," *Cavalier Daily* 64, no. 86 (Mar. 8, 1958): 2.

195. "Spectator Issue Models 'Punch' Termed 'Classic,'" *Cavalier Daily* 64, no. 76 (Feb. 21, 1958): 1.

196. Dabney, *Mr. Jefferson's University*, 290.

197. "Spectator Issue Models 'Punch' Termed 'Classic,'" 1.

198. Andy Ruckman, "President Launches Investigation of 'Spectator,'" *Cavalier Daily* 64, no. 79 (Feb. 27, 1958): 1.

199. Ibid.

200. Andy Ruckman, "Committee Censures Two Student Publications," *Cavalier Daily* 64, no. 87 (Mar. 11, 1958): 1.

201. Dabney, *Mr. Jefferson's University*, 290.

202. Ibid.

203. Fred Quayle, "Students Seek Literary Magazine for University," *Cavalier Daily* 62, no. 83 (Feb. 24, 1956): 2.

204. *University of Virginia Magazine* 1, no. 1 (Spring 1956): 1–3.

205. "Students Respond 'Encouragingly' Towards Magazine," *Cavalier Daily* 62, no. 129 (May 15, 1956): 1.

CHAPTER SEVEN

1. Frederick Rudolph, *The American College and University: A History* (Athens, GA: University of Georgia Press, 1962), 339–340, 427.

2. Virginius Dabney, *Mr. Jefferson's University: A History* (Charlottesville, VA: University of Virginia Press, 1981), 422–423.

3. Dan Heuchert, "Hereford's Half-Century: Former President Remembered as Link between U.Va.'s Past and Future," *InsideUVA Online* (Oct. 1–14, 2004); retrieved from http://www.virginia.edu/insideuva/2004/17/hereford_frank.html, accessed Dec. 1, 2014. See also Dabney, *Mr. Jefferson's University*, 422–466.

4. A series of reports have detailed conditions faced by both African American students and African American faculty and staff since the University became integrated. See University of Virginia Task Force on Afro-American Affairs, "An Audacious Faith: Report of the Task Force on Afro-American Affairs University of Virginia," (June 1987), Accession # RG-20/80/1.871, U.Va.; University of Virginia Office of Equal Opportunity Programs, "An Examination of the University's Minority Classified Staff: The Muddy Floor Report" (June 1996); retrieved from https://blackfireuva.files.wordpress.com/2012/02/an-examination-of-the-universitys-minority-classified-staff-the-muddy-floor-report.pdf, accessed Feb. 15, 2015; and Angela M. Davis and Michael J. Smith, "Embracing Diversity in Pursuit of Excellence: Report of the President's Commission on Diversity and Equity" (Sept. 10, 2004), Accession # RG-20/86/1.041, U.Va. In 2013, Teresa A. Sullivan created the President's Commission on Slavery and the University, to be chaired by Marcus Martin, the vice president and chief officer for diversity and equity, and Kirt von Daacke, professor of history. The commission is charged to "provide advice and recommendations to the President on the commemoration of the University of Virginia's

historical relationship with slavery and enslaved people" and to "explore and report on UVA's historical relationship with slavery, highlighting opportunities for recognition and commemoration."

5. Heuchert, "Hereford's Half-Century."

6. Dabney, *Mr. Jefferson's University*, 428; "State of the University: Q&A with President Teresa Sullivan," *UVA Magazine* (Summer 2011); retrieved from http://uvamagazine.org/articles/the_state_of_the_university/, accessed Feb. 15, 2015.

7. Rudolph, *The American College and University: A History*, 464.

8. Dabney, *Mr. Jefferson's University*, 470.

9. "The Jefferson Society," *Cavalier Daily* 72, no. 37 (Nov. 17, 1961): 1.

10. The goings-on of Skull and Keys and Lambda Pi, particularly their nomination of candidates for major student offices, received considerable coverage in the *Cavalier Daily*. See, for example, Richard Moore, "Political Societies Will Meet Tonight to Choose Candidates," *Cavalier Daily* 72, no. 35 (Nov. 15, 1961): 1.

11. Minutes of JS, Mar. 31, 1967, Minute Book of JS 1966–1970, JS Archives, 23.

12. Minutes of JS, Mar. 3, 1961, Minute Book of JS 1957–1962, JS Archives, 205.

13. Minutes of JS, Oct. 7, 1960, Minute Book of JS 1957–1962, JS Archives, 153.

14. Minutes of JS, Nov. 22, 1963, Minute Book of JS 1963–1966, JS Archives, 15–16.

15. Minutes of JS, Dec. 6, 1963, Minute Book of JS 1963–1966, JS Archives, 19.

16. Minutes of JS, Jan. 15, 1960, Minute Book of JS 1957–1962, JS Archives, 106.

17. Minutes of JS, Dec. 11, 1964, Minute Book of JS 1963–1966, JS Archives, 64.

18. Minutes of JS, Apr. 22, 1960, Minute Book of JS 1957–1962, JS Archives, 124.

19. Minutes of JS, May 12, 1961, Minute Book of JS 1957–1962, JS Archives, 230.

20. Minutes of JS, Apr. 22, 1960, Minute Book of JS, 1957–1962, JS Archives, 124.

21. Minutes of JS, Oct. 23, 1964, Minute Book of JS, 1963–1966, JS Archives, 56.

22. Minutes of JS, Jan. 5, 1973, Minute Book of JS 1972–1974, JS Archives, 33.

23. Minutes of JS, Oct. 30, 1964, Minute Book of JS 1963–1966, JS Archives, 58.

24. Minutes of JS, May 12, 1972, Minute Book of JS 1972–1974, JS Archives, 4.

25. One particularly raucous tradition was observed during this time: the bestowing of the "Kevy Award" to the most obnoxious member of the Society. The honoree was bestowed a (hopefully clean) colostomy bag, from which he was expected to chug a good deal of beer from the Keeper's keg.

26. "Ode to Jefferson Hall," Minute Book of JS 1963–1966, JS Archives.

27. These can be found, respectively, in: Minutes of JS, Oct. 20, 1972, Minute Book of JS 1972–1974, JS Archives, 15; Minutes of JS, Nov. 3, 1972, Minute Book of JS 1972–1974, JS Archives, 17; Minutes of JS, Nov. 9, 1973, Minute Book of JS 1972–1974, JS Archives, 101; Minutes of JS, Nov. 17, 1972, Minute Book of JS 1972–1974, JS Archives, 21; Minutes of JS, Oct. 12, 1973, Minute Book of JS 1972–1974, JS Archives, 91; Minutes of JS, Jan. 18, 1974, Minute Book of JS, 1972–1974, JS Archives, 123; and Minutes of JS, Oct. 22, 1973, Minute Book of JS 1972–1974, JS Archives, 97.

28. Minutes of JS, Jan. 5, 1973, Minute Book of JS 1972–1974, JS Archives, 29.

29. "Origins of Dawn Pilgrimage," *Jefferson Society Journal*, Fall 1986, 2, JS Archives.

30. Minutes of JS, Dec. 15, 1972, Minute Book of JS 1972–1974, JS Archives, 28.

31. Chester R. Titus to William T. Walker, Nov. 5, 1964, JS Archives.

32. Minutes of JS, Nov. 13, 1964, Minute Book of JS 1963–1966, JS Archives, 60.

33. "Selection of Nominees for the Founding Room," 1964, JS Archives.

34. Constitution of the Seven Sours Sippers Society, JS Archives.

35. Ibid.

36. Ibid.

37. "The Selection Process for the Resident of Room 7 West Lawn, the Founding Room of the Jefferson Literary and Debating Society," 1987, JS Archives; Patricia M. Lampkin to Peter Milligan, Feb. 23, 2004, JS Archives; Peter Milligan to Patricia M. Lampkin, Feb. 24, 2004, JS Archives; Peter Milligan to Patricia M. Lampkin, Nov. 30, 2004, JS Archives.

38. "Room 7 Account Founded," *Jefferson Society Journal*, Fall 1986, 3, JS Archives.

39. Dabney, *Mr. Jefferson's University*, 504.

40. For an excellent overview of the different building phases in the University's history, see Office of the Architect for the University, *University of Virginia Grounds Plan, 2008*, "Section I: History"; retrieved from http://www.officearchitect.virginia.edu/GroundsPlan Website/GPNEW/FinalPDF/Sec_1_History.pdf, accessed Feb. 15, 2015.

41. Dabney, *Mr. Jefferson's University*, 504.

42. Thomas Rawles Jones Jr. to Edgar F. Shannon, Mar. 25, 1971, JS Archives.

43. Ibid.

44. Steve Grimwood and Richard Jones, "Students Plan Mass Demonstration against Expansion," *Cavalier Daily* 82, no. 17 (Oct. 13, 1971): 1.

45. Peter H. Shea, "Protests to Continue Despite Shannon's Plea," *Cavalier Daily* 82, no. 20 (Oct. 18, 1971): 1; Ginger Fitz, Beverly Dowell, and Tim Wheeler, "Protest Dwindles Following Sleep-In," *Cavalier Daily* 82, no. 22 (Oct. 20, 1971): 1.

46. "U.Va. Celebrating 75th Anniversary of Alderman Library's Opening," *UVA Today*; retrieved from http://news.virginia.edu/content/uva-celebrating-75th-anniversary-alderman-library-s-opening, accessed Feb. 21, 2015.

47. "Interior Reconstruction Will Restore the Rotunda's Functions," *University Register* (May 11, 1972): 1.

48. Alan Cooper, "U.Va. Rotunda Restoration Due," *Richmond Times Dispatch* (newspaper clipping), JS Archives.

49. Henry Curry, "University Guide Service Proves Very Successful," *Cavalier Daily* 72, no. 35 (Nov. 15, 1961): 2.

50. Cooper, "U.Va. Rotunda Restoration Due"; Henry Curry, "Betts Collection of Old Prints on Exhibit at Alderman Library," *Cavalier Daily* 73, no. 4 (Sept. 26, 1962): 2.

51. "Studies Undertaken to Restore Rotunda, Jefferson Society Formal Ball Will Reestablish Tradition," *Cavalier Daily* 64, no. 106 (May 1, 1964): 1, 4.

52. Restoration Ball Press Release, May 5, 1967, JS Archives.

53. Restoration Ball Planning Document, 1967, JS Archives.

54. Restoration Ball Press Release, 1972, JS Archives.

55. Bob Humphreys, "Rotunda," *Cavalier Daily* 84, no. 119 (Apr. 19, 1973): 1; Carolyn Yeamans, Letter to the Editor, *Cavalier Daily* 84, no. 120 (Apr. 20, 1973): 2.

56. Draft of Restoration Ball Newspaper Story, 1967, JS Archives.

57. Ibid.

58. Ibid.

59. Ibid.

60. Mary Hall Betts to the Society of the Purple Shadows, May 14, 1969, JS Archives.

61. Dabney, *Mr. Jefferson's University*, 520. The JS Archives contain two draft press releases from 1970, one to announce the ball would proceed as planned, and one announcing that the ball would be cancelled because of the unrest. Kathleen D. Valenzi, "Protest! A History of Student Unrest at Virginia, " *UVA Magazine* (Fall 2002): 26–31; see also Alexander Gray, "President Edgar Finley Shannon Jr. and May Days," *Academical Heritage Review* 1, no. 1 (Spring 2010): 95–123.

62. Downing Smith, "Letters to the Editor: Downing Smith Comments on 1970 UVa 'Riot,'" Dec. 27, 2003; retrieved from http://george.loper.org/archives/2003/Dec/783.html, accessed Feb. 15, 2015.

63. Valenzi, "Protest! A History of Student Unrest at Virginia," 28–30.

64. For a detailed and thoroughly researched account of the history of the construction and restoration of the Rotunda, see Office of the Architect, University of Virginia, "Rotunda Historic Structure Report"; retrieved from http://www.officearchitect.virginia.edu/pdfs/history.pdf, accessed Oct. 4, 2014.

65. "Interior Reconstruction Will Restore the Rotunda's Functions," *University Register* (May 11, 1972): 1.

66. Restoration Ball Press Release, 1973, JS Archives.

67. "Eleventh Restoration Ball Scheduled April 27," *Cavalier Daily* 85, no. 111 (Mar. 28, 1974): 1.

68. Patricia Cooper, "Swing Your Partner," *Cavalier Daily* (Mar. 20, 2003); retrieved from http://www.cavalierdaily.com/m/article/2003/03/swing-your-partner/, accessed Feb. 15, 2015.

69. Daniel DeVise, "U.-Va. Rotunda Waits in Line for Repairs," *Washington Post*, Mar. 1, 2011; retrieved from http://www.washingtonpost.com/wp-dyn/content/article/2011/03/01/AR2011030107186.html, accessed Feb. 15, 2015; Abby Meredith, "University Pushes Forward with $51 Million Rotunda Restoration," *Cavalier Daily* (Dec. 2, 2011); retrieved from http://www.cavalierdaily.com/article/2011/12/university-pushes-forward-with-51-million-rotunda-restoration, accessed Feb. 15, 2015.

70. Michelle Davis, "Society Helps Raise Funds for Rotunda," *Cavalier Daily* (Mar. 21, 2011); retrieved from http://www.cavalierdaily.com/m/article/2011/03/society-helps-raise-funds-for-rotunda/, accessed Feb. 15, 2015.

71. Kelly Kaler, "Society Ball Raises Funds," *Cavalier Daily* (Mar. 26, 2012); retrieved from http://www.cavalierdaily.com/article/2012/03/society-ball-raises-funds, accessed Feb. 15, 2015.

72. Dabney, *Mr. Jefferson's University*, 480.

73. Atima Omara-Alwala, "Trailblazing against Tradition: The Public History of Desegregation at the University of Virginia 1955–75"; retrieved from http://xroads.virginia.edu/~ug03/omara-alwala/harrison/Trailblazing.html, accessed Nov. 16, 2014.

74. Ibid.

75. Minutes of JS, Mar. 18, 1960, Minute Book of JS 1957–1962, JS Archives, 117.

76. Omara-Alwala, "Trailblazing against Tradition."

77. Ibid.

78. Ibid.

79. "University Engineering School Will Inaugurate New Honors Program Next Fall for Gifted Students, Students Will Work with Tutors," *Cavalier Daily* 72, no. 36 (Nov. 16, 1961): 1.

80. Wesley Harris, interview with the authors, Nov. 20, 2014.

81. "Jefferson Society to Hear Longley This Evening," *Cavalier Daily* 66, no. 29 (Nov. 4, 1960): 1; "Jeff Society Hears Writer Tonight at 8," *Cavalier Daily* 69, no. 37 (Nov. 15, 1963): 1, 4.

82. Wesley Harris, interview with the authors, Nov. 20, 2014.

83. Ibid.

84. Handwritten notes, obverse of Draft Budget, Spring 1960, JS Archives.

85. Omara-Alwala, "Trailblazing against Tradition."

86. Wesley Harris, interview with the authors, Nov. 20, 2014.

87. Omara-Alwala, "Trailblazing against Tradition."

88. The Thomas Jefferson Chapter of the Council on Human Relations was founded in November 1961 by students from the early generations of African Americans at the University and became a rallying point for black students and their allies, including many of the faculty members with whom Harris became close. See "Human Relations Group Seeks Charter Approval, Student Council to Decide Status of Organization at Next Meeting," *Cavalier Daily* 72, no. 3 (Nov. 9, 1961): 1; Bill Marmon, "Human Relations Charter Approved, Constitution to Prohibit Picketing or Direct Action," *Cavalier Daily* 72, no. 36 (Nov. 15, 1961): 1; and Richard Hughes, "Human Relations Group Speaks at Negro Schools in Enrollment Project," *Cavalier Daily* 74, no. 107 (May 5, 1964): 1, 4.

89. "A Life, a Legacy: Honoring Martin Luther King Jr.," *University of Virginia Magazine* (Spring 2011); retrieved from http://uvamagazine.org/articles/a_life_a_legacy/, accessed Nov. 14, 2014.

90. Ibid.

91. Ibid.

92. Wesley Harris, Lecture to JS, Hotel C West Range (Jefferson Hall), Charlottesville, VA, Feb. 1, 2008, Charlottesville Podcasting Network; retrieved from http://www.cvillepublicmedia.org/jeffsociety/20080201-JS-Harris.mp3, accessed Nov. 16, 2014.

93. Harris, Lecture to JS, Feb. 1, 2008.

94. Wesley Harris, interview with the authors, Nov. 20, 2014.

95. Phyllis Leffler, "Mr. Jefferson's University: Women in the Village!" *Virginia Magazine of History and Biography* 115, no. 1 (2007): 58.

96. Ibid., 65.

97. Ibid., 62.

98. Ibid., 72. The standard gender history of higher education is Barbara Miller Solomon, *In the Company of Educated Women: A History of Women and Higher Education in America* (New Haven, CT: Yale University Press, 1985). See also Lynn D. Gordon, *Gender and Higher Education in the Progressive Era* (New Haven, CT: Yale University Press, 1990); Amy Thompson McCandless, *The Past in the Present: Women's Higher Education in the Twentieth-Century American South* (Tuscaloosa, AL: University of Alabama Press, 1999); Thelin, *A History of American Higher Education*, 142–145, 182–186, 126–129; and, on coordinate education, Rudolph, *The American College and University: A History*, 319–325.

99. Leffler, "Mr. Jefferson's University: Women in the Village!" 79.

100. Ibid., 61.

101. Ibid., 75.

102. Murray McGuire, "Some Objections to the Proposed Co-ordinate Women's College," *University of Virginia Alumni Bulletin* (Jan. 1914); quoted in Leffler, "Mr. Jefferson's University: Women in the Village!" 76–77.

103. Leffler, "Mr. Jefferson's University: Women in the Village!" 62.

104. Sierra Bellows, Carianne King, and Emma Rathbone, "Women at the University of Virginia," *UVA Magazine*, Spring 2011, 20–27.

105. Leffler, "Mr. Jefferson's University: Women in the Village!" 97–98.

106. Holly Smith, "Women Chisel Place from U.Va. Tradition, Chauvanism," *Richmond Times-Dispatch* (June 10, 1973): C1; Dabney, *Mr. Jefferson's University*, 490.

107. Minutes of JS, Jan. 24, 1920, and Feb. 14, 1920, Minute Book of JS 1919–1925, JS Archives, 130, 137.

108. Minutes of JS, Feb. 12, 1971, Minute Book of JS 1970–1971, JS Archives, 101.

109. Minutes of JS, Feb. 12 and 26, 1971, Minute Book of JS 1970–1971, JS Archives, 103, 107.

110. "To whom it may concern," undated, JS Archives.

111. Richard Petty and Bill Patterson, "Coed Threatens Law Suit against Jefferson Society," *Cavalier Daily* 82, no. 64 (Feb. 10, 1972): 1.

112. "Pick Up," Letter to the Editor, *Cavalier Daily* 82, no. 66 (Feb. 10, 1972): 3.

113. Petty and Patterson, "Coed Threatens Law Suit against Jefferson Society," 1.

114. Richard Jones, "Council Seeks Halt to Sex Discrimination," *Cavalier Daily* 82, no. 58 (Jan. 6, 1972): 1.

115. Richard Jones, "Sex Bias Scrutinized by Council," *Cavalier Daily* 82, no. 62 (Feb. 8, 1972): 1.

116. Mayne Moxley, "Jefferson Hall Admits Coed, Strikes 'Male' from By-Laws," *Cavalier Daily* 82, no. 67 (Feb. 15, 1972): 1.

117. Announcement, Feb. 12, 1972, JS Archives.

118. Ibid.

119. Ibid.

120. Moxley, "Jefferson Hall Admits Coed, Strikes 'Male' from By-Laws," 1.

121. Barbara Golden Lynn, interview with the authors, Oct. 29, 2014.

122. Ibid.

123. Mark Curriden, "Meet Barbara and Mike Lynn, Dallas' Legal Power Couple," *Dallas Morning News*, April 27, 2014; retrieved from http://www.dallasnews.com/business/headlines/20140426-meet-barbra-and-mike-lynn-dallas-legal-power-couple.ece, accessed Feb. 15, 2015.

124. Barbara Golden Lynn, Lecture to JS, Hotel C West Range (Jefferson Hall), Charlottesville, VA, Feb. 23, 2007, Charlottesville Podcasting Network; retrieved from http://www.cvillepublicmedia.org/public/js_lynn_070223.mp3, accessed Feb. 15, 2015.

125. "Woman Wins Moomaw Contest," *Cavalier Daily* 83, no. 106 (Apr. 25, 1972): 1.

126. Barbara Golden Lynn, interview with the authors, Oct. 29, 2014.

127. Curriden, "Meet Barbara and Mike Lynn, Dallas' Legal Power Couple."

128. Barbara Golden Lynn, Lecture to JS, Feb. 23, 2007.

129. Barbara Golden Lynn, interview with the authors, Oct. 29, 2014.

130. Robin Lee Ackerman and James M. Guinivan, "Jefferson Society Enters Its Second 150 Years," (1975), 5, JS Archives.

131. Ibid.

132. Minutes of JS, May 11, 1973, Minute Book of JS 1972–1974, JS Archives, 74.

133. For example, Jim Andrews, "Openings Is First Issue of UVM," *Cavalier Daily* 73, no. 4 (Sept. 26, 1962): 1.

134. Dabney, *Mr. Jefferson's University*, 552; "UVM Announces Release of First Christmas Issue," *Cavalier Daily* 73, no. 29 (Nov. 6, 1962): 1.

135. James Guinvan to Thomas H. Justice, July 30, 1974, JS Archives.

136. Stephen C. Jordan to [Anonymous Donor?], Sept. 3, 1990, JS Archives.

137. Articles of Incorporation of U.V.M., Inc., Oct. 23, 1990, JS Archives.

138. Stephen C. Jordan to [Anonymous Donor?], Sept. 3, 1990, JS Archives.

139. Sesquicentennial of the Jefferson Society, Program of Events, Apr. 11–13, 1975, JS Archives.

140. Ackerman and Guinivan, "Jefferson Society Enters Its Second 150 Years."

141. Robin Lee Ackerman to Michael Shortley, June 30, 1975, JS Archives.

142. Historical Report of JS 1974–1975, JS Archives.

CHAPTER EIGHT

1. See Burton Weisbrod, Jeffrey Ballou, and Evelyn Asch, *Mission and Money: Understanding the University* (New York: Cambridge University Press, 2008), 189–193; and David L. Kirp, *Shakespeare, Einstein, and the Bottom Line: The Marketing of Higher Education* (Cambridge, MA: Harvard University Press, 2003), 11–17.

2. Dan Heuchert, "Hereford's Half-Century: Former President Remembered as Link between U.Va.'s Past and Future," *InsideUVA Online* (Oct. 1–14, 2004); retrieved from http://www.virginia.edu/insideuva/2004/17/hereford_frank.html, accessed Dec. 1, 2014; Owen Gallogly, "The 'Merriest Time of All the Year': A History of Easters at the University of Virginia," *Academical Heritage Review* 3, no. 1 (Spring 2012): 7–13.

3. Robin Lee Ackerman and James M. Guinivan, "Jefferson Society Enters Its Second 150 Years," (1975), 5, JS Archives.

4. Ibid.

5. Ibid.

6. Benjamin S. Duval, Jr., newspaper clipping, JS Archives; or, for example, "Jeff Society to Interview," *Cavalier Daily* 73, no. 95 (May 1, 1963): 1.

7. "To whom it may concern," undated, JS Archives.

8. Minutes of JS, Feb. 15, 1957, Minute Book of JS 1957–1962, JS Archives, 1.

9. Minutes of JS, Sept. 23, 1977, Minute Book of JS 1974–1983, JS Archives, 52.

10. "Choyce Amendment Expands Probie Options," *Jefferson Society Journal*, Summer 1982, 1, JS Archives.

11. Constitution of JS, 1982, JS Archives.

12. Donna M. Allmon to Probationary Members, Feb. 1, 1988, JS Archives.

13. Minutes of JS, Feb. 7, 1958, Minute Book of JS 1957–1962, JS Archives, 56; Minutes of JS, Apr. 14, 1961, Minute Book of JS 1957–1962, JS Archives, 222; "Frost Will Lecture in Cabell Hall at 8, Jeff Society Will Sponsor Luncheon in Poet's Honor," *Cavalier Daily* 66,

no. 98 (Apr. 28, 1961): 1; "Novelist Dos Passos to Speak," *Cavalier Daily* 73, no. 4 (Sept. 26, 1962): 1; "Dos Passos Reads Tonight at Meeting, Writer-in-Residence Gives Manuscripts to Alderman," *Cavalier Daily* 74, no. 56 (Feb. 8, 1963): 1; Minutes of JS, Oct. 14, 1988, JS Archives; Letter from Justice William H. Rehnquist to Edward Finley, July 23, 1985, JS Archives. A full listing of speakers since 1992 is available from http://jeffersonsociety .org/about/speakers/.

14. "Bunche Will Speak in Cabell Tomorrow," *Cavalier Daily* 66, no. 51 (Jan. 5, 1961): 1; "Jefferson Society to Present Talk by Official of State Department," *Cavalier Daily* 66, no. 90 (Apr. 14, 1961): 1.

15. "South African Ambassador Scheduled to Give Talk on African Affairs in Newcomb Hall This Evening," *Cavalier Daily* 66, no. 68 (Feb. 24, 1961): 1.

16. Edgar F. Shannon Jr. to JS, Feb. 24, 1961, JS Archives.

17. "Groups Join Jefferson Society in Tshombe Visa Denial Protest," *Cavalier Daily* 72, no. 70 (Feb. 23, 1962): 1.

18. "Intervention in Katanga," *Cavalier Daily* 72, no. 70 (Feb. 23, 1962): 2, reprinted from *Richmond News Leader.*

19. Struelens was the director of the Katanga Information Services, an arm of Tshombe's government in New York City. "Katanga Representative Will Address Society," *Cavalier Daily* 72, no. 104 (May 2, 1962): 1; "Jefferson Society Reports on Congo, Katanga Observers Publish Findings of African Visit," *Cavalier Daily* 73, no. 16 (Oct. 17, 1962).

20. "U.N. Katanga Policy Attacked in Address by Michael Struelens," *Cavalier Daily* 72, no. 111 (May 15, 1962): 1; "Jefferson Society Reports on Congo," 1. See also Joseph Freeman III, "Katanga," *University of Virginia Magazine* 126, no. 1 (Dec. 1962): 18–20.

21. "Yoo Speeches Arouse Discussion, Criticism: Former Bush Administration Official Visits Grounds to Publicize Book; Protestors Deride Political Background," *Cavalier Daily* 121, no. 124 (Mar. 22, 2010): 1.

22. "[Washington] Society History," Washington Literary Society and Debating Union; retrieved from https://pages.shanti.virginia.edu/Washington_Society/about/history/, accessed Mar. 10, 2015.

23. Josh Henson to Washington Society, Dec. 14, 2006, JS Archives.

24. Even though the debate has historically been referred to as the Harrison Trophy debate, for some reason the name changed to the Harrison Cup when it resumed, presumably in part because the plaque itself had long been missing, prior to its rediscovery in 2012.

25. Josh Henson to Washington Society, Apr. 17, 2007, JS Archives.

26. Josh Henson to Washington Society, Dec. 14, 2006, JS Archives.

27. "Diplomacy Debate Firmly Established," *The Jefferson Journal,* Fall 1987, JS Archives.

28. Dennis Hevesi, "Foreign Service Officer R. Smith Simpson Dies at 103," *New York Times,* Sept. 10, 2010, A33.

29. Smith Simpson to the Presidents of the Washington and Jefferson Literary Societies, Oct. 7, 1988, JS Archives.

30. Smith Simpson to Julia King, Apr. 17, 1990, JS Archives.

31. James Guinivan to Angus Macaulay, Dec. 8, 1986, JS Archives.

32. James Guinivan to George Le Sauvage, July 8, 1986, JS Archives.

33. Bok Lee, "Society Takes on Incident," *Cavalier Daily* 102, no. 92 (Feb. 8, 1992): 1; Chris

Wilkinson, "Jeff. Society board member resigns, cites harassment," *University Journal* 14, no. 92 (Feb. 17, 1992): 1; Chris Martin, "Society President Responds to Allegations," *University Journal* 14, no. 93 (Feb 18, 1992): 2; Andrea Dickens, "Isbell explains complaints," *University Journal* 14, no. 93 (Feb. 18, 1992): 1.

34. Stephen Power, "Harassment Claim Settled through Talk," *Cavalier Daily* 102, no. 95 (Feb. 21, 1992): 1.

35. Ashlee Mann, "Jefferson Society: A Better Atmosphere," *Cavalier Daily* 103, no. 129 (Apr. 28, 1993): 4; Committee for Constructive Reform to John Casteen, Apr. 9, 1993, JS Archives.

36. "U.Va. Investigates Charges against Jefferson Society," *InsideUVA* (Apr. 16, 1993); retrieved from http://www.virginia.edu/insideuva/textonlyarchive/93-04-16/1.txt, accessed Dec. 6, 2014; Committee for Constructive Reform to John Casteen, Apr. 9, 1993, JS Archives.

37. Committee for Constructive Reform to John Casteen, Apr. 9, 1993, JS Archives; Brad Willet, "Jefferson Society to Face Allegations," *Cavalier Daily* 103, no. 117 (Apr. 12, 1993): 1.

38. Committee for Constructive Reform to John Casteen, Apr. 9, 1993, JS Archives.

39. Ibid.

40. Willet, "Jefferson Society to Face Allegations," 1.

41. Amy Levin and Greg Volkar, "Bill Points to Society Heads," *Cavalier Daily* 103, no. 116 (Apr. 11, 1993): 1.

42. David Wall, "Allegations Fill Meeting," *Cavalier Daily* 103, no. 122 (Apr. 19, 1993): 1.

43. Greg Greene, "Society's Reputation Blemished by a Few," *Cavalier Daily* 103, no. 118 (Apr. 13, 1993): 2.

44. Daniel Hanlin, "Students Endanger Own Self-Government," *Cavalier Daily* 103, no. 118 (Apr. 13, 1993): 2; "No Faith," *Cavalier Daily* 103, no. 118 (Apr. 13, 1993): 2.

45. Brian Dally, "Society's Transgressions Transcend Call for Judicial Response," *Cavalier Daily* 103, no. 120 (Apr. 15, 1993): 3.

46. Willet, "Jefferson Society to Face Allegations," 1.

47. Vicky Barasch, "Society Violations Weighed," *Cavalier Daily* 103, no. 118 (Apr. 13, 1993): 1.

48. Greg Volkar, "Panel to Look into Society Allegations," *Cavalier Daily* 103, no. 123 (Apr. 20, 1993): 1.

49. "Sanctions Imposed on Jefferson Society: University Investigation Found Alcohol Violations and Discrimination," *InsideUVA* (July 16, 1993); retrieved from http://www.virginia.edu/insideuva/textonlyarchive/93-07-16/3.txt, accessed Dec. 6, 2014.

50. Greg Volkar, "Society Receives Sanction: Members Lose Hotel C, Gain Ombudsman in September," *Cavalier Daily* 103, no. 135 (June 24, 1993): 1.

51. Constitution of JS, Fall 1993, JS Archives.

52. Robert T. Canevari to Michael K. Pullen, Jan. 13, 1994, JS Archives; see also Greg Volkar, "Canevari to Assume Interim Job," *Cavalier Daily* 103, no. 136 (July 1, 1993): 1; Greg Volkar, "Society Will Not Abide by Sanctions," *Cavalier Daily* 103, no. 136 (July 1, 1993): 1; Will Morton, "Jefferson Society Appeals Ern's Sanction," *Cavalier Daily* 103, no. 140 (July 27, 1993): A9; "Again?" *Cavalier Daily* 103, no. 135 (June 24, 1993): 2; Mitchell Aberman, "Jefferson Society's Sharp Wit Reduced to Dull Whining," *Cavalier Daily* 103, no. 135 (June 24, 1993): 2.

53. Jim Morrison, "U-Va. Literary Society Said to Exploit Women," *Washington Post*, June 24, 1993, D2.

AFTERWORD

1. Thomas Spencer Harding, *College Literary Societies: Their Contribution to Higher Education in the United States, 1815–1876* (New York: Pageant Press International, 1971), 295, 297.

2. Ibid., 318.

3. "Society Joins the AACLS," *Jefferson Society Journal*, Spring 1982, JS Archives.

4. Ibid.; Joshua E. Sharf and David S. Louder III to the Association of American Collegiate Literary and Debating [*sic*] Societies, Oct. 7, 1986, JS Archives.

5. Matthew Levin, JS President, to Ernest Ern, Vice President of Student Affairs, Jan. 15, 1988, JS Archives.

6. Inscription, Minute Book of JS 1963–1966, JS Archives, 96.

Index

EDITOR: Siobhan Drummond

DESIGNER: Jill Shimabukuro

PROJECT MANAGER: Sylvia Mendoza

TYPESETTER: Jill Shimabukuro

PRINTER: Sheridan, Chelsea, Michigan

Composed in Robert Slimbach's Arno Pro

Printed on 50lb natural uncoated and 70lb gloss white coated papers

Bound in Arrestox Vellum

NOV - - 2018